CompTIA A+
Core I Exam(220-1001)

Technology Workbook

www.ipspecialist.net

Document Control

Proposal Name	:	CompTIA A+ Core I
Document Version	:	Version 1
Document Release Date	:	12th -Nov-2019
Reference	:	220-1001

Feedback:

If you have any comments regarding the quality of this book, or otherwise alter it to better suit your needs, you can contact us through email at info@ipspecialist.net

Please make sure to include the book's title and ISBN in your message.

About IPSpecialist

IPSPECIALIST LTD. IS COMMITTED TO EXCELLENCE AND DEDICATED TO YOUR SUCCESS.

Our philosophy is to treat our customers like family. We want you to succeed, and we are willing to do everything possible to help you make it happen. We have the proof to back up our claims. We strive to accelerate billions of careers with great courses, accessibility, and affordability. We believe that continuous learning and knowledge evolution are the most important things to keep re-skilling and up-skilling the world.

Planning and creating a specific goal is where IPSpecialist helps. We can create a career track that suits your visions as well as develop the competencies you need to become a professional Network Engineer. We can also assist you with the execution and evaluation of your proficiency level, based on the career track you choose, as they are customized to fit your specific goals.

We help you STAND OUT from the crowd through our detailed IP training content packages.

Course Features:

- ❖ Self-Paced Learning
    - • Learn at your own pace and in your own time
- ❖ Covers Complete Exam Blueprint
    - • Prep-up for the exam with confidence
- ❖ Case Study Based Learning
    - • Relate the content with real life scenarios
- ❖ Subscriptions that Suits You
    - • Get more and pay less with IPS subscriptions
- ❖ Career Advisory Services
    - • Let the industry experts plan your career journey
- ❖ Virtual Labs to Test your Skills
    - • With IPS vRacks, you can evaluate your exam preparations
- ❖ Practice Questions
    - • Practice questions to assess your preparation standards
- ❖ On Request Digital Certification
    - • On request digital certification from IPSpecialist LTD.

About the Authors:

This book has been compiled with the help of multiple professional engineers. These engineers specialize in different fields e.g. Networking, Security, Cloud, Big Data, IoT etc. Each engineer develops content in his/her own specialized field that is compiled to form a comprehensive certification guide.

About the Technical Reviewers:

Nouman Ahmed Khan

AWS-Architect, CCDE, CCIEX5 (R&S, SP, Security, DC, Wireless), CISSP, CISA, CISM, Nouman Ahmed Khan is a Solution Architect working with a major telecommunication provider in Qatar. He works with enterprises, mega-projects, and service providers to help them select the best-fit technology solutions. He also works as a consultant to understand customer business processes and help select an appropriate technology strategy to support business goals. He has more than fourteen years of experience working in Pakistan/Middle-East & UK. He holds a Bachelor of Engineering Degree from NED University, Pakistan, and M.Sc. in Computer Networks from the UK.

Abubakar Saeed

Abubakar Saeed has more than twenty-five years of experience, managing, consulting, designing, and implementing large-scale technology projects, extensive experience heading ISP operations, solutions integration, heading Product Development, Pre-sales, and Solution Design. Emphasizing on adhering to Project timelines and delivering as per customer expectations, he always leads the project in the right direction with his innovative ideas and excellent management skills.

Muhammad Yousuf

Muhammad Yousuf is a professional technical content writer. He is a Certified Ethical Hacker (CEHv10) and Cisco Certified Network Associate (CCNA) in Routing and Switching, holding bachelor's degree in Telecommunication Engineering from Sir Syed University of Engineering and Technology. He has both technical knowledge and sound industry information, which he uses perfectly in his career.

Uzair Ahmed

Uzair Ahmed is a professional technical content writer holding a Bachelor's Degree in Computer Science from PAF-KIET University. He has sound knowledge and industry experience in SIEM implementation, .NET development, machine learning, Artificial intelligence, Python and other programming and development platforms like React.JS Angular JS Laravel.

Afreen Moin

Afreen Moin is a professional Technical Content Developer. She holds a Degree in Bachelor of Engineering in Telecommunications from Dawood University of Engineering and Technology. She has a great knowledge of computer networking and attends several training programs. She possesses a keen interest in research and design related to computers, which reflects in her career.

Heba Dorazahi

Heba Dorazahi is a Technical Content writer. She has completed her Bachelor's Degree with a major in Telecommunication Engineering from Sir Syed University of Engineering & Technology. Throughout her academic studies, she gained extensive research and writing skills. She has done online courses of network security and cryptography to develop her expertise

Free Resources:

With each workbook bought from Amazon, IPSpecialist offers free resources to our valuable customers.

Once you buy this book, you will have to contact us at support@ipspecialist.net or tweet @ipspecialistoff to get this limited time offer without any extra charges.

Free Resources Include:

Exam Practice Questions in Quiz Simulation: With 250+ Q/A, IPSpecialist's Practice Questions is a concise collection of important topics to keep in mind. The questions are especially prepared following the exam blueprint to give you a clear understanding of what to expect from the certification exam. It goes further on to give answers with thorough explanations. In short, it is a perfect resource that helps you evaluate your preparation for the exam.

Career Report: This report is a step-by-step guide for a novice who wants to develop his/her career in the field of computer networks. It answers the following queries:

- What are the current scenarios and future prospects?
- Is this industry moving towards saturation or are new opportunities knocking at the door?
- What will the monetary benefits be?
- Why get certified?
- How to plan and when will I complete the certifications if I start today?
- Is there any career track that I can follow to accomplish specialization level?

Furthermore, this guide provides a comprehensive career path towards being a specialist in the field of networking and also highlights the tracks needed to obtain certification.

IPS Personalized Technical Support for Customers: Good customer service means helping customers efficiently, in a friendly manner. It is essential to be able to handle issues for customers and do your best to ensure that they are satisfied. Providing good service is one of the most important things that can set our business apart from the others of its kind.

Great customer service will result in attracting more customers and attain maximum customer retention.

IPS is offering personalized TECH support to its customers to provide better value for money. If you have any queries related to technology and labs you can simply ask our technical team for assistance via Live Chat or Email.

Our Products

Technology Workbooks

IPSpecialist Technology workbooks are the ideal guides to developing the hands-on skills necessary to pass the exam. Our workbook covers official exam blueprint and explains the technology with real life case study based labs. The content covered in each workbook consists of individually focused technology topics presented in an easy-to-follow, goal-oriented, step-by-step approach. Every scenario features detailed breakdowns and thorough verifications to help you completely understand the task and associated technology.

We extensively used mind maps in our workbooks to visually explain the technology. Our workbooks have become a widely used tool to learn and remember the information effectively.

vRacks

Our highly scalable and innovative virtualized lab platforms let you practice the IP Specialist Technology Workbook at your own time and your own place as per your convenience.

Quick Reference Sheets

Our quick reference sheets are a concise bundling of condensed notes of the complete exam blueprint. It is an ideal and handy document to help you remember the most important technology concepts related to the certification exam.

Practice Questions

IP Specialists' Practice Questions are dedicatedly designed from a certification exam perspective. The collection of these questions from our technology workbooks are prepared keeping the exam blueprint in mind covering not only important but necessary topics as well. It is an ideal document to practice and revise for your certification.

Content at a glance

Table of Contents

15

About this Workbook

This workbook covers all the information you need to pass the CompTIA A+ Core I (220-1001) exam. The workbook is designed to take a practical approach of learning with real life examples and case studies.

- ➢ Covers complete Core I 220-1001 blueprint
- ➢ Summarized content

- ➢ Case Study based approach
- ➢ 100% pass guarantee
- ➢ Mind maps

CompTIA Certifications

CompTIA certification helps to establish and build your IT career. It benefits you in various ways whether you are seeking certification to have a job in IT or want to upgrade your IT career with a leading certification, that is, CompTIA certification.

Figure 1. CompTIA Certifications Pathway

About the CompTIA A+ Core 1 Exam

➤ **Exam Number:** 220-1001 Core I

➤ **Associated Certifications:** CompTIA A+

➤ **Duration:** 90 minutes (90 questions)

➤ **Type of Questions:** Multiple Choice and Practical based Questions

Candidates are encouraged to use this document to help prepare for CompTIA A+ Core 1. In order to receive the CompTIA A+ certification, you must pass two exams: Core 1 (220-1001) and Core 2 (220-1002). CompTIA A+ Core 1 measures the necessary skills for an entry-level IT professional. Successful candidates will have the knowledge required to:

- Assemble components based on customer requirements
- Install, configure, and maintain PCs, mobile devices, and software for end users
- Understand the basics of networking and security forensics
- Properly and safely diagnose, resolve, and document common hardware and software issues
- Apply troubleshooting skills
- Provide appropriate customer support
- Understand the basics of scripting, virtualization, desktop imaging, and deployment

The following topics are general guidelines for the content likely to be included on the exam

1.0	Mobile Devices	14%
2.0	Networking	20%
3.0	Hardware	27%
4.0	Virtualization and Cloud Computing	12%
5.0	Hardware and Network Troubleshooting	27%
	Total-	100%

How to become CompTIA A+ certified?

Step 1: Choose a certification: Explore what is available and choose an IT certification that will benefit you in accomplishing your career target.

To study about various IT career tracks and to choose the best certification for yourself, you can use the "CompTIA Career Roadmap".

CompTIA has four core IT certifications that is; IT Fundamental, A+, Network+, and Security+ that examine your knowledge from the entry to the expert level.

If you have the skills to secure a network & deter hackers and want to become a highly efficient IT Security Tech, then CompTIA Security+ is the right type of certification for you.

Step 2: Learning & Training: Exam preparation can be done through self-study with textbooks, practice exams, and online classroom programs. However, this workbook provides you with all the information and offers complete assessments in one place to help you pass the CompTIA Security+ Exam.

IPSpecialist provides full support to the candidates in order for them to pass the exam.

Step 3: Familiarization with Exam: A great suggestion is to first understand what you are training for. For that, we are providing you not only the exam objectives but practice questions as well, in order to give you a thorough idea about your final exam of certification.

Step 4: Register & Take Exam for Certification: After all the learning process, the next step is to take your test. Certification exams are offered at different locations all over the world. To register for an exam, contact the authorized test delivery partner of CompTIA, contact *Pearson VUE*.

The following are the steps for registration and scheduling an exam:

1. Buy the exam voucher from here "Buy a certification exam voucher".
2. Find and visit a testing center "testing center".
3. Create Pearson VUE account & Schedule your exam. Here is a link for that "Create a Pearson VUE testing account and schedule your exam".
4. You will receive a confirmation email having testing information after the registration process.
5. Prepare for the test.

Step 5: Results: After you complete the exam at an authorized testing center, you will get immediate, online notification of your pass or fail status. If you have passed the exam, a congratulatory email will be forwarded to you with guidelines to access your record.

Make sure to keep a record of the email address you used for registration and score report with exam registration number. This information is required to log in to your certification account.

Chapter 01: Mobile Devices

This chapter will focus on computers such as laptops, smartphones, tablets, and PCs and the troubleshooting of hardware and networks. It will follow the structure of the CompTIA A+ 220-1001 exam blueprint and give a brief introduction on replacement, configuration, and instalment of different components of computing or mobile devices. It will give an overview of opening up a laptop along with the proper steps for disassembling and reassembling a laptop.

Install and Configure Laptop Hardware and Components

Laptops and Notebooks

Laptops or Notebook computers are small computers with all the necessary input and output peripherals packed up in a single portable device. They have all the components that are required by a desktop computer to make it a functional computing device, although some of the components and features are modified to some extent for making it more compact and portable. Like desktop computers, laptops and notebooks use standard operating systems, such as Microsoft Windows, Mac OS, or Linux. Usually a laptop or notebook computer contains the following components:

- Keyboard
- Hard Drive
- Monitor
- CD or DVD Drive
- Memory
- Pointing Device
- Peripheral Ports
- Network Adapter
- Modem
- CPU
- Multiple slots for expansion cards (although, the expansion cards are not the same as those used with desktop computers)

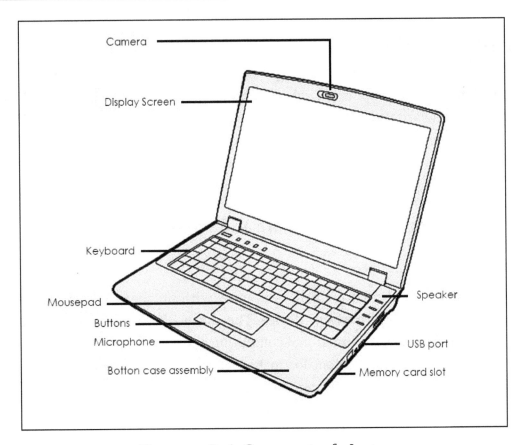

Figure 1-01: Basic Components of a Laptop

Laptops and notebooks are designed to be as small, lightweight, and portable as possible. However, a disadvantage of their small size is that they can be easily stolen.

Netbooks

There is an another class of laptops or notebook computers known as subcompact notebooks or netbooks. Subcompact notebooks are much smaller in size and they also have an integrated monitor. Netbooks are specially designed for wireless internet use such as web browsing, online shopping, email, and cloud computing. These netbooks do not have the processing power or storage capacity of regular notebook computers, which can run local applications and save data. A big advantage of netbooks is that they are very easy to carry, allowing you to travel anywhere with it because of its small size. Netbooks come with operating systems like Linux, Windows XP, Mac OS X, Windows CE, Windows Vista Home Premium or Business, and Windows 7 Starter and Home Premium.

Figure 1-02: Netbook

Replacing Laptop Hardware

Because most notebooks contain custom devices, whenever any of the components to need to be replaced, they have to be purchased by a vendor or manufacturer.

However, mini PCI Cards, PC cards, and some other standardized components, such as memory, can be purchased from any manufacturer. There are also some third-party manufacturers who make replacement components, which are an alternative to original component manufacturers. Most of the time, a PC card can be used to replace a malfunctioning built-in component, but to do this, users have to disable built-in components to prevent conflict between them. Whenever you need to replace an internal component, make sure to follow these general guidelines to ensure the component is properly reassembled:

- Refer to the manufacturer's manual to locate slots or panels through which users can access internal components

- Label and document screw locations to ensure that the screws are extracted and reinserted in their exact locations

- Separate the new parts and the old parts you have removed from inside the case

- Use the correct hand tools when working with laptops or notebooks

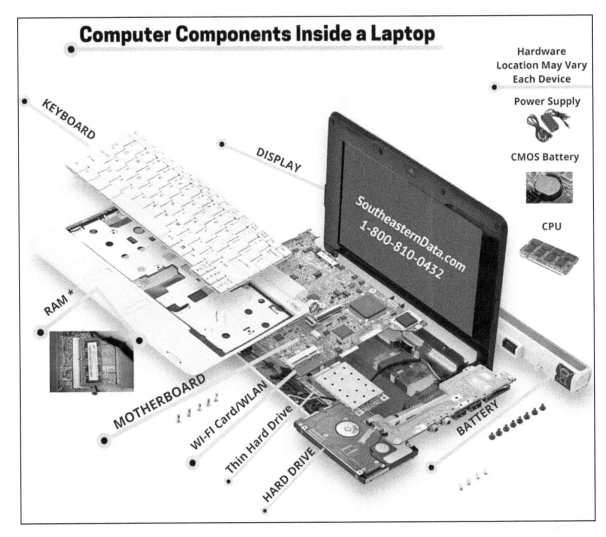

Figure 1-03: Internal Components of a Laptop

The following section deals with replacing of some laptop components:

Keyboard

Laptop keyboards are smaller than standard desktop keyboards. Generally, laptop keyboards include the function keys, alphanumeric keys, and the "system" keys such as "Backspace", "Enter", and so forth.

Steps for Replacing a Keyboard

Following are the general steps for replacing a notebook keyboard:

- Disconnect the laptop from AC power and remove the battery

- Remove the screws that keep the keyboard in place

- Turn the laptop upright

- Open the screen so that the keyboard is visible

- If necessary, remove the bezel that keep the keyboard in place

- To expose the keyboard cable, lift up the keyboard

- Remove any hold-down devices used to keep the keyboard cable in place

- Disconnect the keyboard cable from the system board

- Remove the keyboard

Figure 1-04: Keyboard Replacement

Note

On some laptops, users must remove the display assembly before removing the keyboard.

Installing a Keyboard Driver:

Uninstall the old keyboard driver and reboot the computer before installing the driver for the new keyboard. The old driver may conflict with the new driver, so it is necessary to uninstall it first.

Now, go to the device manager.

Expand the "Keyboard" option.

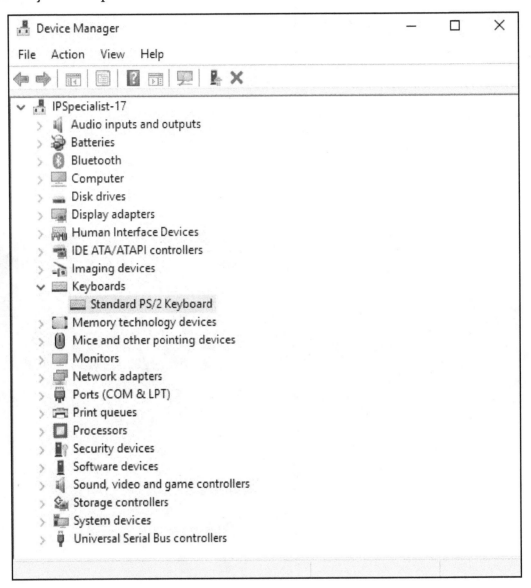

Figure 1-05: Installing a Keyboard Driver

Double click the "Standard PS/2 Keyboard" option. The following windows will pop up:

Figure 1-06: Updating a Keyboard Driver

Now, there are two options for installing the drive: either choose to search for the keyboard driver using Windows Update over the internet, or choose to search for the driver using a disc provided by the laptop manufacturer.

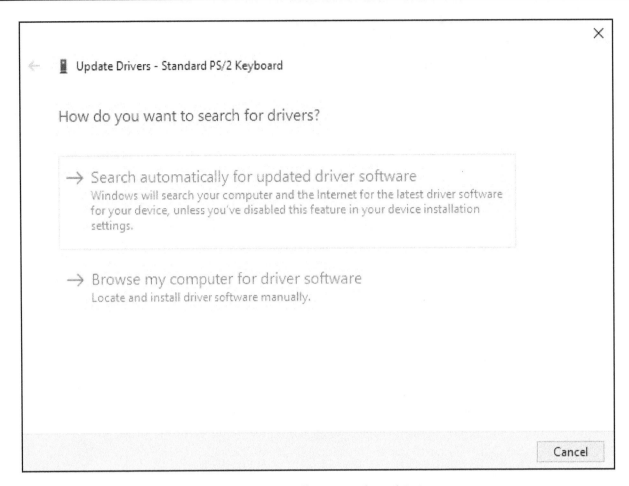

Figure 1-07: Installing a Keyboard Driver

You can either get the driver from the disc that came with the card, or download it from the manufacturer's driver page. Double-click the driver installer file and follow the steps provided by the on-screen instructions. Once the process is complete, the card will be installed and ready to go.

Hard Disk Drive (HDD)

A magnetic disk is a type of storage device that consists of a rotating magnetic disk or a surface with a mechanical arm over it to read, write, rewrite, and access data. The magnetization process is used to read and write the data. The disk stores information in the form of spots, tracks (the circular division of a disk), and sectors (the division of tracks that contains blocks of data). The most common examples of magnetic disks are hard disks, floppy disks, and zip disks.

Hard Disk Drives (HDDs) have been seen as the default storage component in desktops and laptop PCs for decades. Modern hard disk drives are far more efficient and higher-performing than ever, but the basic underlying technology remains the same. Hard disk drives consist of rotating magnetic platters paired with read/write heads that move over the surface of the platter to record or retrieve data. As the speed of platter rotation increases, the hard drive works faster. The hard drive connects

to a system via the SATA or Serial ATA interface. Today's laptop computers have hard drives that consist of hundreds of gigabytes of storage space.

3.5 inches' vs 2.5 inches' vs 1.8 inches'

Usually laptops use 2.5 or 3.5 inch hard drives, which are also used in desktop PCs. Smaller laptops use 1.8 inch hard disk drives. 2.5 inch hard disks are smaller in size compared to the 3.5 inch hardware, but they have less capacity and cache for storing data so they operate at low speed.

The 1.8 inch drive is the smallest of all and contains the least capacity and cache for data storage.

Magnetic disks have been a standard option for years and combine low cost with high capacity. However, they are slower than other options. With magnetic disks and moving parts that can wear down, they are the least reliable of the three options.

Solid-state Drive (SSD)

Solid-state Drives are somewhat similar to hard drives. They also connect to a system via the SATA interface and they store files as other drives do. SSDs use the magnetic platters and read/write heads of hard disk drives, so there are no specific SSD magnetic bits and mechanical parts. SSDs provide the fastest storage with more work load, among all the storage devices. They also access data much faster.

SSDs are durable as they do not have any moving parts, hence, they are not easily prone to damage and can provide high durability.

One of the main disadvantages of SSDs is that they do not give a warning prompt or alert if they fail. Further, SSDs are much more expensive per gigabyte than hard drives

Hybrid Disk Drive/Solid-state Hybrid Drive (SSHD)

Hybrid Disk Drive or Solid-state Hybrid Drive is a blend of hard disk drive and solid-state drive. This ultimate solution provides users with improved storage performance and higher at a lower cost. It uses SDD to improve performance and speed, and uses HDD to improve the storage capacity and reliability of the disk drive.

Adaptive memory technology is used in SSHD. It stores frequently used data in NAND flash memory, which allows quick and easy access to required files.

Type of Hard Drive	Cost	Capacity	Speed	Reliability
HDD	Least expensive	Highest capacity	Slowest due to moving parts	Contains moving parts that can wear over time
SSD	Most expensive	Lowest capacity but improving	Fastest	Has no moving parts
SSHD	Midrange cost	High HDD capacity with fast solid-state cache	Fast solid-state cache with slower magnetic storage	Has moving parts that can wear out but spins less than HDD

Table 1-01: Comparison of HDD, SSD, and SSHD

Steps for Replacing a Hard Disk

Following are the general steps for replacing a laptop or notebook hard drive:

- First, disconnect the laptop or notebook power source or remove the battery
- Refer to the manufacturer's manual for how to disassemble the bottom cover of the laptop
- Remove the battery
- Remove the service door
- Unscrew the two head screws that holds the hard drive to the computer and put them in a secure place as they will be reused to replace the hard drive
- Slide the hard disk drive backward
- Disconnect the cable from its connector using the black tab on the hard disk drive adapter cable
- Lift the edge of the drive using the Mylar tab on the hard disk drive and pull the drive out of the laptop
- Gently remove the hard drive
- Now, remove the four head screws on each side that holds the hard drive to its carrier and place them aside
- Lift and remove the hard drive from the carrier
- Disconnect all the cables from the drive
- Now, put the new hard drive in place

- Reassemble the notebook by reversing the disassemble steps

- Replace the battery and, if required, reconnect the notebook to an external power source

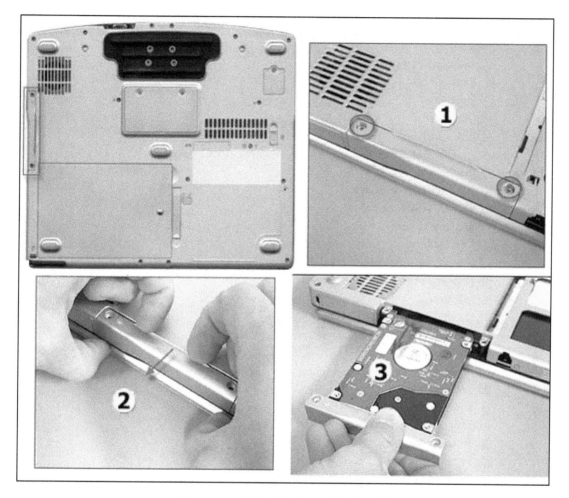

Figure 1-08: Replacing a Hard Disk

Installing the Hard Drive Driver:

Once the drive is replaced, turn on the laptop and enter the system's BIOS/UEFI of the system. Press "F2" or the "DEL" key to gain access to the BIOS/UEFI. Refer to the motherboard manufacturer's manual to ensure using the correct key and exact steps for this purpose.

Go to the "Integrated Peripherals -> SATA" menu or standard "System Settings" menu in the BIOS to see the drives already installed in the system. If the drive controllers are properly connected and enabled, its name should be listed in the BIOS menu.

Reboot the laptop and recheck all the connections if the drive is not in the BIOS menu. Come out of "Setup" and boot Windows normally once you get the hard disk name in the BIOS menu.

Now go to the device manager.

Expand the option of "Disk drives".

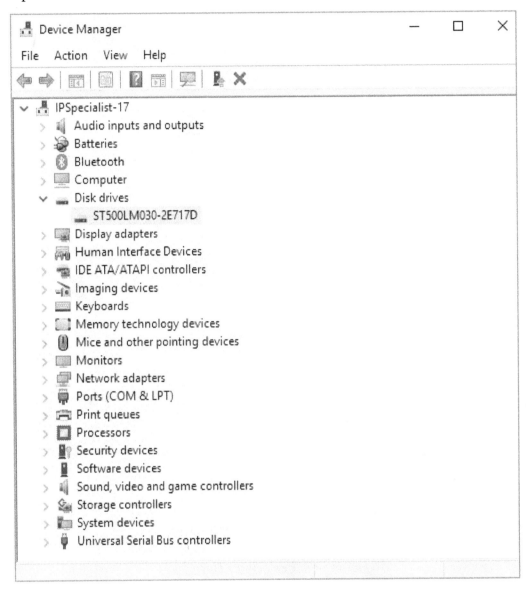

Figure 1-09: Installing the Hard Disk Driver

Here, you can verify the existence of the hard drive driver and whether it is working. A windows will pop up with all the details and updated versions of the hard drive.

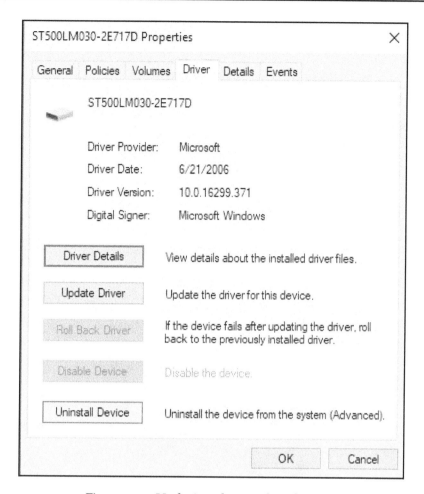

Figure 1-10: Updating the Hard Disk Driver

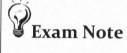 **Exam Note**

Know that laptop hard drive types include SSD, magnetic disk, and hybrid. Also, be aware they have either 2.5- or 1.8-inch form factors.

Memory

Random Access Memory or RAM is a storage location inside a computing device where programs such as Operating System (OS), applications, and recently used data are stored so that they can be easily available for the data processing unit. RAM is the main memory of a computer, and it is faster at reading and writing to memory than other kinds of storage devices such as solid-state drives, hard disk drives, or optical drives. Random Access Memory is volatile, meaning the data in RAM will be retained in RAM as long as the computer is on, but will be lost once the computer is turned off. The OS and other files are reloaded into RAM from other storage devices such as HDD or SSD when the computing device is rebooted. The size of the RAM makes a laptop or notebook run faster. As the size of RAM increases, it allows the computing devices to run more programs simultaneously.

The location of memory modules in different laptops varies greatly. In the past, each laptop model used its own version of memory. But now it is easier to find a memory module in a laptop that uses a standard SODIMM or something similar. When users are calculating the amount of memory they require, they should be aware of the standard process called shared video memory. In a standard process, the graphic card uses a portion of the computer's RAM with on-board memory of its own. Shared video memory consumes less memory for the applications than you might expect.

To configure shared memory in the BIOS:

- Go to the computer's BIOS setup utility

- Access the Integrated Peripherals menu

- Select the "AGP aperture size" option

- Specify the size of RAM to be allotted for shared video memory. You can specify from 8 MB up to 128 MB, depending on the computer. Save the changes

- Exit the BIOS setup utility

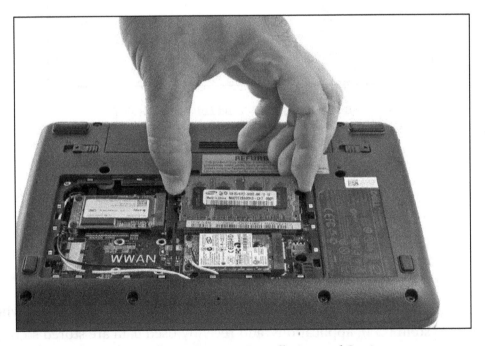

Figure 1-11: Main Memory Installation and Settings

To increase the amount of memory, refer to the laptop's manual. To install memory or any other internal component, first shut down the computer, unplug the power cord, and remove the battery. Do not turn on the computer while installing or replacing any internal component or memory.

Different types of computer memory can be confusing. The following table provides a brief list of memory types, including memory specifically for laptops.

Type of RAM	Description
RAM (Random Access Memory)	Volatile memory not for storage
SDRAM (Synchronous Dynamic RAM)	Combines static RAM and dynamic RAM
SDR SDRAM (Single Data Rate SDRAM)	Single Data rate means internal clock rate and input/output are the same
DDR SDRAM (Double Data Rate SDRAM) DDR2, DDR3, DDR4	DDR4 is the latest generation
DIMM (Dual In-line Memory Module)	Form factor used in desktops
SODIMM (Small Outline DIMM)	Form factor used in laptops

Table 1-02: RAM Review

Follow these steps for a typical memory upgrade:

- Disconnect the laptop from AC power and remove the battery

- Remove any screws or hold-down devices

- Remove the old memory module(s), if necessary. To remove a memory module, pull back the clips on both sides and swing the memory up and out

- Insert the latest memory upgrade, making sure the contacts on the edge of the module make a firm connection with the connector

- Push the cover of the module down until the latches lock in place

- If the memory socket needs screws to secure the memory in place, install them

- To complete the upgrade, close the cover and secure it to complete the upgrade

- Test the upgrade by starting the system and running a memory diagnostic tool

Smart Card Reader

A Smart Card Reader is used to control access control to corporate laptops (do not confuse it with a flash memory card reader). Smart cards are usually plastic with an embedded chip to authenticate a user for access. They are not a common option for home use.

Many mobile devices or laptops include a built-in memory card reader to read flash memory cards. Memory cards are used to store and carry data from devices such as digital cameras, MP3 players, and cell phones, but separate card readers can also be used for this purpose. Users can transfer

information between the memory card and the computing device by inserting the card into the appropriate card reader port.

Steps for Replacing a Smart Card Reader

In order to replace a Smart Card Reader, follow the general steps given below:

- First of all, disconnect the power source and remove the battery of a laptop or notebook

- Remove the bottom cover

- Remove all the storage devices such as optical drive, hard drive, and memory

- Refer to the manufacturer's manual for the correct steps for disassembling the bottom cover plate, hinges, and keyboard

- Remove the wireless WAN module, LAN module, top cover, system board and touchpad button bracket with any prying tool. Refer to the manufacture's manual for the correct steps for your laptop

- Gently lift the left edge of the smart card reader board and slide the tabs on the board out from underneath the retention tabs on the top cover

- Lift the smart card reader's board off the alignment pin on the top cover, remove it and put it aside

- Now, replace the smart card reader board

- To reassemble the laptop, reverse the disassemble steps up to this point

- Reconnect the notebook to an external power source and replace the battery

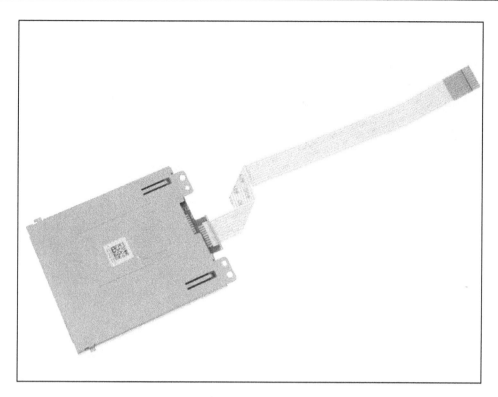

Figure 1-12: Replacing the Smart Card Reader

Installing the Smart Card Reader Drive

Go to the device manager and see the list of all installed drivers.

If a smart card reader drive is installed on the machine, there will be a "Smart Card Readers" option in the list.

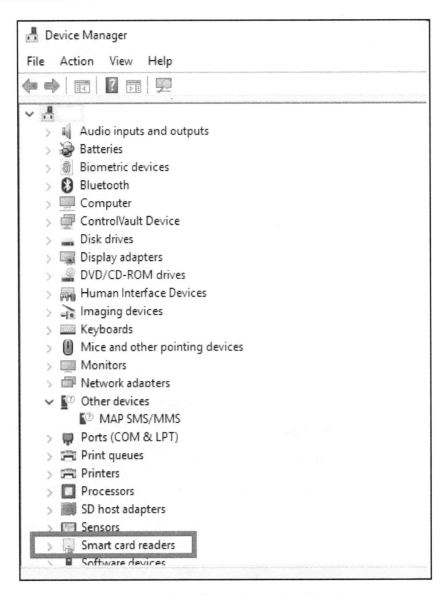

Figure 1-13: Installing a Smart Card Reader

Just double click the option – a window of properties will prompt you to vary the settings of the smart card reader.

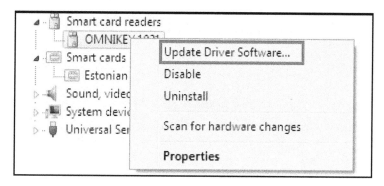

Figure 1-14: Updating a Smart Card Reader

Click on the driver's tab to update or uninstall the driver.

Update the driver, then click one of the two given options in the prompt, and then follow the pop-ups to install the driver.

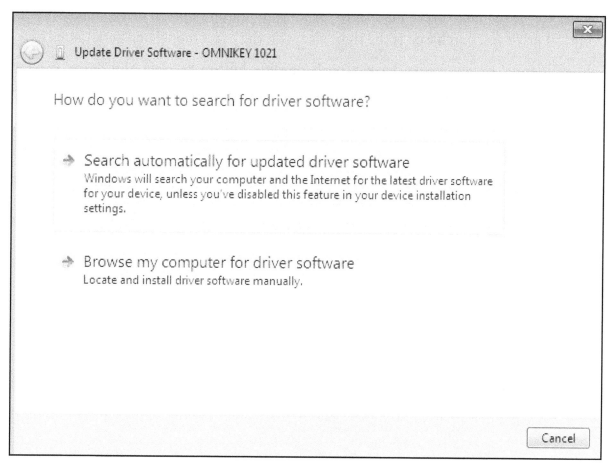

Figure 1-15: Updating a Smart Card Reader Driver's Software

If it is not already downloaded, get the driver from the disc that came with the card or download it from the manufacturer's driver page. Double-click the installer file of the driver and follow the steps

provided by the on-screen instructions. Once the process is finished, the card will be installed and should be in working condition.

Optical Drive

An Optical Drive, also known as a DVD or CD drive, is a type of storage. It serves the same purpose as zip drives. It has a greater storage capacity but a slower access time than a zip drive. It uses laser to read and write to the storage medium.

Steps for Replacing an Optical Drive

In order to replace an optical drive, follow the general steps given below:

- First of all, disconnect the power source or remove the battery of a laptop or notebook

- Remove the bottom cover and the battery

- Refer to the manufacturer's manual to locate your laptop's optical drive. Make sure that the optical drive you purchased is the right size with the exact model and serial number

- Most laptops or notebooks have a push or slide button to eject the drive. Refer to the manufacturer's manual for the correct steps to eject the drive

- Slide out the old optical disk drive and remove it

- Insert the new optical drive in its place

- To reassemble the laptop, reverse the disassemble steps to disassemble up to this point

- Reconnect the notebook to an external power source or replace the battery if required

- Now turn the power ON

Figure 1-16: Replacing an Optical Drive

Installing an Optical Disk Drive

Install the optical disk drive driver by inserting the CD that came with the drive or by downloading driver from the manufacturer's website. Installing the driver may add advanced features that the older drive did not support.

Wireless Card/Bluetooth Module

An internal wireless card is a hardware device that enables the laptop to access high-speed wireless networks.

A laptop with Wi-Fi or Bluetooth uses either an mPCIe expansion card or an M.2 card to offer wireless network support. The M.2 card form factor, also called NGFF (for next-generation form factor) is also used for SSD and other I/O devices. It should be noted that an M.2 card slot made for SSD cannot be used for Wi-Fi or Bluetooth cards.

Steps for Replacing a Wireless Card/Bluetooth Module

If the internal wireless card is no longer functional or a user just wants the laptop's wireless card replaced, follow these general steps:

- First, disconnect the laptop or notebook's power source

- Remove the battery from its compartment

- Remove all attached devices and cables that are connected to the laptop

- Locate the position of the wireless card compartment and remove the cover by unscrewing the screws. Refer to the manufacturer's manual for the correct steps for disassembling the bottom cover plate and locating the wireless card

- Once the cover is removed, locate the position of the two small wires attached to the wireless card. Gently twist and pull up the gold or yellow clips on the end of the wires to detach them from the wireless card

- There are two latch clips on each side of the wireless card that hold the card in its slot. Place your thumbs on the latch clips and press the clips outward to unlatch them. The wireless card will pop up out of the slot

- Now, remove the wireless card from its compartment, holding the sides of the wireless card and gently removing it from the slot

- Now, put in a new wireless card

- To reassemble the laptop, reverse the disassemble steps to disassemble up to this point

- Reconnect the notebook to an external power source and replace the battery

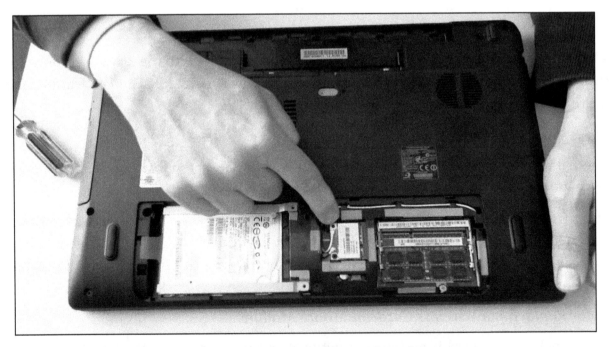

Figure 1-17: Replacing a Bluetooth Module

Installing Your Card's Drivers

Usually, Windows will automatically recognize a new wireless card. Install the downloaded driver by simply following the instructions.

If it is not already downloaded, get the driver from the disc that came with the card or download it from the manufacturer's driver page. Double-click the driver's installer file and follow on-screen instructions provided. Once the process is finished, the card will be installed and should be in working condition.

Cellular Card

Some laptop users need connectivity no matter where they are in the field. For this, cellular access is sometimes required when Wi-Fi is not available; some business-class laptops come with slots for cellular LTE wireless connectivity. Cell providers offer data-only services for data access, but these plans are not set up for calling or messaging.

To enable cellular on a laptop, follow these steps:

- Activate the SIM card

- Insert the SIM card into the laptop, making sure the gold contacts connect.

- If the SIM card does not auto-configure, access the settings by selecting the Cellular option from the Network Connections area in the system tray (Windows 10)

- Select the Cellular tab and choose "Add an APN" (Access Point Name)

- Enable a PIN to specify which users have access to the cellular connection

 Exam Note

If the laptop does not connect to the wireless network, try pressing either the Wi-Fi button, which is either a function key or a standalone button on the keyboard. Ensure you understand the several ways that a laptop can communicate with other computers, including wired and wireless Ethernet, Bluetooth, and cellular WAN connections.

Video Card

A Video Card, also known as graphics card, is used to generate graphics on the laptop's display. All CPUs have a graphics controller, that makes the computer display colorful pictures, videos and basic graphics. However, a video card is an extra device that contributes to the processing of the processor and makes the laptop run faster and more smoothly when dealing with pictures, videos, and movies. Some video cards have their own built-in system memory, which makes processing faster and provides more seamless performance. For this, install the video card in the AGP slots.

Accelerated Graphics Port (AGP) slots are specially designed as a direct connection between the PC's memory and the video circuitry.

Steps for Replacing a Video or Graphics Card

To replace a video or graphics card, follow the steps given below:

- First of all, disconnect the laptop or notebook power source or remove the battery

- Refer to the manufacturer's manual for the correct steps for disassembling the bottom of the laptop

- Use a small flathead screwdriver to open the keyboard cover; remove the cover and put it aside

- Follow the steps under the heading "Keyboard" above to remove the keyboard from the laptop

- Now, pull the keyboard out and put it aside

- Now, disconnect the LCD video ribbon connector from the video card

- Pull the heat sink out of the laptop by removing the screws that protect the heat sink, and put it aside

- Remove the 4 screws that hold the video card to the logic board

- Now, eject the old card from the laptop and install the new video card by placing it in the video card's slot or compartment

- To reassemble the notebook, reverse the disassemble steps up to this point

- Replace the battery and, if required, reconnect the notebook to an external power source

- Now, insert the disc into the CD OR DVD-ROM drive that came with the video card and follow the instructions for installing the video card's driver on the laptop or notebook

Figure 1-18: Replacing a Video Card

Installing the Video Card Driver

Before testing, install a new driver for intel, NVIDIA or AMD so that the software and Windows can effectively communicate with the card.

Uninstall the old graphics driver and reboot the computer before installing the driver for new graphics card. The old driver may conflict with the new driver so it is necessary to uninstall it first.

Get the driver from the disc that came with the card or download it from the manufacturer's driver page. Double-click the driver's installer file and follow on-screen instructions provided. Once the process is finished, the card will be installed and should be in working condition.

Mini PCI

Peripheral Component Interconnects (PCI) are the slots on the motherboard that, from the late 1990's to the early 2000's, were used to attach hardware, modems, or video or sound cards to a computer. The PCI bus was available in both 32-bit and 64-bit versions. There are three types of PCI slot: PCI4, PCI5, and PCI6, along with a CNR slot.

The number of PCI slots are between one and three but they may vary according to the manufacturer and model of the motherboard. Nowadays, very few motherboards have PCI slots, as they have been replaced by PCI-E.

Mini PCI (both card and slot) is much smaller than PCI. Mini PCI has a 32-bit data bus. Mini PCI cards also come in three types: Type I, Type II, and Type III. Types I and II contain 100 pins in a stacking connector, and Type III cards contain 124 pins on an edge connector.

Mini PCIe

Mini PCIe is a newer standard for Mini Cards and is referred to as PCI Express (PCIe) Mini Card, Mini PCI Express, Mini PCI-E, or simply MiniCard. It has replaced the Mini PCI standard on laptop motherboards. Mini PCIe has a 64-bit data bus, which provides much faster throughput. Mini PCI has a 52-pin edge connector.

Steps for Replacing a PCIe Card

To replace any PCIe card, follow the general steps given below:

- First, disconnect the laptop or notebook power source and remove the battery

- Remove all the storage devices such as optical drive, hard drive, and memory

- Refer to the manufacturer's manual for the correct steps for disassembling the bottom cover plate, hinges, and keyboard

- Follow the steps to replace the motherboard (given above in the section on system boards) to access the laptop's motherboard or refer to the manufacturer's manual for the correct steps for accessing the motherboard

- There will be rectangular slots on the motherboard – usually located near the processor

- Each PCI slot contains a bay on the back that is associated with it. Remove the bay by unscrewing the screw that holds it in its place and then lift the card gently

- To install the PCIe card, align the contacts on the bottom of the PCIe card with the PCI slot

- Insert the card by push the card straight down into the slot

- To reassemble the laptop, reverse the disassemble steps up to this point

- Reconnect the notebook to an external power source or replace the battery if required

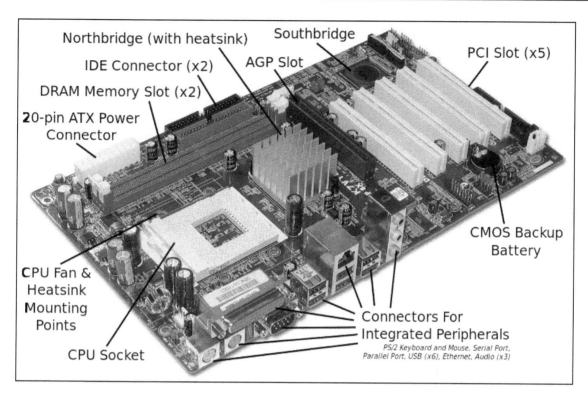

Figure 1-19: Parts of the Motherboard

Installing the PCIe Driver

Turn on the laptop and let the operating system load properly. The card may be automatically detected and installed. Go to the device manager and ensure the availability of the driver on the list of installed devices.

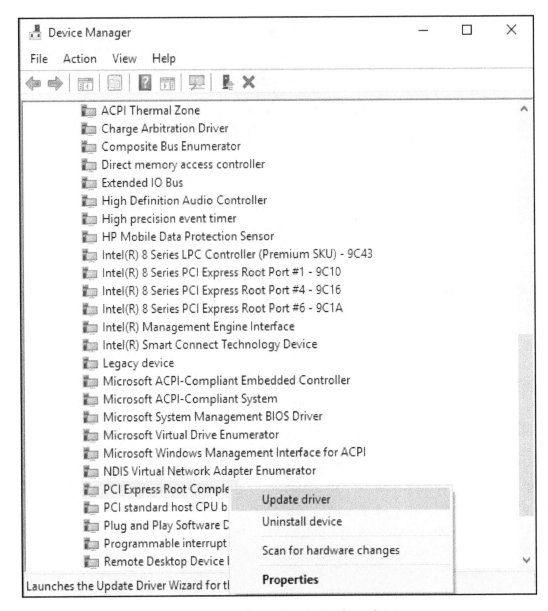

Figure 1-20: Installing the Motherboard Driver

If not, get the driver from the disc that came with the card or download it from the manufacturer's driver page. Double-click the driver installer file and follow on-screen instructions provided. Once the process is finished, the card will be installed and should be in working condition. Restart the laptop after the driver is installed.

Screen

Laptop screens are made up of a thin Liquid Crystal Display (LCD) or an Organic Light-Emitting Diode (OLED) display; any communication peripherals are added separately. Laptop screens are specially designed with a webcam, microphone, Wi-Fi antennas, and often touchscreen digitizers and inverters.

An LCD screen uses a backlight to illuminate light-modulating liquid crystals. LCD screens are customized to different device types, and some have a Wi-Fi antenna attached.

OLED screens are in many ways more advanced than LED screens. They are brighter and use less energy (saving on battery use) and are flexible and foldable. But the screens themselves are much thinner and more subject to cracking or breaking when dropped or mishandled.

Steps for Replacing a Laptop Screen

To replace the screen for any reason, follow the general steps given below:

- First, disconnect the laptop or notebook power source and remove the battery

- Refer to the manufacturer's manual for the correct steps for disassembling the screen

- Locate the round cover stickers that hide the screws on the screen bezel – the case surrounding the screen. These stickers are usually located at the bottom of the bezel, close to the hinges of the screen

- In order to remove the cover stickers, use a sharp, pointed object such as needle or opened safety pin. Stick it between the bezel and the edge of the cover, and then pry the sticker away. Put the cover in a safe place and make sure that the sticky side remains up to retain stickiness when placing it back

- Remove the exposed screws

- Gently pry the screen bezel away from the back of the screen case. The bezel is usually stronger than the back case and has plastic snaps, so you may need to use some force when prying it away, but do not use too much force. Use a thin object or fingernail in the gap around the outside of the screen

- When the bezel is fully removed, you will see the LCD secured by a metal trim frame on the left and right-hand side. Remove the screws that hold the trim frame pieces to the back of the screen case. Now, gently pull the LCD slightly away from the back of the screen case

- Remove the screws from the sides of the trim frame. Most laptops have three screws on each side

- Now, set the LCD face-down onto the keyboard. Make sure not to excessively pull the video cable attached to the back of the LCD

- From the back of the LCD, disconnect the video cable. Pull the cable away from the display gently. Also, remove the tape that secures the video connector to the back of the screen

- Once the broken LCD is removed, simply replace it with a new one. Reconnect the video cable to the connector and replace all the cables and tape as they were

- To reassemble the notebook, reverse the disassemble steps up to this point

- Replace the battery and, if required, reconnect the notebook to an external power source

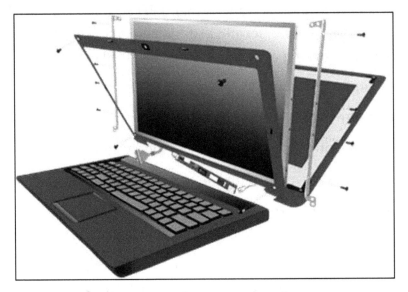

Figure 1-21: Replacing a Laptop Screen

DC Jack

A DC plug or DC connector is an <u>electrical connector</u> that supplies <u>Direct Current</u> (DC) to the computing device. A DC Jack is a hole or other connection (similar to a port) that allows a DC plug to be connected. If the DC jack fails, the laptop's battery cannot be charged and neither can the laptop run on external power.

Steps for Replacing a DC Jack

To replace a DC jack, follow these general steps:

- First, disconnect the laptop or notebook power source and remove the battery

- Now, press and hold down the power button for 40 seconds to discharge the static electricity that can damage the laptop's sensitive components

- Remove the LCD display assembly from the bottom

- Take out the RAM cards. Push out the tabs by the help of a screwdriver and the RAM card will pop up

- Remove all the storage devices such as optical drive, hard drive, and memory

- Refer to the manufacturer's manual for the correct steps for disassembling the bottom cover plate, hinges, and keyboard. Remove the motherboard by unscrewing the screws attaching the motherboard to the chassis

- Detach the motherboard from the fans power cord, and remove from the fan

- Pull out the cords connected to the motherboard and flip the board over. Take the old DC jack out of the motherboard and the chassis (input and output). Insert the new DC jack to the motherboard and chassis

- To reassemble the laptop, reverse the steps up to this point

- Reconnect the notebook to an external power source and replace the battery

Figure 1-22: Replacing a DC Jack

Battery

A battery consists of one or more electrochemical cells that contain positive and negative terminals. It transforms stored chemical energy into electrical energy. When an external load is connected to a battery, electrons go from the negative terminal to the positive terminal, producing an electrical current (electrons) to power the connected device.

Laptops and notebooks contain a battery that provides from 30 minutes to 8 hours' power. These batteries are available in various shapes and sizes. They are specially designed to fit in laptops and notebooks along with other components. They are usually square or rectangular in shape with a connector on one edge. There are three basic types of battery: Nickel Cadmium (NiCad), Nickel Metal-Hydride (NiMH), and Lithium Ion (Li-Ion). Most laptops have Li-Ion batteries because they are lightweight and have a long battery life.

Power adapters with an external power cord and transformer are usually provided for recharging the battery. The power cord has a transformer between the laptop and the outlet. This square or rectangular transformer is referred to as the power brick.

A failed laptop battery can be the source of all sorts of problems for users. Most manufacturers have diagnostic software that reports on the battery's health and estimates how many cycles are left. The

best approach to battery health is to be proactive. If users need to purchase a replacement battery, they should consider a larger-capacity alternative, if such a model is available.

To replace either the battery or the power cord, purchase the one that is specifically designed for that laptop or notebook.

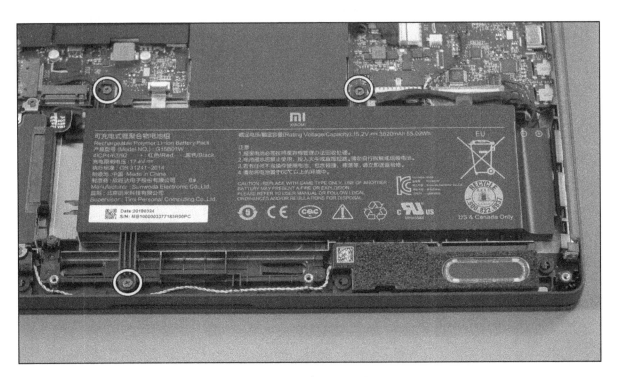

Figure 1-23: Replacing a Battery

To replace a battery, simply remove it from the battery compartment, typically located on the bottom of the notebook. The battery compartment has a slider or button to eject the battery. Manufacturers expect a laptop battery to be replaced after a certain amount of time, which is why they are easy to eject.

Touchpad

A touchpad is a built-in pointing device that is used for giving the computer commands. With the built-in touchpad, users can manipulate the cursor on the screen (just like moving the cursor with the help of a mouse).

Sliding a fingertip around the touchpad sends commands to the computer. Tapping or dragging the fingertip allows a user to perform actions such as copying text, deleting files or making text italic or bold). A physical wired or wireless mouse can also be attached to the laptop.

Steps for Replacing a Touchpad

To replace a laptop touch pad, follow the general steps below:

- First, disconnect the laptop or notebook power source and remove the battery

- Refer to the manufacturer's manual for the correct steps for disassembling the bottom of the notebook, and also to locate the system board

- Gently disconnect the cables of the pointing device. Mark the cables for the left and right mouse buttons to help when reattaching them

- Carefully remove the old pointing device

- Place a new pointing device in its exact location

- Reattach the cables

- Reverse the steps to disassemble a laptop to this point, reassemble the laptop

- Reconnect the notebook to an external power source and replace

Figure 1-24: Replacing a Touchpad

Installing the Touch Pad Driver

Turn on the laptop and let the operating system load properly. The touch pad may be automatically detected and installed. Go to the device manager and ensure the availability of the driver in the list of installed devices.

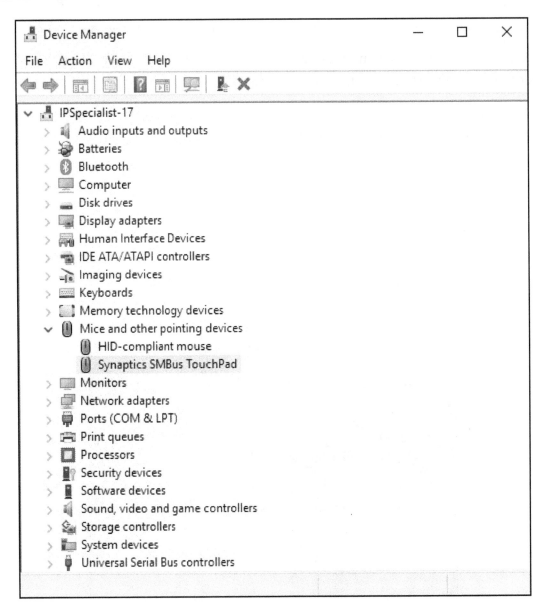

Figure 1-25: Installing a Touch Pad Driver

Plastics/Frames

Plastics or frames are used either to hold something in place or cover certain laptop parts. However, these frames or covers can be damaged easily while disassembling or assembling hardware. Refer to the manufacturer's manual for the replacement of these covers. The outside frame or plastic around a laptop's screen or monitor is known as a bezel.

Steps for Replacing the Plastic/Frame

To replace a laptop's plastic/frame, follow these general steps:

- On the laptop screen, you can see some of the rubber plugs or round corner stickers in the corners of the lid. Usually, there will be either two or four plugs near to the hinges or at the top of the screen

- Locate the round cover stickers or rubber plugs that are hiding the screws on the screen bezel – the case surrounding the screen. These stickers are usually located at the bottom of the bezel, close to the screen hinges

- In order to remove the cover stickers or rubber plugs, use a sharp, pointed object such as needle or open safety pin. Stick it between the bezel and the edge of the cover, and then pry the sticker away. Place these covers in a safe place and make sure that the sticky side stays up to retain stickiness so you can replace them later

- Remove the exposed screws

- Gently pry the screen bezel away from the back side of the screen case. The bezel is usually stronger than the back of the case and has plastic snaps, so use some force when prying it out but be careful not to use too much force. Use a thin prying object or fingernail into the gap around the outside of the screen

- The bezel is secured in place by plastic clips, so remove it carefully

- Now, replace the bezel by pressing its back into place

- To reassemble the laptop, reverse the disassemble steps up to this point

- Reconnect the notebook to an external power source and replace

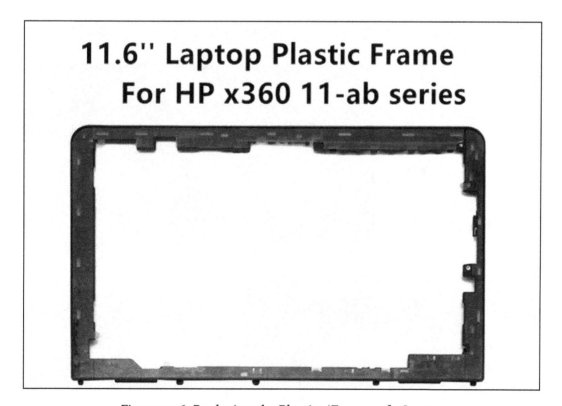

Figure 1-26: Replacing the Plastics/Frames of a Laptop

Speakers

Speakers and a microphone are likely to be built into the laptop or notebook computer. Speakers emit sound and the microphone receives sound.

In order to replace the speakers, find where they are mounted in the laptop or notebook. They are usually located on the inside bottom of the laptop, but some are located in the frame around the LCD screen.

Steps for Replacing a Speaker

Here are the general steps for replacing a speaker:

- First of all, disconnect the laptop or notebook power source and remove the battery

- Refer to the manufacturer's manual for the correct steps for disassembling either the bottom of the notebook, where the system board is located, or the top cover of the notebook, where the LCD screen is located

- Locate the exact position of the speakers, disconnect the cables and gently lift them out

- Now, place the new speakers in their exact location and connect the cables for the new speakers

- To reassemble the laptop, reverse the steps for disassembling up to this point

- Reconnect the notebook to an external power source and replace the battery if required

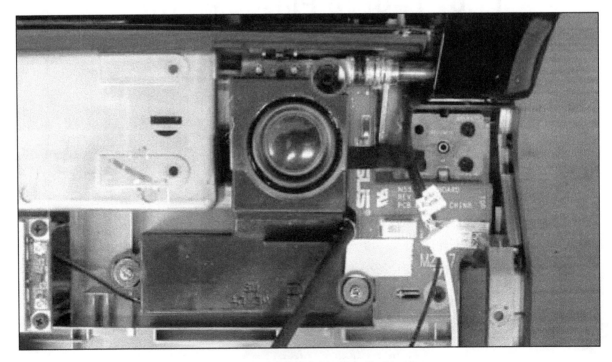

Figure 1-27: Replacing a Laptop's Speakers

Installing a Sound Card:

You must install the sound card within the expansion bus in a laptop. Go for a PCIe sound card if the laptop has only PCIe slots available. Sometimes, the sound card functionality is already integrated into the motherboard. You can connect the CD audio connection to the sound card. This enables the sound to play through the speakers, allowing users to play audio CDs.

Installing the Speaker Driver

Now there are two options for installing the driver for the speakers: either search for the speaker using Windows Update over the internet, or search for the driver using the disc provided by the laptop manufacturer.

Go to the device manager and click on "Audio inputs and outputs".

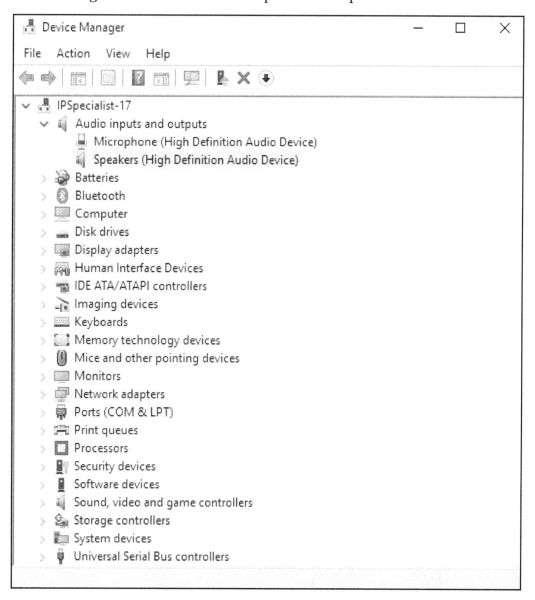

Figure 1-28: Installing the Speaker Driver

Double click on "Speaker/HP (Realtek High Definition Audio)".

A window for "Speaker/HP (Realtek High Definition Audio)" properties will pop up.

Figure 1-29: Updating the Speaker Driver

Click on the "Driver". Click on "Update Driver" to start the Windows search for driver updates.

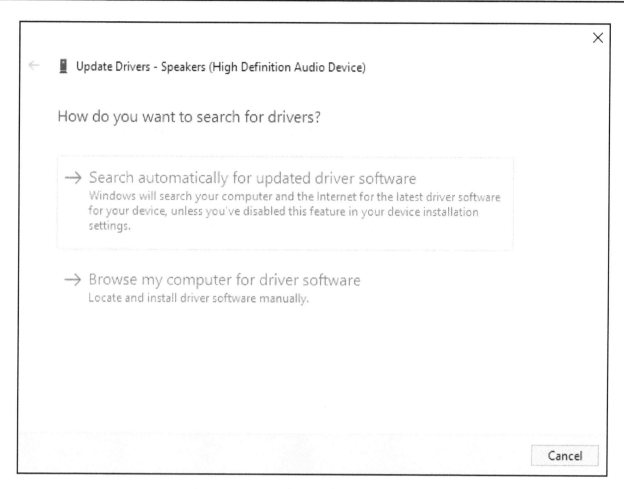

Figure 1-30: Updating the Speaker Driver

Get the driver from the disc that came with the card or download it from the manufacturer's driver page. Double-click the installer file of the driver and follow the steps provided by the on-screen instructions. Once the process is finished, the driver will be installed and should be in working condition.

Configuring the Speakers

Go to "Control Panel".

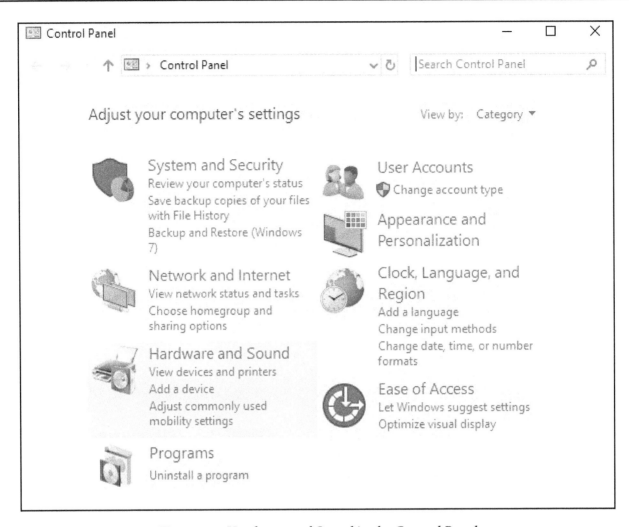

Figure 1-31: Hardware and Sound in the Control Panel

Click the "Hardware and Sound" option.

Select the "Manage audio devices" option in the "Hardware and Sound" section.

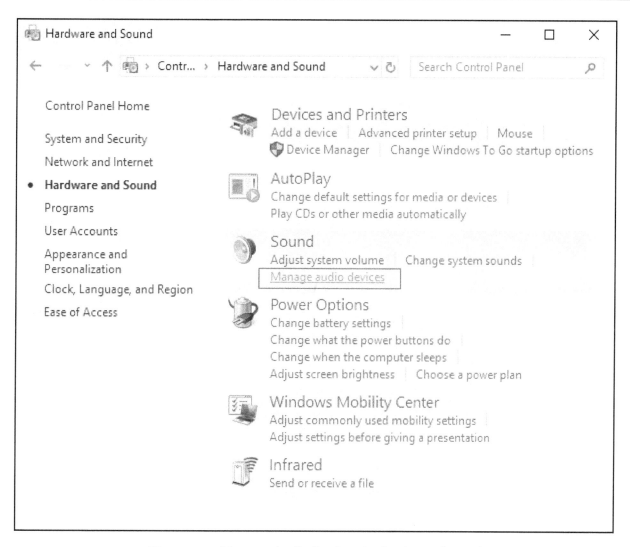

Figure 1-32: Manage Audio Devices in the Control Panel

A sound dialog box will pop up. Double-click the speaker icon.

Go to the properties by clicking the "Properties" button.

Figure 1-33: Speakers' Audio

Figure 1-34: Control Levels

A dialog box for Speakers Properties will pop up. Select the "Levels" tab, and then adjust the slider to vary the volume.

If there is a small red X on the speaker button, your speakers are not active. Click on it to activate the speakers.

Click the "Balance" button.

A Balance dialog box will pop up. Balance the sound between the two speakers using the R(Right) and L(Left) sliders.

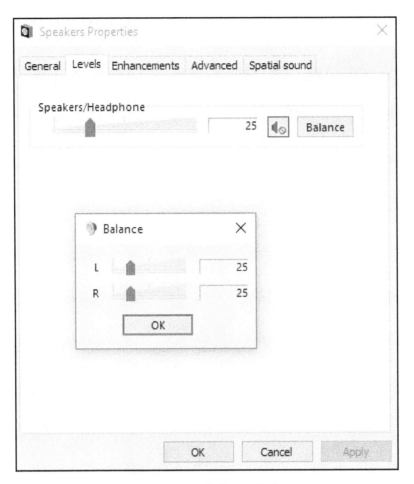

Figure 1-35: Balance Tab

System Board

The System Board is also known as the motherboard, planar board, main-board, or logic board. It provides the electrical connections by which system components can communicate. It connects the hosts with the central processing unit and other subsystems and devices.

Steps for Replacing a System Board

In order to replace the system board, you must first disconnect all components attached to it. The following are the general steps for replacing a notebook system board:

- First of all, disconnect the notebook power source and remove the battery

- Remove all the storage devices such as optical drive, hard drive, and memory

- Refer to the manufacturer's manual for the correct steps for disassembling the bottom cover plate, hinges, and keyboard

- Remove the LCD display assembly from the bottom

- Remove the motherboard cover (plate or shell) that covers the internal components

- Remove all of the internal components attached to the system board, including heat sink, wireless networking adapter, fan, touchpad, modem or other pointing device, and processor

- Now, remove the system board from the notebook. They are usually held in with plastic clips or screws

- Place the new system board in place of the old one, and line up the cut-outs for side ports, such as a USB

- Replace the processor and all the internal components that were attached to the system board

- To reassemble the notebook, reverse the disassemble steps up to this point

- Reconnect the notebook to an external power source or replace the battery if required

Figure 1-36: Replacing a System Board

Installing the Motherboard Driver

A driver called "**chipset**" or "**chipset driver**" needs to be installed first in order to improve the overall working of the motherboard. It makes the motherboard coordinate with the other components of the system. This small file is needed by the operating system to identify the motherboard.

Get the driver from the disc that came with the card or download it from the manufacturer's driver page. Double-click the driver's installer file and follow on-screen instructions provided. Once the process is finished, the card will be installed and should be in working condition.

CPU

The Central Processing Unit (CPU) is the brain of the computer and performs almost all the processing. It controls instructions and flow of data to and from other parts of the computer. A CPU's processing depends on the chipset, which is a group of microchips located on the motherboard. A multicore processor consists of more than one processor core on the same chip. The more cores in the laptop processor, the faster the laptop can perform tasks and the more tasks the laptop can perform simultaneously.

CPUs for laptops and notebooks are specifically designed to consume less power and generate less heat than typical desktop CPUs. Manufacturers like AMD, Intel etc. are continuously working for the improvement and upgradation of their processors.

You need to determine which models are supported by the installed motherboard, before replacing the CPU in a laptop. Laptop motherboards are customized for a limited range of CPUs. A UEFI/BIOS update may allow the successful use of extra CPUs. Before disassembling the laptop, install any required UEFI/BIOS update.

Steps for Replacing a CPU

To replace the processor, heat sink, or system fan, follow these general steps:

- To replace the processor, first update the BIOS. Manufacturers often update their firmware in order to support newer processors

- Now, disconnect the laptop or notebook power source and remove the battery

- Refer to the manufacturer's manual for the correct the steps for disassembling the bottom of the laptop

- Pry up the keyboard cover with a small flathead screwdriver. Remove the keyboard cover and put it aside

- Follow the steps for pulling the keyboard out of the laptop from the section "Keyboard" above

- Pull the keyboard out gently and put it aside

- Now, detach the LCD assembly from the bottom and put it aside

- Remove the plate or shell – the motherboard cover – the covers the internal components

- To gain access to the processor, first remove the other components above the processor such as the graphic card assembly

- Gently remove the heat sink

- Detach and unplug the fan

- Refer to the manufacturer's manual for the correct steps for removing the processor: some processors have a locking bar and some have a locking screw

- Remove any thermal compound residue from the bottom of the processor and heat sink (if you are not replacing the processor)

- Now, apply a thin layer of thermal compound and insert the new processor

- Re-plug and reattach the original or a new system fan

- Attach the original or new heat sink (if it is not already a part of the same cooling assembly as the fan)

- To reassemble the laptop, reverse the disassemble steps up to this point

- Reconnect the notebook to an external power source or replace the battery if required

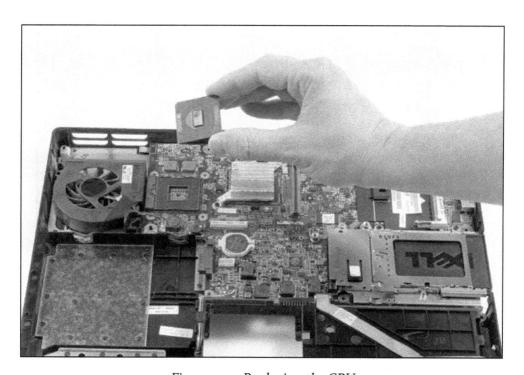

Figure 1-37: Replacing the CPU

Installing a CPU Driver

After replacing the processor, turn ON the laptop. Now go to the device manager.

Expand the "Processors" option.

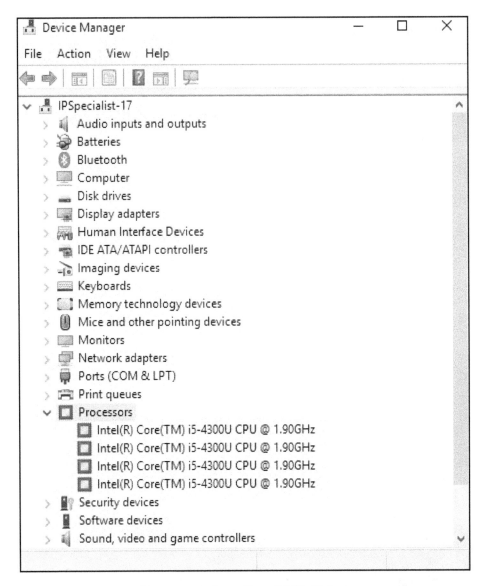

Figure 1-38: Installing CPU's Driver

Click on the "Driver". Then, click on "Update Driver" to start the Windows search for driver updates.

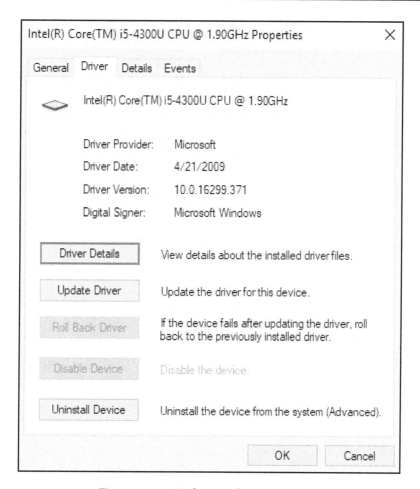

Figure 1-39: Updating the CPU Driver

Click "Update" to update the driver. Now, there are two options for installing a webcam; either search for the webcam using Windows Update over the internet, or search for the driver using the disc provided by the laptop manufacturer.

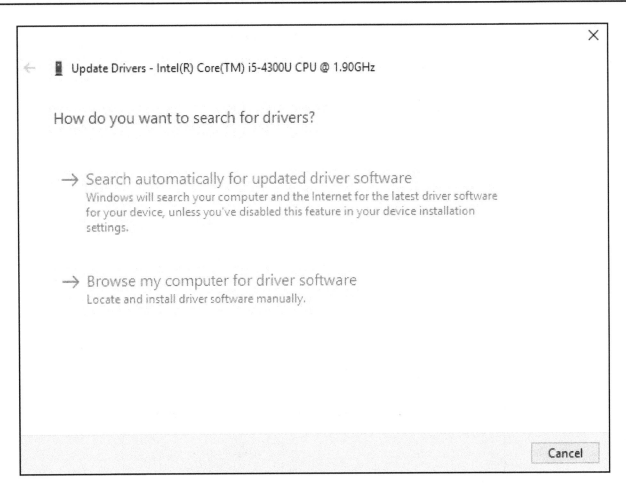

Figure 1-40: Updating the CPU Driver

Get the driver from the disc that came with the card or download it from the manufacturer's driver page. Double-click the driver's installer file and follow the on-screen instructions provided. Once the process is finished, the driver will be installed and should be in working condition.

 Exam Note

Remember: a laptop's video subsystem consists of a screen (example: LED) and a video card (example: Mini PCIe card).

Mind Map of Hardware Replacement

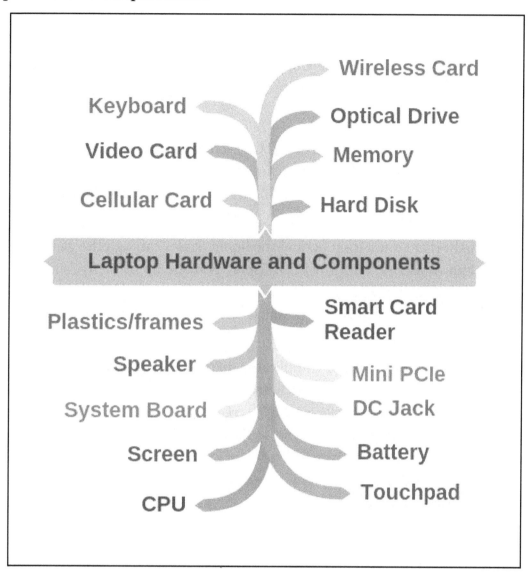

Figure 1-41: Mind Map of Hardware Replacement

Install Components within the Display of a Laptop

The display or monitor of a laptop is an integrated component, just like the keyboard. It is a very thin LCD device. The video adapter is installed in the computing device and converts data into the signals required to form the image on screen. The advanced video adapters produce the signals that are required to display full-color images and video with better picture quality. There are various types of screens and components behind the glass that make it work, and the following sections cover the essentials of screen technology.

Types

It can be a challenging job to replace screens, and it often involves costly and sensitive components. Some vendors provide online documentation to guide users through the whole process of reducing and rebuilding an intact portable into a pile of parts. However, this information is designed mainly for professional computer service staff.

Liquid Crystal Display (LCD)

Laptop usually have thin Liquid Crystal Display (LCD) screens providing users with a display at the native resolution, which means the image matches the exact number of pixels on the screen. The higher the laptop screen's native resolution, the higher the quality of the picture.

In a liquid crystal display, the active part of the monitor is a layer of liquid between two pieces of polarized glass. A light that comes from behind the liquid passes through the glass and illuminates the crystals (also known as shutters). An LCD display is made up of many "shutters", otherwise known as pixels, that open up to become either clear, green, red, or blue. An LCD display uses a separate light source placed behind the LCD Matrix to shine through the "shutters". LCD displays are the most affordable screens.

Replacing LCD screens on laptops can be complicated, particularly if you need to replace the display panel or backlight, or if a Wi-Fi antenna is included in the screen assembly, as is the case with the latest designs. To remove and replace an LCD screen, you need to disassemble the laptop. Replacements can be obtained either from the vendor or from an authorized parts depot. Many vendors require only authorized technicians to remove or replace display panels in portable computers. However, the method of replacing the entire LCD display assembly is simple and can be possible for users to perform in the field.

Steps for Replacing an LCD Screen

- Remove power from the system. Disconnect the antenna leads attached to the adapter if the system has an integrated wireless card
- Remove the keyboard frame and keyboard
- Disconnect the display cable from the system board; this cable transmits power and data to the display assembly. On touchscreen-equipped models, this cable also carries touchscreen data
- Detach the antenna leads from the clips in the top cover, if the system has integrated wireless
- Rotate the display assembly to a 90-degree angle to the base unit
- Remove the screws that secure the display assembly
- Pull the display assembly free from the base unit

Light Emitting Diode (LED)

An LED screen or display usually means an LCD panel, where an array of LEDs (Light Emitting Diodes) provides backlighting.

Screens with an LED display are slightly cooler, thinner, and more energy efficient. LED screens are way slimmer and less costly to run in the long-term.

The disadvantage of LED displays is that they are slightly more susceptible to image retention or screen burn than LCD monitors.

Organic Light-Emitting Diode (OLED)

Organic Light-Emitting Diode (OLED) is a type of display that provides better color reproduction, accuracy, and excellent contrast to the display, while maintaining good viewing angles. OLED is the luxury display option. In OLED, blacks are more vivid than on any other kind of panel. It is much better than LCD at dealing with light and darkness precision.

OLED displays are ideal for movie lovers, content creators, and game lovers who needs fast response time. One of the disadvantages of an OLED display is that it is much more expensive than any of the others. Further, OLEDs consume more power and are susceptible to display burn-in.

It is more difficult to avoid damage during the replacement process when replacing OLED screens, and specialized tools are necessary for the more delicate steps. If an OLED screen needs to be replaced, it may be safer and more cost-effective to take cracked or broken screens to a professional who is equipped to replace them.

The advantages of OLED can be summarized as follows:

- **Brighter:** OLEDs can be larger than other types of screens and offer higher resolutions

- **Thinner and more lightweight:** OLEDs are a good choice for smartphones, tablets and convertible (two-in-one) units that switch between laptop and tablet modes

- **Energy efficient:** Only the lit pixels draw power; with good application design, this can greatly extend battery life

- **Faster refresh rates:** OLEDs can refresh quickly, which makes them a favorite for gamers who value quick response times

Installing a Wi-Fi Antenna Connector/Placement in the Display of a Laptop

A Wi-Fi antenna connector connects an outdoor Wi-Fi antenna to computers wirelessly. It also enhances connectivity and range to the internet and the network.

Place a wireless PCMCIA adapter card into the laptop or computer. If the computing machine does not have an PCMCIA slot, plug a USB wireless adapter into an unused USB port.

A window will pop up. Click on the "Locate and Install Driver Software" option in the pop-up window. Wait until the device is installed on the laptop.

Follow the onscreen prompts to insert the driver CD that came with the device.

During setup, when the prompt to name the wireless network appears, enter the credentials to gain access to the Wi-Fi network.

If a laptop screen is damaged, the Wi-Fi antenna may also be damaged. The inverter is not present in an OLED display, but the remaining components are in the same location.

Webcams

A webcam is a digital video camera that is directly or indirectly connected to a laptop or any other computing device. Webcams are used for taking pictures as well as for high-definition videos. Webcams come with software that first has to be installed on the computer to allow users to record video or stream it to the Web.

If a webcam fails, it can be replaced after performing a partial disassembly of the laptop. However, if a higher-resolution webcam is needed, it is better to use an external webcam that connects to a USB port.

Steps for Replacing a Webcam

In laptops, webcams are typically mounted above the LCD screen inside the display panel. To replace a webcam, follow these general steps:

- First, disconnect the laptop or notebook power source and remove the battery
- From the display panel, gently remove the front bezel. Refer to the manufacturer's manual for the correct steps
- Disconnect the cables and gently remove the webcam
- Insert a new webcam and connect its cable
- Replace the front bezel on the display panel
- To reassemble the laptop, reverse the disassemble steps up to this point
- Reconnect the notebook to an external power source and replace

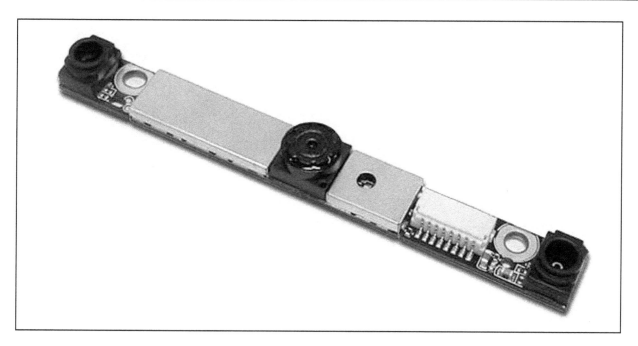

Figure 1-42: Replacing a Laptop Webcam

Installing the Webcam Driver

Go to the start button, open "Control Panel", and double click the "Add a device" option.

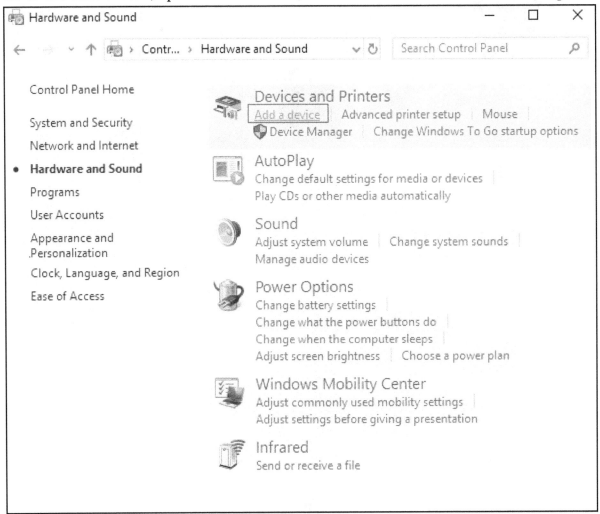

Figure 1-43: Installing a Laptop Webcam

Click "Add a device". A window will pop up and start to search for devices that are connected to the system but are not installed.

If installing a webcam, click on the name of webcam that shows in the search box and then click "Next".

Now there are two options for installing a webcam: either search for the webcam using Windows Update over the internet, or search for the driver using the disc provided by the laptop manufacturer.

The system recovery disc that came with the laptop contains most of the drivers. If you want to add the driver from the disc provided, tick the box next to your chosen option and click "Next" to continue.

<u>Method 1:</u>

If the first option is selected to install a webcam, in order to have an active internet connection for Windows, search from the driver using Windows Update over the internet.

Now, select the "Install the software automatically (Recommended)" option in the "Add a device" application, and click "Next" to begin searching for the webcam driver.

The hardware wizard will search and install the driver on its own on the system recovery disk. Click "Finish" to close the wizard and reboot the PC to get the laptop to recognize the webcam.

Now, allow the computer to install the webcam driver and then reboot the system.

<u>Method 2:</u>

Another option is to use the "system recovery disc" or a driver that has already been downloaded by the laptop manufacturer; users just have to install the driver without going through the Windows Update search feature.

For this option, insert the system recovery disc in the CD/DVD-ROM drive, or place the already downloaded driver in an easily accessible PC file directory, such as in "My Documents" or in any desktop folder.

Select the "Install the software manually" option to browse for the driver's location and install the driver from there. To install the driver, click the "Next" button and then reboot the computer to get the laptop to recognize the new webcam.

Microphone

A microphone is an electronic device that takes audio as an input and converts sound waves into an electrical signal. It is used by the webcam and for other recording purposes when needed.

If a microphone fails, it can be replaced after performing a partial disassembly of the laptop. However, if a higher-quality microphone is needed, it is better to use a microphone as part of a headset connected to an audio port or a USB port.

Installing a Laptop Microphone

Go to the start button, open "Control Panel", and click the "Hardware and Sound" option.

Figure 1-44: Installing a Laptop Microphone

Note
Make sure to have the right driver device for the microphone according to the manufacturer's specifications. If that driver is not recommended for the microphones, download the right driver device from the manufacturer.

Click on the microphone option in the "Control Panel".

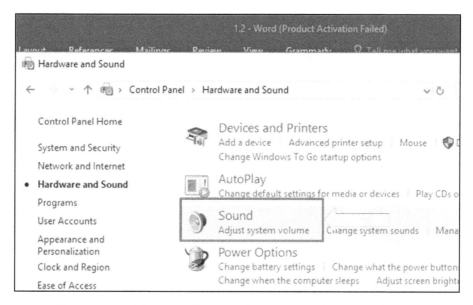

Figure 1-45: Adjusting the Sound System in the Control Panel

A window for sound control panel will pop up. Click on the "Recording" tab, select the microphone option and click "Properties" to update the settings.

Figure 1-46: Laptop Microphone Settings

Figure 1-47: Testing Volume and Microphone

Test the volume control on the computer and make sure the microphone is turned on.

Inverter

The inverter is a power converter that changes low-voltage DC power into the higher voltage AC power required to power a CCFL backlight. If the inverter fails, there is no power to run the backlight. Inverter failure is the most common cause of LCD display failure. However, inverters are relatively inexpensive to replace and they can be purchased for do-it-yourself (DIY) replacement.

Steps for Replacing a Laptop Inverter

LCD panels are fragile and susceptible to damage. If the LCD display is completely black, connect an external monitor to the notebook. If the external monitor is also not working, replace the video inverter card or video adaptor card.

In order to replace a video inverter card, follow these general steps:

- First, disconnect the laptop or notebook power source and remove the battery

- Remove the bottom cover and the battery

- Remove all the storage devices such as optical drive, hard drive, and memory

- Refer to the manufacturer's manual for the correct steps for disassembling the bottom cover plate, hinges, and keyboard

- Remove the LCD panel, and refer to the manufacturer's manual for the correct steps for that type of laptop

- Unscrew the screws that hold the LCD panel in the notebook and remove the bezel

- Open the rear cover from the LCD panel and remove the video inverter card

- Insert a new inverter card in its place

- To reassemble the laptop, reverse the disassemble steps up to this point

- Reconnect the notebook to an external power source and replace

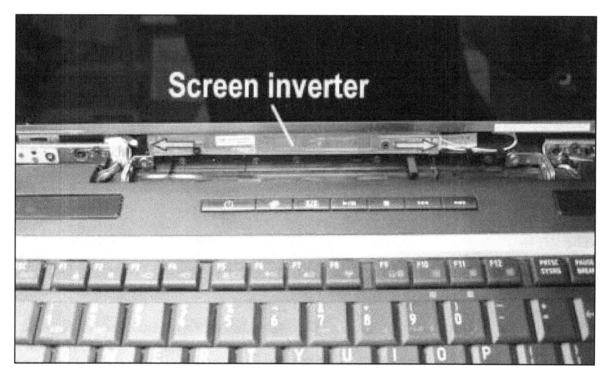

Figure 1-48: Replacing a Laptop Invertor

Digitizer/Touchscreen

The digitizer is the electrical force in the display screen that is touch sensitive. It is located just under the glass of the laptop screen. It senses and responds to touch. The digitizer layer can be replaced separately if it is damaged and the display panel is intact.

Installing a Digitizer/Touch Screen in your Laptop

In order to install a touchscreen or digitizer, follow the steps given below:

- First, determine whether the laptop has a touchscreen or not. In Windows, go to the start menu and search for "View pen and touch info". If the Pen and touch section responds with "No pen or touch input is available for this display", then the laptop does not have a touchscreen

- Check the product specifications for the laptop model on the manufacturer's website

- If the laptop has a touch sensitive screen, you just need to install it. Sometimes the touchscreen does not respond because it is not installed or enabled. Make use of "Device Manager" to install and enable the touchscreen driver

- Go to the start menu, search, and open "Device Manager"

- Click "Human Interface Devices", to expand the list

Right-click the touchscreen device option, and then click "Enable" if the option is available. If the "Enable" option does not display, go to the next step.

Touch the screen to see whether the screen has become touch sensitive or not. If it has not, continue the steps given below:

- Right-click the touchscreen device option, and then uninstall this device

- Reboot the laptop to reinstall the digitizer/touchscreen driver

Touch the screen to see whether the screen has become touch sensitive or not. If it has not, continue with the steps given below:

- Configure the touch display to make the screen similar to a touchscreen

- Go to the start menu, search, and open "Calibrate the screen for pen and touch input"

- Click "Setup" on the Display tab

- Click "Touch" input

Now, follow the on-screen prompts to make the screen a touch sensitive screen.

Touch the screen to see if screen has become touch sensitive or not. If it is still not working, then Windows update might resolve the issue.

Exam Note

Understand that a screen inverter's job is to convert DC voltage from the motherboard into AC voltage to be sent to the backlight. The inverter should not be handled if the laptop is on. Make sure to switch off and unplug the laptop and remove the battery before removing an inverter.

Mind Map of Components Installed in a Laptop for Display

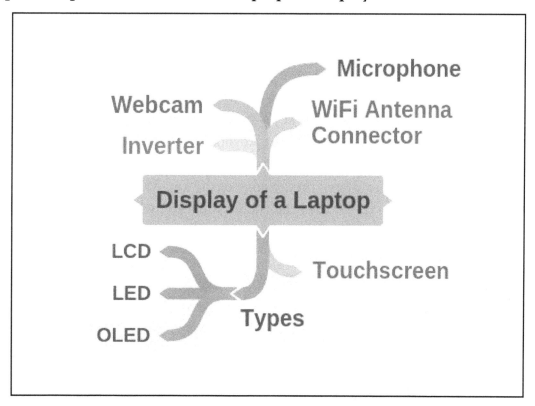

Figure 1-49: Mind Map of Laptop Display Components

Use Appropriate Laptop Features

Recent generations of laptops have become as powerful as and more flexible than desktops. Laptop features have been developed equal to those of larger PCs, but that brought issues that to do with the smaller form factor. The following sections describe the various ways for you to enable a laptop to execute the tasks of a larger computer.

Special Function Keys

Function keys are the set of programmable keys that sit horizontally across the top of the keyboard. In addition to their regular functions, they also perform special tasks assigned by the existing application program.

Laptop keyboards are smaller than standard desktop keyboards. Both types of keyboard have function keys, but some function keys are specific to laptops and are not present on desktop keyboards. In a laptop, there is a special function key at the lower-left side of the keyboard with the name Fn. When this key is pressed, all other function keys such as F1, F2 and so on, can perform functions other than their regular function. Refer to the manufacturer's manual to find out which key combination serves your required purpose for your laptop.

Most laptop keyboards combine two functions on one key, and the user can switch between the two by pressing the Fn key, in much the same way as the Shift key allows the use of numbers and use special characters. To access the functions key's special functions, press the function key "Fn" (generally located in the lower left corner of the keyboard) at the same time as another key to activate the alternate functions. The alternative function is usually written in a different color, in smaller, lighter type and written or drawn on the edge of the key. With the Fn key held down, click any other key (F1, F2, and so on) to perform the the Fn function; when the Fn key is released, the key returns to its normal operation. Fn functions are usually printed below or beside the normal key legend and sometimes in a contrasting color.

Figure 1-50: Laptop Function Keys

Special functions include changing the display's brightness, adjusting the volume, using Num Lock, and switching between the built-in monitor and an external monitor. Refer to your documentation for additional information on other alternate functions that might be included on your keyboard.

Dual Displays

In a scenario where a user requires an additional display such as second monitor or a projector attached to the laptop, they have to enable the laptop's dual display mode.

To do so, hold down the Fn key and press the F key with an image of a monitor that is specific for this particular function. The setting will change from active screen from display to display, or display to projector.

Figure 1-51: Keys to Enable Dual Display on a Laptop

This function is used to direct the display to another laptop screen or to a projector. Refer to the manufacturer's manual to find out which function key serves that purpose for the model of laptop.

Wireless (on/off)

Wireless connections are made with infrared light or radio waves. Wireless networks are used to connect users through hotspots where a wireless internet service is provided by the ISPs. Wireless connections can also be made over satellite or via cellular telephone networks.

In addition, there is a function key that can enable and disable wireless connectivity in the laptop. The function key with an antenna icon on the lower right corner is assigned for this task.

You do not have to hold the Fn key for this function. Simply press the function key for this purpose and enable or disable wireless connection anytime. Refer to the manufacturer's manual to find out which function key serves that purpose for the model of laptop.

Figure 1-52: Keys to Enable Wireless Connectivity on a Laptop

Cellular (on/off)

Cellular connections are made by using a laptop's cellular network PC Card.

There is also a function key that can enable and disable the laptop's cellular (WWAN) connectivity.

For this function, hold the Fn key and then press the function key for this purpose and enable or disable cellular connection anytime.

Refer to the manufacturer's manual to find out which function key serves that purpose for the model of laptop.

Volume Settings

There are usually a couple of function keys that can be used to lower or raise the volume.

These function keys have a blue or grey speaker icon on the lower-right side of the tab. In order to raise or lower the volume, just hold the Fn key and then press the respective function key to achieve desired volume.

Figure 1-53: Keys to Change Volume Settings on a Laptop

Refer to the manufacturer's manual to find out which function key serves that purpose for the model of laptop.

Screen Brightness

There are usually a couple of function keys that can be used to increase or decrease the brightness of the screen.

Figure 1-54: Keys to Adjust Screen Brightness

Refer to the manufacturer's manual to find out which function key serves that purpose for the model of laptop.

> **Exam Note**
>
> Use the Fn key in combination with F1–F12 keys to configure many functions, including media options, Wi-Fi access, brightness, the touchpad, and an external monitor. If available, press the Num Lock key to enable/disable the numeric keypad on the laptop. If the Num Lock indicator light is on, then the numeric key is enabled.

Bluetooth (on/off)

A Bluetooth adapter can be inserted into the USB port. This adapter enables any Bluetooth-compatible device for short-range wireless communication and data synchronization between devices.

The function key that is used to enable and disable wireless connectivity is also used for enabling Bluetooth connectivity on the laptop. The function key that is assigned for this task has an antenna icon on the lower-right corner of the function key.

For this function, it is not necessary to hold the Fn key. Simply press the function key for this purpose and enable or disable the Bluetooth connection anytime. Refer to the manufacturer's manual to find out which function key serves that purpose for the model of laptop.

Figure 1-55: Keys to Enable and Disable Bluetooth on a Laptop

Keyboard Backlight

Some laptops have keyboards that are backlit. They are indispensable for those who work in low lights or dark environments.

Enable the Keyboard Backlight

In order to enable the keyboard backlight, follow these general steps:

- Go to the Start button and select "Control Panel"

- Click "System and Security" in the Control Panel window

- Select "VAIO Control Center" in the system and security window

- Select "Keyboard and Mouse" in the VAIO Control Center window

- Click Backlit KB

- In the Backlit KB screen, place a tick/check in the box next to "Turn backlight on when surroundings dark", to enable the backlight feature in the laptop

Figure 1-56: Enable the Keyboard Backlight on a Laptop

There are also some special function keys and key combinations that enable the keyboard backlight.

Hold down the Fn key and press some other key, for example "ctrl Z" to enable the keyboard backlight. Refer to the manufacturer's manual to find out which function key serves that purpose for the model of laptop.

Touchpad (on/off)

A touchpad is a built-in pointing device that is used to give the computer commands or input. Users can move the laptop cursor on the screen (just like moving the cursor with the help of a mouse) using this built-in pointing device that is in the form of a small button or a touchpad.

Configuring the Touchpad on your Laptop

In order to enable the touchpad, follow the general steps below:

- Go to the Start button and select "Control Panel"

- Click "Hardware and Sound" in the Control Panel window

- Select "Mouse" under Devices and Printers

- Open the mouse properties, select the "TouchPad" or "ClickPad" option or something similar. There will be an option for enabling and disabling the touchpad

- Click the "Enable" option to enable the touchpad and then click "OK"

Touchpad Button

Some laptops have a button near the touchpad that allows users to enable and disable the touchpad whenever required.

Fn Keys

There are some special function keys that allow users to enable and disable touchpad using a key combination. To switch the touchpad off and on, press both of these keys at the same time. Refer to the manufacturer's manual to find out which key combination serves that purpose for the model of laptop.

Screen Orientation

The position of the image on the display screen is referred to as screen orientation. This position or orientation can be changed to suit the position the user is in – sitting or lying. Users can do this by rotating the angle of the image. This rotation can be either done by changing the display setting or by using a key combination.

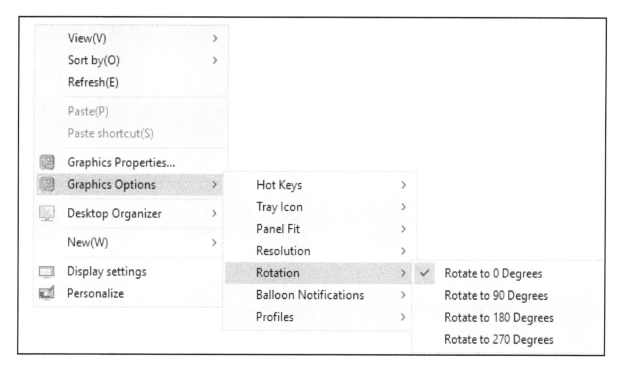

Figure 1-57: Changing a Laptop's Screen Orientation

Refer to the manufacturer's manual to find out which key combination serves that purpose for the model of laptop. For example, in some laptops, Shift+Alt+Arrow keys are used to rotate the screen orientation.

Media Options (Fast Forward/Rewind)

Some laptops offer keys that are associated with the media player. It allows users to forward, rewind, play, or stop the player using a special key combination.

This key combination may include the use of Fn and other function keys. Hold down the Fn key and click the function key according to requirements.

Figure 1-58: Media Option in a Laptop's Function Keys

Refer to the manufacturer's manual to find out which key combination serves that purpose for the model of laptop.

<u>GPS (On/Off)</u>

Computing devices or laptops come with built-in GPS technology. Users just have to enable or disable this feature. This can be done by changing the privacy settings.

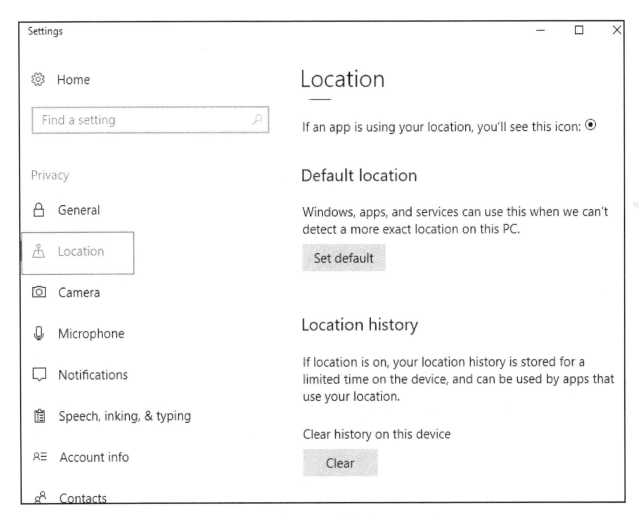

Figure 1-59: Enable or Disable GPS on a Laptop

<u>Airplane Mode</u>

Mobile devices and laptops come with a built-in Airplane mode feature. Users can enable or disable airplane mode by changing the privacy settings.

Go to the Start button and search for "Airplane Mode". The relevant window will pop up.

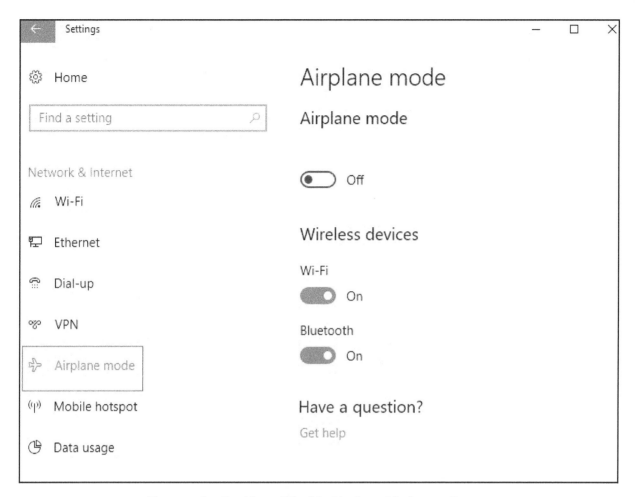

Figure 1-60: Enable or Disable Airplane Mode on a Laptop

Docking Station

A Docking Station extends the capacity of a portable computer by adding features such as:

- One or more expansion slots

- Additional I/O ports, such as Ethernet, display output ports (for HDMI or DisplayPort), Thunderbolt ports, USB ports (USB 2.0, 3.0, USB 3.1 Type C), and others

- Power connection for the laptop

- Connectors for a standard keyboard and mouse

Portable computer suppliers produce most docking stations, although some third-party products are also available. Business-class laptops that support docking stations may have a proprietary expansion bus on the rear or bottom of the computer. However, docking stations for tablets or thin and light laptops might be connected via a high-speed bus such as Thunderbolt or USB 3.0/3.1 or a proprietary data/charging cable.

Installing a Docking Station on your Laptop

In order to connect a laptop to a docking station, follow the steps below:

- First, locate the position of the jack/connector that connects the laptop to the docking device. Connect the laptop to the docking station or port replicator that is compatible with the laptop

- Refer to the manufacturer's manual for the steps for connecting the laptop or notebook to the docking device

- Connect any device such as monitor, keyboard, and mouse to the docking device

- Turn the laptop or notebook on

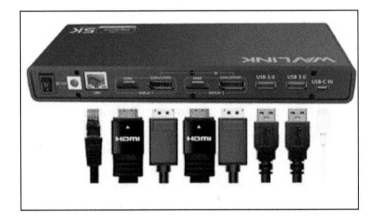

Figure 1-61: Docking Station

Regardless of how a docking station connects to a portable computer, the user can leave desktop-type peripherals attached to the docking station and access them by linking the portable computer to the docking station quickly and easily.

Always turn off the laptop before removing it from the docking station or port replicator, or refer to the manufacturer's manual for the steps for ejecting the laptop from the docking device.

> **Note**
>
> The term mobile docking station is often used to define a device that is used to securely hold a laptop or tablet in place in a vehicle (police, insurance, EMS, and other industries). These devices are not used for additional ports.

Port Replicator

A Port Replicator is a device that can be attached to a laptop or notebook computer. It allows multiple devices such as a monitor, keyboard, and a printer to be simultaneously connected to the laptop. Whenever a user wants to access one or more devices at the same time, the user simply has

to attach the port replicator to the laptop instead of connecting one device at a time. For example, a user can connect a port replicator on a notebook to a USB port and then connect other equipment such as printers, cameras, mice, speakers, and so on, to the port replicator. To host additional displays, the replicator may have DVI and HDMI ports. As features are added, port replicators come to resemble non-proprietary docking stations. The port replicator contains all of the laptop's ports, including serial and parallel ports. In addition, it also contains ports for devices such as Musical Instrument Digital Interfaces (MIDIs) and joysticks.

Physical Laptop Lock and Cable Lock

The portability of a laptop makes them susceptible to being stolen. Therefore, physical security is necessary. Laptops usually come with a special slot known as a lock slot or Kensington Lock.

Figure 1-62: Laptop Lock or Cable Lock

The Kensington lock is also referred to as a K slot or K lock. The lock is used with a small hole that is present on almost every portable computing device. Laptops with a Kensington lock hole can protect the data on their portable device using a Kensington lock.

To avoid data theft, use the password-lock feature in the operating system that requires a password when the keyboard is locked. Press Windows+L on Windows. For maximum security, use some sort of full-disk encryption like Windows BitLocker, MacOS FileVault, or a third-party solution like PGP or Symantec Endpoint Encryption.

Rotating/Removable Screens

Devices with Rotating/Removable Screens is one of the fastest-growing mobile device category. Bridging the gap between tablet and laptop, this category includes all levels of performance from low-end 32-bit processors with 32 GB storage and 2 MB RAM to high-performance multicore 64-bit processors.

Devices with removable keyboards usually have a screen size of less than 12 ins. Such a computer works as a big tablet when used without the keyboard.

Devices with rotating screens have bigger displays and more ports, and they have more powerful processors. Although screen size and port accessibility of these devices rival those of standard laptops, they are not designed to be readily upgradable. Memory, storage, and wireless upgrades typically involve a major disassembly process.

Figure 1-63: Rotating/Removable Screens

 Exam Note

Note the difference: A laptop is placed or "docked" into a docking station. However, a port replicator is connected to the laptop simply to provide additional ports.

Mind Map of Laptop Features and Function Keys

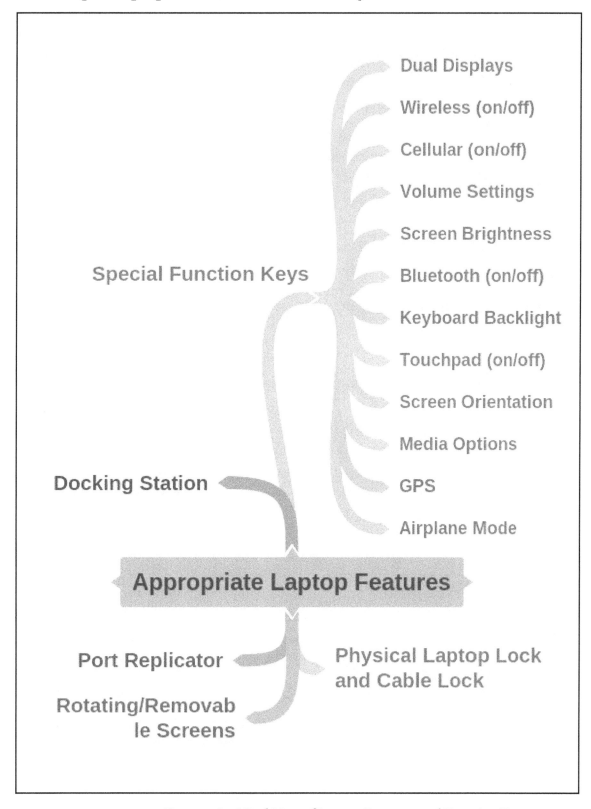

Figure 1-64: Mind Map of Laptop Features and Function Keys

Compare and Contrast the Characteristics of Various Mobile Devices

Manufacturers are constantly developing new applications and mobile devices that further integrate technology into our daily lives. Users more easily accept smartphones, tablets, and wearable technology such as intelligent watches and fitness trackers as part of their daily routine. With the wide range of available products to use or support, it is important to have a working knowledge of their basic functions.

This section compares and contrasts the characteristics of various mobile devices. Mobile device is a general term that is used to describe all handheld computing devices. Mobile devices are extremely portable; users can hold them in their hand and connect anywhere in the world, anytime, while doing anything. Mobile devices can serve almost the same purpose as a desktop, but it allows people to be less location-dependent in both personal and professional life than ever before. Computing with mobile devices has come a long way: from the very first laptop to today's smartphones and the latest devices. Let's have a look at some of the most common examples of mobile devices.

Tablets

The tablet is an evolution of the notebook computer or laptop along with touch sensitive LCD screens, which can be utilized with a stylus or with the fingertips, allowing users to type or enter input on a virtual keyboard. Some tablets also offer a removable keyboard as an additional option. Like laptops, tablets are portable. They can do everything that a traditional computer can do. Usually, tablets are bigger than smartphones and smaller than laptops. On a tablet, a user can browse the internet, stay connected through email, carry out video conferences, watch movies, read e-books, play games, listen to music, share photos, and much more. Here are some of the most common features of a tablet:

- *Mobile OS* is a mobile operating system specially designed to run on mobile devices and other handheld devices. This operating system plays a vital role in determining the features and functions available on a device, for example keyboards, thumb wheel, WAP, text messaging, email, synchronization with applications and much more. The popular mobile OSs are: Android OS, Bada, Blackberry OS, iPhone OS, and Windows Mobile

- *Solid-state Drives* are used by tablets in place of hard-disk drives because they are faster and more durable

- *Wi-Fi Connectivity* in tablets with built-in Wi-Fi allows optimized internet connectivity

Some examples of tablet PCs include Samsung Galaxy Tab, Samsung Nexus, Apple iPad, Surface Pro, Amazon Kindle Fire HD, Microsoft Surface, Lenovo Yoga, and many more.

Smartphones

In recent history, no device has had a greater impact on human communication than the smartphone. Smartphones typically use either Android or iOS operating systems, although some use Windows Mobile.

A smartphone is an advanced version of a traditional cell phone, retaining the same basic features such as phone calls, text messaging, and voicemails. Additionally, smartphones can connect to the internet over a cellular network or Wi-Fi. This means smartphones reduce dependency on computers or desktop PCs for the things people normally do on a computer, such as web browsing, checking emails, online shopping, visiting social networking sites, and much more.

Smartphones are capable of running applications along with basic phone services. They have an operating system with advanced computing capabilities. Some other features include a high-quality digital camera, GPS navigation, and a multimedia player for digital music and video files. Smartphone Operating Systems (OS) enable users to download mobile apps, enhancing the overall phone's functionality.

Wearable Technology Devices

Computing functionalities are not just limited to handheld devices but are now available as wearable devices such as smart watches, fitness monitors, VR/AR headsets, etc. These devices connect to a smartphone via Bluetooth and can be fully charged in as little as 15 minutes.

When choosing wearable technology, it is essential to verify compatibility with the operating system and features of the device. Bluetooth must be enabled on the smartphone before a wearable technology device can connect to it.

Smart Watches

Smart watches are digital watches that do more than just track time. Smart watches use similar technology to Bluetooth to connect to a smartphone. Once a connection is established between a smart watch and a smart phone, an alert or notification will be generated on every email, message, and social media status for any instance, allowing the user to interact with the phone in a unique way. Smart watches can run different apps and digital media, such as radio streams and audio tracks to Bluetooth headphones. Many of these watches have touchscreens, which enables users to access features such as a calculator, compass, thermometer, and much more.

Fitness Monitors

One of the wearable technology devices is the fitness monitor. This can connect to the body as a hand band or watch and give information about the heart rate and more. It provides users with information such as how far they have run, how many steps they have taken throughout the day, or how well they are sleeping at night. By using Bluetooth and Wi-Fi, fitness monitors can monitor the

body state and report the data back to the master device. It measures heart rate and activity in real time along with the activity level.

A fitness monitor such as **Fitbit** can also be fitted with a heart rate monitor, gyroscope, a GPS, and a pedometer. It forms a common profile and sends it to the health and fitness data stored in the cloud and you can use this health data to determine the level of fitness.

VR/AR Headsets

Smart headset uses voice recognition technology and a built in microphone to respond to voice commands. It enables users to dictate and send emails or text messages along with any command and control input.

Smart Cameras

Smart cameras have high resolution touch sensitive screens along with compose, edit, and preview image options. In addition, they are equipped with Wi-Fi or cellular data to allow posting images and videos directly to social media. It may also be equipped with a GPS receiver to allow tagging images with the location it was captured in. These smart cameras are usually embedded in smart phones.

E-Readers

E-readers or e-book readers are mainly designed for reading e-books and magazines in digital and downloadable form. E-readers have either an LCD or E-ink display. E-readers that support ePub and PDF formats are more suitable for graphically rich publications.

- *LCD Display* is a regular screen normally found on laptops and tablet computers. This kind of screen is suitable for viewing books and magazines with graphical content as an LCD screen displays color

- *E-Ink Display or Electronic Ink Display* usually displays content in black and white so has low power consumption. It is designed to look like the actual page of a book. In E-Ink display, text is readable even in full sunlight. E-ink display provides a reading experience with less eyestrain. Some examples of E-readers include Barnes & Noble Nook, Amazon Kindle, and Kobo

GPS

Standalone Global Positioning System (GPS) devices, such as TomTom GO and Garmin provide turn-by-turn vehicle navigation. Although these characteristics are also provided by smartphone mapping applications such as Apple Maps and Google Maps, standalone GPS units are still helpful as they tend to feature bigger displays and an easier user interface (needing less driver interaction).

One potential drawback to the use of standalone GPS devices is the need to update maps. Many of these units do not include map updates in the purchase price, and they have to be purchased individually. If users are running standalone GPS units, they should be familiar with the map update cycles of the devices and with information on subscription renewal.

Mobile Gaming Devices

Mobile gaming devices are handheld, portable, and lightweight video game devices that have built-in game consoles, screen, and speakers. These gaming consoles are specially designed for playing console games wherever a user is, whether moving or at rest. The basic features of handheld gaming devices include: access to online movies, TV shows, online access to free and paid games, web browsing, online and local multiplayer support, social media apps.

 Exam Note

Read and understand the typical specs of a mobile device. Memorize the basic types of hardware used by a smartphone.

Mind Map of Types Mobile Devices:

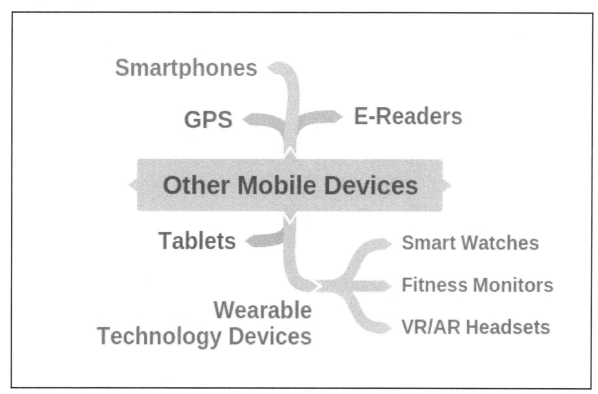

Figure 1-65: Mind Map of Types of Mobile Devices

Connect and Configure Accessories and Ports of Various Mobile Devices

Mobile devices have many of the ports similar to those of PCs but in smaller versions. Proprietary vendor-specific ports are primarily to provide power connections or communication option(s). The following sections review the essential features of these ports in a little more detail.

Connection Types

Many different types of connections, ports, and accessories are available for mobile devices. Connection types can be either wired or wireless.

Wired Connections

Wired connection refers to any physical medium made up of cables. These cables may include coaxial cables, fiber optic cables, copper wire cables, or twisted pair cables. A wired network carries different forms of electrical signal from source to destination. Discussed below are some types of wired connection for communication between mobile devices.

USB

Universal Serial Bus (USB) is one of the most common port users seen in all mobile or computing devices. USB ports are used to transfer data between the mobile device and other devices such as laptops, storage disks, smartphones, etc. This port also sometimes serves as the laptop's charging point, where users can charge their cell phone or other devices such as power banks, etc. USBs have been around for a long time and have gone through several versions and port changes.

The slot or jack in a computing device into which one end of a USB cable is inserted is called the port. The computing device to which a user wants to transfer data or which the user wants to charge (smartphone or tablet) is known as the receptor.

All mobile devices contain two common ports: Micro USB and Mini USB. Micro and mini USBs come in different types. Below are some of the USB types:

USB Type-A or USB-A

This 4-pin connector comes in different types and versions. When charging a device, nearly all charging cables will use a standard Type-A USB port on one end regardless of the connector type used to connect to the device. That enables connectivity to the majority of charging plugs and PCs and laptops in the world.

USB Type B or USB B

Type-B connectors are located at the other end of a typical USB cable that plugs into the slot or port of a peripheral device such as a smartphone, printer, or hard drive.

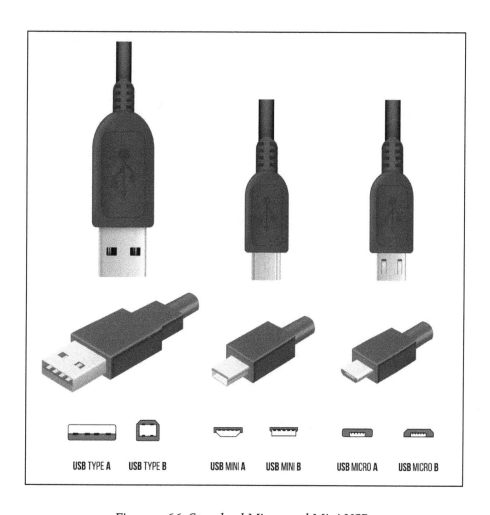

Figure 1-66: Standard Micro and Mini USBs

USB Type-C or USB-C

This type of USB is the newest and latest type of USB port. USB-C has become common for many Android-based smartphones and some tablets. It is much smaller, slimmer, and comes with 24-pins, which allows it to deal with a higher level of current and ensures a faster data transfer.

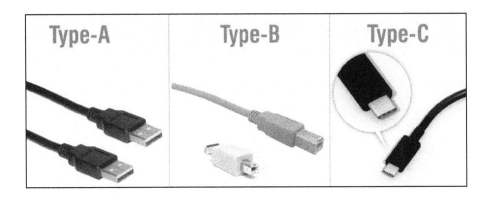

Figure 1-67: Different Types of USB

 Exam Note

Know the ports and connectors of mobile devices. Keep in mind that Android devices will generally use USB-C or Micro-USB, and iOS-based devices will use USB-C, Lightning, or the 30-pin dock connector.

Lightning

The Lightning connector from Apple is a device used for charging. It synchronizes the content, data, audio, and video output. It has an 8-pin connector, which is an advantage over a 30-pin connector. Older iOS devices used the 30-pin connector. However, starting in 2012, Apple standardized the 8-pin reversible Lightning connector for iPhones, iPads, iPods, and other mobile devices. Lightning devices provide the following advantages:

- It can be inserted either way
- It can detect and adapt to connected devices
- It can supply more power
- It is more durable than a USB

Figure 1-68: Lightning Cable and Device

Tethering

Tethering is the process of using the phone or other data-enabled device to get access to the internet with devices that are not able to access it for some reason.

The term tethered is used when one mobile device communicates with another mobile device to access its internet connection. This connection can be established using Bluetooth, 802.11, or a USB cable between devices.

Proprietary Vendor-Specific Ports (Communication/Power)

Many mobile devices contain proprietary ports or vendor specific ports. These ports can either providing power or perform communication.

Here are some examples of proprietary connectors or ports:

- Motorola and Nokia have been using coaxial in some of their power connectors

- The Sony-Ericson's power connector looks like a USB cable but it does not serve the purpose of a USB

- There are many vendors that do not choose to adopt standard connection types for both communication and power. For example, Apple uses a lightning connector for its power but it can detect and adapt to connected devices

Wireless Connection

Wireless Connection is the term used to refer to electromagnetic waves or infrared waves. All wireless devices have antennas or sensors for transmitting or receiving data. Some types of wired connection for communication between mobile devices are discussed below.

NFC

Near Field Communication (NFC) is a technology for short range communication. It allows mobile devices to create a radio communication when in close proximity or touching each other. This technology was earlier introduced to make mobile devices communicate with each other to share information within a short range but now, this technology is also used for making payments at the Point-of-Sale (POS).

NFC can also be used to automatically switch on Bluetooth and transfer files between devices. Apple presently does not allow its devices with NFC to work for file transfers except with iTunes purchasing and Apple Pay. Apple's AirDrop feature uses peer-to-peer Wi-Fi to share files.

NFC works by analyzing tags. These tags are small microchips with antenna that can read. In some cases, The microchip can read and also can be used to write.

Mobile devices must be capable of supporting NFC in order to access their usage. This technology is available in many special applications such as:

- Communication with peripherals

- Communication between toys in gaming

- Reading information stored in tags, in posters and in advertisements

- Making easy Point-of-Sale payments

Bluetooth

Bluetooth is a standard for short-range (up to 10 meters) wireless communication and data synchronization between computing devices. Bluetooth operates in the 2.4-GHz frequency range and it is very easy to configure. It is ideally used for short-range communication. Its speed is low compared to other wireless technologies.

Bluetooth technology helps to create wireless connections between devices such as computers, fax machines, printers, and other peripherals and machines, but it does not provide the long-range communication that a wireless connection does.

By default, Bluetooth is generally disabled on Android devices but is enabled on iOS devices such as iPads or iPhones. To connect a Bluetooth device to a mobile device, Bluetooth must be activated

and the Bluetooth device synchronized to the mobile device. This is known as pairing, or linking. Sometimes a PIN code is required. Once synchronized, the device needs to be connected.

There is usually a Bluetooth icon on the task bar. If the Bluetooth icon is not visible on the taskbar, go to the Start button, then go to the "**Settings**" > "**Devices**" > "**Bluetooth**", and then turn on Bluetooth.

IR

Infrared communication is based on the propagation of light waves for the transmission and reception of data. Some recent and current-model smartphones include capabilities for **built-in IR** (infrared). However, as with older mobile devices, this feature is designed to be used with remote control apps for TV and home theater rather than for data transfer. If your TV can be controlled by smartphone, it has an IR blaster on board.

Hotspot

Hotspot is one more way for providing internet access to mobile devices. Some devices are dedicated to performing solely as a mobile hotspot, but others are also capable of performing as an 802.11 hotspot for other wireless devices in the surrounding area. Hotspot dedicated devices primarily include wireless routers and modems. They provide internet access via a Wireless Local Area Network (WLAN). The function of a hotspot resembles that of a Wi-Fi connection. The signals of a hotspot get weaker as a device moves away far from the central location.

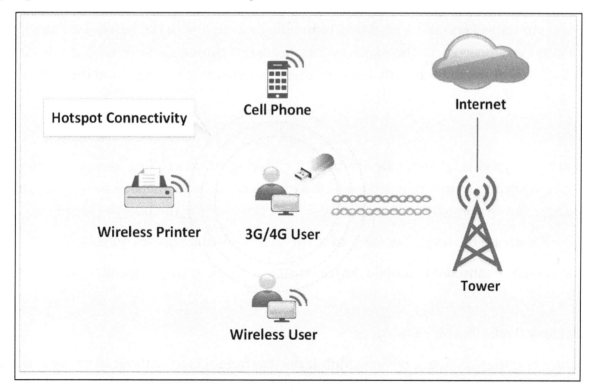

Figure 1-69: Hotspots

Accessories

On their own, mobile devices do not provide the full features of the device. The accessories listed here are aftermarket add-ons that enhance the experience of using a mobile device and, in some cases, physically protect it from damage. In the following section, we discuss some mobile device accessories, their usage, and their impact.

Headsets

Headsets, with an appropriate mike, are necessary for listening to music or for voice and video communications.

They can be connected to a computing device through a wire with a 3.55 mm plug, through a USB, or through Bluetooth to establish a pair between the device and the headset.

Speakers

Speakers and a microphone are likely to be built in to the laptop or notebook computer. Speakers emit sound and the microphone receives sound, helping to record audio files.

Speakers serve the same purpose as headsets. The only difference is that headsets limit the sound to the ears, while speakers emit sound that is audible to everyone in the immediate surroundings. Speakers can be connected in the same way as headsets: through a wire with a 3.55 mm plug, through a USB, or through Bluetooth to establish a pair between the device and the headset.

Game Pads

A gamepad or joypad is an input device used for playing or controlling games. It has multiple buttons and pointing devices that are pressed with the thumbs. Gamepads were first introduced with gaming console systems as a peripheral device for connecting the user to the system.

Gaming pads increase the level of gamers' excitement by providing game control options.

These pads can be connected to mobile devices via a connector or by using a Bluetooth connection.

Extra Battery Packs/Battery Chargers

Batteries are essential for mobile devices. Mobile devices cannot exist without batteries. For a device that needs to be constantly connected, it is best to keep an extra battery and battery charger or

power bank. Where no power outlet is available, these battery packs will provide the necessary power for the device.

There are different types of power pack. Some provide power directly to the device and others store power to recharge the device's battery. These devices differ in terms of the following characteristics:

- **mAh (milliampere-hour) rating:** The higher the rating, the more charge the device can supply before it needs to be recharged

- **Amperage output:** An output rating of 2.1 A or higher is required to charge an iPad or Android tablet

- **Number of USB charging ports:** A portable battery charger may have only one or more charging port. Having two or more USB charging ports can be useful when charging multiple devices

Protective Covers/Waterproofing

Mobile devices have delicate pieces of electronics and to make them more durable, protective and waterproof covers are available to protect the screen and other sensitive parts. Some covers are made of hard plastics while others are made of very thin glass.

Without a protective cover, smartphones and tablets are very susceptible to damage from impact. Broken screens are the most common issue, and a transparent plastic screen protector is highly recommended as it can absorb impact.

Damage to the case may cause other systems to fail. For any tablet or smartphone, a rubberized protective cover with raised edges to protect the screen is a good investment. Look for a cover that has good weather sealing for better protection against humidity.

Credit Card Readers

Smartphone and tablet credit card readers allow credit card transactions nearly anywhere. Readers plug into the 3.5 mm headset jack and are available for magnetic strip cards, chip cards, and NFC (contactless) payment devices. Card chip and swipe readers are becoming very common as we move towards a cashless economy. The Square reader is the most popular and recognizable portable mobile card reader.

Some systems are designed to function as commercial point-of-sale systems, with support for cash drawer and receipt printer. Before choosing a system, make sure it is compatible with the operating system.

Memory/MicroSD

Although the amount of onboard storage in smartphones and tablets has increased in recent years, users who download a lot of media or take a lot of photos can always use more.

All mobile devices have data storage such as HHD, SDD, etc. They also have external slots or jacks where users can connect external memory or storage devices such as SD cards or MicroSD to provide extra memory.

MicroSD or SD card is a type of removable flash memory card used for storing information that users can carry anywhere. Here, SD refers to Secure Digital. It is the smallest memory card of all. These cards can be used in mobile phones and other mobile devices.

There are card readers or adapters that allow the small MicroSD to fit in devices that have slots for all flash memory cards like MiniSD, standard SD, Memory Stick Duo card, and even USB. Nonetheless, these different cards cannot work in parallel. Many MicroSD cards come with a standard SD adapter for users' ease.

Some tablets and smartphones based on Android and Windows have microSD card slots, but there is no upgradeable storage for iOS devices. It may be possible to store some apps on the memory card depending on the operating system a device uses.

Exam Note

Understand the difference between configuring USB tethering and creating a mobile hotspot. NFC is used for close-proximity transactions, such as contactless payments.

Mind Map of Connectivity Types and Mobile Device Accessories

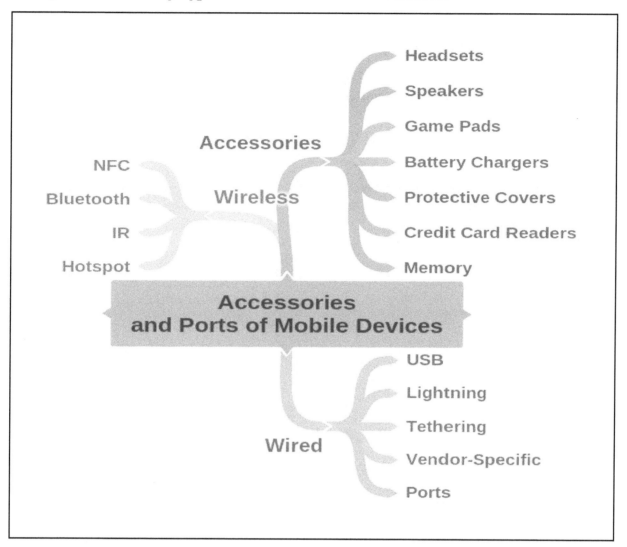

Figure 1-70: Mind Map of Connectivity Types and Mobile Device Accessories

Configure Basic Mobile Device Network Connectivity and Application Support

When individuals are connected to mobile devices, they are able to remain connected to their networks and the internet while they are in movement. Mobile phone users are passed from cell tower to cell tower as they drive down a road, and office workers can move between access points and networks as they take their tablets and mobile devices around buildings. However, these systems are far from perfect. Sometimes, user authentication causes a drop in service or a user wanders out of Wi-Fi coverage and needs access to cellular data. This section covers the connection methods for mobile devices.

Wireless Network (Enable/Disable)

All mobile devices come with a built-in network adapter for receiving Wi-Fi network. Below are some general steps to connect a device to Wi-Fi.

- Connect the laptop or PC to your wireless network
- Go to Control Panel and select "Network and Internet"

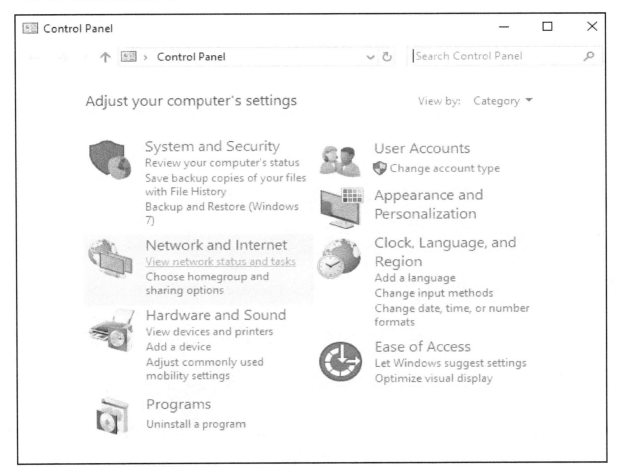

Figure 1-71: Network and Internet Setting in Control Panel

- Select "Network and Sharing Center" in Network and Internet

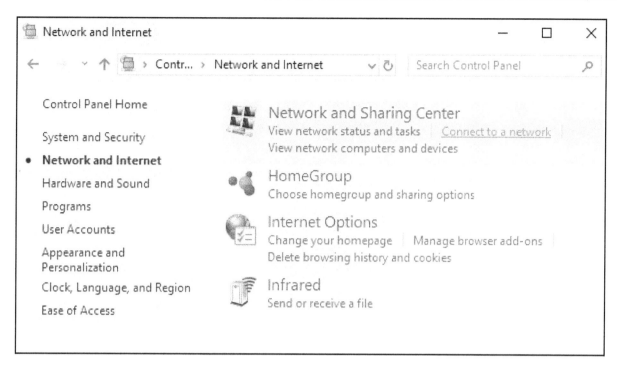

Figure 1-72: Network and Sharing Center in Control Panel

- Click "Connect to a network" in Network and Sharing Center. A window will pop up at the right hand side of the laptop's screen, as shown in figure 1-73

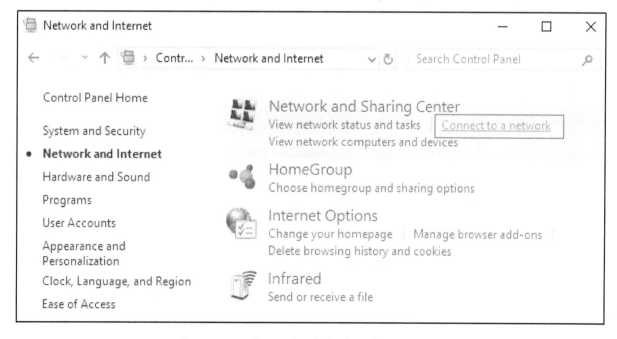

Figure 1-73: Detecting Wireless Connections

- Select the wireless network. Click the "Connect" tab and enter the password to connect

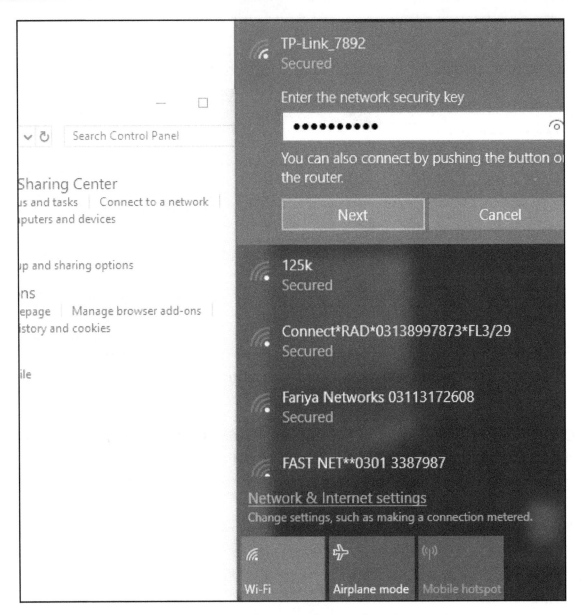

Figure 1-74: Password Settings for Wireless Connection

On entering the correct password, users will connect to the Wireless Internet.

Connect Mobile Devices to the Wireless Network

Here are some general steps for connecting mobile devices to a Wi-Fi network:

- Swipe down the top of the screen
- Tap the apps square located in the top right corner of the mobile to go to the menu or settings
- Tap on the Wi-Fi option given in the menu

- Slide or tap the Wi-Fi ON/OFF button to enable or disable the Wi-Fi connection

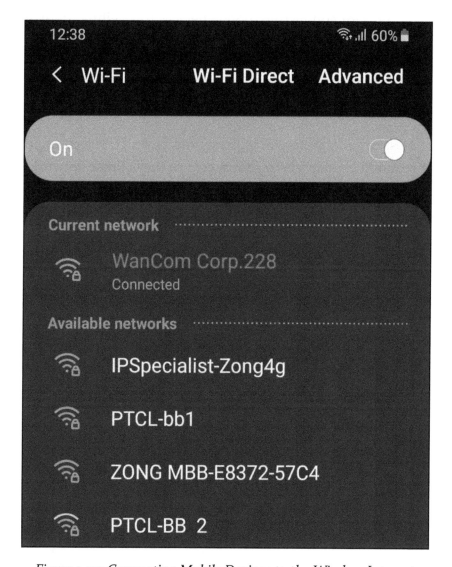

Figure 1-75: Connecting Mobile Devices to the Wireless Internet

These steps can vary according to the type of mobile device.

Cellular Network (Enable/Disable)

Most mobile devices, such as smartphones or tablets come with cellular data capability. However, at the point of sale, users have to decide which cellular network they want to subscribe to. For a certain level of service, users have to sign a contract before they gain access to that particular service. Therefore, the actual configuration is done at the point of sale. Where users purchase a cellular

network over the internet, they need to enter the correct credentials provided by the cellular provider.

Below are some general steps for connecting mobile devices to a cellular network:

- Swipe down the top of the screen

- Tap the apps square located in the top right corner of the mobile to go to the menu or settings

- Tap the "Mobile Data/Cellular" option given in the menu

- There will be a list of cellular networks presented by SSID; select any one of the networks and enter the required credentials to gain access to the cellular network

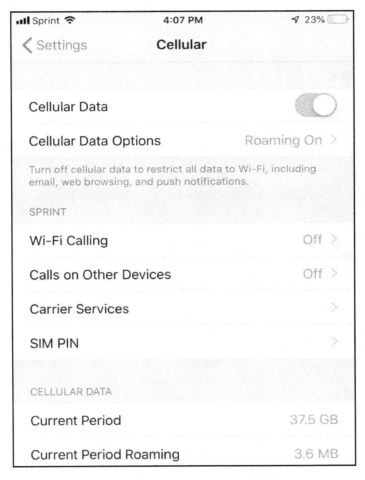

Figure 1-76: Cellular Option in Mobile Devices

Hotspot/Tethering (Enable/Disable)

When the internet is disconnected, users can use the mobile's cellular network connection to gain access to the internet. They can also share this cellular connection with other nearby devices. For example, users can share their mobile phone's internet connection with their desktop PC or laptop where there is no Wi-Fi connectivity. In this case, the phone becomes a mobile hotspot; this process is known as tethering. Credentials, such as a PIN or password are required to get connected, so that

only authorized devices can connect. In order to make your mobile a hotspot, follow the general steps given below:

- Swipe down the top of the screen

- Tap the apps square located at the top right corner of the mobile in order to go to the menu or settings

- Tap "Settings" and go to "Personal Hotspot" and tap or drag the slider to "On"

- In Android phones, go to Settings and select the "Wireless Network" section and choose "Tethering & Portable Hotspot" to enable or disable

- In Windows phones, go to Settings and then go to "Internet Sharing". Drag or tap the slider to "On"

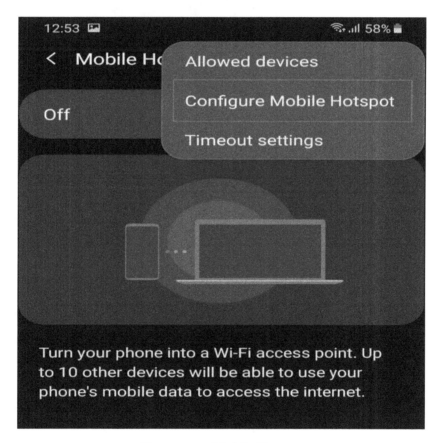

Figure 1-77: Mobile Hotspot

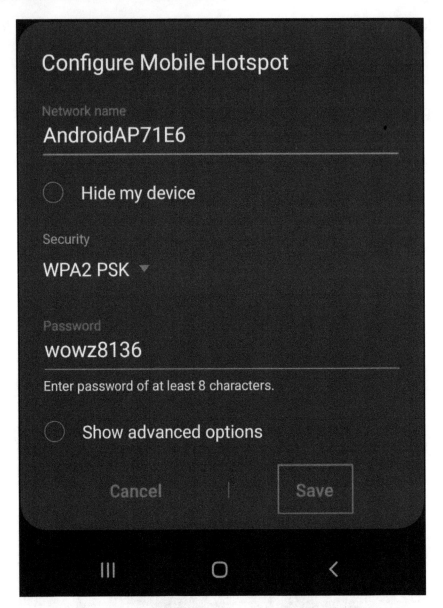

Figure 1-78: Configuration of Hotspot

Note

Some cellular providers charge an additional fee if consumers turn the cellular device into a hotspot or if they use tethering. Check with the mobile service provider for details. Moreover, keep in mind that the data usage of each device connected to a mobile hotspot counts toward the total data allocation. If users are not careful, using a mobile hotspot could cost extra.

Bluetooth

Bluetooth is a short-range, low-speed wireless network technology mainly intended to function between PCs and other devices in peer-to-peer (or ad hoc) mode. Bluetooth operates in virtually the same 2.4 GHz frequency used by IEEE802.11b, 802.11g and 802.11n wireless networks but uses a frequency-hopping spread-spectrum frequency technique to help minimize interference. Bluetooth devices link to each other to form a Personal Area Network (PAN).

Enable Bluetooth

In order to establish a pair between devices, first make sure that Bluetooth is enabled on the computer. Many mobile devices are Bluetooth compatible, but it might be disabled by default in order to save battery. On some laptops, there is a button on the keyboard that switches Bluetooth on or off. Some laptops might have an icon in the System Tray at the bottom-right of the screen. The location of the Bluetooth option depends on the device. If the device is not Bluetooth compatible, users can purchase a separate Bluetooth adapter, which will allow them to pair with other Bluetooth enabled devices.

Enable Pairing

Bluetooth first needs to be enabled to connect a Bluetooth device to a mobile device, then the Bluetooth device needs to be synchronized to the device. This is called pairing, or linking, and sometimes a PIN code is required. Once synchronized, the device needs to be connected. Finally, it is necessary to test the Bluetooth link.

For laptops and other computing devices, go to the Bluetooth settings, click the "Allow Bluetooth devices to find this computer" option, and then click "OK". This allows other devices to discover your laptop or computer.

Find a Device for Pairing

A connection established between two Bluetooth devices is called a pairing. In mobile devices, when both devices have discovered each other, go to the "Settings" and select the other device for pairing. After a moment, a notification will display asking for a pairing code, also called a PIN code. By entering the correct code, a pair will be established between the devices.

Users can also pair a device from a laptop or PC, as long as they are discoverable for other devices. Go to Settings, select "Bluetooth and other devices", click the "Bluetooth" or "Add a device" button in order to establish a pair between them.

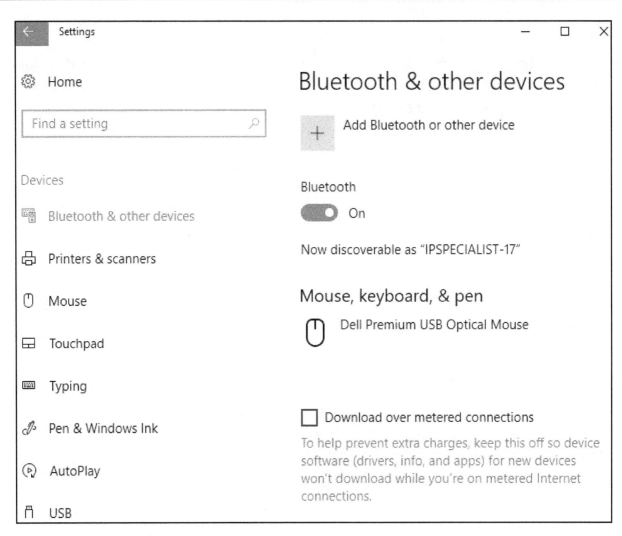

Figure 1-79: Bluetooth Settings for Laptop or Desktop PC

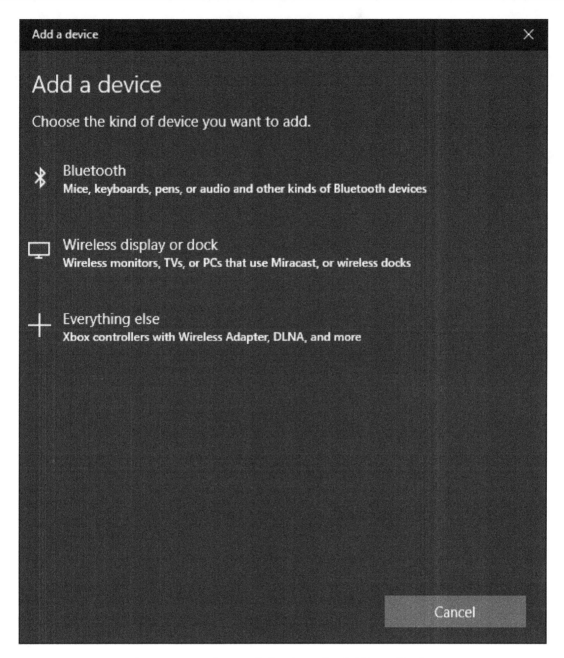

Figure 1-80: Bluetooth Settings for Adding a Device

Windows will present a list of all discoverable Bluetooth devices. Select the one you need and click "Next" to add it.

Enter the Appropriate Pin Code

To initiate a pair, a window will prompt you for a passcode. Make sure that the key on the PC and the device are same. This authenticates and ensures that users are connecting the device to the required machine and not some other machine near the device.

Users have to pass the pairing request to initiate the connection. When pairing a phone, users need to confirm the code on both the phone and the computer. A window will display asking for a pairing code or a PIN code. By entering the correct code, a pair will be established between the devices. This helps prevent other people from pairing with the device when it is in discoverable mode.

Test Connectivity

Bluetooth first needs to be enabled to connect a Bluetooth device to a mobile device, then the Bluetooth device needs to be synchronized to the mobile device. Once synchronized, the device should automatically connect and function at that point. Finally, test the connection by exchanging data between the devices.

Corporate and ISP email Configuration

Although there are various types of communication available to mobile users, email still accounts for an important percentage. Users should know how to configure a mobile device for web-based email services such as Gmail, Yahoo!, and Hotmail. Users should also know how to configure Post Office Protocol Version 3 (POP3), Internet Mail Access Protocol (IMAP), and connections to Microsoft Exchange Servers.

Mobile devices provide Apps for accessing different types of account for social networking, email, streaming and much more. Users just need to enter login credentials to get access these. Emails can either be client-based emails or web-based emails.

Client-based Emails

In Client-based Emails, users need an application or program on the computer properly configured in order to enable email transactions on the device. Examples of client-based emails are Microsoft Outlook, Outlook Express, Pegasus Mail, etc.

Before configuring any client application or program, users need to gather some information from the ISP (Internet Service Provider). The following information will be required from the service provider:

Username – The user's name is often the first part of the email address, but not always. If some other email user already has that name, the first part of the email address will differ. It depends on the ISP and the email addresses that are already taken.

Password - The password is used to access approval or to prove identity to get access to a resource. Passwords corresponds to the Username. Passwords should be as strong as possible.

Email Address – Choose a valid email address, for example: John@IPSpecialist.net.

SMTP Server Address – To begin the email transaction, users need the address of the Simple Mail Transfer Protocol (SMTP) server that receives the outgoing emails and forwards it to an email server. The SMTP address might be in the form of an IP address such as 10.10.10.0 or in the form of a domain

name such as smtp.domainname.com. Contact the service provider to get the actual addresses for the SMTP servers for the email configuration.

POP3

Post Office Protocol version-3 (POP3) is used to retrieve email using TCP port 110; it stores email to the local device.

To set up a POP3 email account, users must know the server that they want to connect to, the port they need to use, and whether security is being employed.

The following steps are for connecting a typical Android smartphone to a POP3 account:

- Go to the Home screen and click on the Menu button. Then select "All Apps"

- Scroll down to see the email app

- Select the desired email service such as POP3, IMAP, or Exchange account. (In this case, select POP3) If the device already has email accounts set up on it, go to Settings and then tap the "Add account" button

- Enter the login credentials (email address and the password of the account) and then tap "Next"

- Configure the incoming settings, if prompted to do so. If desired, change the username to something other than the email address and then type the POP3 server name. This is typically the domain name portion of the email address. If security is being used, select SSL or TLS. Type the port number, which is 110 by default for POP3. Then tap "Next" (for further information, ask the network administrator)

- Configure the outgoing settings. Type the SMTP server. Organizations often use the same server name as for the POP3 server. However, small office/home office (SOHO) users might have to use their ISP's SMTP server. If security is being used, select SSL or TLS. Type the port number, which is 25 for SMTP then tap "Next"

- Configure the account options, such as how often to check for mail and whether to notify when email arrives. Tap "Next". At this point, new email should start downloading

- Finally, give the account an easy-to-remember name and then tap "Done"

Use the following steps to connect an iOS device to a POP3 account:

- Go to the Home screen and click on "Settings"

- Tap "Mail", "Contacts", "Calendars"

- Select "Add Account"

- Select "Other" at the bottom of the list

- Select "Add Mail Account"

- Type the name, email address, and password and tap "Next"

- Select Pop. Then, under Incoming Mail Server, type the POP3 server name and the username. Under Outgoing Mail Server, type the SMTP server, then tap "Save"

- The system verifies the address and password. If successful, the process is completed. If not, make sure that everything was typed correctly and that the correct parameters, such as the type of server and security, have been configured.

Background

Post Office Protocol 3 (POP3) is the latest version of a standard protocol for receiving email. POP3 is a client/server protocol where the internet server receives and holds emails for clients. Periodically, users check the mail-box on the server and download any mail, possibly using POP3. This standard protocol is integrated into most popular email products such as Outlook Express and Eudora. It is also built into the Netscape and Microsoft Internet Explorer browsers.

Outlook is designed by Microsoft as an alternative to Google Gmail. Basically, users can add the outlook account to any email client that supports POP3 or IMAP, such as Microsoft Outlook Professional, Windows Mail, Android or iOS mail apps, etc. Depending on the email client application, users can add and configure their Outlook email account as a POP3 account or as an ActiveSync/Exchange service.

Challenges

On February 16, 2016, Microsoft updated Outlook 2016, upgrading the email client's version number to 16.0.6568.2025. According to Microsoft's description, this patch was supposed to add a few feature improvements, including support for a new troubleshooting tool. But instead, POP3 users faced a lot of trouble. One forum poster complained of receiving 10,000 duplicate emails, which tipped the scales on the user's bandwidth quota.

Problems started showing up when complaints about duplicate emails appeared in a Microsoft forum, while another forum thread linked this same problem with an Outlook 2016 update issued by Microsoft.

The greatest pitfall of POP3 is the implementation among email clients. POP3 is intended to delete mail on the server as soon as the user has downloaded it. Typically, Microsoft Outlook is configured to leave a copy on the server for a certain amount of time. This is what causes the problem of duplicating email.

Solutions

Microsoft acknowledged the problem on February 25, 2106 and released Knowledge Base Article 3145116, which provides two workaround options. If possible, POP3 users can either configure their email accounts to use IMAP instead of POP3, or can revert to a version of Outlook 2016 before the February 16 update, which would be version 16.0.6366.2068. The Knowledge Base article contains instructions for both approaches.

Conclusion

Getting duplicate copies of an email message is a rather common issue that can happen while using a POP3 email client such as Outlook. There are several possible reasons why this can happen, beyond incorrect rule settings. The Microsoft Outlook executable is not restricted to a single running instance. If several instances are running, duplicate requests to the POP3 server may lead to downloading a similar message twice. In other cases, leaving a duplicate of the message on the server or having two POP3 accounts for the exact same profile may cause the same message to be received more than once.

IMAP Server Address

Internet Message Access Protocol (IMAP) is used to retrieve email using TCP port 143 when several people check the same account or a user wants email access from multiple devices.

If users link to a Microsoft Exchange mail server, that server name often takes care of receiving and sending email. Users may need to understand the domain of which the Exchange server is a member.

Port and SSL Settings

Secure Sockets Layer (SSL) is used to encrypt data between an email client and the email server. Secure email sessions need to use SSL or TLS on port 443. Ports must be defined for the incoming and outgoing email servers along with the security settings. By default, port 25 is used for outgoing emails, but users can vary port settings according to requirements. There is also an option for making emails secure using either SSL or TLS. Make changes according to administrator requirements.

MIME

Multi-purpose Internet Mail Extensions (MIME) is an extension of the email protocol. This protocol allows people to exchange different kinds of data files on the internet other than email message text, such as images, audio, video, application programs, ASCII text, and other kinds of data. This protocol allows new file types to be added to "mail" as a supported Internet Protocol file type.

Email servers put the MIME header at the starting of any web transmission. Clients use this header to choose a relevant "player" application for the type of data that header indicates.

S/MIME

Secure/Multi-purpose Internet Mail Extension (S/MIME) is a standards-based protocol for sending and receiving authentic, secured and verified email messages. It provides email encryption by using certificates based on public/private-key. Only the intended recipient can open and read the email, and they can be sure that the email is from an authorized sender.

Mind Map of Basic Mobile Device Network Connectivity

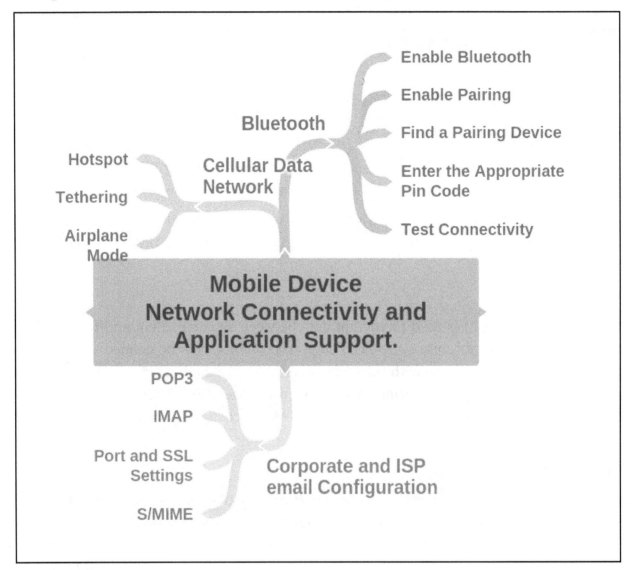

Figure 1-81: Mind Map of Basic Mobile Device Network Connectivity and Application Support

Integrated Commercial Provider Email Configuration

Users can install the suitable app from their device's app store to set up web-based services such as Apple's iCloud, Google/Inbox (Gmail), Microsoft's Outlook or Exchange Online, and Yahoo! Mail.

Android devices, for instance, come with a built-in Gmail application, so a user can immediately access Gmail without having to use the browser. Apple iOS phones enable connectivity to Gmail, Yahoo! ICloud Mail, Exchange, Outlook, AOL and many other email providers.

Connecting to these services is simple and works in the same manner as using a desktop computer or laptop. The following are the general steps for manually configuring an email account on a mobile device:

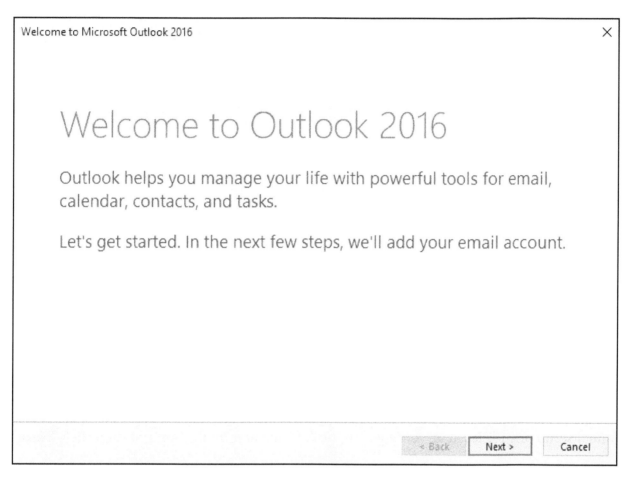

Figure 1-82: Configuring Microsoft Outlook

Go to the "Add an Email Account" dialog box.

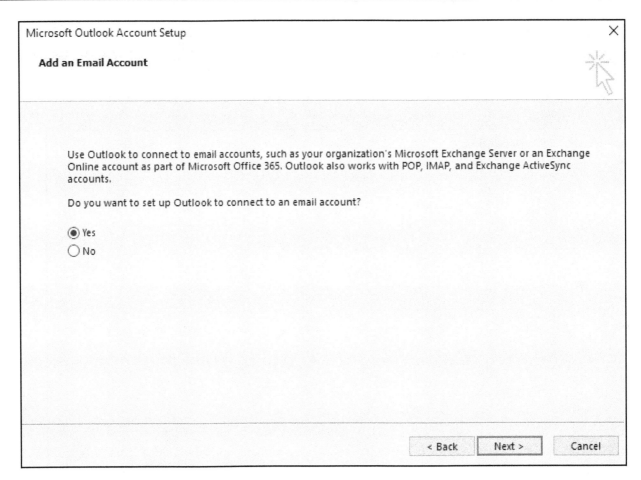

Figure 1-83: Configuring Microsoft Outlook

Click "Manual setup or additional server types" in the Add account dialog box and then click "Next".

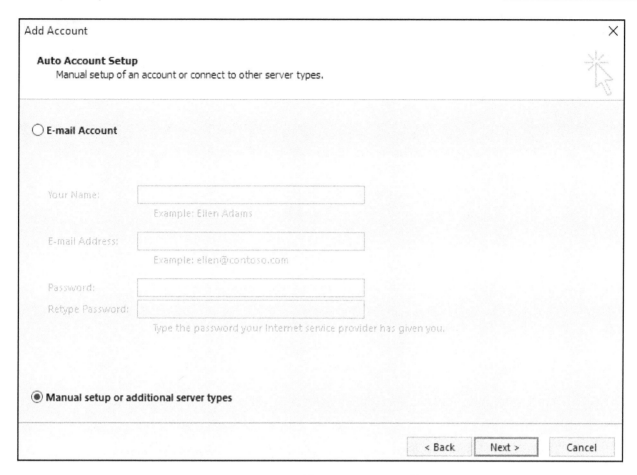

Figure 1-84 Add account manually

Click "POP or IMAP" and then Tap "Next".

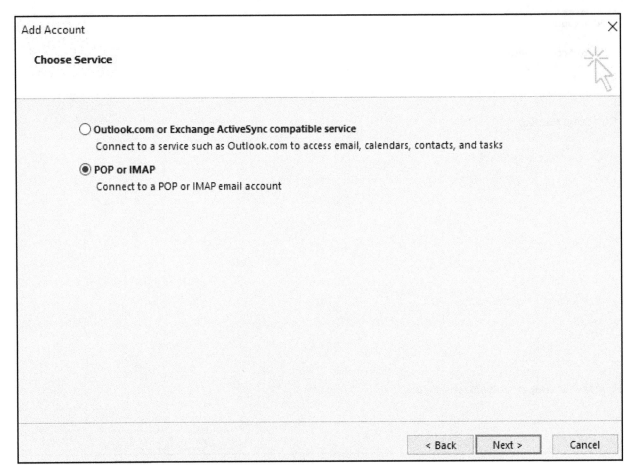

Figure 1-85: Configuring POP or IMAP in Microsoft Outlook

A window will pop up:

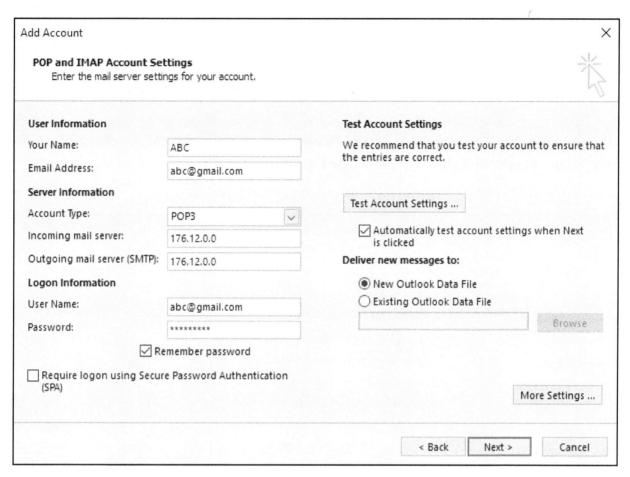

Figure 1-86: Configuring Name, Email address, POP, SMTP Server

Configure the following information under User Information:

- Type the full name in the "Your Name" box

- Type email address in the "Email Address" box

Configure the following under Server Information:

- Select the email account type in the "Account Type" box – either POP3 or IMAP

- Type the name (e.g. www.ipspecialist.net) or IP address (e.g. 176.12.0.0) of the server provided by the ISP in the "Incoming mail server" box

- Write the IP address or name of the server provided by the ISP in the "Outgoing mail server (SMTP)" box

Configure the following under "Logon Information":

- Type user name in the "User Name" box

- Enter the password provided by ISP in the "Password" box

- Tick the "Remember password" check box for Outlook to remember the email account password

Tick the required logon by using the "Secure Password Authentication (SPA)" check box to log on by using Secure Password Authentication if the ISP asks you to do so.

Click on the "More Settings…" option and the following window will pop up:

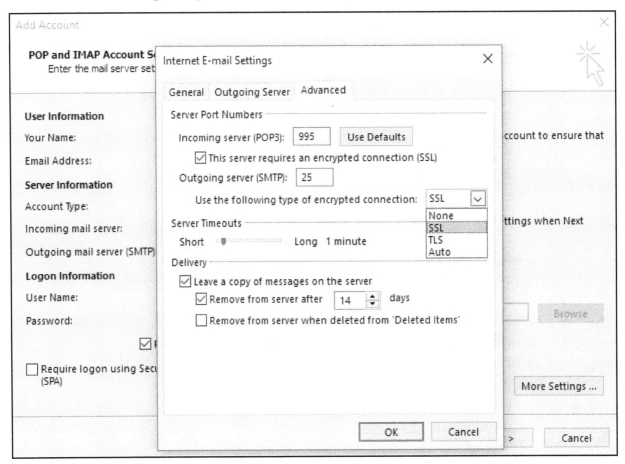

Figure 1-87: Configuring Ports in Microsoft Outlook

In the pop-up shown above, select the ports according to requirements and further select the encrypted connection of the required type such as SSL or TLS.

Click "Next".

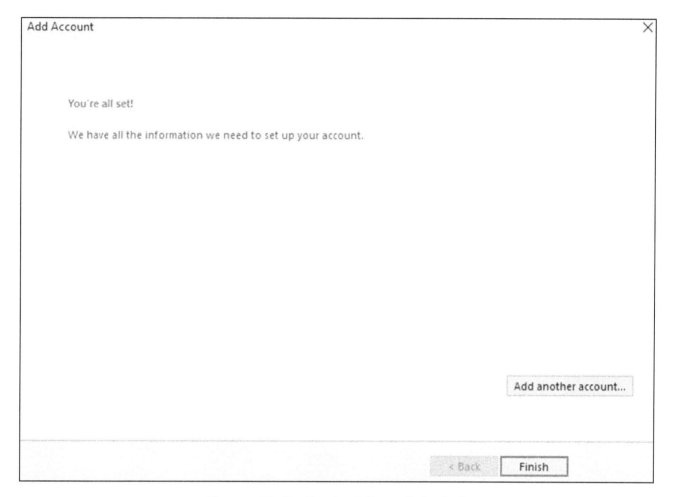

Figure 1-88: Configuring Microsoft Outlook

Click "Finish".

To configure S/MIME, follow the general steps given below.

Go to the account info and select "Options".

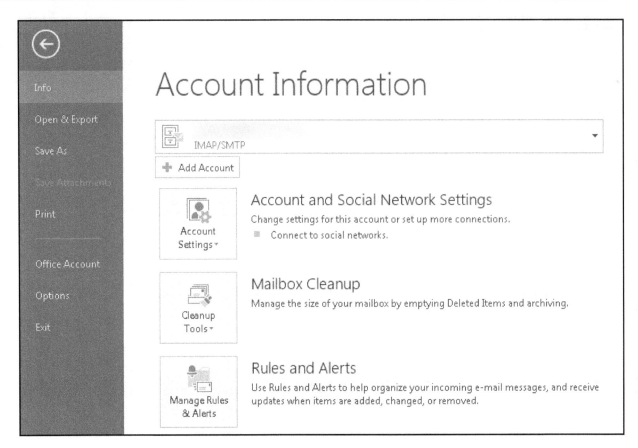

Figure 1-89: Configuring S/MIMIE in Microsoft Outlook

In the "Outlook Options" tab, select "Trust Center" on the left-hand corner of the tab.

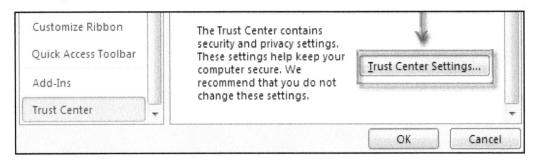

Figure 1-90: Configuring S/MIME Features in Microsoft Outlook

Go to "Trust Center Settings...."

Select "Email Security" on the left of the Trust Center's tab.

Now, select "Settings..." in the Trust center's tab.

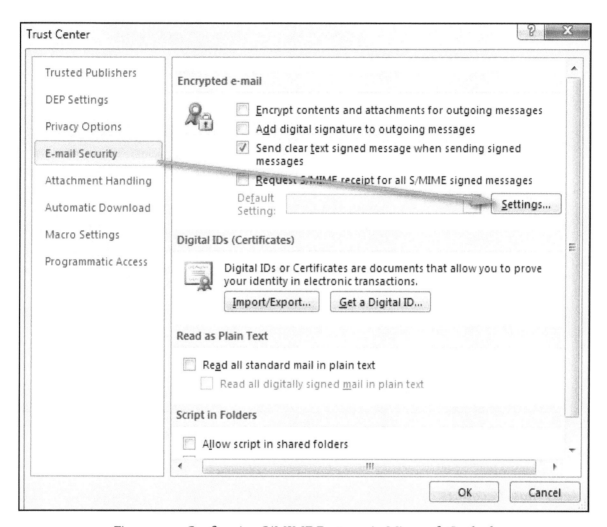

Figure 1-92: Configuring S/MIME Features in Microsoft Outlook

The following windows will pop up to get the digital ID of the user. Get the digital ID online and make the email transaction secure and authentic.

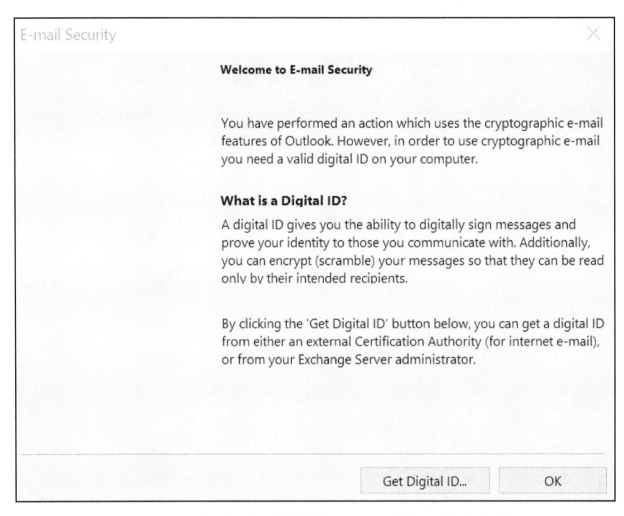

Figure 1-93: Configuring S/MIME Features in Microsoft Outlook

Web-based Email Accounts

Web-based Email accounts, such as Outlook.com, Gmail, iCloud, or Yahoo mail, do not require a sending and receiving server to be specified. Users just need to enter the correct credentials to gain access to emails. The operating system of the mobile device already knows the incoming and outgoing mail server ports and addresses for these general systems.

Web-based mail enables users to access their emails as long as they are connected to the internet or a web browser. Users cannot compose, send, or read an old email offline. In order to gain access to web-based email services, all users need to do is to register for a free account. Begin the email transaction by logging in using credentials such as Login ID/Username and Password. After accessing email, users can compose, send, receive, forward, reply, and delete the email files.

Some of the well-known free web-based email services are:

- Yahoo

- Gmail

- MSN

- iCloud

- Google/Inbox

- Exchange Online

iCloud

iCloud allows consumers to store data such as documents, photos, and music on remote servers for downloading to iOS, MacOS or Windows devices, to share and send information to others, and handle their Apple devices when lost or stolen.

iCloud also offers the means to wirelessly back up iOS devices directly to iCloud, rather than relying on Mac host or Windows computer manual backups using iTunes. By connecting accounts via AirDrop wireless, service users are also able to share photos, music, and games.

Google/Inbox

Inbox began primarily as a web-based service that later became accessible for iOS and Android as a dedicated application. However, there was no support for desktop computers and the only choice was to use Inbox from a browser. Google discontinued Inbox in March 2019 and has slowly integrated some of Inbox's best features into Gmail.

Exchange Online

Exchange Online is the host version of Microsoft's Exchange Server messaging platform that organizations can purchase as a standalone service or by subscribing to Office 365. Exchange Online provides businesses with a majority of the benefits that on-premises Exchange deployments provide.

Yahoo

Yahoo mail is one of the most popular free email services. Yahoo Mail provides free email accounts with one TB online storage at the yahoo.com, ymail.com and rocketmail.com domains.

Yahoo Mail offers a rich web-based application on mobile devices, allowing for a full archive and some offline searching. With these characteristics, iPhone and Android phones get indigenous apps, contact integration, attachment support, and more.

> **Background**
>
> Yahoo! Mail is an email service introduced through the American parent company Yahoo! in 1997. Yahoo Mail provides four distinct email plans: three for private use (Basic, Plus, and Ad Free) and one for business. Yahoo! Mail had 281 million customers by December

2011, making it the world's third biggest web-based email service. Since 2015, its webmail has also supported managing non-Yahoo email accounts.

Challenges

During the second half of 2016, the internet service business Yahoo! revealed two data breaches of customer account information. The first data breach reported in September 2016, occurred sometime in late 2014 and affected over 500 million Yahoo! user accounts. A different data breach was recorded in December 2016, occurring earlier around August 2013. At first, it was believed that the data breach had affected over 1 billion user accounts. Later, in October 2017, Yahoo! stated that all 3 billion of its user accounts had been impacted. Both breaches are regarded as the largest in the history of the internet. Further, Yahoo! revealed that the late 2014 breach possibly used manufactured web cookies to falsify login credentials, enabling hackers to gain access to any account without a password. So, what were the consequences of Yahoo data breach?

Solutions

According to Yahoo!, the 2014 data breach was carried out by a "state-sponsored hacker" and the organization argues that such "intrusions and thefts by state-sponsored hackers have become increasingly prevalent across the technology sector". Yahoo! did not, however, name any country.

Yahoo! was criticized for the late disclosure of the data breaches and its security measures, and is presently facing several lawsuits as well as investigation by representatives of the United States Congress. The breaches affected Verizon Communications' acquisition of Yahoo! and resulted in a $350 million reduction in the final price on the deal, which closed in June 2017.

Yahoo! agreed to pay $50 million in damages and to provide two years of free credit-monitoring services to 200 million individuals whose email addresses and other personal data were stolen.

Conclusion

Yahoo! took measures to strengthen its systems after the attacks. The company encouraged its clients to change passwords associated with their Yahoo! account and any other digital accounts linked to their Yahoo! email and account.

Smartphone Updates

Mobile device cellular providers periodically send updates to smartphones for upgrading. Whenever a smartphone update is released, users will get a notification to proceed with the update. The most common types of update include OS updates, baseband/radio firmware updates and the Preferred Roaming List (PRL).

OS Updates

Installation of OS updates resolves system problems and adds more features to the smartphone. An OS takes more than half an hour to proceed.

For installation, go to the "Settings" app, select "Settings" in "IOS" -> "General" -> "Software update" and then follow the pop ups to install the latest update.

PRI Updates/PRL Updates/Baseband Updates

The Preferred Roaming List (PRL) is a type of database stored in the mobile device. It allows the device to be able to roam or get service from outside the cellular network. It contains all the necessary information for connecting mobile devices to the cellular service towers. Normally, mobile users do not update the PRL list; but doing so may enable the phone to connect to the roaming carriers better. Users can update the PRL list on their mobile device by dialing a particular feature code provided by their cellular or service provider.

Radio/Baseband Firmware

The part of the phone that modulates and demodulates is called the modem. It sends and receives data and performs conversions between analog and digital data. This is also referred to as radio or the device's baseband.

Sometimes, the cellular provider sends the message or notification about the updates to the firmware on every release. However, sometimes users might not get the notification, in which case they have to look into "updating the firmware". To do this, users should refer to the manufacturer's manual or online guide, as this process involves complex steps that differ depending on the type of device.

IMEI vs. IMSI

Inside smartphones and other mobile devices are some specific identification numbers that differentiate one cell phone from the other.

IMEI: International Mobile Equipment Identification (IMEI) is the standard used to identify a physical phone device. This code serves as a tracking number for the device. The IMEI can be used to block access to a stolen device. CDMA networks (Sprint, Verizon, and US Cellular) use MEID numbers in the same way as IMEI numbers. Some vendors refer to these numbers as IMEI/MEID numbers.

IMSI: International Mobile Subscriber Identification (IMSI) is a standard used to identify a SIM (Subscriber Identification Module) card. All mobile phones contain a SIM card. It is usually stored in the phone or tablet's SIM card jack or holder.

If a cell phone is stolen, the owner may contact the provider of the cell phone and request that the phone be blocked. The cell phone provider usually has an IMEI number record and can block the phone from use even if the SIM card is changed. Support for cell phone blocking by IMEI number varies from provider to provider and from country to country.

Exam Note

Understand how to connect to a Wi-Fi network in Android and iOS. Know how to configure Bluetooth devices in Android and iOS. Know what airplane mode is and how to configure it on Android and Apple devices. Understand that the IMEI ID identifies the device and the IMSI ID identifies the user of the device.

VPN

Virtual Private Network (VPN) is an encrypted communication channel or tunnel between two remote sites over the internet.

VPN is a logical network that allows connectivity between two devices. Those devices can either belong to the same network or connect over a wide area network. Now, let's go deep down into the word VPN. The term "Virtual" here refers to the logical link between the two devices, as the VPN link does not exist separately but uses the internet as a transport mechanism. The term "Private" refers to the security that VPN provides to the connection between the two devices. As the medium of transport is the internet, which is not secure, VPN adds confidentiality and data integrity. It encrypts the data and prevents alteration or manipulation of data from an unauthorized person along the route.

Types of VPN

- Remote access VPN
- Site-to-site VPN

Remote Access VPN

A remote access VPN allows a networking device to connect to a corporate office when it is outside. These devices, commonly known as end devices, include smartphones, tablets, laptops etc.

For example, when a user wants to build a VPN connection from their personal computer to the corporate headquarters or any other branch of an organization, it is referred to as a remote-access VPN connection. Remote-access VPNs use IPsec or Secure Sockets Layer (SSL) technologies for their VPN. Many organizations use Cisco's AnyConnect client for remote access SSL VPNs.

Site-to-Site VPN

A site-to-site VPN securely connects two or more sites that want to connect over the internet. For example, when a corporate office wants to connect to its head office or multiple branches that want to connect to each other, it is referred to as a site-to-site VPN. Site-to-site VPNs usually use IPSEC as a VPN technology.

Connecting Mobile Devices to a VPN

In order to create a VPN connection in mobile devices, go to the setting app of mobile devices to enable the VPN configuration utility.

In order to configure an iPhone for VPN connection, follow the general steps given below:

- Go to "Settings" -> "General" -> "VPN"
- Tap "Add VPN Configuration"

Then follow the steps that appear during establishment of the VPN to set up the connection.

In order to configure an Android phone for VPN connection, follow the general steps given below:

- Go to the "Settings" app
- Select "More" in the "Wireless & Networks" section
- Select "VPN"

Mind Map of Basic Mobile Device Network Connectivity

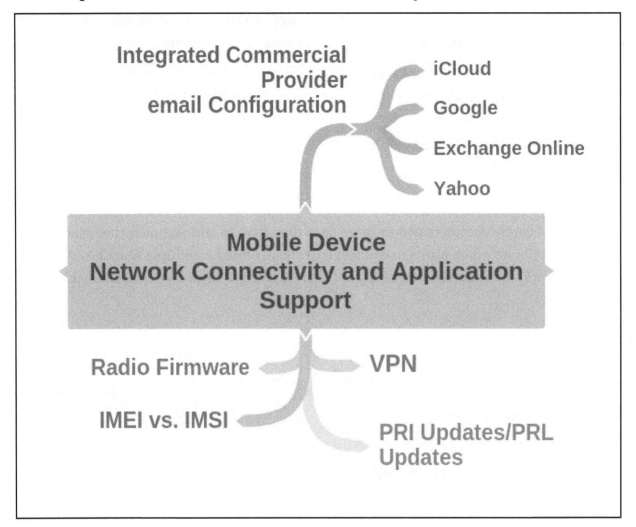

Figure 1-94: Mind Map of Basic Mobile Device Network Connectivity and Application Support

Perform Mobile Device Synchronization

Keeping things in sync means that different devices have the same information. Synchronization is used to bring files in line with each other and to force devices to coordinate their data. Synchronization can be done through a particular operating system, browser, email provider, application, and/or third-party vendors.

Synchronization Methods

Data synchronization is the process of maintaining and exchanging data between two or more devices. It ensures that only the actual state of data is used in all synchronized devices from source to destination. Data synchronization can also help to maintain a backup, as an insurance policy against losing data if one of the devices is lost or stolen. For example, computing devices such as

desktops, tablets, and cell phones are used in continuous rotation; consumers use all their devices simultaneously. In some cases, users draft an email or a document on one device and have to refer to that document from another device. In order to make that possible, the data needs to be synchronized between the computing devices.

Users either can synchronize data to another desktop PC or laptop or to a cloud service. People commonly use one or more of the following synchronization methods for mobile devices.

Synchronize Data to the Cloud

Each cloud provider closely designs a system for user data synchronization, and distinct data types may need a different level of synchronization. Mostly, cloud storage helps to make decisions related to how often information is synchronized to clients. Transfers are sometimes scheduled by time and sometimes triggered by events such as changes to a document. When required, with Google Drive documents, multiple users can access group editing documents simultaneously.

Dropbox is one of the most popular examples of cloud storage services. All the data users place into a Dropbox folder is backed up online and can be downloaded to any other device that is logged in to Dropbox using the same account.

It is a data sync utility because the folders users store on Dropbox are replicated to all their mobile devices and computers; they just have to sign in to their Dropbox account.

Phone OSs make it painless and easy to back up using their preferred provider, but they can also use other cloud backup providers, regardless of the phone model.

Similarly, there are synchronization apps for Android and IOS such as OneDrive and iCloud. OneDrive is Microsoft's cloud storage system; it is used by default for data synchronization and backing up Windows Phones. iCloud is for Android and Windows phones.

> **Note**
>
> Keep in mind that data backup is different from data synchronization. For example, users might back up an Android-based device's apps, call history, contacts, device settings, SMS text messages, and other items that are normally stored locally. Users can back this data up to a server on the cloud owned by the mobile device's manufacturer, or they can use a separate service such as Google Drive. Either way, this is done separately from synchronization.

Figure 1-95: Data Synchronization to the Cloud

Synchronizing Data to a Desktop

A mobile device can synchronize by connecting to a computer via USB or by using Wi-Fi or Bluetooth. For local data synchronization, use the USB cable that is attached or connected to an AC adapter for charging the smartphone. Remove the USB cable from the AC adapter and connect the adaptor end, which is usually a standard USB connector, to the computer and connect the other end, which is usually a type B or C USB, to the device.

Synchronizing Data to an Automobile

Users can also synchronize data to mobile devices such as smartphones or tablets. They can either do this with a connector cable or through an internet connection using Wi-Fi or a cloud-based service.

On smartphones, this connector cable will usually be a micro USB connector of type B or C; on an iPad and some other tablets, this connector is called a Lightning connector.

Synchronizing through iPhones and iPads

There are apps and software such as Apple iTunes or iCloud for syncing an iPad and iPhone to a PC or Mac. iTunes comes with all Apple computers. iCloud enables users to configure cloud-based storage for a mobile device where they just have to specify what kind of data they want to be synched in the cloud, for example contacts, photos, bookmarks, videos, etc.

Synchronizing through Android Devices

For synchronizing Android devices, users have the choice of Google and the one provided by the cellular service provider. If you select Google for data synchronization, all contacts and data will be automatically synced and backed up to Google over the internet, either through a Wi-Fi or cell connection.

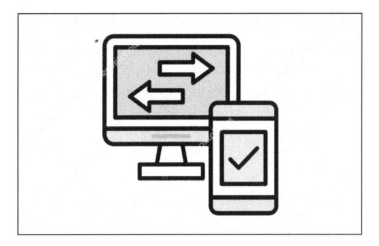

Figure 1-96: Synchronizing Data through Mobile Devices

Types of Data to Synchronize

Contacts

Contacts are considered one of the most important parts of any mobile or calling device. Contacts are usually stored in the SIM or synchronized accounts of the mobile phone or device. Contacts can be synchronized from email applications such as a Gmail account in order to keep a backup. The contact list can also be saved to external memory cards or transferred to some other device or computer for maintaining a backup. All newly added data will be added to the backup once data synchronization is enabled. Users can even get their contact list in a new phone when they log in to the synchronized email account.

Applications

App synchronization is one way to back up data, but it does not provide backup for an operating system. A mobile device should have the system backed up in case an operating system update failure, a virus infection, or inability to remove malware. Many apps are available that allow users to back up a mobile device remotely. Backup and restore techniques in the mobile environment are just as important as they are in the desktop arena.

Emails

Emails are considered one of a person's most confidential and sensitive documents as they contain all their business and personal data transactions. Emails need to be synchronized so that they can be accessed from anywhere, anytime. They can be synchronized by using the IMAP or IMAP server along with the security types such as SSL/TLS or STARTTLS to ensure that there will be no data loss or manipulation of the email. Other data such as documents, audio, and video will be synchronized as well, so users can gain access to them anywhere.

Pictures

Pictures include clicks of happy moments of someone's life, logos, signatures, important seals, and all of an organization's visual data. They are also a person's highly confidential files. Transferring images from one device to another is not always possible, so synchronization is a useful alternative to Image transfer. There are plenty of software for this purpose, for example Google's Picasa, Flickr, integral programs, etc. for serving this purpose. Pictures synchronization software is therefore considered a necessary application for all mobile devices.

Music

Many people love listening to music and they want to access their music collection anywhere at any time, so music playlist synchronization is a preference for almost all music listeners. People do not just want synchronized playlists. They also want the same environment settings and personalized equalizer. The music playlist and settings can be synchronized by using different applications and software such as Windows Media Player or ITunes.

Videos

Videos are also important data as they can contain corporate presentations, seminars, or even recordings of special events such as weddings. Therefore, video synchronization is another important aspect in the synchronization process. Videos, audios, music playlists and settings can be synchronized using different applications and software such as Music Station launched by Windows.

Calendar

Android devices can easily connect to the Google account and keep all calendars synced across computers and devices. Users can do this on the calendar app that is installed on the device, or they can use an app like Google Calendar. Events that users create on one connected device will automatically appear on any other device that the account is connected to.

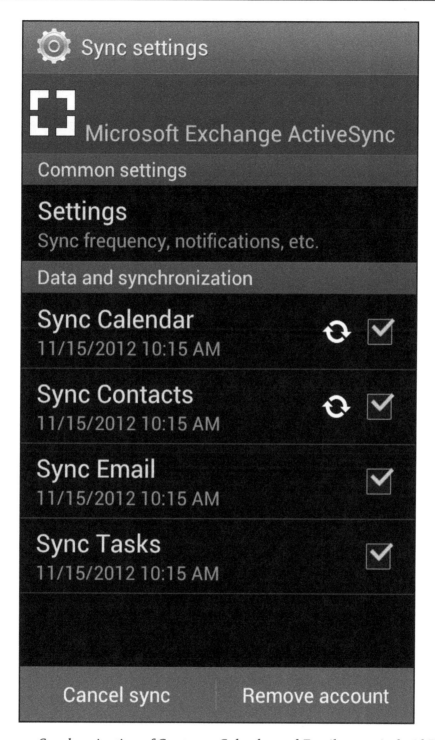

Figure 1-97: Synchronization of Contacts, Calendar and Email on an Android Device

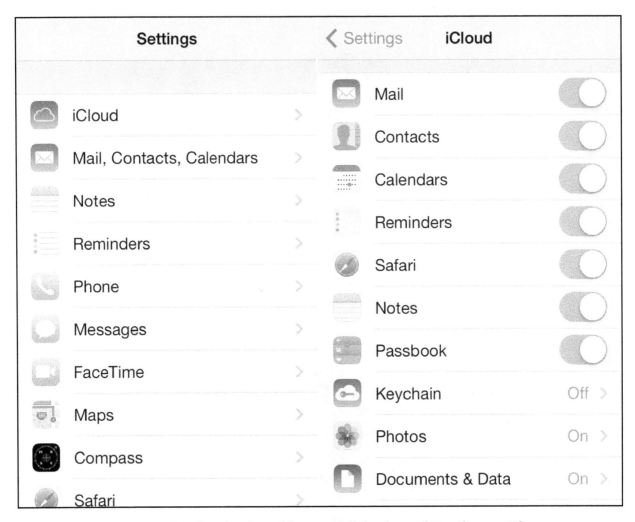

Figure 1-98: Synchronization of Contacts, Calendar and Email on an iPhone

Bookmarks

The Google Chrome browser allows synchronization of bookmarks. Bookmarks are important to synchronize where users need to refer back to a website they have saved when using another device. When users need to sync bookmarks, they should turn on sync to the Google account; all the profile information such as Bookmarks, History and Open Tabs, Passwords, AutoFill Info and Credit Cards, Settings and Preferences will be saved to the Google account.

Follow the general steps to sync information:

- Open the "Chrome" app on the computer or mobile device
- Go to the right corner of the address bar, tap "More" and go to "Settings"
- Click on the account name
- Click "Sync"
- Turn off the option "Sync Everything"

Documents

Document Sync improves productivity and effectiveness by allowing users to synchronize files across managed mobile devices. To ensure data security, documents are safely stored in the cloud and on their devices.

Google software is commonly used to synchronize data between an Android device and other devices. Google Drive can be used to store and share documents for free.

Social Media Data

Social Media Data synchronization enables keeping all the social media accounts such as Facebook, Twitter, Instagram, etc. synchronized on different devices, making content transfer across all accounts easy.

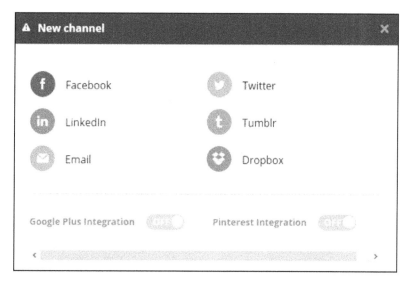

Figure 1-99: Synchronization between Various Social Media Accounts

E-books

E-book synchronization allows users to move freely between devices when reading books. Users do not have to manually figure out which page they were on with a book when reading it on some other devices. The E-book's highlights and bookmarks can be synchronized by using different applications and software like Google play books and Bluefire Reader.

Passwords

Every web browser out there has the ability to store passwords and possibly synchronize them. Third-party programs are also available that act as password vaults that can be accessed from anywhere because they are stored in the cloud. However, due to safety considerations, most organizations frown at this practice. Generally, if a password vault is to be used, a locally saved one will be the most secure. But, even locally stored vaults (such as KeePass) can be set up on the internet. If a password vault has to be used for synchronization purposes and it has to be on the cloud, then some additional security procedures should be implemented.

 Exam Note

Know the various ways to synchronize data between an Android and a PC. Know the various ways to synchronize data between mobile devices and PCs or Macs. Implement strong master passwords for any password vaults.

Mutual Authentication for Multiple Services

Single Sign-On (SSO) is a technique in which a user needs only one set of credentials to gain access to multiple resources.

SSO issues a security token (credentials, usually username and password) for the initial login and then users can log in to multiple applications using the same set of credentials or security token. It makes operations easier for the user as they do not need to remember different credentials for different applications. It is also useful where a single user has to maintain individual credential pairs for different service providers, which can be done by obtaining a set of credentials from a trusted authority. Each authorized user of an organization can use this set of credentials to authenticate him/herself and then gain access to multiple service providers. Basically, it serves two security purposes, i.e., credential privacy and soundness. Soundness will not let an unauthorized user gain access to the resource. Credential privacy ensures that these credentials will not be fully recovered by any dishonest user or service provider.

The local folder, called vaults in Windows, enables users to save credentials automatically whenever users sign in to websites, servers, and certain applications. It makes the users of these locally stored credentials provide a single sign-on (SSO), i.e., a user only has to provide credentials once and can gain access to multiple resources.

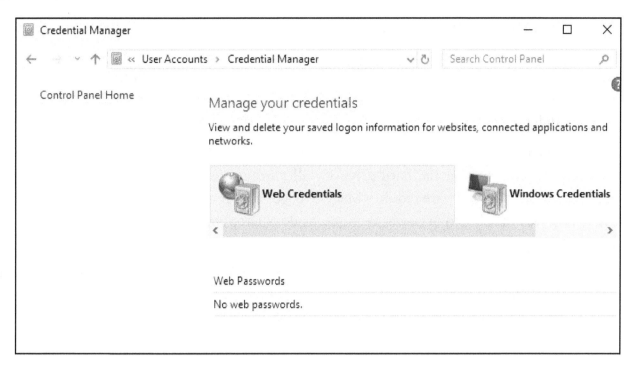

Figure 1-100: Options for Credentials Management

This Credential Manager applet, in Control Panel, enables users to directly manage their credentials. The "Edit" option enables users to change their user name and password.

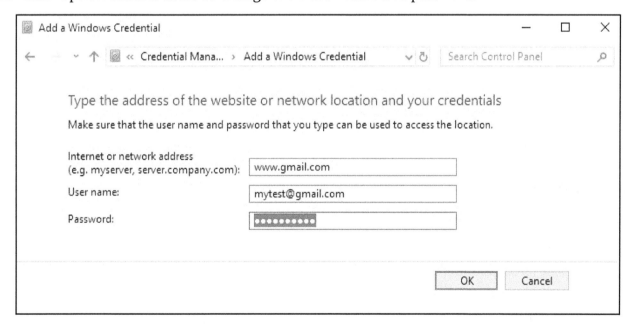

Figure 1-101: Settings for Credentials Management

Software Requirements for Installing a Synchronization Application on a PC

A file synchronization software or application is a program or service that provides a convenient way to automatically synchronize data <u>files</u> between more than one mobile device or computer. Whenever users log in to a file syncing software or app, all the sync files will be available for them to see, open, delete, edit, copy, stream, and so on.

Most desktop synchronization software requires 4 GB or more of RAM, at least one USB 2.0 port, and 300 MB of free space on the hard drive for all current versions of Windows. Most MacOS desktop synchronization software requires MacOS 10.5 or higher and a USB port available, although some may require MacOS 10.9 or newer versions, as does Dropbox for example.

Synchronization algorithms are used to synchronize data between devices such as desktops, laptops, remote FTP/SFTP, USB drives, and various online data storage services. The following are data synchronization software and applications:

- Allway Sync
- Box Sync
- FreeFile Sync
- Good Sync
- Sync Toy
- Sync Back

Connection Types to Enable Synchronization

The connection types can be either wired, for example a connection cable, such as a USB cable, lightning device, or wireless such as cellular and Bluetooth. USB and Wi-Fi are the most common connection types for synchronizing software, especially on mobile devices.

Connecting to Wired Networks

For a wired data synchronization, use the USB cable that is attached or connected to an AC adapter for charging the smartphone. Detach the USB cable from the AC adapter and connect the end that is connected to the adaptor, which is usually a standard USB connector, into the computer and connect the other end, which is usually a USB type B or C, to the device.

On smartphones, this connector cable is usually a micro USB connector of type B or C; on an iPad and some other tablets, this connector is a lightning connector.

Connecting to Wireless Networks

All mobile or computing devices such as laptops, smartphones, and tablets come with a built-in network adapter for Wi-Fi networks, cellular data networks, or both. They can also establish Bluetooth connections for connecting and synchronizing to nearby devices.

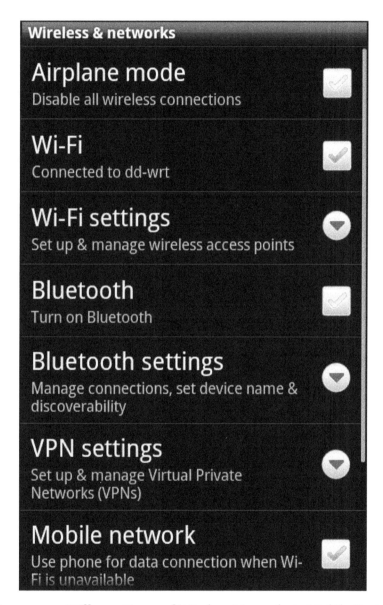

Figure 1-102: Different Types of Wireless Networks in Mobile Devices

Mind Map of Data Synchronization between Mobile Devices

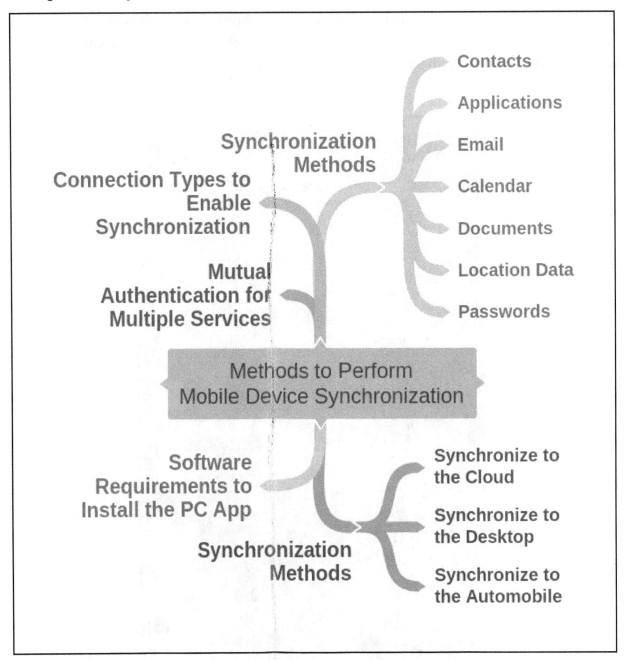

Figure 103: Mind Map of Data Synchronization between Mobile Devices

Summary

Install and Configure Laptop Hardware and Components

- Laptops or portable computers have integrated displays, keyboards, and pointing devices, making them easy to carry and easy to use in confined spaces

- The keyboard is the main input device on a laptop or a PC

- Laptops use double data rate (DDR) memory

- Laptops are designed to operate on battery power, but laptops can run only several hours on these batteries

Install Components in a Laptop Display

- Different laptop displays are LCD, LED, and OLED

- Two display technologies are inverter and digitizer

- The inverter is a power converter that coverts low-voltage DC power into the higher-voltage AC power

- The digitizer detects touch and transmits it to the laptop processor

Use Appropriate Laptop Features

- Recent generations of laptops have become as powerful as and more versatile than desktops

- A laptop will have many special function keys

- Function keys allow us to enable, disable, and adjust many of the important features of a laptop

- Docking stations and port replicators allow users to enhance laptops to be more like workstations

Compare and Contrast the Characteristics of Various Types of other Mobile Devices

- Most mobile devices store their long-term data to solid-state flash memory. They do not use SATA for connectivity

- LPDDR4 is a common type of RAM used in mobile devices for short-term storage

- A standalone GPS device or a smartphone equipped with a GPS app can display maps and give directions

Connect and Configure Accessories and Ports of other Mobile Devices

- Many different types of connections, ports, and accessories are available for mobile devices

- An SSD is a solid-state drive, which generally means a hard drive that is installed to a PC or laptop

- A SIM is a subscriber identity module that securely stores authentication information about the user and device

- Tethering can allow a desktop computer or laptop to share a mobile device's internet connection

Configure Basic Mobile Device Network Connectivity and Application Support

- An incoming mail server (such as POP3 or IMAP) and an outgoing mail server (SMTP) are required for POP3 and IMAP email connections

- Mobile hotspot technology enables a mobile device to share its internet connection with other Wi-Fi-capable devices

- International Mobile Subscriber Identity (IMSI) is used to identify the device user

- Virtual Private Networking (VPN) technology is used to make secure connections tunneling though the radio network of provider

Perform Mobile Device Synchronization

- Data synchronization is the process of maintaining and exchanging data between two or more devices

- USB is the most prevalent connection method used when synchronizing data from a mobile device to a PC

Practice Questions

1. Which of the following storage devices involves magnetization process to read and write the data?

   a) Solid State Drives (SSD)

   b) Hard Disk Drives (HDD)

   c) Optical Drives

   d) Flash Drives

2. Which of the following storage drives blend the features of both Hard Disk Drives and Solid State Drives?

   a) Hybrid Drives

   b) Optical Drives

   c) Flash Drives

   d) All of the above

3. Which of the following storage locations has volatile memory?

a) Hybrid Drives

b) Optical Drives

c) Read Access Memory (RAM)

d) Solid State Drives

4. In which of the following slot the video cards are installed?

a) Pin Gird Array (PGA)

b) Line Grid Array (LGA)

c) Accelerated Graphics Port (AGP)

d) None of the above

5. Which of the following is a type of display for laptops and desktop PCs?

a) LED

b) LCD

c) OLED

d) All of the above

6. What is a set of programmable keys that are horizontally present on the top of the keyboard performing some special tasks called?

a) Function Keys

b) Numeric Keys

c) Special Keys

d) Arrow Keys

7. To gain access of the special functions of the function keys, you need to press _____ key along with some other key to allow alternate functions.

a) Num Lock Key

b) Space Key

c) Fn Key

d) Shift Key

8. The _____ is a device that contains all of the laptop's ports, including serial and parallel ports to connect multiple devices to the laptop.

a) Port Replicator

b) Docking Station

c) All of the above

d) None of the above

9. Which of the following technologies is specially designed for reading E-books and magazines that are in digital and downloadable form?

a) E-Readers

b) Tablets

c) Smartphones

d) All of the above

10. Which of the followings is a type of wired connection?

a) USB

b) Bluetooth

c) NFC

d) Hotspot

11. Which of the followings is an example of client based email?

a) Gmail

b) Yahoo!

c) Microsoft Outlook

d) Flickr

12. Which of the followings is a web based email?

   a) Gmail

   b) Yahoo!

   c) MSN

   d) All of the above

13. Which of the following information is required for configuring a client based email?

   a) Username

   b) SMTP address

   c) POP address

   d) All of the above

14. Which of the following ports is used for outgoing emails?

   a) 26

   b) 24

   c) 25

   d) None

15. Which of the followings is an extension of email protocol that is used to exchange media such as images, audio, video, application programs, ASCII text and other kinds of data?

   a) SMTP

   b) MIME

   c) POP

   d) None

16. Which of the following updates allow the device to be able to roam or get service from outside of your cellular network?

    a) OS Updates

    b) PRI Updates

    c) Firmware Updates

    d) None of the above

17. Which of the followings is a type of data synchronization with cloud?

    a) Dropbox

    b) One Drive

    c) ICloud

    d) All of the above

    e) None

18. Which of the following data can be synchronized between devices?

    a) Contacts

    b) Pictures

    c) Music

    d) Emails

    e) All of the above

19. In which of the following techniques, a user needs only one set of credentials to gain access of multiple resources?

    a) Multiple Sign-On (MSO)

    b) Thumb Impression

    c) Two Factor Authentication

    d) Single Sign-On (SSO)

20. Which of the followings is the standard used to identify a physical phone device?

a) International Mobile Equipment Identification (IMEI)

b) SIM (Subscriber Identification Module)

c) International Mobile Subscriber Identification (IMSI)

d) None of the above

Chapter 02: Networking

Networking support requires a sound knowledge of how different types of computer networking hardware and software work together to enable communication between computing devices. CompTIA offers many networking certifications such as Network+, Server+, and so on, but to become successfully A+ certified, candidates must have good basic networking skills. The A+ certification exams cover two fields of networking; networking theory and hardware, and networking at the Operating System (OS) level. This chapter focuses on the networking theory and the networking hardware area of A+ exams.

After the successful completion of this chapter, candidates will understand the several networking devices and protocols, both wired and wireless, that need to be mastered to become a successful network technician.

Compare and Contrast TCP and UDP Ports, Protocols, and their Purposes

Communication over a TCP/IP based network is performed using various protocols, for example FTP to transfer files, HTTP to visit web pages, and POP3 or IMAP to send and receive emails. Each of these protocols possess a default port number corresponding to it. TCP and UDP both use port numbers to listen and respond to requests for communication using numerous protocols. These will be discussed in the following sections.

Ports and Protocols

21-File Transfer Protocol(FTP)

The File Transfer Protocol (FTP) is a standard protocol for transmitting files between a client and server on a computer network. It can work in active or passive mode and uses TCP to control the connection. In active mode, the connection is initialized by the user. It informs the server about the port that it intends to use in order to receive data. In active mode, (although port 21 is used for command and control) the data will be sent out on port 20 that serves as the FTP servers data port. Passive mode is used in situations where inbound user TCP connections are not possible. Firewalls generally block inbound connections by default. Here, the user sends a PASV command to the server and the server determines which user port can be used for the transfer.

Using FTP to transfer files is helpful in the following ways:

- It transfers files between two different networks easily

- It can resume a file transfer session even if the connection is dropped, as long as the protocol is configured appropriately

- It enables connection between geographically separated areas

Exam Note

Although users can use an operating system's built-in FTP client for file uploads and downloads with both secured and unsecured FTP sites, users should consider using third-party FTP products such as FileZilla (https://filezilla-project.org). Such programs enable users to create a customized setup for each FTP site they visit and store passwords, server types, and other necessary information. They also enable faster downloads than typical web browsers running in ftp:// mode.

22-Secure Shell (SSH)

Secure Shell (SSH) opens a secured network channel that promotes confidentiality and integrity for network services over an unsecure public network using public key cryptography. This makes it a cryptographic network protocol. It is used to secure remote network logins and other confidential data. Passwords cannot be intercepted because the encryption is established before the login is required.

23-Telnet

Telnet was designed to support remote logins and communication between computers. It provides a functional command prompt on the remote host. These are plaintext and communication channel, making them subject to interception. Telnet does not encrypt data. SSH has generally replaced Telnet and these connections.

Telnet is a remote access protocol for building a connection with a remote machine over the TCP/IP network.

Exam Note

A remote computer must be configured to accept a Telnet login. Generally, TCP port 23 on the remote computer must be open before login can take place.

25-Simple Mail Transport Protocol (SMTP)

SMTP is an internet standard protocol that permits the transmission and delivery of emails over the internet. Most email software is designed to use SMTP for communication purposes when sending emails. It only works for outgoing messages. So when an email has to be sent, the address of its

Internet Service Provider's SMTP sever has to be given. The actual mail transfer is done through Message Transfer Agents (MTA). So the computer user must have a user MTA and the server MTA. SMTP actually defines the MTA user and the server on the internet. SMTP uses TCP port 25 for internet mail transmission.

 Exam Note

When configuring email settings on a client, check with the ISP or organization that provides internet access for the correct settings. Users have to know the server type(s) used (SMTP, POP3, or IMAP), the ports used (default values may be changed by some ISPs), the username and password for the email service, and the security settings (for example, whether SSH is used).

53-Domain Name System (DNS)

The Domain Name System (DNS) is the process where internet domain names are located and translated into Internet Protocol (IP) addresses. The domain name system maps the name people use to locate a website to the IP address that a computer uses to locate a website.

DNS uses two protocols TCP and UDP on port 53. DNS servers update themselves using and maintaining a list of known hosts to address translations in a distributed database, while obtaining unknown or moved domains. This supports the hierarchical nature of domains, and the naming of domains and sub-domains.

80-Hypertext Transfer Protocol(HTTP)

Web browsers use the Hypertext Transfer Protocol (HTTP) for internet communications and can be considered the basis of the World Wide Web. It uses the client/server method, where a user uses a Uniform Resource Locator (URL) to locate and request information from the target server of the resource. A typical URL begins with http:// (or increasingly https://) followed by the Fully Qualified Domain Name (FQDN) of the desired resource. URLs to websites can be distributed between parties in messages containing the address, which can be converted into clickable links called hyperlinks in reference to the hypertext communication being used. HTTP uses TCP/UDP port 80 and sends unencrypted data by default, this is inherently insecure.

110-Post Office Protocol (POP) Version 3

Receiving email is executed over several different protocols. There are two main protocols available depending on the service. The first is Post Office Protocol with the latest version called POP3. POP3 protocol uses port 110 by default and is responsible for the management of messages on the server (saving or deleting them). Deleting the message after delivery is the default mode. Leaving messages on the server is helpful if multiple devices are used for messaging.

143-Internet Message Access Protocol (IMAP)

Internet Message Access Protocol (IMAP) is a standard protocol for accessing email on a remote server from a local client. IMAP is an application layer Internet Protocol using the underlying transport layer protocols to establish host-to-host communication services for applications. This allows the use of a remote mail server. The well-known port address for IMAP is 143.

The IMAP architecture encourages users to send and receive emails through a remote server, without support from a particular device. This type of email access is ideal for travelers receiving or answering emails from their home desktop or office computer.

This term is also known as interim mail access protocol, interactive mail access protocol, and internet mail access protocol.

443-Hyper Text Transfer Protocol Secure (HTTPS)

HTTPS is the secure version of HTTP. It is the protocol over which data is sent between the users' browser and the website they are connected to. It means all communications between the users' browser and the website are encrypted. HTTPS protocol, also called HTTP over SSL/TLS, is a web communication protocol designed to secure communications over computer networks by encrypting it through SSL/TLS. The purpose of HTTPS is to ensure the integrity, protection, and privacy of the data exchanged between a server and a client (usually a browser). It also authenticates websites and confirms its trustworthiness.

 Exam Note

Most browsers connecting with a secured site also display a closed padlock symbol onscreen.

3389-Remote Desktop Protocol (RDP)

Remote Desktop Protocol (RDP) is a secure network communications protocol designed for remote management, as well as for remote access to virtual desktops, applications, and RDP terminal servers. From Windows XP onward, RDC is available. Using RDP on TCP/UDP port 3389, RDC is able to bring the fully functional remote machine's desktop and programs to a device. This requires the client and the server software to be configured on Microsoft products, but versions are available for most OSs. Users can use their home or office computer on their iPhone by connecting their phones remotely with their system.

137-139-Network Basic Input/Output System (NetBIOS)

NetBIOS permits computers and applications to communicate with hardware and allows data to be transmitted properly over a network. NetBIOS communicates on ports 137, 138, and 139. For

example, Microsoft Windows computers that are named in a workgroup and not a domain, use NetBIOS names converted to IP addresses.

If a user's firewall blocks any of these ports, they may get errors when their computer communicates with another computer that utilizes NetBIOS (such as, Microsoft Windows). To prevent these errors or warnings, users must provide access on these ports.

 Exam Note

If traffic on ports 137–139 is blocked, users must use the device's IP address to access shared files or printers. When these ports are open, users can use the name of the device to access its shared files or printers.

445-Service Message Block (SMB)

SMB is a protocol used for sharing access to files, printers, serial ports, and other resources on a network. It can also carry transaction protocols for inter-process communication. SMB predates active directory and is the basis of Microsoft's Windows for workgroups networking capability. Based on NetBIOS, it can run on UDP ports 136,138 and TCP ports 137, 139 as NetBIOS over TCP/IP. It can also operate directly on TCP port 445. While being one of the oldest networking protocols, it has been continuously improved, and the 3.0 version implemented with Windows 8 (3.02 in 8.1) supports improved performance in virtualized data centers. It is common in many network applications and embedded devices, with newer versions supporting an end-to-end AES encryption. Users may also see this service as a Common Internet File System (CIFS) or samba depending on the operating system.

427-Service Location Protocol (SLP)

The Service Location Protocol (SLP) is a protocol or method of arranging and locating the resources (such as printers, databases, schedulers, disk drives) in a network. SLP is intended to give users an easy-to-use interface to a network's resource information. The protocol defines and monitors communications and operations that take place among entities called user agents (subscribers or workstations), service agents (peripherals and resources), and directory agents (peripherals and resources within service agents).

548- Apple File Protocol (AFP)

The Apple File Protocol (AFP) version 3.0 and higher uses TCP/IP ports 548 or 427 to support the proprietary Apple sharing protocol used in an AppleTalk network. A non-Apple network can only access data from an AppleShare file server by first translating into the AFP language. AFP over TCP/IP, a flavor of AFP, allows users to access AFP servers over TCP/IP networks. The protocol can use URLs with this structure afp//server/path. At the time of writing, AFP is migrating to SMB.

67/68-Dynamic Host Configuration Protocol (DHCP)

Dynamic Host Configuration Protocol (DHCP) is a network management protocol used to dynamically assign an Internet Protocol (IP) address to any device, or node, on a network so they can communicate using the IP. As the most common IPv4 or IPv6 TCP/IP addressing method, DHCP is responsible for the complete client configuration on a TCP/IP network. On an operating network, there is usually an assigned DHCP server. SOHO implementations use the router provided by the ISP to perform this process. What DHCP does is assign or lease a unique IP address to each host. The duration of the lease is determined by the network administrator or weekly by default. It will define the internet gateway and Domain Name Server to be used. This means that the machine may not get the same IP address when rebooted or is otherwise disconnected. The DNS and Gateway settings will remain same. The DHCP server has an available pool of IP addresses available to assign to clients (hosts) who attempt to connect to the network. The client broadcasts a UDP discovery packet for an address to all connected networks. All DHCP servers offer an address to the client then the client accepts the offer from the nearest server by requesting a lease, and that server then leases the address to the client. The address assignment process is same for both IPv4 and IPv6 addresses. In the interest of regularity, the ports used are UDP 67 for the server and UDP 68 for the client.

389-Lightweight Directory Access Protocol (LDAP)

Lightweight Directory Access Protocol (LDAP) is a software protocol for enabling anyone to locate organizations, individuals, and other resources such as files and devices in a network, whether on the public internet or on a corporate intranet. LDAP is a version of Directory Access Protocol (DAP). The protocol serves to provide access to an IP network, and maintains a distributed directory of users, applications, available network services, and systems throughout an IP network. It is based on the x.500 standard's directory services using the Directory Access Protocol (DAP), which relies on the 7 layer OSI model. LDAP uses only a portion of the x.500 standard set and uses the latest and more relevant four layer internet protocol suite on port TCP/UDP 389 in the application layer. by gathering all the required network information including users and their credentials, LDAP servers can be used to quickly validate user access. LDAP can achieve specific and detailed responses to queries about the network with precisely detailed information based on the parameters of the request. In addition to its own Distinguished Name (DN) object identification, LDAP can ask DNS servers to locate other LDAP servers.

161/162-Simple Network Management Protocol (SNMP)

Simple Network Management Protocol (SNMP) is an application-layer protocol used to manage and monitor network devices and their functions. SNMP provides a common language for network devices to relay management information within single and multivendor environments in a Local Area Network (LAN) or Wide Area Network (WAN). SNMP is one of the most popular network management protocols used to monitor and configure network nodes such as printers, routers,

hosts, and servers, to name a few, using a network manager on TCP/UDP ports 161 and 162. The latest version of SNMP3 includes security enhancements that authenticate and encrypt SNMP messages as well as protect packets during transit.

 Exam Note

Remember these protocols and their corresponding port numbers for the 220-1001 exam.

Compare/Contrast TCP and UDP Protocols

There are two types of Internet Protocol (IP) traffic. TCP (Transmission Control Protocol) and UDP (User Datagram Protocol). TCP is a connection-oriented protocol, which ensures end-to-end reliable packet delivery with efficient flow control, full-duplex operation, multiplexing, and data streaming services. TCP belongs to transport layer protocol (layer 4). UDP is a simple, connectionless Internet Protocol. Multiple messages are sent as packets in chunks using UDP. Unlike TCP, UDP adds no reliability, flow-control, or error-recovery functions to IP packets. Because of its simplicity, UDP headers contain fewer bytes and consume less network overhead than TCP.

Transmission Control Protocol (TCP)

There are two types of IP (Internet Protocol) traffic, TCP (Transmission Control Protocol) and UDP (User Datagram Protocol). TCP belongs to the Transport Layer protocol (layer 4). It is a connection-oriented protocol, which ensures end-to-end reliable packet delivery with an efficient flow control, full-duplex operation, multiplexing, and data streaming services.

User Datagram Protocol (UDP)

UDP (User Datagram Protocol) is another type of Transport Layer (Layer 4) protocol. It is very efficient for multicast or broadcast types of network transmission. UDP is a connectionless protocol. Unlike TCP, UDP adds no reliability, flow-control, or error-recovery functions to IP. UDP is used in several well-known application-layer protocols, including Domain Name System (DNS), Simple Network Management Protocol (SNMP), Network File System (NFS), and Trivial File Transfer Protocol (TFTP).

The following table compares the TCP and UDP protocols:

Parameters	Transmission Control Protocol (TCP)	User Datagram Protocol or Universal Datagram Protocol (UDP)
Connection	TCP is a connection-oriented protocol	UDP is a connectionless protocol
Function	A message makes its way across the internet from one computer to another. This is connection based	UDP is also a protocol used in message transport or transfer. This is not connection based, which means that one process can send a load of packets to another and that would be end of the connection
Usage	TCP is suited for applications that require high reliability, and transmission time is relatively less critical	UDP is suitable for applications that need fast, efficient transmission, such as games. UDP's stateless nature is also useful for servers that answer small queries from huge numbers of clients
Use by other Protocols	HTTPs, HTTP, SMTP, FTP, Telnet	DHCP, DNS, SNMP, TFTP, VOIP, RIP
Ordering of Data Packets	TCP rearranges data packets in a specified order	UDP has no appropriate order, as all packets are independent of each other. If ordering is required, it has to be managed by the application layer
Speed of Transfer	The speed for TCP is slower than UDP	UDP is faster because error recovery is not attempted. It is a "best effort" protocol
Reliability	There is an absolute guarantee that the transferred data will remain intact and arrive in the same order in which it was sent	There is no guarantee that the sent messages or packets will arrive at all
Header Size	TCP header size is 20 bytes	UDP header size is 8 bytes
Common Header Fields	Source port, Check Sum Destination port	Source port, Check Sum Destination port
Streaming of Data	Data is read as a byte stream, no distinguishing indications	Packets are sent individually and are checked for integrity only if they arrive.

	are transmitted to signal message (segment) boundaries	Packets have definite boundaries, which are honored upon receipt, meaning that a read operation at the receiver socket will yield an entire message as it was originally sent
Weight	TCP is heavyweight. TCP requires three packets to set up a socket connection, before any user data can be sent. TCP handles reliability and congestion control	UDP is lightweight. There is no ordering of messages, no tracking connections, etc. It is a small transport layer designed on top of the IP
Data Flow Control	TCP does Flow Control. TCP requires three packets to set up a socket connection, before any user data can be sent. TCP handles reliability and congestion control	UDP does not have an option for flow control
Error Checking	TCP does error checking and error recovery. Erroneous packets are retransmitted from the source to the destination	UDP does error checking but simply discards erroneous packets. Error recovery is not attempted
Fields	1. Sequence Number, 2. AcK number, 3. Data offset, 4. Reserved, 5. Control bit, 6. Window, 7. Urgent Pointer 8. Options, 9. Padding, 10. Check Sum, 11. Source port, 12. Destination port	1. Length, 2. Source port, 3. Destination port, 4. Check Sum
Acknowledgment	Acknowledgment segments	No Acknowledgment
Handshake	SYN, SYN-ACK, ACK	No handshake (connectionless protocol)

Table 2-1: Comparison of TCP and UDP Protocol

Mind Map of Ports and Protocols

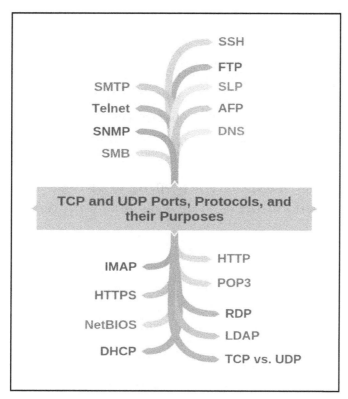

Figure 2-1: Mind Map of Ports and Protocols

Compare and Contrast Common Networking Hardware Devices

Networking devices are physical devices that are required for interaction and communication between devices on a computer network. Network devices include routers, switches, access points, cloud-based network controllers, firewalls, network interface cards, repeaters, hubs, cable/DSL modems, BridgePatch panels, Power over Ethernet (PoE), and Ethernet over Power.

These network devices are defined below.

Routers

A router is a network device that forwards data packets from one network to another. It is based on the address of the destination network in the incoming packet and an internal routing table. The router determines which port (line) to send out the packet (ports typically connect to Ethernet cables). Routers operate at the network layer of the OSI model.

The biggest advantage of a router is that it can determine the best path for data to take in order to get to its destination. They are slower than bridges because they are more intelligent devices; they analyze every packet, causing packet-forwarding delays. They are also expensive because of this intelligence.

An example configuration for a router to configure an interface is *Cisco IOS Software, 7200 Software (C7200-ADVENTERPRISEK9-M), Version 15.2(4)S7.*

Switches

A switch is a device used on a computer network to physically connect devices together. Multiple cables can be connected to enable network devices to communicate with each other. A switch operates at layer 2 of the OSI model. Switches operate very similar to hubs, which got their name because they connect several computers (usually twisted-pair Ethernet networks). However, switches receive on one port and not every other port as hubs do. Rather, switches examine the header of the incoming packet and forward it properly to the right port and only that port. This reduces overhead and thus performance as there is essentially a virtual connection between sender and receiver.

There are two types of switch:

- Managed Switch
- Unmanaged Switch

Managed Switches

A managed switch allows connected network devices to communicate with each other and gives the network administrator greater control over managing and prioritizing LAN traffic. It manages the data transferring over a network and security access to the data by using protocols like SNMP (Simple Network Management Protocol), which monitors all devices connected to the network. A managed switch uses SNMP to dynamically present a current status on network performance through a graphical interface, which is easier to understand and use for monitoring and configuration. SNMP allows remote management of the network and connected devices, without having to physically work on the switch.

Unmanaged Switches

An unmanaged switch allows devices connected to a network (LAN) to communicate with each other. It is a plug-and-plug switch that does not require or allow any user intervention, configuration, or setup to be usable. An unmanaged switch is developed with a standard configuration that cannot be altered.

Access Points

An Access Point is a device that creates a Wireless Local Area Network, or WLAN, usually in an office or large building. An access point connects to a wired router, switch, or hub via an Ethernet cable, and projects a Wi-Fi signal to a designated area. For example, if users want to enable Wi-Fi

access in a company's reception area but do not have a router within range, they can install an access point near the front desk and run an Ethernet cable through the ceiling back to the server room.

Advantages of Using Wireless Access Points

When both employees and guests connecting to desktops, laptops, mobile phones, and tablets, 20 devices on a wireless network add up quickly. At 60 simultaneous connections each, access point gives you the freedom to scale the number of devices supported on the network. That is only one of the advantages of using these network enhancers—consider these points:

- Business-grade access points can be installed where users can run an Ethernet cable. Newer models are also compatible with Power over Ethernet Plus, or PoE+ (a combination Ethernet and power cord), so there is no need to run a separate power line or install an outlet near the access point

- Additional standard features include Captive Portal and Access Control List (ACL) support, so users can limit guest access without compromising network security, as well as easily manage users within the Wi-Fi network

- Select access points include a Clustering feature—a single point from which the IT administrator can view, deploy, configure, and secure a Wi-Fi network as a single entity rather than a series of separate access point configurations

Cloud-based Network Controller

Cloud-based networking has appeared in the past few years as the next generation of computer networks. Administrators can manage wireless LANs and branch offices that are located anywhere on the internet from a central point using a cloud-based controller. With wireless networking becoming more popular than wired-based networks, cloud management solutions are expected to expand.

Firewall

A firewall is a network security device that monitors incoming and outgoing network traffic and decides whether to allow or block specific traffic based on a defined set of security principles.

Firewalls have been a first line of defense in network security since the 1980's. They establish a barrier between secured and controlled internal networks that can be trusted and untrusted external networks, such as the internet. A firewall can be both hardware or software.

Firewall Types

Proxy Firewall

An old type of firewall device, a proxy firewall serves as the gateway from one network to another for a specific application. Proxy servers can provide additional functionality such as content caching and security by preventing direct connections from an external network.

Stateful Inspection Firewall

Now thought of as a "traditional" firewall, a stateful inspection firewall allows or blocks traffic based on state, port, and protocol. It monitors all activity from the opening of a connection until it is closed. Filtering decisions are made based on both administrator-defined rules as well as context, which refers to using information from previous connections and packets belonging to the same connection.

Unified Threat Management (UTM) Firewall

A UTM device typically combines, in a loosely coupled way, the functions of a stateful inspection firewall with intrusion prevention and antivirus. It may also include additional services and often cloud management. UTMs focus on simplicity and ease of use.

Next-Generation Firewall (NGFW)

Firewalls have been developed beyond simple packet filtering and stateful inspection. Most organizations are deploying next-generation firewalls to block modern threats such as advanced malware and application-layer attacks.

According to Gartner Inc.'s definition, a next-generation firewall must include:

- Standard firewall capabilities such as stateful inspection

- Integrated intrusion prevention

- Application awareness and control to see and block risky apps

- Upgraded paths to include future information feeds

- Techniques to address evolving security threats

Threat-Focused NGFW

These firewalls include all the capabilities of a traditional NGFW and also provide advanced threat detection and remediation.

With a threat-focused NGFW, users can:

- Know which assets are most at risk with complete context awareness

- Quickly react to attacks with intelligent security automation that sets policies and hardens their defenses dynamically

- Better detect evasive or suspicious activity with network and endpoint event correlation

- Greatly decrease the time from detection to clean up with retrospective security that continuously monitors for suspicious activity and behavior even after initial inspection

- Ease administration and reduce complexity with unified policies that protect across the entire attack continuum

Network Interface Card (NIC)

A Network Interface Card is a circuit board installed in a computer so that it can be connected to the network. A network interface card provides the computer with a dedicated, full-time connection to a network. The NIC contains the electronic circuitry required to communicate using a wired connection (such as Ethernet) or a wireless connection (such as Wi-Fi). A network interface card is also called network interface controller, Local Area Network (LAN), or network adapter.

Repeater

A repeater is a network device that operates at the physical layer of the OSI model. Repeaters can be used to regenerate or replicate signals between similar network segments.

They are used in transmission systems to regenerate analog or digital signal distorted by transmission loss. An important point about repeaters is that they do not amplify the signal when the signal becomes weak. They copy the signal bit by bit and regenerate its original strength.

Hub

When referring to a network, a hub is the most fundamental networking device that connects various PCs or other system devices together. Dissimilar to a network switch or switch, a network hub has no directing table or knowledge of where to send data and communicates all network information over every association.

A hub, also called a network hub, is a typical association point for devices in a system. The hub contains numerous ports. At the point when a bundle touches base at one port, it is duplicated to alternate ports with the goal that all fragments of the LAN can see all parcels.

The Difference between Hubs and Switches

A switch is utilized to interface different system sections. A network switch is a small device that combines various PCs inside one neighborhood (LAN). A hub interfaces numerous Ethernet devices together, influencing them to go about as a solitary section.

Exam Note

Sharing all traffic in a LAN created traffic jams for the computers. One solution that came along was the now-legacy Ethernet bridge, which divided a LAN into two parts. The Ethernet bridge was the original wireless bridge

Cable/DSL Modem

A modem is a device for converting serial data (typically EIA-232) from a computer into an audio signal suitable for transmission over a telephone line. Computer information is stored digitally, whereas information transmitted over telephone lines is transmitted in the form of analog waves.

Bridge

A bridge is a device that connects a Local Area Network (LAN) to another Local Area Network that uses the same protocol (such as, Ethernet or token ring). A bridge operates at the data link layer of the OSI model. A bridge is a repeater with the add-on functionality of filtering content by learning the MAC addresses of source and destination. It is also used for interconnecting two LANs working on the same protocol. Transparent bridges and source routing bridges are types of bridges.

Patch Panel

A patch panel is also referred to as a patch field or jack field. It is a mounted hardware assembly that contains a set number of ports to connect and manage the incoming and outgoing fiber or copper cables. In a typical data center infrastructure, patch panels are often placed in a wiring closet to connect racks with each other. Each rack contains at least one patch panel, the back end of which is connected to the back end of the other one. Users will need patch cords to connect servers or network switches to the ports on the front end of the patch panel in each rack.

Power over Ethernet (PoE)

Power over Ethernet (PoE) is a technology for wired Ethernet LANs (Local Area Networks) that allows the electrical current necessary for the operation of each device to be carried by the data cables rather than by power cords. PoE technology sends 10/100/1000 Mbps of data and 15W, 30W, 60W, and up to 90W of power budget to devices over Cat5e and Cat6 Ethernet cables to a maximum distance of 100m.

PoE Injector

A PoE Injector is a device that is also known as "midspan". It injects power onto an Ethernet cable. The injector adds power to data coming from a non-PoE switch. It has an external power supply. Injectors allow admins to populate and properly support LANs with both compliant and non-compliant devices.

Splitter

A splitter is another power device that goes in the opposite direction to the injector. It has two output cables: one supplies data and the other supplies power. It is used to deploy remote non-PoE devices with no nearby AC outlets.

A splitter allows a non-compliant device to upgrade to PoE. By plugging into the network connection, it can pull power and convert it into low-voltage ranges as required.

The Difference between a PoE Injector and a PoE Splitter

The difference between an injector and a splitter is that a PoE injector sends power to PoE equipment that receives data through existing non-PoE switches. A splitter also supplies power, but it does so by splitting the power from the data and feeding it to a separate input that non-PoE compliant devices can use.

Ethernet over Power

One method for creating an Ethernet network without switches, hubs, or crossover cable is using electrical outlets. Ethernet over Power (EoP) sends network data to EoP modules plugged into power outlets to extend Ethernet networks. Most EoP modules support wireless connectivity as well. Using EoP requires two EoP modules. One module plugs into a power outlet near the internet modem – an Ethernet cable connects from the internet modem to the EoP module. A second EoP module connects near the home or business device that has trouble connecting to the internet due to a lack of Ethernet wiring or weak RF signal. By connecting an Ethernet cable between the standard device and the EoP module, the device will get internet access.

Mind Map of Networking Hardware Devices

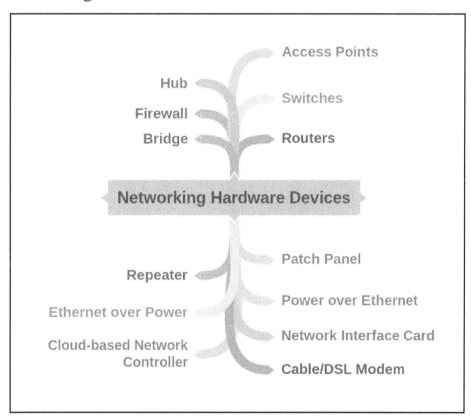

Figure 2-2: Mind Map of Networking Hardware Devices

Install and Configure a Basic Wired/Wireless SOHO Network

Wireless Ethernet networks, commonly known as IEEE 802.11, is the specified name for a group of wireless technologies compatible with wired Ethernet. These technologies are referred to as wireless LAN (WLAN) standards. Wireless Ethernet is also known as Wi-Fi, after the Wireless Fidelity (Wi-Fi) Alliance (www.wi-fi.org), a trade group that supports interoperability between different vendors of wireless Ethernet hardware.

The following section describes factors to consider when implementing and configuring these wireless technologies in a SOHO platform.

Lab 2.1: Configure the Basic Router/Switch

In the previous section, we described the concepts of router and switch. We implemented these concepts on the router/switch in the diagram below:

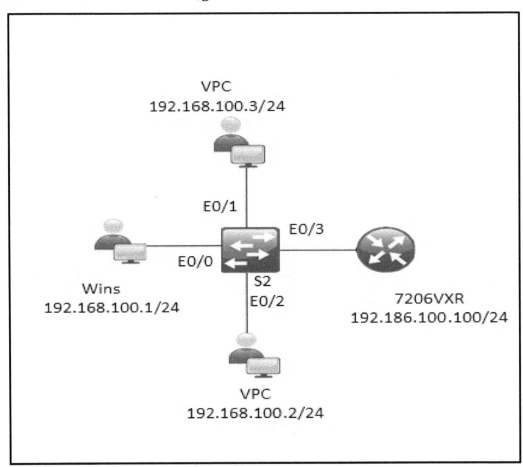

Figure 2-3: Configuring Router and Switch

Enter "enable" on the user privilege mode.

--- System Configuration Dialog ---

Would you like to enter the initial configuration dialog? [yes/no]: **no**

Router> **enable**

//Enter configure terminal to enter the global configuration mode

Router# **configure terminal**

Enter configuration commands, one per line. End with CNTL/Z.

Router(config)#

Use hostname command to specify the name for the router.

Router(config)# **hostname Cisco_7206VXR**

Cisco_720VXR(config)#

//Enter the configuration mode for Ethernet interface on the router

Cisco_7206VXR(config)# **interface ethernet 1/0**

//Set the IP address and subnet mask

Cisco_7206VXR(config)# **ip address 192.168.100.100 255.255.255.0**

Cisco_7206VXR(config)# **duplex ?**

  full Force full duplex operation

  half Force half-duplex operation

Cisco_7206VXR(config)# **duplex full**

Cisco_7206VXR(config)# **no shutdown**

Cisco_7206VXR(config)# **exit**

*Feb 21 09:36:34.119: %LINK-3-UPDOWN: Interface Ethernet1/0, changed state to up

*Feb 21 09:36:35.119: %LINEPROTO-5-UPDOWN: Line protocol on Interface Ethernet1/0, changed state to up

According to the results shown below, duplex mismatch has been observed on the interface Ethernet1/0:

*Feb 21 09:36:35.595: %CDP-4-DUPLEX_MISMATCH: duplex mismatch discovered on Ethernet1/0 (not half duplex), with Switch Ethernet0/3 (half duplex).

According to the results shown below, duplex mismatch has been observed on the interface Ethernet0/3:

*Feb 21 07:38:27.496: %CDP-4-DUPLEX_MISMATCH: duplex mismatch discovered on Ethernet0/3 (not full duplex), with Router Ethernet1/0 (full duplex).

Enter the privilege mode by entering the enable command.

Switch> **enable**

//Enter configure terminal to enter the global configuration mode

Switch# **configure terminal**

Enter configuration commands, one per line. End with CNTL/Z.

Switch(config)#

//Enter the configuration mode for Ethernet interface on the switch

Switch(config)# **interface ethernet 0/3**

Switch(config-if)# **shutdown**

*Feb 21 07:38:41.309: %LINK-5-CHANGED: Interface Ethernet0/3, changed state to administratively down

*Feb 21 07:38:42.317: %LINEPROTO-5-UPDOWN: Line protocol on Interface Ethernet0/3, changed state to down

Switch(config-if)# **duplex full**

Switch(config-if)# **no shutdown**

*Feb 21 07:38:47.437: %LINK-3-UPDOWN: Interface Ethernet0/3, changed state to up

*Feb 21 07:38:48.437: %LINEPROTO-5-UPDOWN: Line protocol on Interface Ethernet0/3, changed state to up

Switch(config-if)# **exit**

Switch(config)#

Use hostname command to specify the name for the switch.

Switch(config)# **hostname Cisco_L2_Switch**

Cisco_L2_Switch(config)#

Note: IPSpecialist offers free downloadable vRacks for CompTIA A+ certification. You can practice the above configuration in Lab 2-1.

Access Point Settings

A Small Office/Home Office wired or wireless router can provide a secure connection for users to access the internet and local network resources. Sometimes, it can increase the chance of an attack if SOHO routers are not configured properly.

To configure the access point settings, connect to the router with an Ethernet cable or wirelessly, using the vendor's instructions on the default IP address. To connect, open a browser and enter the IP address of the router and press "Enter". Set up the router on the pop-up window.

IP Addresses

For the above topology diagram, we used the 192.168.100.0/24 network. This network can support 254 nodes as shown below:

192	168	100	0
8bits	8bits	8bits	8bits
11000000	10101000	1100100	00000000
Network bits			Host bits

Network Address: 192.168.100.0/24

Broadcast Address: 192.168.100.255/24

Host Address Range: 192.168.100.1 – 192.168.100.254

Lab 2.2: NIC Configuration

We discussed the Network Interface Card (NIC) in the previous section. Now, we have to configure the NIC. Both wired and wireless NICs have some optional parameters that can be manually configured. Access these parameters by right-clicking the NIC within the Networking and Sharing Center option of the Control Panel and following the steps mentioned below.

Log in to the Windows PC connected to the network as shown in the above topology diagram.

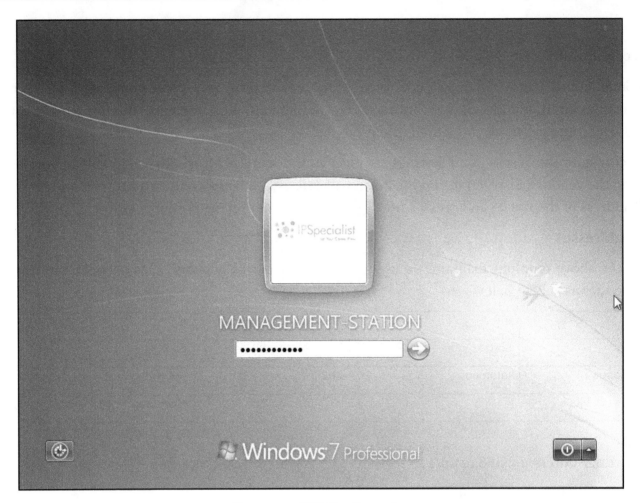

Figure 2-4: NIC Configuration

Go to Control Panel and click on "Network and Internet".

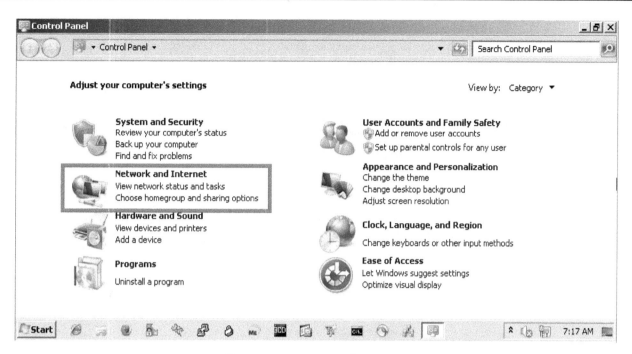

Figure 2- 5: NIC Configuration

Click on "Network and Sharing Center".

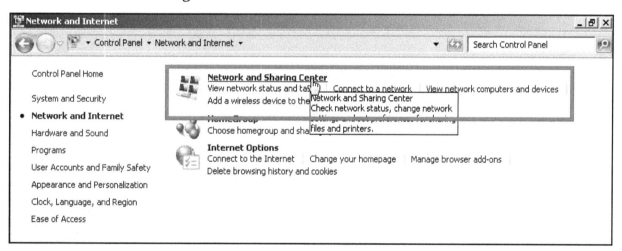

Figure 2- 6: NIC Configuration

Click on "Change adapter settings".

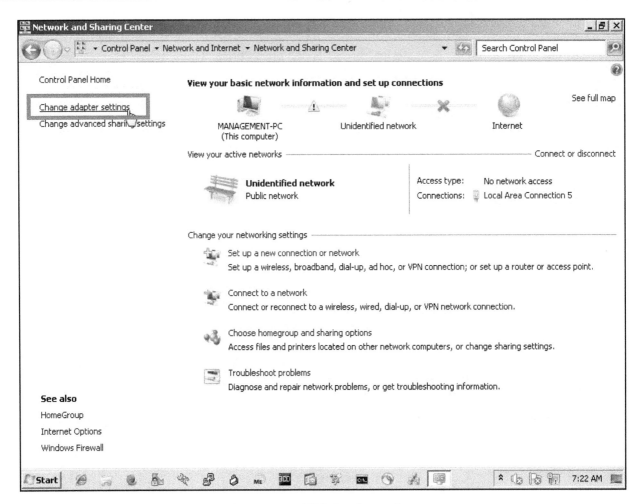

Figure 2- 7: NIC Configuration

Click on "Local Area Connection" >"Properties" > "Configure" > "Advanced"

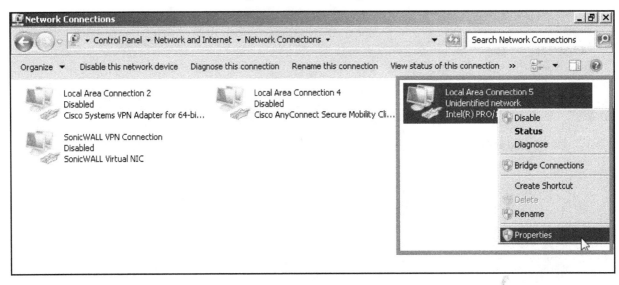

Figure 2- 8: NIC Configuration

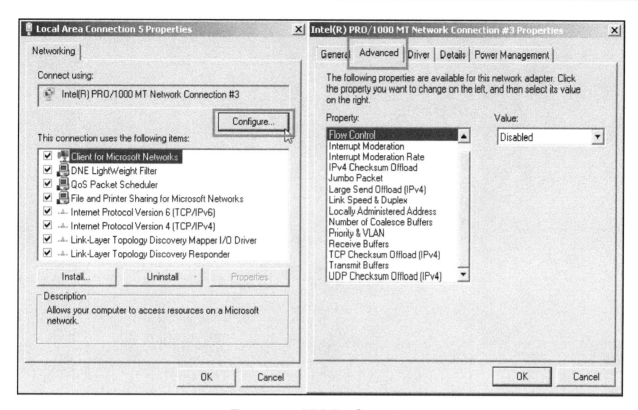

Figure 2- 9: NIC Configuration

End-user Device Configuration

End-user device is a technical term referring to IT hardware that your team uses during work, in off-hours, for any other purposes. Some examples of end devices are as follows:

- Network printer

- VoIP phones

- Computer, laptops, web server, file server

- Security cameras

- Mobile handheld devices

End-user Device Management

End-user device management protects business data and the network. Management of end-user devices includes installing and updating operating systems and application patches, maintaining up-to-date security, and managing user accounts.

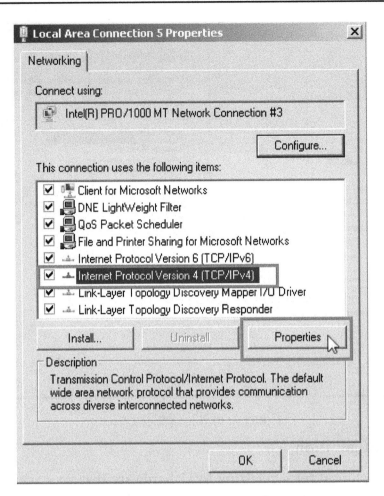

Figure 2-10: End-user Device Configuration

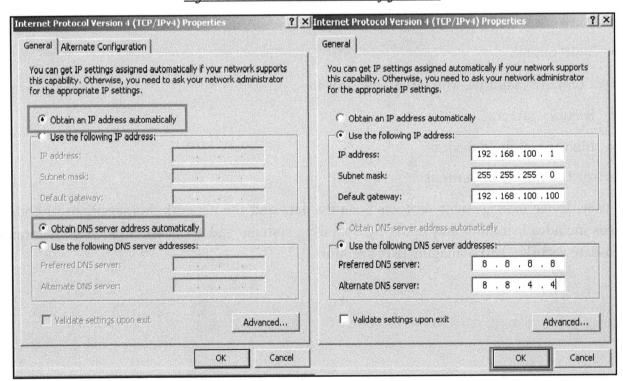

Figure 2-11: End-User Device Configuration

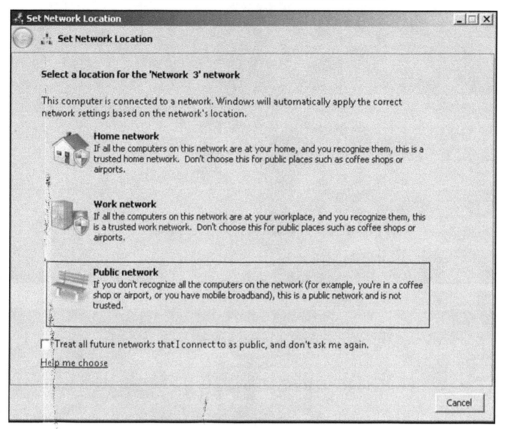

Figure 2-12: End-User Device Configuration

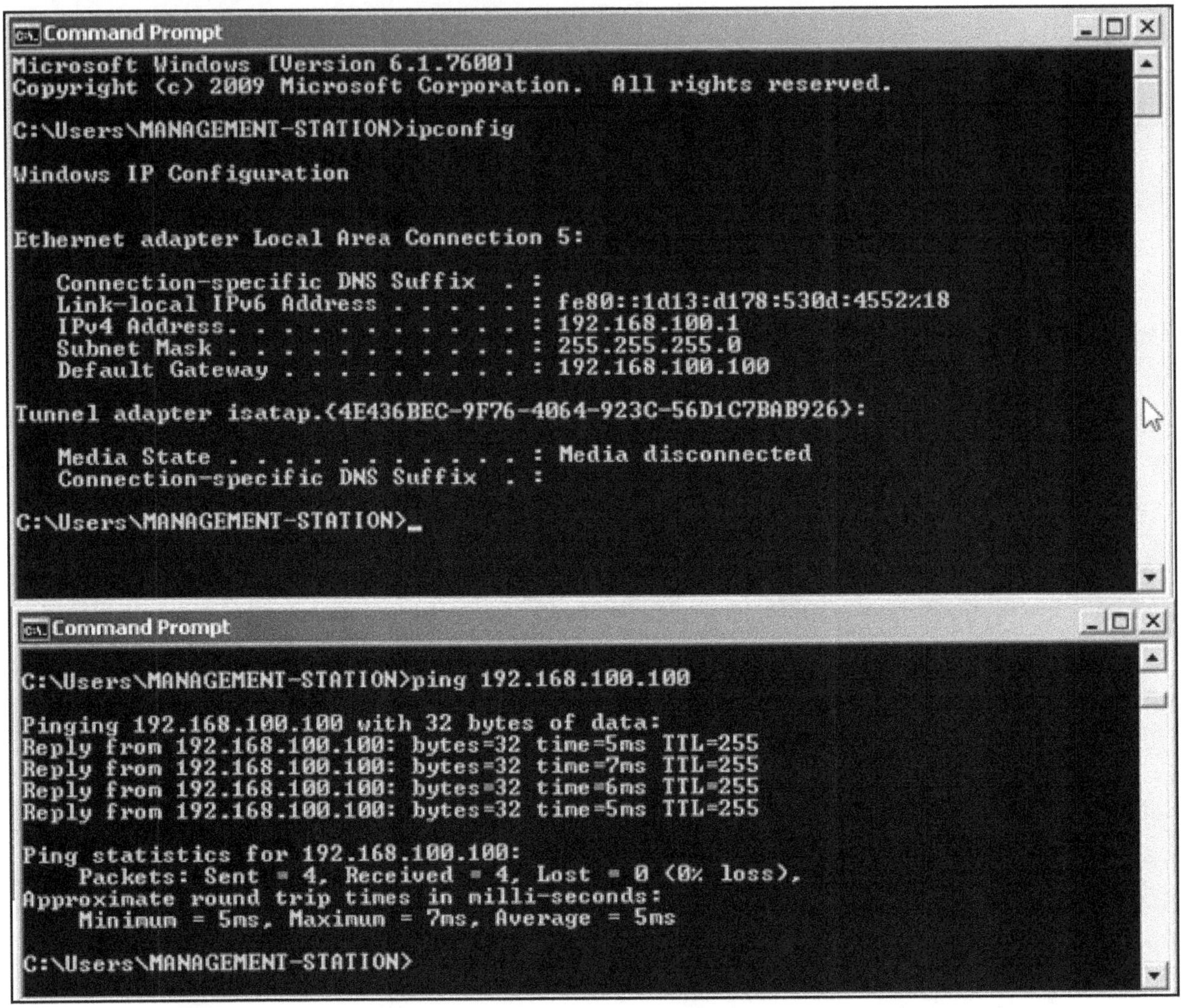

Figure 2-13: End-user Device Configuration

Note: IPSpecialist offers free downloadable vRacks for CompTIA A+ certification. You can practice the above configuration in Lab 2-1.

Internet of Things (IoT) Device Configuration

The internet has rapidly connected people together and in recent years and many things that people use are, not unexpectedly, connected to the internet, making life easier. Areas for IoT devices are ever-expanding and include phones, cars, home appliances, door locks, switches, cameras, and many others. Millions of devices are now talking to each other and also sharing data, and the quantity of such devices is expected to grow exponentially.

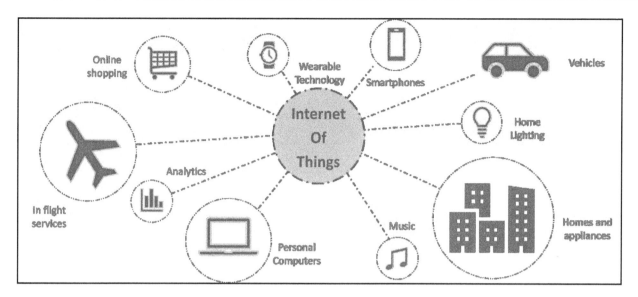

Figure 2-14: Internet of Things

IoT devices are managed by the software that can be installed on computers or mobile phones. Usually a vendor of an IoT product introduces an application to operate and manage the devices.

Some of the Internet of Things are described below:

Thermostats

A thermostat is a small device that contains sensors and is used to regulate temperature. A smart thermostat is a programmable incorporated thermostat capable of connecting to an Internet Protocol (IP) network. Through an IP connection, users can remotely send instructions to an internet thermostat to turn it on or off or personalize its settings using a thermostat device app interface.

Figure 2-15: Thermostat Device App Interface

Light Switches

Smart light switches are connected to the existing Wi-Fi network to provide wireless control of your lights from anywhere in the world. Simply place the light switches and download the support app on your phone or tablet and start controlling your lights as you wish.

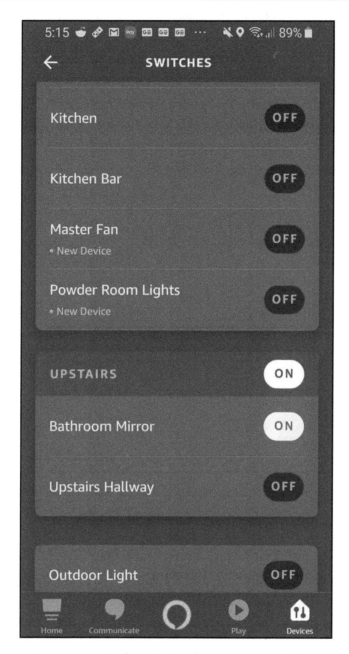

Figure 2-16: Light Switches Device App Interface

Security Cameras

Wireless security cameras, also known as wireless IP cameras, collect and stream data over the wireless network. As such, IP cameras connect to home Wi-Fi networks allowing you to view security footage from anywhere. With IP security cameras, you can view the area where the security cameras are placed by typing the IP addresses of the security cameras from anywhere around the globe.

Door Locks

A smart door lock is a Wi-Fi or Bluetooth-enabled smart home device that allows users to lock and unlock a door by sending secure signals from a mobile application on their smartphone, computer, or tablet. Smart locks provide a new home security experience with the ability to customize who can access your home and when and who can lock or unlock your door from anywhere with your smartphone.

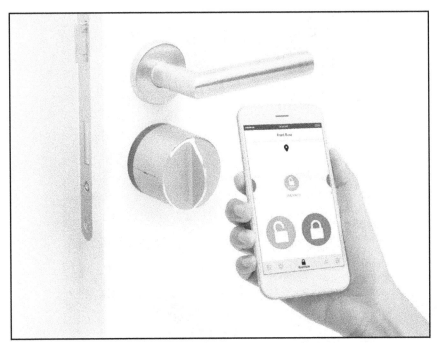

Figure 2-17: Door Locks App Interface

Voice-enabled Smart Speakers/Digital Assistants

A smart speaker is a device that can not only play favorite music, but can provide answers from verbally introduced questions and even control parts of home through a built-in virtual assistant feature. This means that a smart speaker can serve as a central information source for weather, dictionary, traffic, directions, etc. It can also serve as a home assistant that can control common household tasks, such as environmental control (thermostat), lighting, door locks, window shades, security monitoring, and more.

Figure 2-18: Smart Speaker

Cable/DSL Modem Configuration

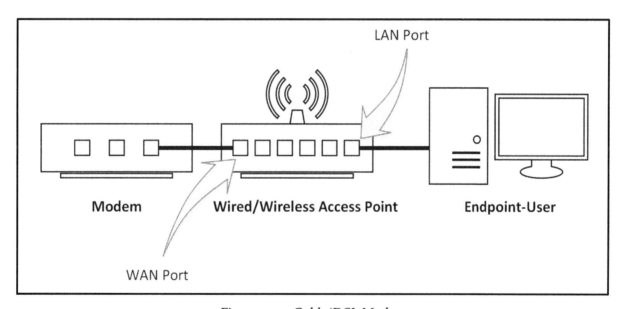

Figure 2-19: Cable/DSL Modem

Installation of TP-Link Router to Work with a Cable Modem

Here are some steps to follow:

Step 1

Log into the router's web-based utility.

Step 2

Configure the WAN Connection type.

After logging into the router, click "Network">"WAN" on the menu.

Select "Dynamic IP" as the WAN Connection Type on the right side of the web page.

Step 3

Check the WAN part on the Status page. If it shows an IP address (similar as below), that means the connection between the router and the modem is established. If there is no WAN IP address, please move to step 4.

Step 4

Click "Network"->"MAC Clone". Click "Clone MAC Address", then click "Save".

Firewall Settings

Most small office/home office users depend on two different types of firewall: a software firewall and a hardware firewall. Software firewalls include those in the Operating Systems, such as the Windows Firewall Service, and those in other security packages such as anti-virus software. These firewalls generally allow only normal traffic in and out by default. Hardware firewalls provided by the LAN/WAN router are used to connect to the internet. They can generally be controlled through the software provided by the vendor.

In the following section, firewall settings will be implemented on the HUAWEI HG8247H router.

DMZ

A DMZ (Demilitarized Zone) is a special local network configuration designed to develop security by separating computers on each side of a firewall. DMZ can be set up either on home or business networks, except their usefulness in homes is limited.

Open the web browser and type the IP address of the device in the address bar (**192.168.100.1**). Press "Enter".

The default user name and password are:

User name: root

Password: IP$pecialist!@#

Click "OK" to log into the device.

Now, configure the DMZ.

For the HUAWEI HG8247H router:

Click "Forward Rules" > "DMZ Configuration" > "Enable DMZ", then click "Apply".

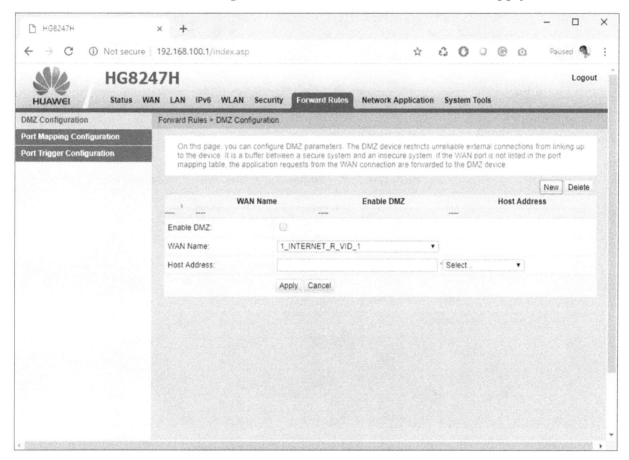

Figure 2-20: DMZ Configuration

 Exam Note

Use static IP addresses for any devices that use port forwarding or the DMZ to ensure that the correct device is being specified. Dynamic IP (server-assigned DHCP) addresses can change according to the number of devices on the network and based on whether some devices leave the network and then return to it.

Port Forwarding

Port forwarding is a process that is used to allow external devices access to computer services on private networks.

In the case of port forwarding, a user would only require forwarding ports from the internet/WAN to the same on the http server.

Click on "Forward Rules" > "Port Mapping Configuration" > "Enable Port Mapping", then click "Apply".

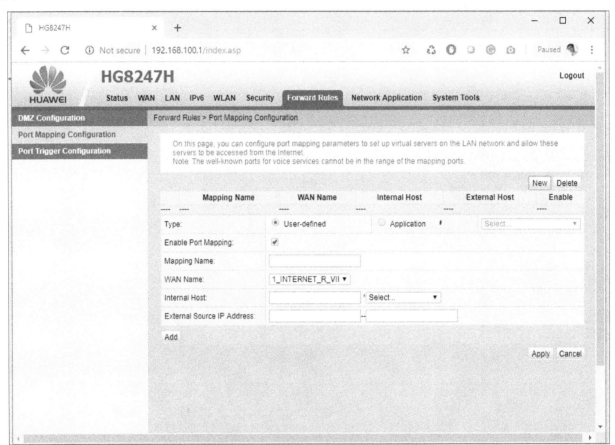

Figure 2-21: Port Mapping Configuration

NAT

Network Address Translation (NAT) is the process of modifying IP addresses as information moves across a router. Usually, this functionality is built into a router. It hides an entire IP address space e.g., 192.168.0.1 through 192.168.0.255 on the LAN. Whenever an IP address on the LAN wants to communicate with the internet, the private IP address is translated to the public IP address of the router, for example, 68.54.127.95.

SOHO routers perform NAT automatically when connected to an IPv4 network. NAT is not required on an IPv6 network because IPv6 is much more secure and has no shortage of IP addresses.

Universal Plug-and-Play (UPnP)

This technology is used for configuring device drivers in a Windows environment that is primarily geared to home users, but can also give advantages to many small and medium-sized businesses. UPnP uses existing protocols and technologies in an approach that makes networking

connectivity a lot simpler for non-technical users. UPnP supports automatic discovery of devices and needs no manual configuration. When a UPnP-enabled device connects to a UPnP-aware router, the device automatically acquires an IP address and announces its name to the rest of the network. UPnP-compliant devices can also announce their capabilities to other devices upon request.

Click on "Network Application" > "UPnP Configuration" > "Enable UPnP", then click "Apply".

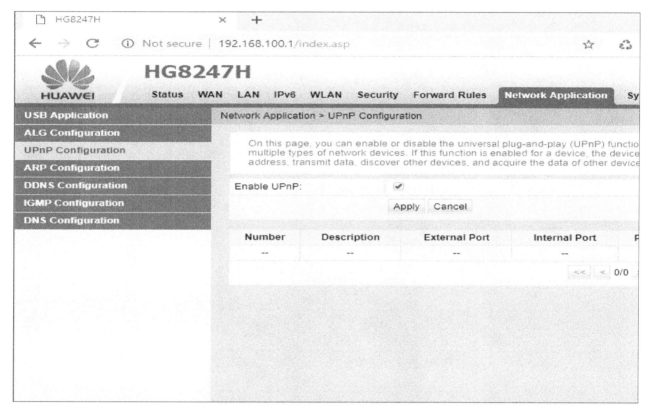

Figure 2-22: UPnP Configuration

Whitelist/Blacklist

A Media Access Control (MAC) address is an identifier for a computer or other devices. This page allows administrations to manage users by MAC address. They can filter users by MAC addresses and/or keep a log of devices connected to the router.

The MAC Filter enables generating a list of devices that have either selected access (whitelist) or no access (blacklist) to the local network.

In whitelist mode, the router will restrict LAN access to all computers except those contained in "MAC filter list" panel. In blacklist mode, listed devices are completely blocked from the local network address.

MAC Filtering

Now, configure the MAC filter.

A MAC filter list adds devices to either your blacklist or whitelist, simply by inputting each device's MAC address.

Click on "Security" > "MAC Filter Configuration" > "Enable MAC Filter" > "Filter Mode", then click "Apply".

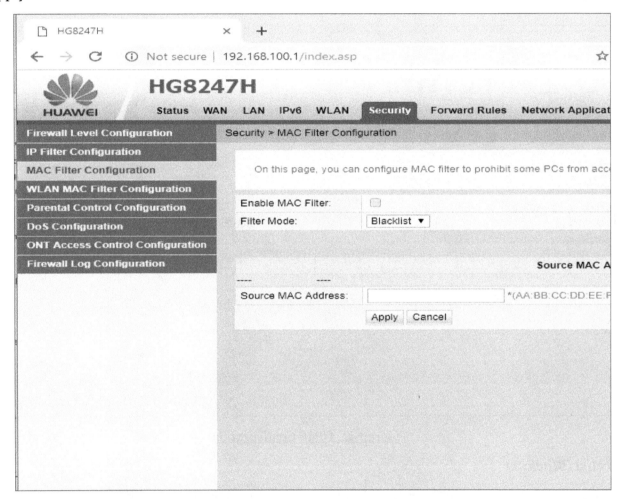

Figure 2-23: MAC Filter Configuration

QoS

Quality of Service (QoS) is an important feature to enable on any network that offers streaming media, gaming, or VoIP services. QoS prioritizes real-time and streaming traffic. Depending on the router, QoS can simply be turned on and off, or it can be modified by specifying services to prioritize, whether to optimize for gaming, or to use uplink/downlink speeds. QoS can be configured by an ISP or by a router. If your ISP is already performing QoS optimization, any changes you make on your router will not affect your traffic.

Wireless Settings

Encryption

Encryption makes your traffic unintelligible to outsiders and insiders who do not have the public key. Since their pairing with 802.11x wireless traffic, encryption techniques have continuously evolved to keep ahead of the threats. Creation with WEP (Wireless Encryption Protocol), which started with a 40-bit key, was rapidly compromised. Consequently strengthened to 128-bits, WEP was still vulnerable. WPA (Wi-Fi Protected Access) was a short-term solution executed to address the shortcomings of WEP. WPA can be used on legacy hardware demanding only software or firmware upgrades and be mutual with additional encryption standards such as TKIP (Temporal Key Integrity Protocol). WPA-2 is a further secure implementation of WPA, that can use both TKIP and more advanced AES (Advanced Encryption Standard). The only drawback is that users of legacy wireless interfaces will have to upgrade to use AES. When configuring a router, it is wise to implement WPA2 with TKIP and AES to permit devices that cannot support AES to fall back to TKIP. AES is a fast and secured form of encryption that keeps curious eyes away from our data. TKIP is an older encryption protocol introduced with WPA to change the very-insecure WEP encryption at the time. TKIP is actually relatively similar to WEP encryption. TKIP is no longer considered secure.

In the below image, you can see that, built on the operating system and hardware, the encryption types accessible will vary.

Click on "WLAN"> "WLAN Basic Configuration"> "Encryption Mode".

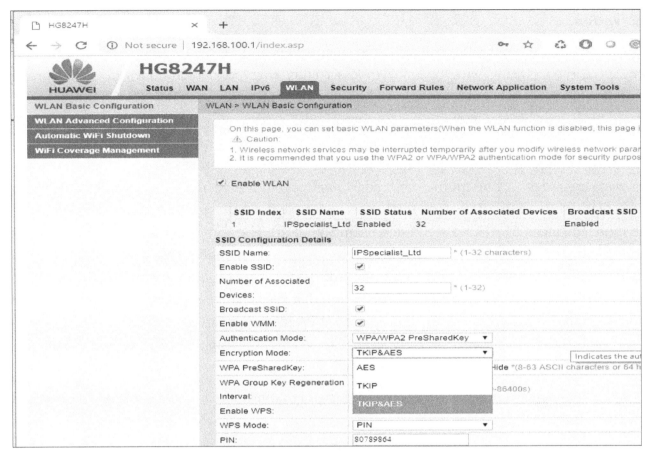

Figure 2-24: WLAN Basic Configuration

Channels

The channel identifies the portion of the wireless frequency used by the access point and connected devices. Use a channel that does not overlap or conflict with other access points in the area. A simple rule to minimize conflicts is to remember that the frequencies used by channels 2-5 compete with the frequencies used by channels 1 and 6, while the frequencies used by channels 7-10 compete with the frequencies used by channels 6 and 11. Many access points have an automatic feature that detects other access points and chooses the channel based on which channel is free.

The image given below shows how to configure the channel:

Click on "WLAN" > "WLAN Advanced Configuration", then click "Apply".

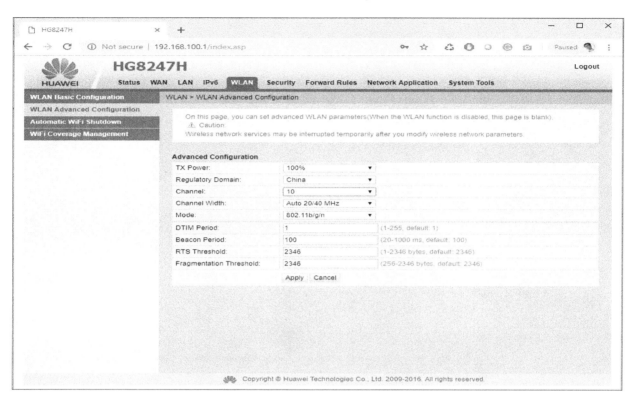

Figure 2-25: WLAN Advanced Configuration

Quality of Service (QoS)

This is a network mechanism for reserving the network resource (bandwidth) in order to offer better service and give higher priority to the network traffic flows, such as video conferencing, online gaming, Bittorrent, VoIP, and other bandwidth consuming applications.

To implement simple QoS on a home or SOHO router, you will usually be given the choice to set QoS priority built on application, port, protocol, IP, or Mac address, and so on.

Click on "Status" > "WAN Information".

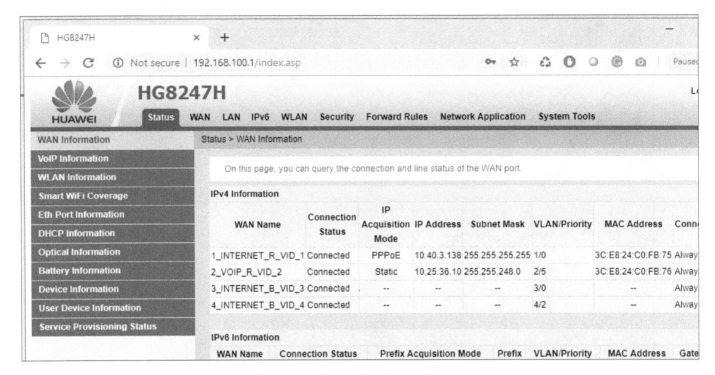

Figure 2-26: QoS Configuration

Mind Map of Install and Configure Wired/Wireless SOHO Network

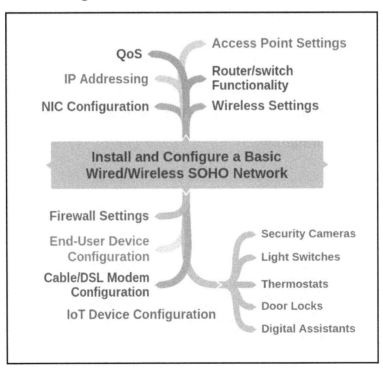

Figure 2-27: Mind Map of Install and Configure Wired/Wireless SOHO Network

Wireless Networking Protocols

Wireless networking protocol is a set of communication protocols called TCP/IP. TCP/IP is a collection of various protocols that have their own purpose or functions. These protocols have been established by international standards and are used in almost all platforms around the globe to ensure that all devices on the internet can communicate successfully. Wi-Fi is an acronym for describing the use and implementation of 802.11 Wireless Local Area Networking Protocols (WLANs). 802.11 protocols define a working set of standards for vendors of wireless networking equipment to abide by in order to help ensure interoperability between devices from different vendors. There are several types of 802.11 standards, 802.11 (a/b/g/n/c/ac) networking protocols, which are described below:

802.11a

802.11a is a 802.11 standard. The 802.11a protocol is in a whole different frequency range between 5.725 GHz and 5.850 GHz. By broadcasting in the 5 GHz range, 802.11a devices run into less competition and interference from household devices. 802.11a is also capable of transmitting speeds of up to 54 Mbps.

802.11b

Another 802.11 standard is the 802.11b protocol, currently in use for wireless networking. Equipment using 802.11b is comparatively inexpensive. It operates on a 2.4 GHz band and allows for wireless data transfers of up to 11 Mbps. Unfortunately, so do many other devices, such as cordless phones and baby monitors, which can interfere with the wireless network traffic.

802.11g

The 802.11g standard is a fast standard that was introduced after 802.11b. It still uses the same 2.4 GHz shared by other common household wireless devices, but 802.11g is capable of transmitting speeds of up to 54 Mbps. Most wireless networks are based on either 802.11b or 802.11g. Equipment designed for 802.11g can still communicate with 802.11b equipment.

802.11n

802.11n builds upon previous 802.11 standards by adding Multiple-Input Multiple-Output (MIMO) that uses multiple antennas to achieve greater throughput than its predecessors. The speed is 100 Mbits/s (even 250 Mbit/s), and hence up to 4-5 times faster than 802.11g. 802.11n also offers a better operating distance than current networks.

This technology effectively twins the range of a wireless device. Therefore, a wireless router that uses 802.11n may have twice the radius of coverage as an 802.11g router. This means a single 802.11n router may cover an entire household, whereas an 802.11g router might require additional routers to bridge the signal.

802.11ac

The 802.11ac standard for Wi-Fi wireless networking is more advanced than the 802.11n standard. 802.11ac represents the 5th generation of Wi-Fi technology. 802.11ac offers better network performance and capability implemented through more advanced hardware and device firmware. 802.11ac was designed to perform similar to Gigabit Ethernet. 802.11ac offers theoretical data rated up to 1 Gbps through the combination of wireless signaling enhancements, in particular channels that utilize a wider expanse of signal frequencies, and a larger number of MIMO radios and antennas to enable more simultaneous transmissions.

802.11ac operates in the 5 GHz signal range, as do most previous generations of Wi-Fi that utilized 2.4 GHz channels.

 Exam Note

Wi-Fi-certified hardware is an 802.11-family wireless Ethernet hardware that has passed certifications established by the Wi-Fi Alliance. Most, but not all, 802.11-family wireless Ethernet hardware is Wi-Fi certified.

Frequencies

Frequency is the rate of radio signal for sending and receiving communication signals measured in hertz (hz) cycle per second. The common frequencies are used for Wi-Fi communication are 2.4 Ghz and 5 Ghz. Each frequency provides its wireless network.

2.4GHz

The advantages and disadvantages of 2.4 GHz are given below:

Advantages	Disadvantages
• It is cheaper to manufacture devices that use this frequency. As a result, this frequency has become standard and all Wi-Fi enabled devices can use this network • It has a much better range than a 5 GHz wireless network. This is due to the fact that the radio waves are able to penetrate solid objects (such as walls and floors) much better than the 5 GHz radio waves	• It has a lower bandwidth than the 5 GHz network • Devices such as cordless phones and microwaves use the same 2.4 GHz radio waves as a wireless router. If you have such devices at home, they can cause interference with the radio waves from the router, causing the network's bandwidth to be reduced • More devices support this frequency so there is more congestion in this frequency, which may cause issues with bandwidth

Table 2-2: Advantages and Disadvantages of 2.4 GHz

5 GHz

The advantages and disadvantages of 5GHz are given below:

Advantages	Disadvantages
• It has a much higher bandwidth than the 2.4 GHz network • This network is not used by common wireless devices such as cordless phones, therefore, there will be no or very little interference to cause a reduction in bandwidth	• It is more expensive to manufacture devices that use this frequency, therefore, only few wireless devices can use this network • It has a much lower range than the 2.4 GHz wireless network. Being the higher frequency of the two, it is not able to penetrate solid objects as well as 2.4 GHz radio waves • As this is a newer standard and more expensive to implement, so fewer devices support this frequency

Table 2-3: Advantages and Disadvantages of 5 GHz

Channels

Every wireless network transmits and receives data on a certain frequency, or channel. The wireless spectrum is distributed into 11 channels ranging from 1-11 channels. When installing a router on a 2.4 GHz wireless network, it is important to select an appropriate channel for the signal. To avoid interference, use non-overlapping channels. Only channels 1, 6, and 11 do not overlap with other channels, so it is best to use one of these three. With APs that have a 2.4 GHz antenna, up to 14 channels are available, depending on where in the world the wireless network is deployed. In the United States, only 11 channels are used; they are listed in the table below:

Channel Number	Frequency (GHz)
1	2.412
2	2.417
3	2.422
4	2.427
5	2.432
6	2.437
7	2.442
8	2.447
9	2.452
10	2.457
11	2.462

Table 2-4: Wireless Frequency Channels

Bluetooth

Bluetooth is a radio communication technology that enables low-power, short distance wireless networking between phones, computers, and other network devices. Bluetooth is another wireless standard. Bluetooth devices transmit at relatively low power and have a range of only 30 feet or so. Bluetooth networks also use the unregulated 2.4 GHz frequency range and are limited to a maximum of eight connected devices. The maximum transmission speed only goes to 1 Mbps.

Bluetooth technology was designed primarily to support networking of portable consumer devices and peripherals that run on batteries, but Bluetooth support can be found in a wide range of devices including:

- Cell phones
- Wireless keyboard
- Wireless speakers
- Computers
- Printers

Near-Field Communication (NFC)

Near-Field Communication (NFC) allows data to be exchanged between devices through short-range, high-frequency wireless communication technology by combining the interface of a smartcard and reader into a single device.

Nokia smartphones, Google Android smartphones and Apple iPhones have the ability to exchange data such as web links and directions as well as make payments for products using NFC technology.

What does it do?

- Transfers data rapidly between two devices such as a phone and an NFC reader
- Allows users to make purchases quickly using their phone and an NFC reader
- Operates within a radius of a few centimeters
- Will be used in Google Android and Nokia phones
- NFC chips cost pennies to develop

Radio-Frequency Identification (RFID)

Radio-Frequency Identification (RFID) technology allows remote and automated gathering and sending of information between RFID tags or transponders and readers using a wireless link.

One of the major benefits of radio-frequency identification is that information exchanged between tags and readers is rapid, automatic, and does not require direct contact or line of sight. RFID readers may be handheld units or fixed units connected to a remote computer system.

RFID tags are used for tracking expensive industrial and healthcare equipment, medical supplies, cattle, and vehicles.

RFID operates using small pieces of hardware called RFID tags or RFID chips. These chips incorporate an antenna to transmit and receive radio signals. Chips (tags) may be attached to or sometimes injected into target objects.

RFID systems operate in any of four radio frequency ranges:

- 125 to 134.2 kHz

- 13.56 MHz

- 856 MHz to 960 MHz

- 2.45 GHz

The reach of an RFID reader varies depending on the radio frequency in use and also physical obstruction between it and the chips being read, from a few inches (cm) up to hundreds of feet (m). Higher frequency signals generally reach shorter distances.

NFC is an extension of RFID technology band, which is being developed to support mobile payments. NFC utilizes the 13.5 MHz band.

Zigbee

Zigbee communication is built for control and sensor networks on the IEEE 802.15.4 standard for Wireless Personal Area Networks (WPANs). The communication standard defines physical and Media Access Control (MAC) layers to handle many devices at low-data rates.

Zigbee's WPAN operates on 868 MHz, 902-928 MHz and 2.4 GHz frequencies. The data rate of 250 kbps is best suited for periodic as well as intermediate two-way transmission of data between sensors and controllers. Zigbee is a low-cost, low-powered mesh network widely deployed for controlling and monitoring applications where it covers 10-100 meters within range. This system is less expensive and simpler than other proprietary short-range wireless sensor networks, such as Bluetooth and Wi-Fi. Zigbee networks are extendable with the use of routers and allow many nodes to interconnect with each other for building a wider area network.

Z-Wave

Z-Wave is a wireless protocol. It is a wireless technology specifically designed for control and monitoring in residential environments; it is used in many products that monitor and control your homes. A z-wave network can interconnect up to 243 appliances. Z-wave uses the low frequency of 868.42 MHz. There are protocols using the same frequency, for example, proprietary protocols and Zigbee. These protocols are closed source, while z-wave is a more open home automation protocol.

3rd Generation

3G refers to third generation wireless technology. It comes for wireless videophones and high-speed internet access for mobile devices. 3G wireless networks are capable of moving data at speeds of up to 384 kbps. Average speeds for 3G networks will range between 64 Kbps and 2.4 Mbps.

3G provides a few improvements over 2.5G or previous networks:

- Enhanced video and audio streaming
- Videoconferencing support
- Several times higher data speed
- Web and WAP browsing at higher speeds
- IPTV (TV through the internet) support

3G is a collection of technologies and standards that includes W-CDMA, WLAN, and cellular radio, among others.

Technology	Standards	Speed
1G (Analog)	Radio signals	Greater than 14.4 Kbps
2G (Digital)	TDMA & CDMA	14.4 Kbps. A common wireless data speed in the United States that is often slower than a 14.4 Kb modem
3G (Digital)		64 Kbps-384 Kbps and expected to reach speeds of more than 2.4Mbps
Pre-4G		WiMax 75 Mbps. Range 30 Miles

Table 2-5: 3G Technologies

Requirements for using 3G technology

In contrast to Wi-Fi, you must be subscribed to a service provider to get 3G network connectivity. This type of service is often called a network plan or data plan.

Your device is connected to the 3G network over its SIM card (in the case of a mobile phone) or its 3G data card (which can be of altered types, like PCMCIA, USB etc.), both of which are usually delivered or sold by the service provider.

Some devices now support the 4G technology. However, in many parts of the world, mostly in rural areas, 3G remains a support service.

4th Generation

4G refers to fourth generation wireless technology. 4G technology is mainly the extension in 3G technology with more bandwidth and services provided. 4G offers a downloading speed of 100 Mbps and the same features as 3G with additional services such as Multi-Media Newspapers, greater clarity on TV programs, and sending data much faster than previous generations. LTE (Long Term Evolution) is considered 4G technology. 4G is being established to accommodate the QoS and rate requirements set by forthcoming applications like Multimedia Messaging Service (MMS), wireless

broadband access, mobile TV, video chat, Digital Video Broadcasting (DVB), HDTV content, minimal services like data and voice, and other services that use bandwidth.

5th Generation

5G technology stands for fifth generation mobile technology. A 5G network offers affordable broadband wireless connectivity (very high speed). Currently, the term 5G is not officially used. Researches are being carried out on the use of 5G for improvements in Worldwide Wireless Web (WWW), Real wireless world, and Dynamic Adhoc Wireless Web (DAWN). 5G focuses on (Voice Over IP) VoIP allowed devices so that a user will experience a high level of call volume and data transmission.

Long Term Evolution (LTE)

LTE is currently the fastest available type of wireless network. The purpose of LTE is to continually evolve, for the better, in the areas of capacity and speed due to the increasing demands on wireless usage. LTE is marketed as a 4G (fourth generation) wireless service and currently, it is the fastest method for connecting with a mobile device. The main feature of an LTE network is that it transforms voice data into data frames to transfer pieces of information in the same way as other types of data are sent. It has merged the two services into one type, removing the traditional phone service mechanism. This alliance of phone and internet utilities brings an enhanced experience to users. With LTE, it is more beneficial to have one connection instead of different connections for altered services.

Mind Map of Wireless Networking Protocols

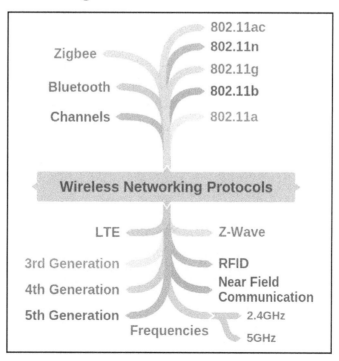

Figure 2-28: Mind Map of Wireless Networking Protocols

Properties and Purposes of Services Provided by Networked Hosts

In this section, we will describe the properties and purposes of services provided by network hosts.

Server Roles

Servers can be configured to perform a number of roles. The applications that the server is running specify the particular server's role. Servers typically need services and additional features installed to perform their specific role. Compared to workstations, servers have more disk space and memory and faster processors. The server roles determine the hardware that servers require. Some common server roles are defined below:

Web Server

A web server is used by companies to deliver web-based content over HTTP. This can be done privately in the case of an internally accessed company webpage, or publicly over the internet. The term web server can refer to hardware or software, or both of them working together.

In terms of hardware, a web server is a computer that stores web server software and a website's component files (e.g., images, HTML documents, and JavaScript files). It is connected to the internet and supports physical data interchange with other devices connected to the web.

In terms of software, a web server includes several parts that control how web users access hosted files. An HTTP server is a piece of software that understands URLs (web addresses) and HTTP (the protocol your browser uses to view webpages). It can be accessed through website domain names it stored (such as Mozilla.org), and delivers their content to the end-users' devices.

File Server

A file server is mainly used to establish a central location where users can store and share stuff such as documents, media files, and spreadsheets that can be stored and accessed. The computer hosting the service is attached to the local network. A Network Attached Storage (NAS) device is often used in this type of application. This is not the same as an internet-based file server that uses FTP protocols or more appropriately an FTP server. It is accessed by using FTP client software.

Print Server

A print server is a network of connected, shared devices that manage and distribute print "jobs" to the printers it controls. The management of the jobs is accessible by users and administrators in the form of a queue that contains all jobs received by the server and their status. While computers still serve as print servers in many networks, there are also standalone wired and wireless network-based printers that contain built-in print servers.

DHCP Server

A DHCP server is a network server that automatically provides and assigns IP addresses, default gateways and other network parameters to client devices. It relies on the standard protocol known as dynamic host configuration protocol to respond to broadcast queries by clients.

A DHCP server automatically sends the required network parameters for clients to properly communicate on the network. DHCP servers usually assign each client with a unique dynamic IP address, which changes when the client's lease for that IP address expires.

The DHCP server has an address range assigned to it for the purposes of providing addresses to hosts without duplication along with any other necessary data like subnet masks or gateway information.

DNS Server

A DNS server is of the DNS domain name which stores IP addresses.

When a user types a host address or URL into their browser address bar, the DNS resolver will contact a DNS server to find the IP address connected to the hostname and take this back to the user so that they can look at the website or device they want to access.

Proxy Server

A proxy server is a computer system or an application, used to hide the IP address of the client computer so that it can surf anonymously – this is mostly for security reasons. A proxy server can act as intermediary between the user's computer and the internet to prevent an attack or unexpected access. As the name implies, a proxy server is an intermediary between the PC or device and the internet. This server makes requests to websites, servers, and services on the internet. A proxy server is used for cache, auditing, security and access control. It also enhances access.

Mail Server

A mail server, also referred to as an email server, is a server that handles and delivers email over a network, usually the internet. A mail server can receive emails from client computers and deliver them to other mail servers. A mail server can also deliver emails to client computers.

Types of Mail Server

There are two main types of mail server: an incoming mail server and an outgoing mail server. Outgoing mail servers are SMTP servers that send traffic to other mail servers end route to the destination. Delivery to the destination client is achieved using one of two incoming server types, Post Office Protocol 3 (POP3) or Internet Message Access Protocol (IMAP). When users send using an SMTP mail server, they will receive using either a POP3 or IMAP server.

Authentication Server

An authentication server is an application running on a server, e.g., Active Directory. This internet or network application handles authentication by providing a user or device access to selected resources on the network as determined by the administrator.

Syslog

Users can read system messages from a switch's or router's internal buffer. It is the most popular and efficient method of seeing what is going on with the network at a specific time. But the best method is to log messages to a *syslog* server, which stores messages from users and can even time-stamp and sequence them for users. It is easy to set up and configure.

By using syslog, users can display, sort, and even search messages, all of which makes it a really great troubleshooting tool. The search feature is especially powerful because users can use keywords and even severity levels. Plus, the server can email admins based on the severity level of the message.

Network devices can be configured to generate a syslog message and forward it to various destinations. These four examples are popular ways to gather messages from Cisco devices:

- Logging Buffer (on by default)

- Console Line (on by default)

- Terminal Lines (using the terminal monitor command)

- Syslog Server

All system messages and debug output generated by the IOS is sent from the console port by default and is logged in buffers in RAM. To send a message to the VTY lines, use the *terminal monitor* command.

The Cisco router sends a general version of the message to the syslog server, which is formatted into something like this:

Seq no: timestamp: %facility-severity-MNEMONIC: description

The system message format can be broken down in this way:

Seq no: This stamp logs messages with a sequence number, but not by default. If users want this output, it has to be configured.

Timestamp: Date and time of the message or event, which again will show up only if configured.

Facility: The facility to which the message refers.

Severity: A single-digit code from 0 to 7 that indicates the severity of the message.

MNEMONIC: A text string that uniquely describes the message.

Description: A text string containing detailed information about the event being reported.

Real World Scenario

Background

Today, many small companies and organizations such as non-profits, units of governmental and educational institutions, etc. consider that running their own mail server has become an unmanageable task due both to the large number of inbound spam and to the continuous attempts by spammers to send outbound spam through their mail servers.

Challenges

Organizations often lack internal technical resources to configure and run a mail server properly and to deal with these threats. Because of this, many organizations decide to outsource their email service to external parties.

Outsourcing does not come without cost; even when the outsourced service appears to be free, it can include hidden costs. For small organizations that want reliable, confidential email systems, the decision of whether to outsource or not can be a tough one.

Solutions

Functioning a secure, spam-filtered mail server for a small organization is not terribly difficult if these guidelines are followed:

- **Choose a good ISP or Hosting Provider**

ISPs vary immensely in how well they keep spam and abuse under control on their network. To confirm that an ISP or hosting company is properly handling spam and abuse, use the number of resources available to check the status of its IPs and domains, and identify how well it responds to abuse reports sent to its RFC-mandated abuse contact email address.

If a security hole has allowed a server to become a vehicle of abuse, it would be really appreciated if the ISP is notified in a professional and timely way rather than the issue being ignored. Consider changing the ISP if the current ISP does not appear to handle abuse and security issues properly.

- **Reject as much inbound spam as possible**

There are many projects that provide several IP address and domain databases that, if properly used, lower the amount of inbound spam reaching mailboxes to a very low level without blocking a significant number of legitimate emails.

- **Avoid outbound spam**

The release of spam is caused either by a person or unit within an organization that decides to send spam, or by a security issue that allows other people to send spam from the company's IP address. The first case does not have a technical solution.

The incredible amount of spam caused by security issues falls into one of the following four categories:

1. Malware Trojans and viruses

2. Open relay

3. Compromised accounts

4. Compromised web servers

> • **Monitor the logs**
>
> Allocate a small amount of time or fixed automated mechanisms, based for instance on email counts and the proportion of undelivered messages, to keep the mail server monitored. Do not forget that spam sent via web server will leave residue in the web server logs rather than the mail server logs, and that spam sent by malware generally bypasses the mail server and leaves no residue in the logs.
>
> ### Conclusion
>
> We believe that an in-house mail server remains a feasible solution for small organizations, and it should be the preferred option when privacy/confidentiality issues are considered important. While it is true that a system administrator knowledgeable in operating the mail system is necessary, this task should not be overwhelming once the points above are covered. All considered, running your own mail server may be a very good use of resources.

Internet Appliance

UTM

Unified Threat Management (UTM) is a solution to reduce costs and administrative overheads by integrating multiple security features such as the router, firewall, content filters, and more into a single hardware appliance with the ability to protect the network from unwanted or malicious traffic. It is generally located between the internet and the protected network.

Intrusion Detection System (IDS)

An Intrusion Detection System (IDS) is a security solution that provides real-time detection of malware. It analyses data traffic without effecting the packet flow. Here, the traffic is continuously monitored and any malicious activity is reported to the management. An IDS works passively as it works on the copied traffic, so it cannot stop or respond to an attack. An IDS works in cooperation with other devices such as routers and firewalls to react to such attacks.

Intrusion Prevention Systems (IPS):

An Intrusion Prevention System (IPS) works somewhat similar to an IDS as it provides real-time monitoring and analyzing of data traffic. An IPS analyses the content and payloads of layer 3 and layer 4 data traffic to make sure that there is no malicious content inside. It provides more sophisticated monitoring of the data stream as it does not allow any untrusted packet to enter a network. This sophisticated analysis enables the IPS solution to detect, stop, and mitigate attacks that try to bypass firewall devices. An IPS works in inline mode, so it can stop attacks from reaching their target, but it also affects the data stream packet flow.

The main difference between an IDS and IPS is that the IPS responds immediately to an attack and does not allow any malicious traffic to bypass the network device, whereas the IDS just does passive monitoring. It detects the malware but allows malicious traffic to reach its destination; it does not address mitigation techniques for such attacks.

End-point Management Server

An end-point management server maintains records of devices using the network and makes sure that they adhere to the security parameters of the entire network. End-points are the end users' devices that are uses in the network. It is necessary that any devices on the network adhere to security policies to keep the network secure. End-point servers can manage security policies for all the different devices and can consolidate data into one dashboard for the network security administrator.

Legacy/Embedded Systems

An embedded system is the use of a computer system within a mechanical or electrical system of some sort, usually to provide a means of control. "Legacy" implies to an old system that has led to a newer version with no major revision.

Mind Map of Properties and Purposes of Services Provided by Network Hosts

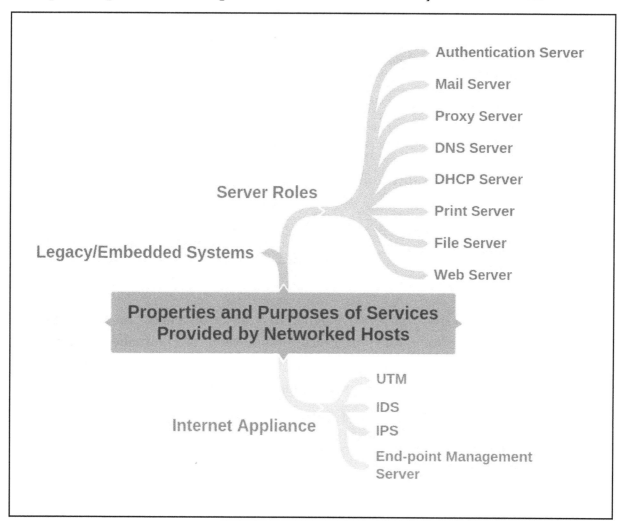

Figure 2-29: Mind Map of Properties and Purposes of Services Provided by Network Hosts

Common Network Configuration Concepts

Computer network technologies have expanded at a rapid pace. Keeping track of all the different technologies and protocols can be alarming, but a fundamental understanding of communication processes is essential for a computer technician. This will become even more true as the use of computers for communication increases and as the number of devices connected to each other grows exponentially. The following sections cover some of the most commonly used networking terms and technologies.

IP Addressing

An IP (Internet Protocol) address is a unique address that identifies a device on an IP network. This address is made up of 32 binary bits that can be divided to a host portion and a network portion with the help of a subnet mask. The 32 binary bits are broken into 4 octets (1 octet= 4 bits). Basically, each octet contains one to three digits. These numbers are separated with a single dot (.). The four numbers in an octet can range from 0 to 255.

IP addresses are sub-divided into different classes: A, B, C, D, and E.

CLASS	ADDRESS RANGE	SUPPORTS
Class A	1.0.0.1 to 126.255.255.254	Large networks with many devices
Class B	128.1.0.1 to 191.255.255.254	Medium-sized networks
Class C	192.0.1.1 to 223.255.254.254	Small networks (fewer than 256 devices)
Class D	224.0.0.0 to 239.255.255.255	Reserved for multicast groups
Class E	240.0.0.0 to 254.255.255.254	Reserved for future use or Research and Development Purposes

Table 2-6: Classes of IP Address

There are two types of IP address: Static and Dynamic.

Static IP Addresses

Static IP addresses are IP address that, once assigned to a device on a network, never change. They provide a simple and reliable route for communication and serve as a permanent internet address. This type of addressing is cost effective but can carry, a high security risk. They are mostly used by email, web and gaming servers unconcerned about hiding their location.

The following are some advantages of static IP addresses:

- They benefit businesses more than home users

- They are good for generating or hosting computer servers

- They are better for devoted services such as mail, web server, and FTP

- They make it easier for geolocation services to accurately locate you

Dynamic IP Addresses

Dynamic IP addresses are assigned to a computer when it is connected to the internet. Each time the device logs on to a network, it is assigned a different address. These are temporary IP addresses. Dynamic addresses are more secure than static IP addresses as they are harder to track.

The following are some advantages of dynamic IP addresses:

- They do not cost anything extra

- They are automatic, maintenance free and reliable with very little work required at your end

- They are the most effective use of IP addresses for your ISP

 Exam Note

Routers, wireless gateways, and computers that host an internet connection shared with Windows Internet Connection Sharing or a third-party sharing program all provide DHCP services to other computers on the network.

Automatic Private IP Addressing (APIPA)

Automatic Private IP Addressing (APIPA) was originally developed by Microsoft, but it is now a standard (RFC 3927) that is also supported by MacOS and Linux. APIPA assigns an IP address and mask to the computer when a DHCP server is not available. The IP addresses assigned are 169.254.0.1 to 169.254.255.254 with subnet mask 255.255.0.0. No more than one computer gets the same IP address. APIPA continuously requests an IP address from the DHCP server at 5-minute intervals. If users can connect to other computers on the local network but cannot reach the internet or other network, it is probably because the DHCP server is down and Windows has automatically assigned an APIPA address.

To determine whether APIPA is configured, open a command prompt window and type ipconfig /all. If the words "Autoconfiguration Enabled Yes" appear, APIPA is turned on. If the last word is "No", APIPA is disabled.

The following is a screenshot of the APIPA configuration:

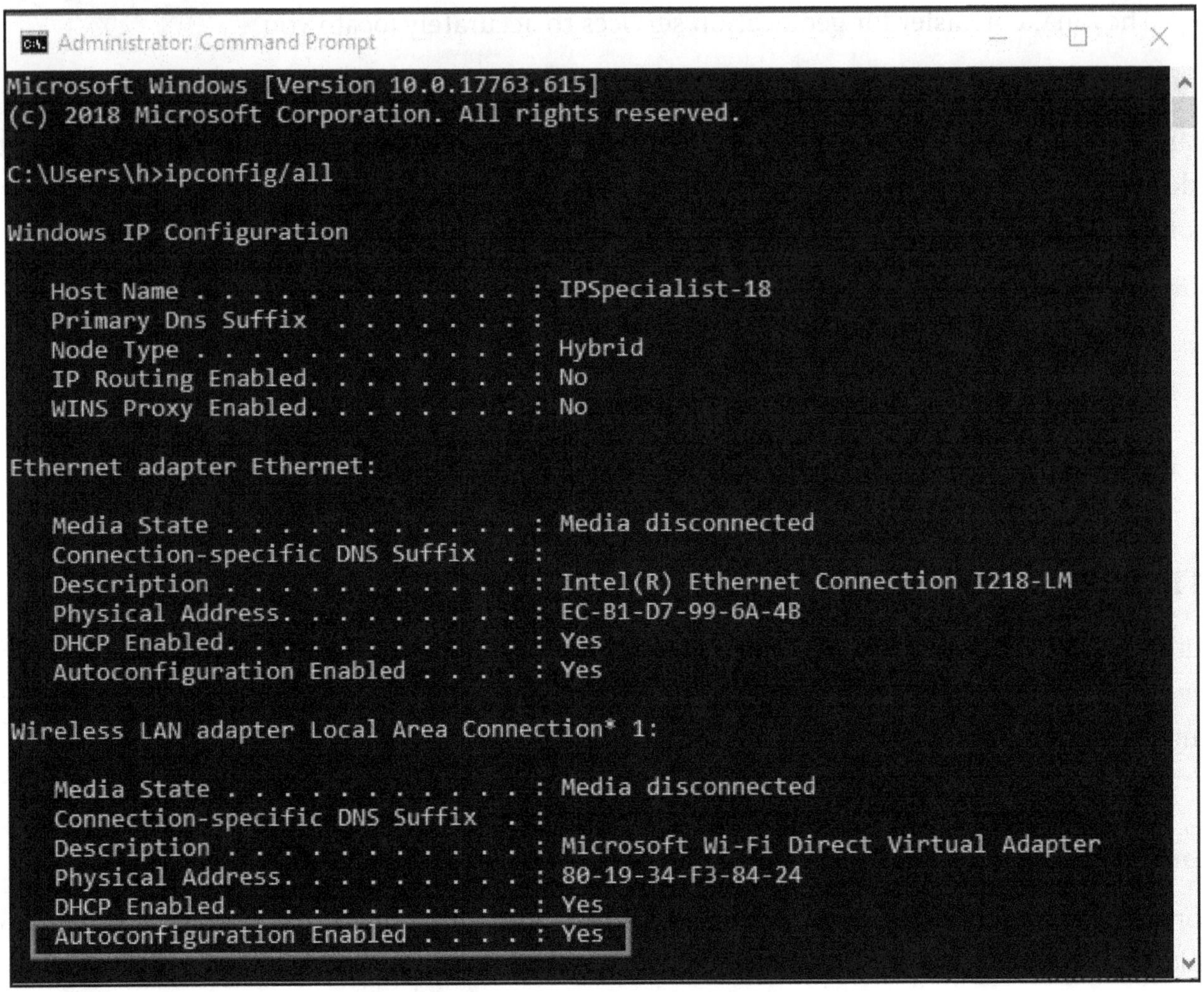

Figure 2-30: APIPA Configuration

Link-local Addresses

A link-local address is a Unicast IPv6 address that is automatically assigned to any interface using the link-local prefix FE80::/10 and EUI-64. Link-local addresses are used for Stateless Auto-Configuration and Neighbor Discovery Protocol.

DNS

The Domain Name System (DNS) is the process where internet domain names are located and translated into Internet Protocol (IP) addresses. The domain name system maps the name people use to locate a website to an IP address to the name a computer uses to locate a website.

DHCP

Dynamic Host Configuration Protocol (DHCP) is a network management protocol used to dynamically assign an Internet Protocol (IP) address to any device, or node, on a network so they can communicate using IP. As the most common IPv4 or IPv6 TCP/IP addressing method, DHCP is responsible for complete client configuration on a TCP/IP network. On an operating network, there is usually an assigned DHCP server. SOHO implementations use the router provided by the ISP to perform this function. What DHCP does is assign or lease a unique IP address to each host. The duration of the lease is determined by the network administrator or is weekly by default. It will define the internet gateway and Domain Name Server to be used. This means that the machine may not get the same IP address when rebooted or otherwise disconnected. The DNS and Gateway settings will remain the same. The DHCP server has an available pool of IP addresses available to assign to clients (hosts) who attempt to connect to the network. The client broadcasts a UDP discovery packet for an address to all connected networks. All DHCP servers will offer an address to the client, then the client will accept the offer from the nearest server by requesting a lease, and that server will lease that address to the client. The address assignment process is same for both IPv4 and IPv6 addresses. In the interest of regularity, the ports used are UDP 67 for the server and UDP 68 for the client.

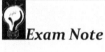

Exam Note

For the 220-1001 exam, make sure you understand the difference between static and dynamic IP addressing and where to go within a given operating system to set or change client-side DHCP, DNS, subnet mask, and default gateway settings.

IPv4 vs. IPv6

Developed in the 1970's, Internet Protocol (IP) is the most popular open-system protocol used for communicating across interconnected networks. IP is a primary network layer (layer 3) protocol that carries addresses and controls information to route the packets.

IP version 4 (IPv4) and IP version (IPv6) are the two versions of IP address, and they have many features, as set out below:

IPv4	IPv6
This is the underlying technology that makes it possible for us to connect our devices to the Web. Whenever a device accesses the internet (whether it is a PC, smartphone, Mac, or any other device), IPv4 is assigned with a numerical IP address. To send data from one computer to another through the Web, a data packet must be transferred across the network containing the IP addresses of both devices	Similar to IPv4, it provides the numerical IP addresses necessary for internet-enabled devices to communicate

IPv4	IPv6
IPv4 uses a 32-bit long (4 bytes) address, which is composed of a network and a host portion based on the address class. Address classes are classified as A, B, C, D, or E depending on initial limited bits. The maximum number of IP addresses is 2^32 or 4,294,967,296	IPv6 uses a 128-bit long (16 bytes) address, 64 bits for the network number and 64 bits for the host number. The host portion of an IPv6 address will be derived from a MAC address. IPv6 is more complicated than IPv4. The IPv6 addresses are represented by 8 groups of four hexadecimal digits with the groups being supported by colons. For example, 3001:0dc7:0047:0000:6a4e:0260:8335
The IP header includes a checksum	The IP header does not include a checksum
IP Sec support is optional	IP Sec support is required in a IPv6 implementation
ICMP router discovery is used to determine the IPv4 address of the best default gateway and is optional	It uses ICMPv6 Router Solicitation and Router advertisement to determine the IPv6 address of the best default gateway and is a required function
Addresses must be configured either manually or through DHCP	Address can be automatically assigned using stateless address auto-configuration, DHCPv6, or manually configured
It uses the host address (A) resource records in the Domain Name System (DNS) to map host names to IPv4 addresses.	It uses host address (AAAA) resource records in the Domain Name System (DNS) to map host names to IPv6 addresses
For QoS, IPv4 supports both differentiated and integrated services	IPv6 also supports both differentiated and integrated services. IPv6 provides a flow label that can be used for more granular treatment of packets

Table 2-7: IPv4 Vs. IPv6

Real World Scenario

Background

As the global system for sending and receiving data packets across the internet, the Internet Protocol is the basis of all digital communications. However, the current internet Protocol version 4 (IPv4) is rapidly running out of available IP addresses for the number of new devices and for the increasing number of users.

In some countries, major mobile networks are impelling IPv6 adoption. In India (Reliance JIO – 87%), Japan (NTT – 7%, KDDI – 42% and Softbank – 34%), and the USA (T-Mobile USA – 93%, Verizon Wireless – 84%, AT&T Wireless – 57%, and Sprint – 70%) national mobile networks take very high ranks of IPv6 deployment.

Challenges

IPv6 has progressed from the "Innovators" and "Early Adoption" stages of deployment, and is now in the "Early Majority" stage. The cost of an IPv4 address is near its expected peak, and cloud service providers are beginning to charge for IPv4 addresses while leaving IPv6 services free from additional charges for address space.

> **Solutions**
>
> Some mobile networks have decided to adopt IPv6-only to simplify network operations and limit the cost. In India, Reliance JIO started deploying IPv6 after its local internet registry occupied all spaces of IPv4 address. Reliance has been forced to buy IPv4 address space as a result, but for business reasons prefers not to.
>
> Gradually, IPv4 has become an unnecessary cost and a speculative asset. An IT department or CIO faced with buying IPv4 addresses should question whether the expense is worth its value. Increasingly, the answer is that it is not. A company would do better, in the long run, to sell the address space it holds and utilize that money for storing IPv6 deployment, and connecting to an upstream Internet Service Provider (ISP) that will use translation processes to connect to the remaining IPv4-only content.
>
> In February 2017, Reliance reported that about 90% of its LTE customers were using IPv6, and represented about 80% of their traffic. Their principal content partners, Google, Facebook, and Akamai, who relay their content using IPv6 in that network, claimed this was ambitious. Reliance activated over 200 million subscribers with IPv6 connectivity in just 9 months, between September 2016 to June 2017.
>
> **Conclusion**
>
> For those companies and networks that have yet to make the upgrade, the best time to start the IPv6 deployment process is now, and there are many resources available online for support.

Subnet Mask

Subnet mask is a 32-bit long address used to differentiate between network address and host address in an IP address. Subnet mask is always used with an IP address. Subnet mask has only one goal: to identify which part of an IP address is the network address and which part is the host address.

For example, how to distinguish the network partition and host partition from the IP address 192.168.1.4. Here, we need the subnet mask to work out the network address and host address.

In decimal notation, subnet mask 255 represents the network address and value 0 [Zero] represents the host address.

In binary notation, subnet mask ON bit [1] represents the network address while OFF bit [0] represents the host address.

In Decimal Notation

IP address   192.168.1.4

Subnet mask   255.255.255.0

The network address is "192.168.1" and the host address is "4".

In Binary Notation

IP address 11000000.10101000.00000001.00000100

Subnet mask 11111111.11111111.11111111.00000000

The network address is "11000000.10101000.00000001" and the host address is "00001010".

Advantages of Subnetting

- Subnetting breaks a large network in smaller networks and smaller networks are easier to manage

- Subnetting reduces network traffic by removing collision and broadcast traffic, that overall improves performance

- Subnetting allows users to apply network security polices at the interconnection between subnets

- Subnetting allows users to save money by reducing requirements for IP range

Gateway

Gateway is a network device that establishes a connection between a local network and an external network with a different structure. It connects two dissimilar networks. Basically, it is a node on a network that serves as an entrance to another network.

Computers that control traffic on the company's network or on a local internet Service Provider (ISP) are gateway nodes. A network gateway can be implemented in software, hardware, or in a combination of both. In an enterprise network, a computer server acting as a gateway node often also acts as a proxy server and a firewall server. A gateway is often linked with a router, which knows where to direct a given packet of data that arrives at the gateway, and a switch, which furnishes the actual path in and out of the gateway for a given packet. It expands the functionality of the router by performing data translation and protocol conversion.

Users will sometimes see the term, "default gateway" on network configuration screens in Microsoft Windows. The default gateway is a device that passes traffic from the local subnet to devices on other subnets. It often connects a local network to the internet, although internal gateways for local networks also exist.

Virtual Private Network (VPN)

A Virtual Private Network (VPN) is an encrypted communication channel or tunnel between two remote sites over the internet. A VPN is a logical network that allows connectivity between two devices. That devices can either belong to the same network or be connected over a Wide Area Network. Going deep down into the term VPN, the word "Virtual" refers to the logical link between the two devices. As the VPN link does not exist separately, it uses the internet as a transport mechanism. The word "Private" refers to the security a VPN provides for the connection between the two devices, as the medium of transport is the internet, which is not secure. A VPN adds confidentiality and data integrity. It encrypts data and prevents its alteration or manipulation by unauthorized people along the path.

The advantages of using VPNs are as follows:

Security: A VPN uses one of the most advanced encryption and hashing algorithms to provide confidentiality and integrity. Although the latest web browsers have native support for SSL, Cisco's AnyConnect SSL client software also provides an SSL-based VPN solution. The second most common option is IPsec. It is used for Site-to-Site VPN implementation.

Cost: Connecting remote offices to the most feasible internet service provider and then using VPN for secure connection is by far the most cost effective solution compared to point-to-point leased lines.

Scalability: Setting up VPN connectivity of a newly established remote office with a corporate office is quicker in terms of setup than using leased lines.

Types of VPN

The two types of VPN are:

- Remote access VPN

- Site-to-site VPN

Remote Access VPN

A remote access VPN feature allows an endpoint to connect to an organization's secure LAN network. These endpoint devices include smartphones, tablets, laptops, etc.

For example, consider an employee who works from different remote locations providing real-time data to the organization. The organization wants to provide a secure communication channel that securely connects the remote employee to the organization's internal network. A remote-access VPN provides the solution by allowing the remote employee's device to connect to corporate headquarters or any other branch of that organization. This is referred to as a remote-access VPN connection. Remote-access VPNs use IPsec or Secure Sockets Layer (SSL) technologies for securing the communication tunnel. Many organizations use Cisco's AnyConnect client for remote access SSL VPNs.

Site-to-Site VPN

A site-to-site VPN securely connects two or more sites that want to connect together over the internet, for example, a corporate office that wants to connect to its head office or multiple branches that want to connect to each other. This is referred to as a site-to-site VPN. Site-to-site VPNs usually use IPsec as a VPN technology.

Virtual Local Area Network (VLAN)

A VLAN is a group of devices in which one or more LANs are configured to communicate as if they were attached to the same wire, when in fact they are located on a number of different LAN segments. Because VLANs are built on logical rather than physical connections, they are extremely flexible.

A Virtual Local Area Network (VLAN) is a broadcast domain that users create on a switch. This domain also coordinates to a TCP/IP subnet. Switches are multiport bridges that allow users to create multiple broadcast domains. Each broadcast domain is like a distinct virtual bridge within a switch. Each virtual bridge that users create in the switch defines a new broadcast domain (VLAN). Traffic cannot pass directly to another VLAN (between broadcast domains) within a switch or between two switches.

Here are some reasons why we should use VLANs in our network:

- VLANs increase the number of broadcast domains while decreasing their size

- VLANs reduce security risks by reducing the number of hosts that receive copies of frames that the switches flood

- Users can keep hosts that hold sensitive data on a separate VLAN to improve security

- Users can create more flexible network designs that group the users by department instead by physical location

- Network changes are achieved with ease by just configuring a port into the appropriate VLAN

Network Address Translation (NAT)

Private addresses are used to allow devices to communicate within an organization locally. However, private IPv4 addresses are not routable over the internet. In order to access devices and resources outside of a local network, a private address must first convert into a public address. The mechanism of translating private addresses into public addresses is called Network Address Translation (NAT). This makes a device with IPv4 a private address with which to communicate over the internet.

NAT is one of the most widely used features in Cisco and other vendor's networking devices. Consider the following diagram, which acts as a reference for the discussion in this section:

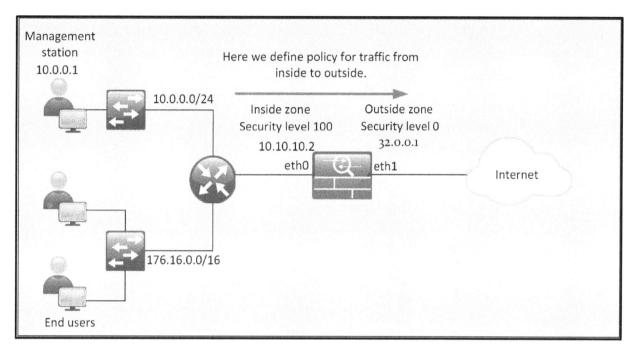

Figure 2-31: NAT

As shown in the above diagram, end-users along with the management network is using a private addressing scheme as defined in RFC 1918. If an end user wants to communicate with another end user over the internet, a public IP address would be needed. The firewall will not have any connectivity problem because of the globally reachable IP address 32.0.0.1/30 assigned to one of its interfaces. In order to allow the internal or trusted network to communicate with the public internet, the NAT feature is used either by the firewall or the router. This can be done by swapping the source address field in the IP header of the originating packets with either its own global address or with the pool of global addresses (assigned by service providers).

The implementation of NAT or PAT not only hides thousands of users behind a single or group of global IP addresses, it also helps in mitigating many types of attack. Without knowing which global IP address is assigned to the internal device, connecting with a specific internal device from the outside world is even more difficult.

NAT Terminology: In Cisco's implementation of NAT, either in routers or firewalls, very specific terminology is used, for example, inside local, outside global etc. The following table summarizes NAT/PAT terminology.

NAT Term	Description
Inside Local	The original IP address of the host from a trusted network. For example, 172.16.0.5 has been assigned to end users in the diagram above
Inside Global	The global address is either from a router interface IP or from a pool, which will represent the client out on the internet

Outside Local	The IP address with which a device is known on the internet. For example, the IP cameras, which are configured to be accessed from anywhere on the internet
Outside Global	The real IP address of the host device, which is configured to be accessed over the internet, like the private IP address of an IP camera, which can be accessed via some global IP address

Table 2-8: NAT Terms

The following diagram further explains the NAT process:

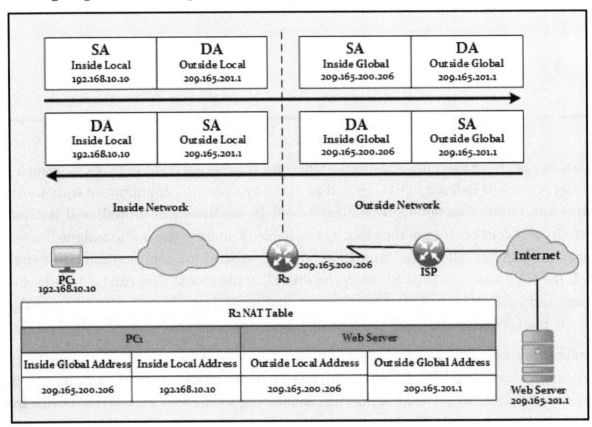

Figure 2-32: NAT Process

Mind Map of Network Configuration

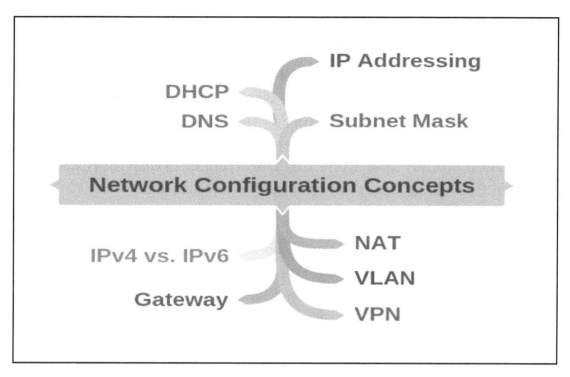

Figure 2-33: Mind Map of Network Configuration Concepts

Internet Connection Types, Network Types, and their Features

A variety of methods for accessing the internet have come and gone over the year since it was established.

In this sections, we are going to discuss the internet connection and network types and their features.

Internet Connection Types

There are various ways to connect to the internet: cable, DSL, Dial-up, Fiber, Satellite, ISDN, Cellular, Tethering, Mobile hotspot, and a line-of-sight wireless internet service. Some of the most commonly used internet connections are defined below.

Cable

Cable provides an internet connection. It is a broadband high speed internet connection that is always on. There are different speeds depending on whether you are uploading data transmissions or downloading. Cable modems can support voice and data and it can be wired or wireless based on preference. Cable speeds ranges from 512 k to 20 Mbps.

Digital Subscriber Line (DSL)

Digital Subscriber Line (DSL) is an internet connection. It uses existing 2-wire copper telephone lines connected to one's home service and is delivered at the same time as the landline telephone

service. DSL uses a router to transport data and the range of connection speed, depending on the service offered, is between 128 k and 8 Mbps.

The latest versions of the technology use different techniques to achieve higher speeds. One method is Symmetric Digital Subscriber Line (SDSL). The symmetry referred to in its name applies to the equal upload and download rates and its theoretical speeds of up to 22 Mbps. Another method is Asymmetrical Digital Subscriber Line (ADSL), where the upstream and downstream are not the same. This enables the provider to adjust the data rate according to what the customer is willing to pay, maxing out at 640 kbps upstream and up to 24 Mbps downstream.

Dial-up

Dial-up connections require users to link their telephone line to a computer in order to access the internet. This is also referred to as analog. Dial-up requires a modulated digital signal from a computer to the analog waveform used by phone lines, then on the receiving end, the signal is converted back to digital. Its speed starts at 14.4 Kbps, increasing to 28.8 Kbps. The increases in speed were considered ground-breaking in the pro-broadband era.

Exam Note

Generally, the term modem (modulator/demodulator) refers only to a device that connects to the telephone line and performs digital-to-analog or analog-to-digital conversions. However, other types of internet connections such as DSL, wireless, satellite, fiber, and cable internet also use the term modem, even though they work with purely digital data. When used by itself in this book, however, modem refers only to dial-up (telephone) modems.

Fiber

Fiber optics is an internet connection that transfers data fully or partially through fiber optic cables. "Fiber" refers to the thin glass wire inside the larger protective cable. "Optic" refers to the way that the type of data transfers light signals. It provides the highest bandwidth available in a range up to 43 terabits per second, depending on the provider. Fiber optic networks can deliver speeds up to 1 Gbp (1000 Mbps). Fiber optics can deliver bandwidth ideal for virtually anything you do online, including:

- Streaming TV and movies
- Downloading music and videos
- Playing real-time multiplayer games online

- Connecting many devices, such as mobile devices, computers, smart TVs, at the same time

Satellite

Satellites access the internet through a satellite orbiting the earth in a geosynchronous orbit. The massive distance that a signal travels from earth to satellite and back again provides a delayed connection compared to cable and DSL. There are 400 satellites orbiting in this manner. Most are communication satellites delivering video, voice, data, and internet. Satellite connection speeds are around 512 k to 2.0 Mbps.

<u>Why we use Satellite</u>

If other connections, for example cable or DSL, are not available in your area, you might use satellite internet. If you are on dialup, then satellite internet will be an "upgrade" in the sense that satellite internet is considered to be much faster.

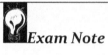*Exam Note*

Satellite connections can also be made between buildings to allow for high-speed exchange of data. In this scenario, a satellite dish would need to be installed on each building, and the dishes would need to be in direct line of sight of each other. Internet access can also be offered in this manner.

Integrated Service Digital Network (ISDN)

An Integrated Service Digital Network (ISDN) is a set of communication standards that allows users to send voice, data, and video over a single line, while providing at least two instantaneous connections. ISDN is the process for transferring voice data with some specific services accessible for data. It makes entry to packet switched networks accessible because it is a circuit switched telephone network system. Therefore:

- It delivers better quality of voice data than an analog phone

- It provides 64 Kbits/s and in some countries it provides 128 Kbits/s for both uploading and downloading

- The ISDN-B channel is responsible for providing a greater data rate and it is suitable for digital services that exist on layer 1, layer 2, and layer 3 of the OSI reference model

<u>The Advantages of ISDN</u>

Here are some advantages of ISDN:

- ISDN facilitate the use of multiple digital channels. These channels can work simultaneously through the same single copper wire pair

- The digital signals broadcast across telephone lines

- ISDN delivers a high data rate of digital scheme, which is 56 kbps

- ISDN network lines are able to switch between multiple devices on a single line, for example, computers, cash registers, credit cards readers, faxes, and many other devices. All these devices can work appropriately and be associated on a single line

- ISDN takes only 2 seconds to launch a connection while other modems take 30 to 60 seconds

Exam Note

Most telephone companies have largely eliminated ISDN in favor of DSL, which is much faster and less expensive for internet connections.

Cellular

Cellular technology is the largest wireless internet connection accessed through cell phones. The speeds vary depending on the provider. 2G cellular is actually slower than dial-up on paper but users should not expect more than 50 Kbps on this connection. The most advanced and common connections are 3G and 4G speeds. 3G is a significant improvement when properly implemented and has speeds between 200 k and 4 Mbps. 4G, however, has speeds between 100 Mbps and 1 Gbp. 4G LTE is the fastest combination of them all and users are likely to encounter more LTE implementations than WiMAX.

Tethering

Tethering is a way of providing internet access allowing users to connect their cell phone to a laptop or desktop computer through USB or Bluetooth so that devices can use the phone's cellular connection for mobile connectivity to another device. This connection shares one-to-one connection. It is useful when immediate and essential connectivity is required as it offers limited bandwidth and, if used over a Bluetooth connection, the battery will take a big hit.

Mobile Hotspot

Hotspots are technology that offer internet access over a Wireless Local Area Network (WLAN) by way of a router that then connects to an internet service provider. Hotspots use Wi-Fi technology, which allows electronic devices to connect to the internet or exchange data wirelessly through radio waves. Hotspots can be phone-based, and either charged or free to the public. In most cases, the device sharing the hotspot will have its internet capability disabled. Bandwidth will not replicate the full capacity of the host and battery life will be impacted.

Line-of-Sight Wireless Internet Service

Line-of-sight internet provides an over-the-air internet connection to buildings that have a clear line of sight to a dedicated mast. Satellites and long range wireless internet transmissions require an obstruction-free line of sight between devices.

Network Types

There are several types of computer network, all classified by their purpose. Networks can be wired, wireless or both. They are defined below.

Local Area Network (LAN)

A Local Area Network is used when one or more computers or wireless devices are connected and are sharing resources and services with each other. LANs can be built with relatively inexpensive hardware, such as network adapters, hubs, and Ethernet cables. The smallest LAN may use only two computers while the largest LANs can accommodate thousands of computers. A LAN typically relies mostly on wired connections for increased speed and security. A LAN can also be a part of wireless connections. It is high speed and relatively low cost.

Wide Area Network (WAN)

A Wide Area Network (WAN) is the opposite of a LAN. A WAN occupies a very large area, such as an entire country or the entire world. A WAN can contain multiple smaller networks, such as LANs or MANs. The technology is high speed and relatively expensive.

Personal Area Network (PAN)

A Personal Area Network (PAN) is a very short range network consisting of personal devices. A typical PAN would include one or more computers, peripheral devices, telephones, video game consoles, and other personal entertainment devices. Generally, this is a Bluetooth configuration and could be made up of personal heart and activity monitors connected to a cell phone. The cell phone can in turn connect to a laptop's Bluetooth and create another PAN.

Metropolitan Area Network (MAN)

A Metropolitan Area Network (MAN) consists of a computer network across an entire city, a college campus, or a small region. A MAN is larger than a LAN, which is typically limited to a single building or site. A MAN is often used to connect several LANs together to form a large network. They are reliable and redundant, and are sometimes referred to as a Campus Area Network (CAN).

Wireless Mesh Network (WMN)

A Wireless Mesh Network works on the concept of mesh networking that can be applied to both wireless networking and be physical. It is a communication network that has increasingly attracted Internet Service Providers (ISPs) because of its rapid growth and development of wireless technologies. It provides a high bandwidth network coverage. The main advantages of a WMN are that it is self-organizing or self-configuring, has increased reliability, low deployment costs, interoperability, and scalability.

Mind Map of Internet Connection Types

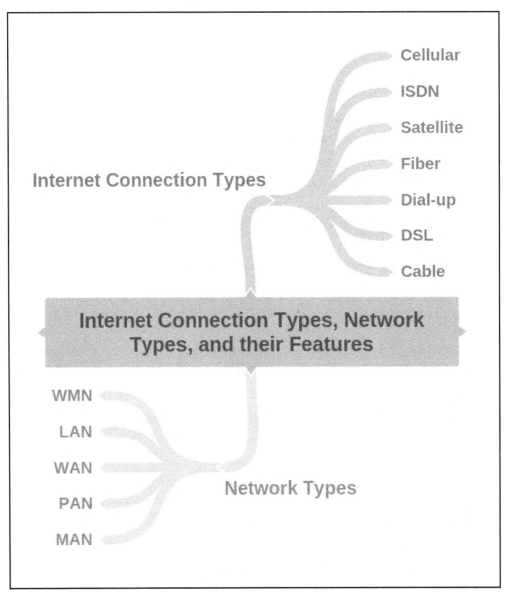

Figure 2-34: Mind Map of Internet Connection Types

Networking Tools

When physical network is being deployed on a building, it is useful to stock up on key networking tools for running, terminating, and testing cables.

In this section, we will discuss the range of networking tools and how they work. All networking tools are described below.

Exam Note

When working with computers and computer network equipment, standard household tools are not adequate for the job. A specialized network technician's toolkit is necessary for quality work. A quick internet search for "networking toolkit" will provide a full range of options and prices. Networking toolkits are available from nearly everywhere that sells computers and accessories.

Crimper

A crimper is a tool that is used to cut a network cable or to secure the connector to the end of the cable. The metal pins are folded down onto the cable wires, piercing the sheath and holding the wire, making connectivity with the copper wire below. If a cable is broken, the crimper can be used to cut the wires to the correct length and to fit a new connector.

Cable Stripper

This is similar to the crimper and the two terms are often used interchangeably. A cable stripper has a circular doughnut-style blade. This is used to remove only the outer sheath and not used to fit the connector.

Multimeter

A multimeter, which is used to test voltage and current and to diagnose problems with a cable, can be analog or digital. They have three modes and can measure current, voltage, and resistance.

A multimeter has two probes, one of which makes a setting on the multimeter. Both probes can be put together to make a connection. To measure the voltage on a circuit, check whether the dial is set to read the correct scale (otherwise the meter may be damaged), and hold the probes across the component you want to check (such as a resistor). To measure the current, the meter is placed in sequence before the component that users want to check. To measure resistance, hold the probes at either side of the component.

Tone Generator and Probe

A tone generator and probe is a network installation and troubleshooting tool used for tracing wires through difficult or unreachable locations. A signal is emitted by the tone generator at one end of a cable, which is easily detected by the probe at the other end. The tone generator and probe can be used to locate a specific cable in a mess of cable, identify wiring faults, and determine line polarity and voltage in network and modular telephone lines.

Cable Tester

Before a cable can be used, it needs to be checked to see if it has good connectivity. A cable tester is a hardware device that can be connected to both ends of the cable to check that a signal can be sent from one end and received on the other. They are used to verify that the cable has been attached, or crimped, properly.

A cable tester is the cable certifier. This certifier is used when laying cables within building infrastructure and confirms that the cables conform to building and electrical regulations. It not only checks for a voltage but it also checks the level of signal, ensuring good connectivity along the cable. A cable tester is less expensive than a network multimeter.

Loopback Plug

A loopback plug is a 10-inch wire device with a connector used for diagnosing transmission problems. It plugs into a port, such as a parallel, serial, or Ethernet port and crosses the transmit line to the receiving line so that outgoing signals can be redirected back into the computer for loopback testing.

Techniques of a loopback plug are:

- Testing access lines for transmission from the serving switch center without manual assistance

- Installing a patch cable that ,may be applied automatically, manually, remotely or locally

- Testing a communication channel with only one end point so that any transmitted message is received by the same communication channel

Punch Down Tool

A punch down tool is a small hand tool used by telecommunication and network technicians for inserting wire into insulation-displacement connectors on patch panels and surface mount boxes. It is used to connect the twisted pair cable to a patch panel or to secure the cable to the back of the wall jack.

WiFi Analyzer

It is common to use a simple smartphone with a Wi-Fi analyzer app installed. This will show the different Wi-Fi networks within range and report on the signal strength of each and which channels

are in use. A Wi-Fi analyzer is a device that can monitor the wireless network environment and help identify potential issues. It can also identify the best channel to use for a wireless network and identify the best location for wireless access points on the network.

Mind Map of Networking Tools

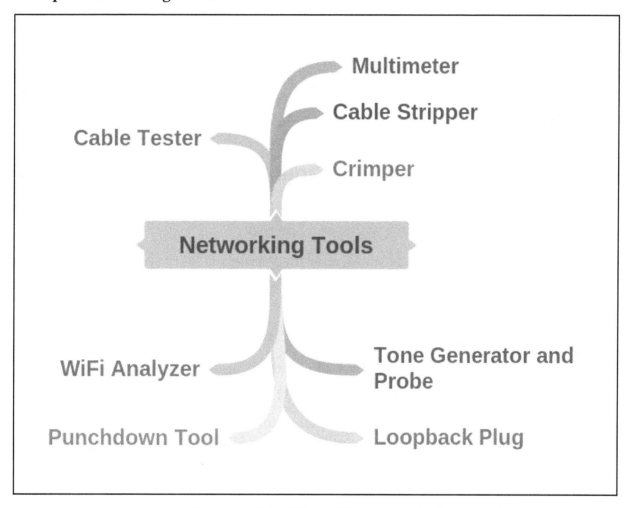

Figure 2-35: Mind Map of Networking Tools

Summary

Compare and Contrast TCP and UDP Ports, Protocols, and their Purposes

- Communication over a TCP/IP based network is performed by using various protocols, such as FTP to transfer files, HTTP to visit web pages, and POP3 or IMAP to do with email

- TCP and UDP both use port numbers to listen and respond to requests for communication using numerous protocols

- TCP is a connection-oriented protocol that ensures end-to-end reliable packet delivery with an efficient flow control, full-duplex operation, multiplexing, and data streaming services

- UDP is very efficient for multicast or broadcast types of network transmission. It is a connectionless protocol, and unlike the TCP, UDP adds no reliability, flow-control, or error-recovery functions to IP

Compare and Contrast Common Networking Hardware Devices

- Networking devices are physical devices that are required for interaction and communication between devices on a computer network

- Network devices include routers, switches, access points, cloud-based network controllers, firewalls, network interface cards, repeaters, hubs, cable/DSL modems, BridgePatch panels, Power over Ethernet (PoE), and Ethernet over Power

Install and Configure a Basic Wired/Wireless SOHO Network

- Wireless Ethernet network, commonly known as IEEE 802.11, is the specified name for a group of wireless technologies compatible with wired Ethernet

- Wireless Ethernet is also known as Wi-Fi, after the Wireless Fidelity (Wi-Fi) Alliance (www.wi-fi.org), a trade group that supports interoperability between different vendors of wireless Ethernet hardware

Wireless Networking Protocols

- The wireless networking protocol is a set of communication protocols called TCP/IP. It is a collection of various protocols that have their own purpose or functions

- These protocols have been established by international standards and are used in almost all platforms around the globe to ensure that all devices on the internet can communicate successfully

- Wi-Fi is an acronym for describing the use and the implementation of 802.11 Wireless Local Area Networking Protocols (WLANs). 802.11 protocols define a working set of standards for vendors of wireless networking equipment to abide by in order to help ensure interoperability among devices from different vendors

- 802.11 (a/b/g/n/c/ac) networking protocols are the various types of 802.11 standard

Properties and Purposes of Services Provided by Networked Hosts

- Servers can be configured to perform a number of roles

- The applications that a server runs specify the particular server's role

- Some common server roles are web server, file server, print server, DHCP server, DNS server, proxy server, mail server, authentication server, syslog

Common Network Configuration Concepts

- Computer network technologies have expanded at a rapid pace, and keeping track of all the different technologies and protocols can be alarming, but a fundamental concept of the communication processes is essential for a computer technician

- This will become even more true as the use of computers for communication increases and as the number of devices talking to each other grows exponentially

- The most commonly configured networking terms and technologies are IP addressing, DNS, DHCP, Subnet mask, Gateway, VPN, VLAN, NAT

Internet Connection Types, Network Types, and their Features

- A variety of methods for accessing the internet have come and gone over the years since it was established

- There are various ways to connect to the internet: cable, DSL, Dial-up, Fiber, Satellite, ISDN, Cellular, Tethering, Mobile hotspot, and line-of-sight wireless internet service

- There are several types of computer network, classified in order to identify their purpose. They can be wired, wireless or both

Networking Tools

- When a physical network is being deployed in a building, it is useful to stock up on key networking tools for running, terminating, and testing cable

- Some of the important networking tools are crimper, cable stripper, ultimeter, Tone generator and probe, cable tester, oopback plug, punch down tool, Wi-Fi analyzer

Practice Questions

1. How many types of Internet Protocol(IP) are there?

    A. Two

    B. Three

    C. Four

    D. Five

2. Which of the following is connection-oriented protocol that ensures end-to-end reliable packet delivery with efficient flow control, full-duplex operation, multiplexing, and data streaming service?

A. Transmission Control Protocol(TCP)

B. User Datagram Protocol (UDP)

C. Internet Protocol (IP)

D. None of the above

3. What are the usage of User Datagram Protocol (UDP)?

  A. It is suited for applications that require high reliability, and transmission time is relatively less critical

  B. It is suitable for applications that require fast, efficient transmission, such as games. UDP's stateless nature is also useful for servers that answers small queries from huge numbers of clients

  C. Both of the above

  D. None of the above

4. What is the full form of FTP?

  A. File Transfer Protocol

  B. File Transport Protocol

  C. File Transparent Protocol

  D. None of the above

5. What is Secure Shell (SSH)?

  A. It opens a secure network channel that provides confidentiality and integrity for network services over an unsecured network using public key cryptography

  B. It is used to secure remote network logins and other confidential data

  C. It is designed to support remote logins and communication between computers

  D. All of the above

6. Which of the following is a remote access protocol for creating a connection with a remote machine over TCP/IP network?

  A. Secure Shell (SSH)

  B. File Transfer Protocol (FTP)

  C. Telnet

  D. Simple Mail Transport Protocol (SMTP)

7. What is Simple Mail Transport Protocol (SMTP)?

A. It is used in a client/server configuration to transfer files

B. It is used to secure remote network logins and other confidential data

C. It is allowing the transmission and delivery of email over the Internet

D. None of the above

8. What is Domain Name System (DNS)?

A. It opens a secured network channel that promotes confidentiality and integrity for network services over an unsecured network using public key cryptography. This makes it a cryptographic network protocol. It is used to secure remote network logins and other confidential data

B. It is the way that Internet domain names are located and translated into Internet Protocol (IP) addresses

C. It uses the client/server method where a client uses a Uniform Resource Locator (URL) to locate and request information from the target server of the resource

D. None of the above

9. Which of the following is a secure network communication protocol designed for remote management, as well as for remote access to virtual desktops, and applications?

A. Apple File Protocol (AFP)

B. Remote Desktop Protocol (RDP)

C. Telent

D. None of the above

10. What is the full form of SMB?

A. Service Message Block

B. Simple Mail Block

C. Sender Message Block

D. None of the above

11. What is Service Location Protocol (SLP)?

A. It is a protocol used for sharing access to files, printers, serial ports and other resources on a network

B. It can also carry transaction protocols for interprocess communication

C. It is a protocol or method of organizing and locating the resources (such as printers, databases, schedulers, disk drives) in a network

D. All of the above

12. What is Dynamic Host Configuration Protocol (DHCP)?

A. It is a network management protocol used to dynamically assign an Internet Protocol (IP) address to any device, or node, on a network so they can communicate using the IP

B. It is the way that Internet domain names are located and translated into Internet Protocol (IP) addresses

C. It uses the client/server method where a client uses a Uniform Resource Locator (URL) to locate and request information from the target server of the resource

D. None of the above

13. Which of the followings is a network device that forwards data packets from one network to another?

A. Switch

B. Router

C. Hub

D. Firewall

14. How many types of switches are there?

A. Two

B. Three

C. Four

D. Five

15. What is a Firewall?

A. It is a network management protocol used to dynamically assign an Internet Protocol (IP) address to any device, or node, on a network so they can communicate using IP

B. It is the way that Internet domain names are located and translated into Internet Protocol (IP) addresses

C. It is a network security device that monitors incoming and outgoing network traffic and decides whether to allow or block specific traffic based on a defined set of security rules

D. None of the above

16. What is the acronym of NIC?

A. Network Interface Card

B. Network Internal Card

C. Network Interface Controller

D. Near Interface Card

17. Which of the following contains the electronic circuitry required to communicate using a wired connection (such as Ethernet) or a wireless connection (such as Wi-Fi)?

A. Power over Ethernet (PoE)

B. Patch Panel

C. Network Interface Card (NIC)

D. None of the above

18. Which of the following types of IP address never change, when once they are assigned to a device on a network?

A. Static IP Address

B. Dynamic IP Address

C. Both of the above

D. None of the above

19. What are the advantages of dynamic IP address?

A. It does not cost you anything extra

B. It is automatic, carefree and reliable with very little work on your end

C. It is the most effective use of IP addresses for your ISP

D. All of the above

20. What are the advantages of subnetting?

A. It breaks large network in smaller networks and smaller networks are easier to manage

B. It reduces network traffic by removing collision and broadcast traffic, that overall improves performance

C. Both of the above

D. None of the above

21. What is Gateway?

    A. It is an encrypted communication channel or tunnel between two remote sites over the internet

    B. It is a network device that establishes a connection between the local network and external network with different structure; it connects two dissimilar networks

    C. It expands the functionality of the router by performing data translation and protocol conversion

    D. All of the above

22. Which of the following is an encrypted communication channel or tunnel between two remote sites over the internet?

    A. Gateway

    B. Subnet Mask

    C. Virtual Private Network (VPN)

    D. None of the above

23. How many types of VPN are there?

    A. Two

    B. Three

    C. Four

    D. Five

24. Which of the following features allows an endpoint to connect to the secured LAN network of an organization?

    A. Site-to-site VPN

    B. Remote access VPN

    C. VLAN

    D. None of the above

25. What is Near Field Communication (NFC)?

A. It is a radio communication technology that enables low-power, short distance wireless networking between phones, computers and other network devices

B. It allows data to be exchanged between devices through short-range, high-frequency wireless communication technology by combining the interface of a smartcard and reader into a single device

C. It was designed primarily to support networking of portable consumer devices and peripherals that run on batteries

D. All of the above

26. Which of the following statements states that information exchange between tags and readers is rapid, automatic and does not require direct contact or line of sight?

A. Radio-Frequency Identification (RFID)

B. Near-Field Communication (NFC)

C. Bluetooth

D. Channels

27. Which of the followings uses existing 2-wire copper telephone line, which is connected to one's home service, and is delivered at the same time as landline telephone service?

A. Cable

B. Digital Subscriber Line (DSL)

C. Dial-up

D. Tethering

28. What are the advantages of Integrated Service Digital Network (ISDN)?

A. It is to facilitate the user with multiple digital channels. These channels can work simultaneously through the same one copper wire pair

B. The digital signals broadcasting across the telephone lines

C. It delivers high data rate as of digital scheme, which is 56kbps

D. All of the above

29. What is tethering?

A. It offers internet access over a Wireless Local Area Network (WLAN) by way of a router that then connects to an Internet service provider

B. It is a way to provide internet access, which allows you to connect your cell phone to a laptop or desktop computer through USB or Bluetooth, it also provides mobile connectivity to a device from other devices using the phone's cellular connection

C. It provides an over-the-air Internet connection to buildings that have a clear line of sight to a dedicated mast

D. None of the above

30. Which of the following concepts of mesh networking can be applied to both wireless networking and physical?

A. Wide Area Network (WAN)

B. Local Area Network (LAN)

C. Wireless Mesh Network (WMN)

D. Metropolitan Area Network (MAN)

Chapter 03: Hardware

This chapter will give a broad overview of computer hardware, provide detailed information on the System Board, and provide a detailed look at storage devices.

Understanding the physical aspects of computing is an essential requirement for a certified support technician. While most working technicians become specialized in a few areas of hardware support, it is important to demonstrate a broad knowledge of the different components of computing on the A+ exam. This chapter covers the CompTIA A+ 220-1001 exam objectives related to knowledge of hardware.

Basic Cable Types, Features, and Their Purposes

In computing, the range of cable types can be overwhelming, especially since cable technology is in a constant state of evolution. Individuals need to know not only the types of cable but also the different versions of some types. This section organizes cables by their purpose, which should help to keep them straight. While some cables are uncommon and rarely encountered, readers need to be familiar with all of the types in this section.

Network Cables

A cable is the physical medium through which data or information moves between different networking devices. There are currently many types of cable and the choice of cable is dependent on the network's topology, its protocol, and its size.

Cable types are broken down into two categories: electricity-using cables and light-using cables. Twisted pair and coaxial cables have copper wires as their transmission medium along which electricity is sent. Fiber optic cable, on the other hand, has glass or plastic as the transmission medium and light (photons) is sent along the cables.

The following types of cable will be discussed in this chapter:

- Ethernet
- Twisted Pair Cable
- Coaxial Cable
- Fiber Optic Cable

Ethernet

In computer networking, the most widely used method or standard for data communication is Ethernet IEEE 802.3. It is popular because it maintains a good balance between ease of setup, speed, use, and cost. Demand for greater speed for data communication is daily increasing and Ethernet 802.3 has improved its speed. Ethernet connections are normally used for providing wired

connectivity to computers, but it also provides a backbone for many other data communication systems.

Ethernet cables carry small voltage pulses over a single frequency (1 is voltage, 0 is no voltage). This is known as baseband transmission. It is bidirectional, which means hosts can send and receive information on one cable. In cable categories, various capabilities are indicated. For example, 10BASE-T indicates the cable carries 10 Mbps on a baseband signal over twisted pair (TP) cables.

Currently, there are four types of Ethernet architecture. They differ by the speed at which they operate. The speed at which an Ethernet cable operates is referred to as bandwidth, or the network's data rate. This data rate is measured in bits per second (bps).

The following tables shows the features of the four main types of Ethernet:

Ethernet Types	Features
10-Gigabit Ethernet also called 10GbE	This is the fastest of all Ethernet standards. It provides a data rate of 10 Gbps (gigabits per second), which is 10 times faster than Gigabit Ethernet
1000-Mbps Ethernet or Gigabit Ethernet	This works at a speed of 1000 Mbps (1000 megabits per second, which is equal to 1 gigabit per second). This standard is used for large or heavy traffic, high-speed LANs and overloaded server connections
100-Mbps Ethernet or Fast Ethernet	This operates at a speed of 100 Mbps
10-Mbps Ethernet	This was the first Ethernet version and was developed by the Xerox Corporation in the 1970s and later known as Ethernet IEEE 802.3. It operates at a speed of 10 Mbps

Table 3-01: Main Types of Ethernet

The different speeds at which they operate and the versions of Ethernet cables usually specify which type of wire should be used.

A network's actual bandwidth can be degraded by data processing delays in a network. These delays are referred to as latency and it can be caused by a variety of factors, such as when a device becomes overloaded with data and cannot operate well. The overall impact of latency on network performance can last for a few seconds or can be constant. It depends on the source of the delay.

In Ethernet standards, baseband signaling is known as "BASE", and it refers to the fact that only Ethernet traffic or signals are carried on the cable or wire. Application of the different Ethernet standards is based on the medium that each standard uses.

BASE Standards	Features
BASE-R standards	Operates over fiber optic cables
BASE-W standards	Operates over fiber optic cables; here the "W" refers to Wide Area Network and WAN PHY refer to WAN at Physical Layer (WAN PHY). BASE-W Ethernet frames are encapsulated inside SONET frames. BASE-W standards include the same types of fiber and they support the same distances as 10GBASE-R standards
BASE-T standards	Operates over twisted pair cable, either shielded or unshielded
BASE-C standards	Operates over shielded copper twisted pair cable. Now Ethernet installations also use unshielded twisted pair (UTP) cables or fiber optic cables. Older Ethernet installations used either 50-ohm RG8/U coaxial (known as thick Ethernet and 10Base5) or 75-ohm RG58A/U coaxial cables also referred to as thin Ethernet and 10Base2. However, they are both now obsolete

Table 3-02: Base Standards

Elements of the Ethernet Cable

The Ethernet IEEE 802.3 LAN consists of the following main elements:

Interconnecting Media

The interconnecting media is the media through which the signals travel within the Ethernet network system. The properties of the medium determine the speed at which the particular data may be transmitted or received. The types of interconnecting media include:

- **Coaxial Cable:** This was the first type of interconnecting media used for Ethernet

- **Twisted Pair Cables:** Two types of twisted pair wires are used for Ethernet cables: Shielded Twisted Pair (STP) or Unshielded Twisted Pair (UTP). Usually shielded cable is used as it reduces data errors
- **Fiber Optic Cable:** The use of fiber optic cable is increasing rapidly as it provides very high data rates of communication.

Nodes of the Network

The nodes of a network are the points to and from which the communication is sent. The following are the categories of network nodes:

- **Data Communications Equipment (DCE):** Also referred to as Intermediate Network Devices or Intermediate Nodes. Devices under this category send and receive data frames across the network. Devices include routers, repeaters, switches, modems and other communication interface units
- **Data Terminal Equipment (DTE):** These devices include the end devices at either the source or the destination. Devices such as PCs, file servers, print servers etc. fall under this category

Categories of Ethernet Cables

Ethernet cables come in many different categories: Category 3, Category 5, Category 5e, Category 6, Category 6a, and Category 7. Each category has different specifications, for example, different data transmission speeds, different shielding from electromagnetic interference, and different possible bandwidth frequency range. The category of the cable is usually printed on the cable's covering or sheath. The following table summarizes the different types of Ethernet cable:

Category	Cable Type	Data Transmission Speed	Maximum Bandwidth	Features
Category 3	UTP	10 Mbps	16 MHz	This is one of the oldest 10BASE-T Ethernet installations. It is also known as Station wire or Cat 3. It still exists in two-line telephone systems
Category 5	UTP	10/100 Mbps	100 MHz	It is the successor to the Category 3 but it provides higher data transfer rate (100BASE-TX)

Category 5e	UTP	1000 Mbps or 1 Gbps	100 MHz	This is an advanced version of Cat5 that reduces unwanted signals from the carriers and provides better data rates (100BASE-TX)
Category 6	UTP or STP	1000 Mbps or 1 Gbps	250 MHz	This improves the overall transmission performance of data. It provides a higher signal to noise ratio
Category 6a	STP	10,000 Mbps or 10 Gbps	500 MHz	This is an advanced version of Cat6 as it provides data rates or up to 10,000 Mbps and it effectively doubles the maximum bandwidth to 500 MHz
Category 7	SSTP	10,000 Mbps or 10 Gbps	600 MHz	Category 7 cable, Cat7 or Class F, is a shielded cable, which provides speed of up to 10 Gbps or 10,000 Mbps and increased bandwidth of up to 600 MHz. Cat7 cables are made up of screened, shielded twisted pair (SSTP) of wires with the more extensive layers of insulation and shielding. They are more difficult to bend
Category 7a	SSTP	10,000 Mbps or 10 Gbps	1000 MHz	This is an advanced version of Cat7 that increases the bandwidth up to 1000 MHz

Table 3-03: Types of Ethernet Cables

Category 5

Category 5 Ethernet cable is also known as Cat5 or Fast Ethernet. It is considered the first fast Ethernet cable.

- Cat5 is an unshielded twisted pair (UTP) cable
- Cat5 carries data at a higher transfer rate
- Cat5 cables can support 10/100 Mbps, which means it can operate at either 10 Mbps or 100 Mbps speeds
- Cat5 contains four twisted pairs of wires but it only uses two of these pairs
- Cat5 can also be used for video and telephone signals along with Ethernet data

Category 5e

Category 5e Ethernet cable is also known as Cat5e. This Ethernet standard is an advanced version of Cat5 Ethernet cable where the "e" stands for enhanced.

- Cat5 is an unshielded twisted pair (UTP) cable
- Cat5 is capable of reducing crosstalk or the unwanted transmission signals inside data channels
- Cat5e cables can support 10/100 Mbps, which means it can operate at either 10 Mbps or 100 Mbps speeds
- Cat5e contains four twisted pairs of wires and it uses all four pairs, which enables Gigabit Ethernet speed
- Cat5e increases the bandwidth up to 100 MHz
- Cat5e cables are backward-compatible with Cat5 cables and can be used in modern network installations

Category 6

One of the major differences between Category 5e and the newer Category 6 (Cat6) is in transmission performance.

- Cat6 cables can handle data up to 1000 Mbps or 1 Gigabit Ethernet with a bandwidth of up to 250 MHz
- Cat6 cables are more improved as they contain thinner wires and better insulation
- Cat6 provides a higher signal-to-noise ratio and is suitable for environments where there is higher electromagnetic interference
- Cat6 cables are available in both shielded twisted pair (STP) or unshielded twisted pair (UTP) wires
- Cat6 cable is backward-compatible with Cat5 and 5e cable

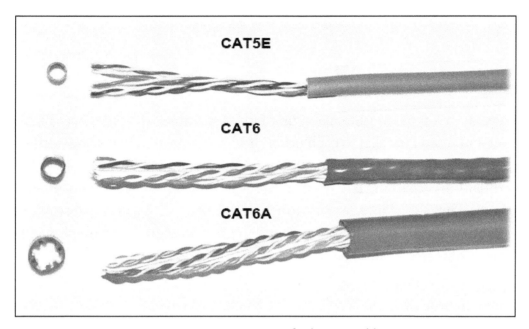

Figure 3-01: Categories of Ethernet Cables

Plenum

Plenum cable contains a special fire-resistant outer covering or sheath that does not burn so quickly. When burned, the plenum cable generates less smoke and less toxic chemicals and is usually self-extinguishing. Plenum cable is designed for use in plenum space (that is space used for HVAC air exchanges), such as ventilator shafts, under floors, or between a suspended ceiling and the permanent ceiling.

Plenum cables are usually costly but can be a necessity in sensitive areas where cables are prone to burn or be damaged. Usually network cables are covered with a polyvinyl chloride (PVC) outer sheath to protect the cable.

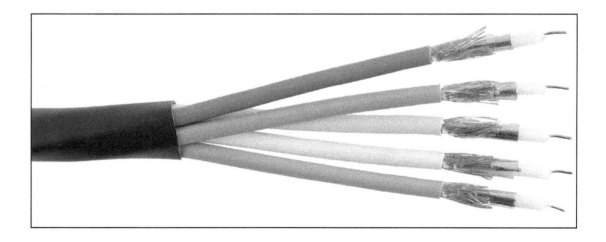

Figure 3-02: Plenum Cables

Twisted Pair Cable

A twisted pair cable is a type of cable made up of two separate insulated wires that are twisted or wound together and placed parallel to each other. It has four pairs of wires and each wire is twisted with its pair, so usually there are two pairs of four wires surrounded by a flexible jacket. It transfers both voice and data information. The twist in the wires cancels out electromagnetic interference and decreases noise and signal interference from outside sources. Twisted pair cables are the most cost-effective cabling option but it also introduces high attenuation and lower bandwidth. There are two basic types of twisted pair cable:

- Unshielded Twisted Pair (UTP)
- Shielded Twisted Pair (STP)

Unshielded Twisted Pair (UTP)

This cable has four pairs of wires and a protective jacket covering the pairs. Each pair is twisted or wound with a different number of twists per inch. This practice eliminates interference from other pairs. The transmission rate increases as the twists of the pairs become tighter. There are 6 basic categories of UTP cabling:

	Speed	Application
Category 1	1 Mbps	Telephone wire for voice only
Category 2	4 Mbps	Telephone and local talk
Category 3	16 Mbps	10BaseT Ethernet
Category 4	20 Mbps	Token Ring
Category 5	100 Mbps (2 pairs),1000 Mbps (4 pairs)	100BaseT Ethernet, Gigabit Ethernet
Category 5e	1000 Mbps (4 pairs)	Gigabit Ethernet
Category 6	10,000 Mbps	Gigabit Ethernet

Table 3-04: Types of UTP Cabling

UTP is the least expensive cable and is commonly used in Ethernet installations, but it is susceptible to electrical or radio frequency interference. The standard connector for UTP cable is an RJ-45.

Figure 3-03: Unshielded Twisted Pair Cables

UTP has a few disadvantages:

- UTP can run only 100 meters (328 feet) before signal attenuation happens, which is signal weakening or degrading
- Its outer plastic jacket has no shielding, making it susceptible to electromagnetic interference (EMI) and vulnerable to unauthorized network access in the form of wiretapping

Shielded Twisted Pair (STP)

Shielded twisted pair cable come in three different configurations:

1. Each pair of wires is individually covered with foil
2. All pairs of wires (as a group) are covered with foil or any other shield inside the main jacket covering
3. There is a covering on both; a covering around each individual pair and a covering around the group of wires. This practice is referred to as double shield twisted pair

STP prevents Electromagnetic Interference (EMI) and crosstalk. STP cable can also be used to provide grounding. STP cables also help to increase the maximum distance of the cables.

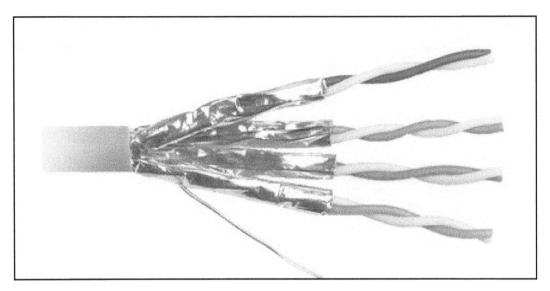

Figure 3-04: Shielded Twisted Pair Cables

STP has a few disadvantages:

- STP involves higher costs both of product and installation
- The shielding needs to be grounded to work effectively

Keep in mind that all server rooms and wiring closet equipment such as patch panels, punch blocks, and wiring racks should be permanently grounded before use.

T568A and T568B

The T568A and T568B are TIA standards that correspond to the wiring designs that are widely used with computers. The T568A or T568B standards are often interchangeable. T568A and T568B refer to the two color code schemes that are used for wiring RJ45 modular plugs. The only difference between the two schemes is that the green and orange pairs are interchanged.

However, the T568A wiring scheme is the most preferred wiring scheme for this standard because it supports backward compatibility with both one pair and two pair USOC wiring schemes. Although the T568B standard resembles the older ATA&T 258A color code, it supports backward compatibility to only a single pair USOC wiring scheme.

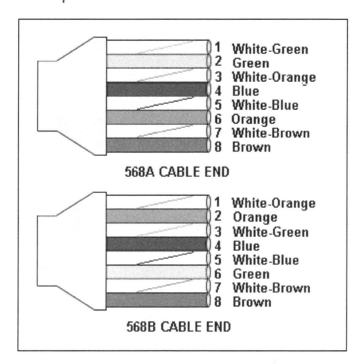

Figure 3-05: 568A and 568B Cable Ends

Straight Through Cable

Straight-through cable is a CAT5 cable with RJ-45 connectors attached at each end. In straight-through cable, both the ends of the cable have the same pin out and both ends of the cable follow the same color code. Straight-through cable is also known as a patch cable. Straight-through cables are used to connect computers and various end devices to networking devices such as switches and hubs.

Straight-through cables (the more common patch cable) do not connect the same devices (for example, they connect from a computer to a switch). T568B is the typical wiring standard in twisted pair cables; T568A is the less common standard.

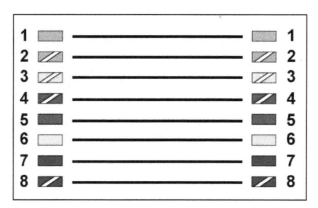

Figure 3-06: Straight-through Cable

Crossover Cable

A crossover cable is CAT5 cable where one end of the cable is configured as T568A and the other end is configured as T568B. Pin 1 is crossed with Pin 3 of the other side and Pin 2 is crossed with Pin 6 of the other side. Crossover cables are used to connect two or more computers.

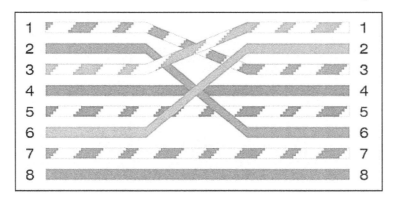

Figure 3-07: Crossover Cable

Fiber

Fiber uses light for transmission rather than pulses of electrical signals so it is not susceptible to electromagnetic interference (EMI). It provides faster transmission compared to other types of cable. Fiber is more costlier than copper and requires more experience to install, but it provides the benefit of longer distances for large amounts of data and can be used in areas where electrical interference would cause copper cable problems. Fiber is used mainly as a backbone between networks due to the cost.

Figure 3-08: Fiber Optic Cables

A "mode" in a fiber is a single light wave passing through fiber cabling. There are two types of fiber in fiber optic cables:

<u>Single Mode Fiber (SMF)</u> – allows only a single beam of light or light wave to pass through the cable. However, it provides faster data transmission over longer distances.

<u>Multimode Fiber (MMF)</u> - allows multiple beams of lights or light waves to pass simultaneously through the cable. However, it has a larger diameter than single mode fiber. Each light wave utilizes a particular portion of the fiber cable for transmission.

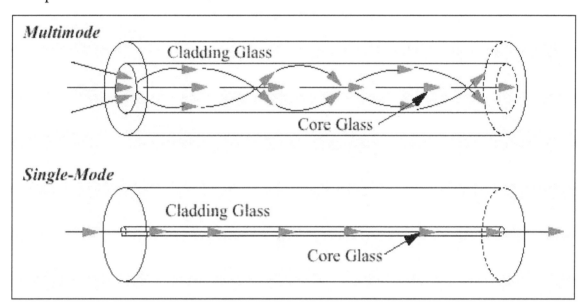

Figure 3-09: Modes of Fiber Optic Cable

<u>Fiber Optic Cables</u>

For optical fiber data communication, generally two cables are required: one for sending data and another for receiving data. Hence, different types of connectors will be used to connect the cable to the transmitters, receivers, or other devices. The followings are the four basic types of connector used with optical fiber cable:

Straight-Tip (ST) – This is a round and straight connector that is used to connect fiber cable to network devices. It has a twist type coupling.

Subscriber Connector (SC) – This is a square snap coupling of about 2.5 mm in width. It is used for providing cable-to-cable connections or to provide connections between cables and network devices. It is like video or audio jacks, as it latches with a push and pull action.

Lucent Connector (LC) – This is also known as a local connector. It is 1.25 mm in size, which is half of the SC connector size and it also has a snap coupling.

Mechanical Transfer Registered Jack (MT-RJ) – It is easier to work with this connector as it looks like an RJ-45 network connector and it is the least expensive of them all.

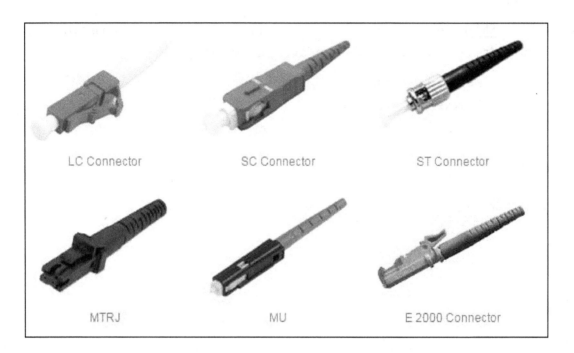

Figure 3-10: Fiber Optics Cable Connectors

Coaxial Cable

Coaxial cabling consists of a single copper conductor at its center, a plastic layer over the conductor to provide insulation between the braided metal shield, and a central conductor. The metal shield prevents or blocks any outside interference from motors, fluorescent lights, and other computers. They are a high frequency transmission cable where data is transmitted electrically through the inner conductor. Its transmission capacity is 80 times greater more than twisted pair wires.

This cable is surrounded by a single conductor of insulating material, which is surrounded by a copper screen, and lastly by an exterior plastic sheath. Some networking technologies still use coaxial cable; for example, cable internet connections use RG-6 coaxial cable (and possibly the older RG-59 cable).

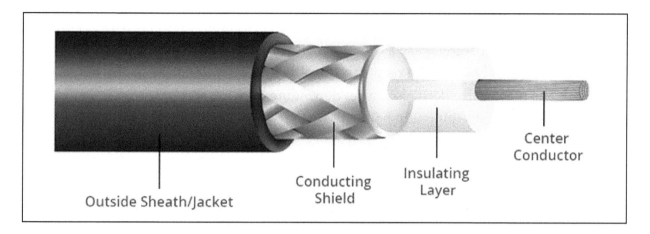

Figure 3-11: Coaxial Cables

Although the coaxial cable insulation is very difficult, it greatly prevents signal interference. Further, it can support greater cable lengths between network devices than twisted pair cable. There are two types of coaxial cable:

- Thin coaxial
- Thick coaxial

Thin Coaxial Cable

This cable is also known as thinnet or 75-ohm cable. Ethernet signals are used for carrying 10BASE2 Ethernet. The 2 refers to the maximum segment of 200 meters' length of cable. The coaxial cable used with 10BASE2 is referred to as RG-58. It was used for low-cost Ethernet networks before the advent of UTP cable.

Thick Coaxial Cable

This cable is also known as thicknet or 50-ohm cable. It is used for carrying Ethernet signals over thick coaxial cable of 10Base5. The 5 refers to the maximum segment of 500 meters' length. It has an extra protective plastic cover over the center conductor that keeps moisture away from the cable. The drawback of thick coaxial is that it is difficult to install as it does not bend easily and it is costly compared to twisted pair wires. Some common applications of coaxial cables include:

- Delivering TV signals or video signals
- Video applications as it has higher bandwidth
- Connecting computers in a network
- Providing transmission of data along with anti-jamming capabilities and protecting signals from interference

Speed and Transmission Limitations

RG-6 cable can usually operate as far as 500 to 1000 feet. The maximum distance varies because several factors play into how far the data can travel before attenuation (e.g. the frequency used, protocol used, and so on). Its speed also varies depending on what sort of transmission is sent over it. A typical RG-6 cable has a minimum bandwidth of 1 GHz that can loosely translate to 1 Gbps, but the data throughput will most likely be capped at an amount below that. For example, cable internet providers often cap it at between 30 Mbps and 50 Mbps, and some fiber optics providers (who may change the cable type from fiber optics to coaxial at home or business) may cap it at anywhere between 100 Mbps and 500 Mbps. All of this varies depending on the provider and how many services are transferred across the same line.

Characteristic	100BaseFX	1000BaseSX	1000BaseLX	10GBaseER
Speed	100 Mbps	1,000 Mbps	1,000 Mbps	10,000 Mbps
Distance (multi-mode)	412 meters	220 to 550 meters	550 meters	(not used)
Distance (single-mode)	10,000 meters	(not used)	5 km	40 km

Table 3-5: Fiber Speeds and Limitations

Video Cables

Video cables are specially designed for desktop monitors or TV screens to output visual information. One end of the video cable is plugged into the computer's display adapter or graphics card and the other end of the cable is connected to a video input channel on a monitor. Desktop computers use a variety of video cables, such as Video Graphics Array (VGA), an early standard video cable used by many monitors, DVI, S-Video, and HDMI. They are used to send video or graphics information to the display screen. HDMI is the only video cable that supports and sends audio signals as well. S-Video, DVI, and HDMI cables are not only used with the computers but are also used to connect game consoles, DVD players, and other video devices to TVs.

VGA

Video Graphics Array (VGA) is the standard of video adapter that was introduced in the late 1980's. VGA works by sending analog signals to the display, which results in the production of a wide range of color. VGA is an obsolete technology today, due to more advanced technology and software

packages that are far more capable than VGA. Some software packages still require VGA as a minimum requirement for installing the software package, and VGA adapters are still in use today on many advanced video adapters that support more advanced video modes, although newer adaptors and connectors are also available. VGA mode usually consists of a combination of 640 × 480 pixels, where pixels are referred to as the tiny dots that produces an image, with 16 to 256 colors.

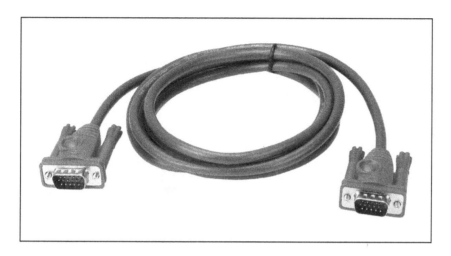

Figure 3-12: VGA Cable and Connector

The VGA connector is also known as a DE-15 connector or 15-pin D-Sub connector. It is used for connecting both traditional monitors and many LCDs or flat-panel displays. It has three rows with five pins in each row. This connector is also called the Video Electronics Standards Association (VESA), by the organization that introduced this standard. The connector at the monitor end is male, and the connector at the video adapter (at the computer end) is female. A male connector consists of pins and a female connector has a port or socket that receives the pins.

SVGA

An enhanced version of VGA is Super VGA, or SVGA, which typically refers to 800×600 VGA resolution. The SuperVGA (SVGA) cable is quite similar to VGA. The plug is D-shaped and always blue, with two locking screws one either side to hold the plug tight in place. The pins are arranged in three rows, each carrying five pins.

HDMI

High-Definition Multimedia Interface (HDMI) is a relatively new interface standard. It is being used with devices that require high-definition digital video signals as an output, such as Digital Television (DTV) players, DVD/Blu-ray players, set-top cable or satellite service boxes, digital cameras, camcorders, and other devices. It provides a bandwidth of up to 10.2 Gbps and combines video and audio signals into an uncompressed signal. HDMI is now integrated into many desktop computers, in place of DVI. Further, it provides a Digital Rights Management (DRM) feature, which is referred

to as High-Bandwidth Digital Content Protection (HDCP), to control and prevent illegal copying of Blu-Ray discs. HDMI supports 3D video and high-speed Ethernet communications as well.

There are 5 different types of HDMI connector: Type A, B, C, D, and E, where type A and B are regular HDMI connectors (original specification). The types will be discussed in the following section.

Figure 3-13: HDMI Cable and Connectors

Mini HDMI

There are two types of small HDMI connectors that are specially designed to be used in laptops and other small devices. The first type that is designed for laptops is called the Type C Mini-HDMI connector (version 1.3 specification). It has 19 pins. The second connector that was designed for other small devices is the Type D Micro-HDMI connector (Version 1.4 specification). The Type E-Automotive Connection System HDMI was also introduced for video systems installed in vehicles or cars. Type E contains both a cable and connector designed for the load or stresses present on equipment installed in cars.

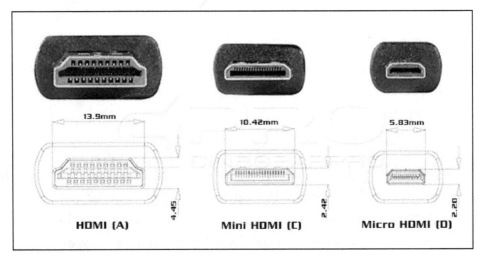

Figure 3-14: Types of HDMI Cable and Connectors

DisplayPort

DisplayPort is the newest standard of digital display interface introduced by VESA. It supports both audio and video signals and provides HDCP copy protection. It is royalty-free to manufacturers and has popular proponents, such as AMD, Apple, Intel, Hewlett-Packard, and Dell. DisplayPort got acknowledgement when Apple introduced its new MacBooks with DisplayPort, replacing DVI. DisplayPort supports DisplayPort Content Protection (DPCP) for preventing the copy of DVDs.

DisplayPort's cable is less than 1/4" thick, which is much slimmer than previous cables, even the connectors are much smaller and do not contain thumbscrews like DVI plugs. DisplayPort is available in two sizes: Standard and Mini DisplayPort.

Figure 3-15: Display Port Cable and Connector

However, the drawback of DisplayPort is that it neither supports all the color options supported by HDMI nor is it compatible with DVI, whereas HDMI is backward compatible with DVI. Some manufacturers place both HDMI and DisplayPort in the same devices to make it more efficient. DisplayPort cables are up to 15m long, but quality decreases with length.

DisplayPort is currently available in three versions:

- DisplayPort 1.1: Maximum data transfer rate of 8.64 Gbps
- DisplayPort 1.2: Maximum data transfer rate of 17.28 Gbps; introduces mini-DisplayPort connector, and support for 3D
- DisplayPort 1.3: Maximum data transfer rate of 32.4 Gbps with support for 4K, 5K, and 8K UHD displays

DVI

The Digital Visual Interface port, or DVI port, is a digital video port that is used by many LED and LCD displays with a 25" or smaller diagonal measurement. There are five variations of Digital Video Interface (DVI), each with a different pin arrangement on the connectors and each transmitting a different kind of signal. All different types of standard DVI connector measure about 1" by 3/8" in size with a variety of pin configurations. Users can distinguish between the five variations by looking at the connector.

Figure 3-16: DVI Cable and Connectors

DVI-A

The analog mode of DVI is referred to as DVI-A. This connector supports analog signals only. It consists of four pins placed around the blade of the main pin grid area. It is available in two varieties of pin configuration: the first consists of eight pins arranged in a 3 × 3 grid, where the position of the 9th pin is empty; the second consists of two sets of two pins with equal spaces between them.

DVI-D

The digital mode of DVI is referred to as DVI-D. This connector supports digital signals only and is available in two varieties: Single Link and Dual Link. The DVI-D Single Link connector consists of two 3 × 3 grids, with 9 pins in each grid, while the DVI-D Dual Link consists of a single grid with 24 pins. The dual link can support higher resolution video modes by doubling the bandwidth in the cable.

DVI-I

DVI-Integrated, or DVI-I, is interchangeable and supports both DVI-A and DVI-D signals and can work with both analog and digital displays. It is also available in Single Link and Dual Link versions. The connector resembles with the DVI-D counterparts, along with the four pins around the blade to support analog mode of DVI.

DVI supports various screen resolutions and color densities depending on which type of DVI is used. Common resolutions of DVI include 1280 × 1024 Super XGA (SXGA) with 85 Hz, 1920 × 1200 Wide UXGA (WUXGA) with 60 Hz, and 2560 × 1600 Wide Quad XGA (WQXGA) with 60 Hz. In order to support various modes of DVI, there are several types of connector.

When users want to connect the cable to any interface, they have to compare the adapter card with the connector. There is also a need to match the pins for making proper connections.

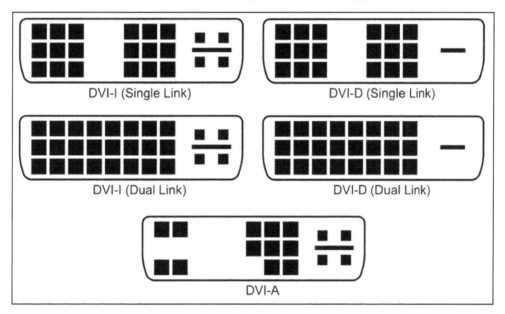

Figure 3-17: Types of DVI Cables and Connectors

Mini-DVI vs Micro-DVI

The Mini-DVI connector is widely used by Apple and is about the same width as a standard USB connector but twice the thickness. It consists of 8 pins arranged in four rows. There is smaller version of DVI, the Micro-DVI connector, that was greatly used by ASUS and Apple.

Multipurpose Cables

The following section deals with the different types of multipurpose cable.

Lightning

This is an 8-pin connector replacing the predecessor of the 30-pin dock. As with USB-C, it is possible to insert the Lightning connector face up or face down. It supports speeds of USB 3.0.

Lightning is a proprietary port built into Apple devices such as the iPad and iPhone. It is an 8-pin connector that replaced the predecessor of the 30-pin dock. As with USB-C, the Lightning connector can be inserted face up or face down. It supports speeds of USB 3.0. Lightning provides more functions than standard microUSB, and users can directly access and control accessories on the iPhone screen over this port from another device.

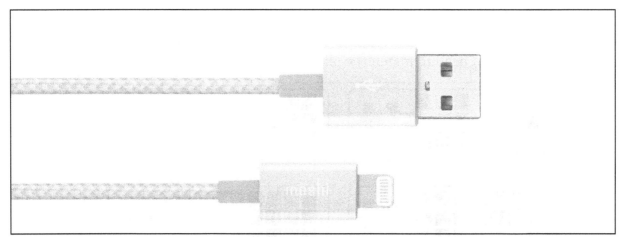

Figure 3-18:

Lightning Cable and Connectors

Thunderbolt

Thunderbolt was launched by Intel in 2011. Thunderbolt was initially adopted by Apple, which uses it in the latest and existing MacBook product lines. Thunderbolt is a high-speed interface capable of supporting hard disk drives, SSDs, HDTVs up to 4K resolution, and other types of I/O device. It combines elements of PCI Express and DisplayPort technologies. Versions 1 and 2 use the Mini DisplayPort connector and version 3 uses the USB Type-C connector. Thunderbolt is also available on some high-end desktop motherboards using Intel chipsets.

Thunderbolt uses two separate channels with 10 Gbps throughput on the same connector in both directions. The advanced version of Thunderbolt, i.e., Thunderbolt 2 or the next generation of Thunderbolt, increases the throughput of data up to 20 Gbps. This throughput is 40 times faster than USB 2.0, 4 times faster than USB 3.0, and 25 times faster than FireWire 800.

Figure 3-19: Thunderbolt Cable and Connectors

Versions	Data Transfer Rate	Connector Type	PCI Express Version Required
Thunderbolt 1	10 Gbps	DisplayPort	Version 2.0
Thunderbolt 2	20 Gbps	DisplayPort	Version 2.0
Thunderbolt 3	40 Gbps	USB Type-C	Version 3.0

Table 3-06: Comparison of Thunderbolt Versions

USB

The USB port allows data transfer between a device and computer and usually powers the device as well. The Universal Serial Bus (USB) interface has now become the primary choice of interface for PCs, replacing both parallel and serial ports and even replacing SCSI and FireWire/IEEE 1394. All modern manufactured PCs and laptops contain at least one USB port, located usually on the front, as well as on the back of a desktop PC case, and on either side and at the back of a laptop.

USB is itself an external bus that connects to the PCI bus of PC. The speed of data transfer of a USB device depends on the version of the USB port. USBs have been available in several versions of the USB standard; the most common are 1.0, 1.1, 2.0, and 3.0.

USB Version	Name	Data Transfer Rate
USB 1.1	Low-Speed	12 Mbps
USB 2.0	High-Speed	480 Mbps
USB 3.0	SuperSpeed	5 Gbps
USB 3.1	SuperSpeed+	10 Gbps
USB 3.2 (USB-C)	SuperSpeed+	10/20 Gbps

Table 3-07: Comparison of USB Versions

USB 1.0 and 1.1

The low speed version of USB standard 1.0 and 1.1 transmits data up to 1.5 Mbps while the full-speed 1.1 standards can transmit data up to 12 Mbps. Data communications are under the control of the host system and can flow in both directions, but one at a time. This one-way single transmission is called half-duplex communication.

Hi-Speed USB 2.0

USB 2.0 standard transmits data at high speeds of up to 480 Mbps or 60 Mbps in half duplex. USB peripherals and hubs are downward compatible with hardware with the older standard, but when users connect an older device into a Hi-Speed USB port or attach a Hi-Speed USB device to a full-speed USB 1.1 port, the overall speed will become lower with a maximum of 12 Mbps.

SuperSpeed USB 3.0

The 3.0 standard of USB or SuperSpeed USB was introduced in 2008 and is now widely used on modern PCs and laptops. USB 3.0 transmits data at up to 625 MBps or 5 Gbps, which is ten times faster than the speed of USB 2.0 and is also faster than the speed of recent 300 MBps eSATA. USB 3.0 can communicate in both directions; hence it supports full-duplex communication. The symbol "SS" corresponds to the SuperSpeed USB 3.0 port. Manufacturers now integrate fast ports of USB 3.0 into chipsets on recently manufactured computers. USB 3.1 is actually two standards in one:

- USB 3.1 Gen 1 is the new name for USB 3.0. Anytime you see a reference to USB 3.0, keep in mind that USB 3.1 Gen 1 is the same standard. Although USB 3.1 Gen 1 is the same standard as USB 3.0, vendors continue to use the original USB 3.0 name
- USB 3.1 Gen 2 has new USB 3.1 features. USB 3.1 Gen 2 (often referred to simply as USB 3.1) runs at speeds of up to 10 Gbps (2x the speed of USB 3.0/USB 3.1 Gen 1). It is backward compatible with USB 1.1, 2.0 and 3.0/3.1 Gen 1

Figure 3-20: Types of USB Cables and Connectors

Mind Map of Basic Cable Types

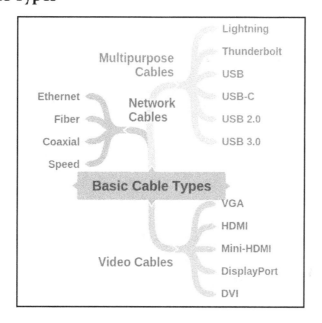

Figure 3-21: Mind Map of Basic Cable Types

Peripheral Cables

Peripheral devices such as keyboards, mice, digital cameras, and external hard drives can be connected to a computer by using peripheral cables: Modern types of peripheral cable include Universal Serial Bus (USB). USB is a standard interface that is present on almost every modern computer. Many desktop computers contain more than one USB port that enables several USB devices to connect to the computer simultaneously. FireWire or IEEE 1394 is a popular data transfer technology introduced by Apple Computer that resembles USB in functionality and is often used for connecting external hard drives and digital camcorders. FireWire ports are available on Mac computers.

Serial

Serial means that the data bits flow in one row, one after the other, over the cable. Serial connections were designed for the comparatively low speed of telephone modem communication but were also used for other devices, such as keyboards, mice, and other peripheral devices.

Usually, serial ports and cables were compared to parallel ports and cables, where various bits flow at once. Serial cables conformed to the RS-232 standard. Printers were the most common devices to be connected with parallel ports, but now most printers are connected with USB cables or via Ethernet cables on networks.

USB cables have replaced serial cables, but it is possible to use a USB to serial adapter to connect to an older machine, if necessary.

Figure 3-22: Serial Cables and Connectors

Hard Drive Cables

Hard drive cables are built to carry data to and from the motherboard. As data rates have increased, cable designs have changed to maintain the data speeds. The main types of hard drive cables include SCSI, IDE, and Serial ATA cables.

SCSI cables are obsolete now, whereas IDE and SATA are widely used cables today. IDE cables are thick, ribbon-like cables that can be used to attach up to two IDE hard drives to the motherboard. Serial ATA cables are much smaller than IDE cables and many motherboards have several Serial ATA ports available.

SATA

At one time, hard drives were connected to motherboards with Advanced Technology Attachment (ATA) cables. These cables had a ribbon-like appearance, with various wires carrying data between the bus and the hard drive. Serial ATA (SATA) provides serial connectivity and hot plugging. It increased data transfer rates up to 1.5 Gbits/second, but its modern version can transfer data up to 6 Gbits/second.

Serial ATA (SATA) cables are next-generation serial cables that carry high-speed data. SATA cables are used inside computer cases and offer not only the benefit of high speed but the advantage of better airflow inside the box.

External SATA (eSATA) wires make it possible to mount external drives at the same data rate. To protect the cable and the data, eSATA has better shielding. To avoid the use of thinner SATA cables from being used outside the case, eSATA cables have a different connecter.

A SATA data cable is usually 1-meter long with 9 pins. SATA cables can fit easily in small devices and provide better air cooling. Connectors are either straight or angled; the angled ones are used for lower profile connections. A mini SATA connector is used to connect small storage drives, and an e-SATA connector is used to connect external devices to the computer.

A SATA cable can support only one connection per connector. The latest versions of SATA can support data rates of up to 3 Gbps and 6 Gbps respectively. One further advantage of SATA cables is that these peripherals are the least expensive peripherals in the market.

Figure 3-23: SATA Cables and Connectors

IDE or PATA

Integrated Drive Electronics (IDE), popularly known as Parallel Advanced Technology Attachment (PATA), supports parallel communication for data transfer. Initially IDE consisted of 40-pin and 80-ribbon cables, whereas modern IDE contains 28 pins. It transfers data at a rate of 16 bps, and operates on a plug-and-play basis. It allows the connection of two devices in a single channel. The modern versions of IDE or PATA allows a data rate of up to 133 Mbps. They have replaced SCSI by providing better speed and cost effectiveness.

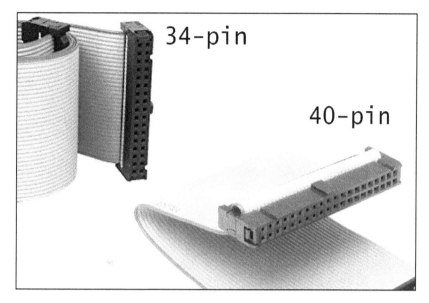

Figure 3-24: PATA Cables and Connectors

SCSI

Small Computer System Interface (SCSI) was designed as a parallel technology that could operate faster than IDE and other connections. Today, a common type of SCSI is Serial Attached SCSI (SAS), which can transfer data as fast as 22.5 Gbps.

SCSI was the earliest standard for connecting hard drives with the computer. It used a flat ribbon connector with 50 pins. Several versions of SCSI have been released since then, and some low end PCs still use them because of their low cost. The SCSI interfaces used today perform serial communication, that provides faster transmission compared to the parallel communication.

SCSI allows 7 to 15 devices to be connected simultaneously. Modern SCSI devices are backward compatible and can transfer data up to 80 megabytes/second.

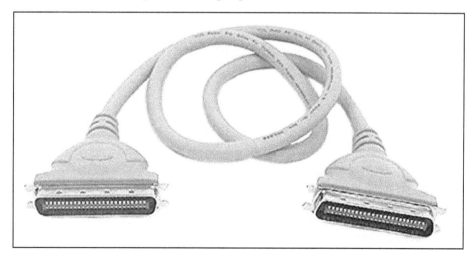

Figure 3-25: SCSI Cables and Connectors

Adapters

With technology advancements, there tends to be a moment when the old overlaps with the new, or when competing technologies need to find a way to get along. During an upgrade cycle, physical cable adapters are often the short-term (and economical) response to technical compatibility issues. This section briefly describes the three types of cable adapters.

DVI to HDMI

Because HDMI uses the same video signals as DVI, DVI to HDMI cables or adapters are widely available. Usually only the video transmits through these adapter cables, but some newer graphics cards enable HDMI audio over DVI, which eliminates the need for a separate sound cable connection.

HDMI is backward compatible with the DVI standard. The video adaptor of DVI can work with an HDMI monitor by using an appropriate cable and converter. However, with the DVI video adaptor, remote control, audio, 3D, and Ethernet features provided by HDMI are easily achievable. On the bright side, only one specially designed cable with an HDMI connector on one end is needed to get all these features.

Figure 3-26: DVI to HDMI Converter

Type A HDMI is electrically compatible with DVI-D Single Link. Type B supports the same, along with the support of very-high-resolution displays, such as WQUXGA (3840 × 2400). Type B HDMI is electrically compatible with DVI-D Dual Link.

USB to Ethernet

USB to Ethernet adapters allow a device without an Ethernet port to connect to a wired network. These common connectors are available in a wide range of prices and qualities. There are adapters that can convert an RJ-45 Ethernet cable to USB and vice versa. These adaptors can save users from having to replace hardware in the desktop or add functionality to a machine. The older adapter that served this purpose was the PS/2 to USB adapter.

Figure 3-27: USB to Ethernet Converter

DVI to VGA

DVI-I includes both VGA compatible analog video and DVI digital video. The DVI-I to VGA adapters allow VGA displays to work with DVI-I ports on video cards.

The DVI to VGA convertor or adaptor resolves digital versus analog issues. As VGA supports analog signaling and DVI, it can use either analog or digital. The VGA or DE-15 standard interface only uses an analog connection type and cannot handle digital signals, whereas DVI-I is integrated to carry either digital or analog signals. Therefore, users may require a digital to analog or vice versa converter to bridge the gap between analog and digital signals.

Figure 3-28: DVI to VGA Converter

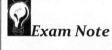
Exam Note

If a computer cannot connect to the network, check the network cable first. Ensure that the RJ45 plug has a solid connection.

Mind Map of Basic Cable Types

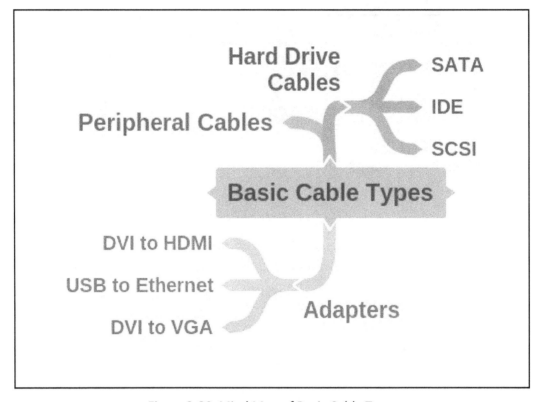

Figure 3-29: Mind Map of Basic Cable Types

Identify Common Connector Types

This section deals with the various types of electrical connectors. A connector or an electrical connector is an electro-mechanical component that is used to connect electrical terminations. It is used to establish an electrical connection between two or more electronic devices, components, or assemblies. There is a vast variety of electrical connectors with their individual roles that can be used in different applications.

Before looking at the different types of connector, users must be aware of the terminology of electrical connectors.

Terminology for Cable Connectors

The following is a list of some common terminology used to describe connectors.

Gender

The gender of a connector defines whether it is a plug or a jack into which the plug is inserted. Gender involves two types of connectors:

Male connector: This is usually a plug with a solid pin as a center conductor. This is usually for providing input to the connected device.

Female connector: This is usually a slot, port, or jack. It contains a center conductor with a hole to accept the male conductor pin.

Figure 3-30: Male and Female Connector

Polarity

The orientation in which the plug and jack should be connected is referred to as polarity. This polarity prevents the jack and the plug from being connected from the wrong side, and this trait is referred to as keyed or polarized.

Contact or Connections

The metal parts of the electrical connector (in both male and female) that establish an electrical connection is referred to as contact.

Figure 3-31: Connector Contacts

Pitch

Many types of connectors contain an array of contacts. The distance between the center of one contact to the center of the next contact is referred to as the pitch of the connector. Many connectors look similar but they are differentiated by their pitch, which makes it easy to purchase the right connector.

Mount

The term mount can refer to the orientation of the jack in a connector, for example, board mount, panel mount, or free-hanging. It also specifies the angle of the connector relative to its attachment, straight or right-angled, and it specifies how it should mechanically connect, through a hole solder tab or surface mount.

Strain Relief

Whenever a connector is connected to a cable or board, the contacts of the connector can be fragile. It is therefore a good idea to provide some sort of strain relief to take the weight of the force on the connector.

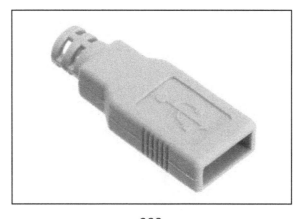

Figure 3-32: Self Relief

Common Types of Cable Connectors

The following is an introduction to the different types of cable connector.

RJ-11

RJ-11, or Registered Jack-11, is a connector for cable that consists of two to four wires. It is used to attach phone cables (with RJ-11 plug) to analog modems (with RJ-11 jack) and it is also used in wall-mounted phone jacks. Technically, the two connectors of either two wires or four wires are of the same size, but the two-wire connector is an RJ-11 and the four-wire connector is an RJ-14.

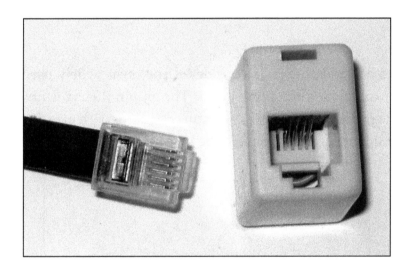

Figure 3-33: RJ-11

RJ-45

RJ-45, or Registered Jack-45, is a connector for cable that consists of eight wires. An RJ-45 is slightly larger than an RJ-11 connector. RJ-45 connectors are commonly used to attach twisted-pair cables to Ethernet network cards.

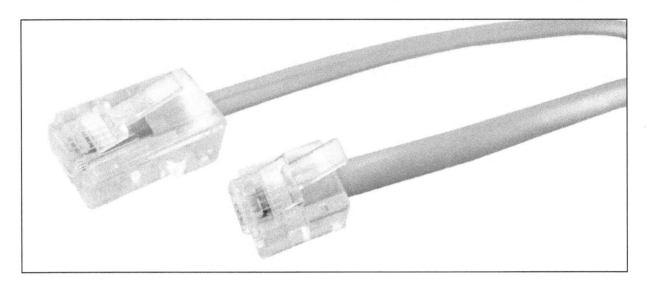

Figure 3-34: RJ-45

RS-232

RS-232 or Recommended Standard-232, is considered the most widely used data communication standard. It is used for cable of either 9 or 25 pins. The 25-pin RS-232 is now known as the legacy parallel connector. The 9-pin connector was a D-sub connector with an arrangement of pins in two rows, i.e., 5 pins in the upper row and 4 pins in the lower row.

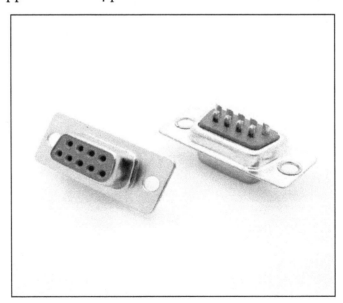

Figure 3-35: RS-232

BNC

BNC, or Bayonet-Neill-Concelman or British Naval Connector, is a cable connector used to attach coaxial cables (with BNC plug) to a BNC port in some other device. This connector is round and

allows a quick connect and disconnect with a twist-lock mechanism to keep the cable in place. BNC connectors have a conducting pointed pin that corresponds to a receiver socket in the port. BNC connectors are used for CCTV cameras and for some kinds of video projectors.

Figure 3-36: BNC

RG-59

Coaxial cables use the term RG, Radio Guide, to differentiate between the different kinds of cables. The number preceding the term RG specifies the different traits of the coaxial cable, such as the size of the conductor, its width, its properties, and more.

The RG59 connector is used for cable that is thinner (contains thinner conducting material or gauge) and is recommended where low bandwidth and lower frequency applications are required such as CCTV installation and analog video signals. This type of 75-ohm cable is not used in LANs but is used in video installations. Typical distances are 750 feet (225 m) to 1000 feet (305 m). It can carry frequencies up to 1000 MHz.

Figure 3-37: RG-59

RG-6

An RG-6 connector is used for cable of a heavier gauge and has shielding and insulation for high-bandwidth and high-frequency applications such as the internet, cable TV, and satellite TV signals. This is the type of cable least likely to be used in a network. It is a 75-ohm cable suitable for distributing signals for cable TV, satellite dish, or rooftop antenna. It has better shielding than RG-59, so it is larger in diameter. Typical distances are 1000 feet (305 m) to 1500 feet (457 m). It can carry frequencies up to 2200 MHz.

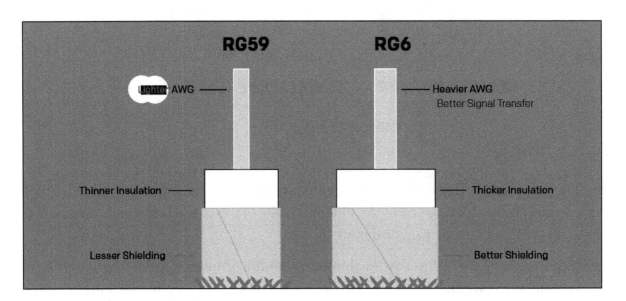

Figure 3-38: RG-59 vs RG 6

USB Connectors

USB ports can be either upstream ports or downstream ports. An upstream port is used to connect to a computer or another hub. A USB device such as a printer or flash drive connects to a downstream port. Downstream ports are commonly known as USB Type-A and USB Type-B.

USB-A Connectors

<u>USB-A female connector:</u> This is the standard "host" connector type. This port or jack is found on hubs, computers, or any other device that has peripherals plugged into it.

<u>USB-A male connector:</u> This is the standard "peripheral" connector type. A USB-A male connector is the most widely used connector and most cables have one terminal with a USB-A male connector.

USB-B Connectors

The USB-B female connector is a standard slot or jack for peripheral devices. It is somewhat bulky but robust in performance. This connector is usually a through-hole board mount jack, for maximum throughput and reliability.

The USB-B male connector or plug is a popular type and can be found at the end of a USB cable. USB-B cables are inexpensive and ubiquitous.

Figure 3-39: Different Types of USB

USB-Mini Connectors

The USB-Mini connector was introduced as a reduced size USB connector for smaller devices.

<u>USB-Mini Female Connector:</u> These are usually found on smaller peripherals such as older cell phones, MP3 players, and small external hard drives.

<u>USB-Mini Male Connector:</u> These are plug connectors, are extremely common, and can be found cheaply almost anywhere.

USB Type-A Mini

Used by USB On-The-Go (OTG) peripheral devices such as tablets and smartphones to function as host devices for mice and keyboards.

USB Type-B Mini

Used by external hard drives, digital cameras, USB hubs, and other equipment.

USB-Micro Connectors

The USB-Micro connector is a recent addition to the standard USB connector family. The size reduction factor is there, but USB-Micro adds a fifth pin in the connector, allowing it to be used in USB applications where a device may want to operate as either a peripheral or a host depending on the requirement of the application.

USB-Micro Female Connector: This jack or slot is found on MP3 players and digital cameras. It is now a standard charge port for all new smart phones, cellular phones, and tablet computers, which means that data cables and chargers are becoming more common by the day.

USB-Micro Male Connector: USB-Micro male connectors are of two types: one is used for modifying the USB Micro female port to a USB-A female port, to be used in USB-On-The-Go capable devices, and the other is used for connecting a device with a USB-Micro port as a peripheral to a USB host device.

USB Type-A Micro

Used by USB On-The-Go (OTG) devices such as tablets and smartphones.

USB Type-B Micro

Used by almost all Android devices as a standard charging plug and jack.

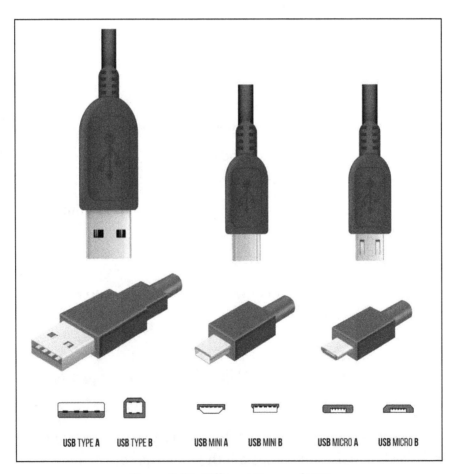

Figure 3-40: Different Types of USB

USB-C

The C USB connector type appears slightly bigger than micro USB. It provides a faster data transfer speed and higher throughput to ensure a faster recharge along with data transfer rates from 5 Gbps to 10 Gbps. It can provide up to 100 W of power for recharging devices.

The USB Type-C connector is the latest connector and will eventually replace the Type-A and Type-B connectors. With older devices, it is possible to use an adapter in order to attach a Type-C connector. Many USB 3.0 ports are Type-C connectors, but they do not have to be. USB 3.1 (Gen 2) and USB 3.2 require USB Type-C connectors.

With its double ended connector cables, USB type C is capable of replacing connector cables in cameras, laptops, smartphones, game controllers, HDMI, printers, scanners, and whatever computing device you use.

Figure 3-41: USB C

DB-9

The DE-9, also known as DB-9, is an analog connector of the D-sub miniature (D-sub) plug and jack family with 9 pins (for the male connector) and 9 holes (for the female connector) for desktop computers and other communication devices. DB9 connectors were widely used for serial peripheral devices such as joysticks, keyboards, mice, and cable assemblies for data connectivity.

Some other common applications of DB-9 cable connectors include:

- Token Ring Network Adapters
- Serial Communication
- Asynchronous Data Transfer (standardized as RS-232C)

- IBM Video Interfaces
- UPS Cables

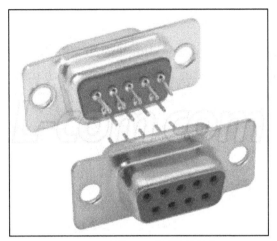

Figure 3-42: DB-9

Lightning

Older iOS devices (up through the iPhone 4 series and third-generation iPad) used the 30-pin connector. However, starting in 2012, Apple standardized the 8-pin reversible Lightning connector for iPhones, iPads, iPods, and other mobile devices. The Lightning connector is used for both charging batteries and transferring data. The data transfer rates are about the same as the USB 2.0 standard.

The Lightning cable is a small cable with a standard USB-A adapter on one side and a thin Lightning adapter on the other side. The Lightning connector not only transmits power but it can also be used to send and receive digital information.

Figure 3-43: Lightning Cable

SCSI

Small Computer System Interface (SCSI) is a group or set of standard electronic interfaces that enable computers to communicate with peripheral hardware devices like CD-ROM drives, disk drives, tape drives, scanners, and printers.

SCSI was first designed as a parallel technology that could run faster than IDE and other connections. Today, a common type of SCSI is Serial Attached SCSI (SAS), which can transfer data as fast as 22.5 Gbps (SAS version 4).

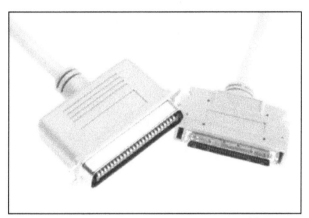

Figure 3-44: SCSI Cable

eSATA

The eSATA port is used for connecting external storage devices such as hard drives or optical drives and is commonly found on laptops. eSATA can transfer data at 600 MB/s. Devices can connect at a maximum of approximately 6.6 feet (2 m). If the internal hard drive has crashed, an external drive connected to an eSATA or USB port can be used to boot and troubleshoot the system.

SATA cables are 7-pin cables and both the ends of a cable are flat and thin. One end of the cable plugs into a port on the motherboard, usually called SATA, and the other end plugs or inserts into the back of a storage device such as a SATA hard drive. External hard drives can also be attached by using SATA connections, this is referred to as eSATA.

Figure 3-45: eSATA Cable

Molex

Molex is a connector used to provide power to storage devices such as hard drives, optical drives, and other internal peripherals.

In Molex, the female connector is found on the end of the cable and it resides inside a plastic shell. Similarly, the male pins on the male connector are placed inside a plastic shell. The Molex connectors are not a good choice for those connections that will be frequently changed as these connectors are press-fit only and extremely tight.

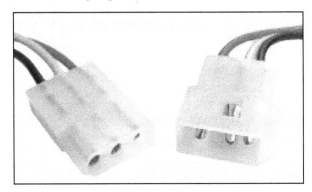

Figure 3-46: Molex Cable

> 💡 **Exam Note**
>
> Be able to identify device connectors. This includes but is not limited to SATA, eSATA, USB, Molex, and SCSI.

Mind Map of Common Connector Types

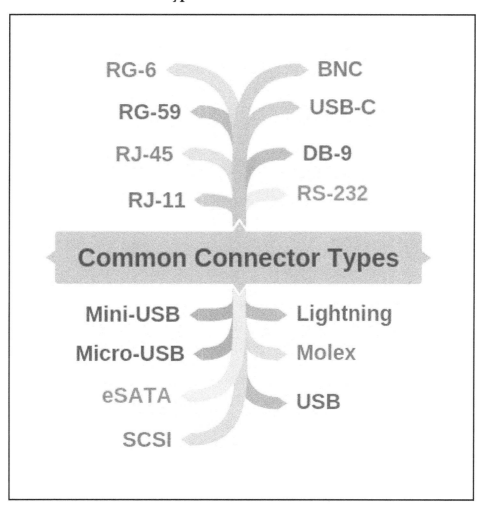

Figure 3-47: Mind Map of Common connecter types

Install RAM Types

There are many types of RAM, but this section will focus on two types of RAM to cover the exam objectives: desktop RAM and laptop RAM. Generally, desktops use Dual-Inline Memory Modules (DIMMs), and laptops use small-outline DIMMs (SODIMMs). They both use RAM that is based on Double Data Rate (DDR) technology. The original DDR got its name because it doubles the data

per cycle compared to older types of RAM. A typical data transfer rate for DDR version 1 was 1600 MB/s.

RAM Types

A motherboard contains special sockets or slots for the system's memory. These special sockets accept different types of RAM chips that are attached to small circuit boards called memory sticks or memory modules. There have been various types of these memory modules, but the ones that are in use today are all some sort of Dual Inline Memory Module (DIMM). Different types of DIMM include Double Data Rate (DDR), DDR2, DDR3, and Small Outline DIMM (SODIMM).

Typically, there are two types of RAM:

- Static RAM (SRAM)
- Dynamic RAM (DRAM)

SRAM

Static RAM (SRAM) is very fast in accessing data compared to DRAM, but it is also very expensive. For this reason, most PC manufacturers use SRAM just for caches. A cache memory stores frequently accessed data or instructions for the CPU's use. On modern systems, the L1, L2, and L3 caches are all built into the processor's package.

DRAM

Dynamic RAM (DRAM) was introduced to combat the high cost of SRAM. Although DRAM chips are slower in accessing data than SRAM chips, they are still much better in speed compared to accessing data from a hard drive. They store several hundreds of megabytes of data or even gigabytes on a single chip.

A DRAM chip is a tiny spreadsheet with billions of cells, arranged in rows and columns. The number of columns refers to the bus width of the RAM; a 64-bit chip consists of 64 columns. Every "cell" in a DRAM chip comprises one capacitor and one transistor to store a single bit of information.

Because of the high capacity and low cost, manufacturers prefer DRAM to be used as "main" memory (system memory) in the computing device.

SDRAM

More advanced, DRAM operates at speeds assigned by the motherboard's system clock or system timer. As it is synchronized with the system timer or system clock, it is known as synchronous DRAM, or SDRAM. Usually SDRAM works at the same speed as the system timer, but advanced types of SDRAM work at a multiple of that speed and are referred to as Double Data Rate (DDR) SDRAM.

SODIMM

Small Outline Dual Inline Memory Module (SODIMM) is a laptop memory module that is smaller in size compared to the regular memory module (DIMM) used for desktop computers. SODIMM is about half the size of a Dual Inline Memory Module (DIMM), and it measures about 2 5/8. Although it is smaller in size, it has the same microchips and circuitry as other memory modules. Its small size makes it compatible for fitting in small computing devices such as laptops, netbooks, high end printers, or small form factor PCs. Initially, SODIMMs were 30 pins, but later expanded to 72 pins. Next, SODIMMs had 100 pins along with a 32-bit data bus. Now, laptops contain 64-bit, 204-pin SODIMMs.

SODIMMs have notches (as with DIMMS) inside that means they only fit into their respective keyed SODIMM slots. The 144-pin SODIMMs have a single notch just off center. The 200-pin SODIMMs have at least three notches at different locations, depending on the DDR level. Now, users can get 200-pin DDR1, DDR2, and DDR3 SODIMMs, and all have a single notch that is off center and is at a different location for each type of SODIMM such as DDR1, DDR2, and DDR3. In newer laptops, SODIMM has 204 pins, with a notch on different locations depending on the manufacturer's choice.

MicroDIMM

MicroDIMM is a RAM module that is specially designed for smaller notebooks, laptops, or netbooks. It is about half the size of a SODIMM and provides higher-density storage.

Installing of SODIMM Memory

Users can install RAM on a laptop if it has a RAM slot. If there is no RAM slot, users can replace the existing RAM module with a denser module. If users are looking to install RAM or a memory module, follow the general steps for memory installation given below:

- Before beginning the installation process, place an antistatic wrist strap around the wrist and attach the other end to the ground or an unpainted metal part of the computer. Alternatively, use an antistatic glove
- First, disconnect the power source or remove the laptop or notebook battery charger and all exterior devices and cables
- Remove the bottom cover and the battery
- Refer to the manufacturer's manual for the correct steps for disassembling the laptop to locate the compartment that contains the SODIMM slot
- Gently open the compartment that has the SODIMM slot
- Generally, laptops have one or two memory slots and these slots are numbered. Start filling the slots with the lowest number first
- Now, remove the old module to replace by pressing down the retaining clips that are located on the sides of the module. Pull out the module gently, by lifting its edge at an angle of 45 degrees. Make sure not to touch the chips or contacts of the module

- Now, put the old memory module in an antistatic bag
- Take out the new memory module and align the notch of the memory module with the memory slot. Gently insert the memory module in the memory slot at an angle of 45 degrees. Note: Hold the memory module from its edge and do not touch any of its chips or contacts
- Press the memory module carefully flat down until the clamps of the module lock into place
- Now, close the compartment, reinsert the battery, and reconnect the power cables and other devices

Figure 3-48: Installing SODIMM Memory

- Turn on the laptop and configure the memory in BIOS setup if required, normally it is not required. Users can refer to the manufacturer's manual for its configuration
- Carry out a normal start up in Windows and go to the control panel and check system properties to ensure the new memory is there

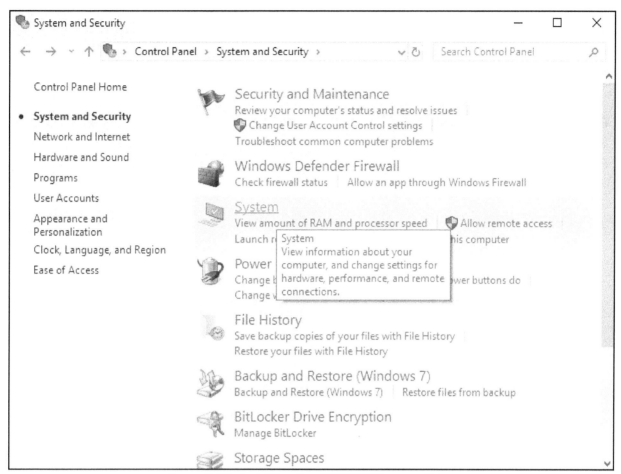

Figure 3-49: Installing the SODIMM Memory Driver

The following windows will let users know about the installed Windows, installed RAM, processor, and its size.

Figure 3-50: Installing the SODIMM Memory Driver

DDR

Double-data rate SDRAM (DDR1 SDRAM), also known as DDR SDRAM, doubled the speed of data processing compared to the standard SDRAM. It processes data by accessing the module with the rate of twice per clock cycle. Here, users can get even faster access to memory by combining DDR memory with dual-channel or triple-channel architecture.

DDR SDRAM's module or stick is labeled with a module specification such as PC1600, PC2100, PC2700, or PC3200. This labeling defines the total bandwidth or speed rating (in MHz) of the memory. The numeric value in the label refers to the MHz speed at which the DDR SDRAM memory operates, which should be synchronized with the motherboard's clock speed. The stick or module of DDR SDRAM memory consists of 184-pin DIMM with a notch on any one end to make it only fit into the appropriate DIMM slot or socket on a motherboard. It requires only a 2.5V power supply.

DDR2 SDRAM

Double-data-rate two SDRAM (DDR2 SDRAM) provides improvements in electrical characteristics, for example, it can handle faster clock rates, consume less power, and replace the original DDR standard. It provides bandwidth rates starting from 400 MHz and it increases speed by adding buffers and clock doubling the I/O circuits on the chips.

There are defined specifications for the chips and modules. The table below shows the speed standards that come from the combination of chip and module for DDR2 SDRAM.

DDR2 Chip Specification	Chip Operating Speed	I/O Clock Speed	DDR2 Module Specification
DDR2-400	100 MHz	200 MHz	PC2-3200
DDR2-533	133 MHz	266 MHz	PC2-4200
DDR2-667	166 MHz	333 MHz	PC2-5300
DDR2-1066	200 MHz	400 MHz	PC2-6400
DDR2-1066	266 MHz	533 MHz	PC2-8500

Table 3-08: Speed Standards for DDRAM2

DDR2 sticks are compatible only with motherboards that have a special 240-pin slot or socket. The location of DDR2 stick notches is different from DDR1. A DDR2 consumes only 1.8V and a DDR1 consumes 2.5V.

DDR3 SDRAM

Double-data-rate three SDRAM (DDR3 SDRAM) has a more improved module and chip, as they provide double bandwidth and consume far less power than the previous SDRAMs. Like the DDR2, the DDR3 DIMM contains 240 pins. They are the same size as DDR2 but they come with a different key notch to prevent users from placing the wrong modules into DDR3 slots or sockets. DDR3 modules can upgrade its efficiency by using dual-channel architecture; it can get much better by using memory controller chips (MCCs) that support a triple-channel architecture.

Like DDR1 and DDR2 are defined. The table below shows the speed standards that come from the combination of chip and module for DDR3 SDRAM.

DDR2 Chip Specification	Chip Operating Speed	I/O Clock Speed	DDR2 Module Specification
DDR3-800	100 MHz	400 MHz	PC3-6400
DDR3-1066	133 MHz	533 MHz	PC3-8500
DDR3-1333	166 MHz	667 MHz	PC3-10600
DDR3-1600	200 MHz	800 MHz	PC3-12800

| DDR3-1866 | 233.33 MHz | 933.33 MHz | PC3-14900 |
| DDR3-2133 | 266.66MHz | 1066.66 MHz | PC3-17000 |

Table 3-09: Speed Standards for DDRAM3

The DDR3L is referred to as the low-voltage version of DDR3 and it operates at 1.35V, which is relatively low compared to the 1.5V or 1.65V standard DDR3. Low-voltage RAM is ideal where there is a big number of RAM working together, as in a server farm or data center. It saves electricity and runs cooler. It is compatible with the slot or socket of regular DDR3 but the motherboard should support DDR3L to make it work.

DDR4 SDRAM

DDR4 is the most improved version of DIMMs. It is faster, provides higher density, and consumes lower voltage than DDR3. DDR4 comes with 288-pin DIMMs. DDR4 changes the pattern of accessing channels by using a point-to-point architecture where each channel connects to a single module. This is a departure from the multichannel architectures of DDR1, DDR2, and DDR3, so it is not compatible with slots that take earlier types.

DDR SDRAM Standard	Date Rate (MHz)	Bus Clock (MHz)	Pre-Fetch	Data Rate (MT/s)	Transfer Rate (GB/s)	Voltage (V)
SDRAM	100-166	100-166	1n	100-166	0.8-1.3	3.3
DDR	133-200	133-200	2n	266-400	2.1-3.2	2.5
DDR2	133-200	266-400	4n	533-800	4.2-6.4	1.8
DDR3	133-200	533-800	8n	1066-1600	8.5-14.9	1.35/1.5
DDR4	133-200	1066-1600	8n	2133-3200	17-21.3	1.2

Table 3-10: Comparison of SDRAM, DDR, DDR2, DDR3 and DDR4

A circuit that controls the RAM in a system is known as the Memory Controller. The Memory Controller and the RAM are connected through a series of wires. Collectively, they are referred to as a Memory Bus. The Memory Controller also determines the memory speeds or clock rates for the memory stick or module. For example, if the Memory Controller supports a max clock rate of 3333

MHz, then the system will only be able to use 3333 MHz even if users install a 5555 MHz memory module. One way to increase the system's RAM, is to access RAM by using more than one channel. However, multichannel is a trait of the motherboard not of the RAM. Use a multichannel-enabled motherboard in the system to gain speed improvements.

Single-channel Architecture

A single module of RAM operates on a single data channel of 64 bits. This architecture provides single-channel bandwidth and is used when only one DIMM is installed or when the memory capacities of more than one memory module (DIMM) are not the same.

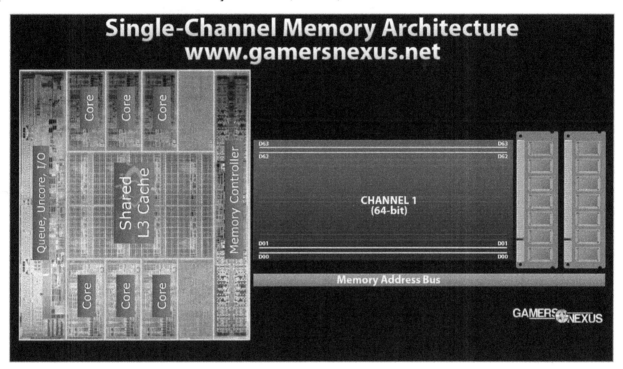

Figure 3-51: Single-channel Architecture

Dual-channel Architecture

Dual-channel memory, also known as dual-channel architecture, is a chipset (of DDR, DDR2, DDR3) on the motherboard that improves RAM performance by providing two dedicated high-throughput data channels. The channels allow reading from and writing to memory to take place on two different channels.

To install DIMM in a motherboard's slot to make use of dual-channel architecture, make sure to get memory modules in identical pairs. For example, if a user wants to add 2 GB of memory to the system, get two, exactly identical, 1 GB memory modules (DIMMs) instead of one 2 GB memory module (DIMM). The pair of RAM must be installed in identical modules across a set of slots. In almost all motherboards, memory slots are color-coded to specify the memory channel, for example, two black RAM slots and two blue RAM slots. The memory in the two black slots must be identical

in features, capacity, and all the other aspects, and the memory in the two blue slots must also be identical.

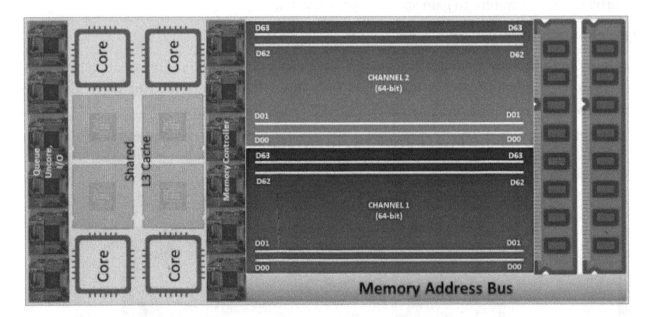

Figure 3-52: Dual-channel Architecture

Triple-channel Architecture

Triple-channel architecture provides three dedicated channels for reading from and writing to memory to improve the overall speed of accessing data. For triple-channel memory, motherboards contain three identical slots but the motherboard handles them as if they were a single slot logically. It triples the available bandwidth of the memory.

Quad-channel Architecture

Quad-channel Architecture multiplies the bandwidth memory by 4 (quadruples). As with dual-channel architecture and triple-channel architecture, memory should be installed in a set of four DIMMs.

Error Correcting Memory (ECC)

Error Correcting Code (ECC) is a method used to detect and then correct single-bit memory errors. A single-bit memory error is an information error in output that greatly impacts the system's performance.

Two types of single-bit memory errors exist: hard errors and soft errors.

Hard Errors – These may occur because of physical factors, such as physical stress, voltage stress, excessive temperature variation upon the memory bits.

Soft Errors – These may occur when there is an error in reading or writing any data, for examples, if radioactive or cosmic rays decay, it causes bits in the memory to flip or variations in voltage on the motherboard. Usually bits store their original programmed value in the form of an electrical charge. This type of circumstances or interference can change the charge of the memory bit, which results in an error.

For financial organizations or data centers where data corruption, errors, and/or system failure cannot be tolerated, ECC memory is the ideal choice of memory.

Data is transmitted and received in the form of a data stream or binary code, which is a set of bits either 0 or 1. For example, 10110001 is the binary code for moving between memory and CPU. The ECC memory adds an extra bit at the end of this binary code, which is known as a parity bit. Now the modified binary code will look like this: 101100010. This additional bit will be used to identify errors in the binary code.

Parity vs Non Parity

If the sum of all the 1's in a stream of binary code is an even number (excluding the parity bit), then the stream of binary code is called even parity. Error-free code always has even parity.

Memory chips that do not add a ninth bit in a data stream for parity checking is referred to as non-parity memory. The term also refers to the memory that does not use Error-Correcting Code (ECC).

Exam Note

Follow the RAM speed and compatibility guidelines. Faster memory can be added to a PC with slower memory installed, but the system will run only at the speed of the slowest module present. RAM types cannot be mixed.

Mind Map of RAM Types

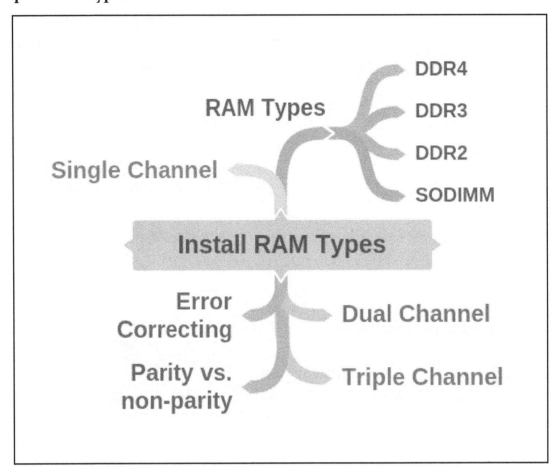

Figure 3-53: Mind Map of RAM Types

Select, Install, and Configure Storage Devices

Optical Drives

An optical drive or optical disc drive is a drive that is used to accept, read, and write data to Compact Discs (CDs), Digital Versatile Discs (DVDs), or Blu-ray discs.

These drives are backward compatible with previous disc formats: DVD drives can accept and read CDs, whereas Blu-ray drives can accept and read all three types of disc, CDs, DVDs, and Blu-rays. There is a difference in the terminology, which differs between optical and magnetic media. In magnetic media, the spelling of a "disk" ends with a "k" and in optical media the spelling of a "disc" ends with a "c".

The standard CD, DVD, or Blu-ray disc is about 4.75 inches or 12 cm in diameter, but there are also mini-discs that are about 3.125 inches or 8 cm in diameter. The surface of the disc is smooth and shiny with one colored or labeled side and one plain side but in the case of double-sided discs, both

sides are equally shiny. The music, video, or data is stored on the disc using microscopic raised and depressed areas called pits and lands, respectively, which are shielded by a protective transparent layer. Pits and lands are used to represent binary 1 and 0. A light sensor and a laser beam are used to read the data from the disc. Optical storage is portable, but you can access data much faster from a hard drive than from an optical disc and the capacity of the optical disc is generally much smaller than commonly available hard drives. This section deals with some of the different types of optical discs.

CD Drives

Compact Disc drives (CD drives) are known to be the first generation of optical drives. Initially, they came as music CDs and people used them for listening to music, but later they were used to store digital data as well. CDs can hold up to 80 minutes of audio and up to 700 MB of data.

CD-ROM vs CR-R/CR-RW

Discs with music or software are called Compact Disc–Read-Only Memory (CD-ROM) discs, which means that they are only readable and you cannot write or modify the content. Data can be writeable on two types of blank CD drive:

CD-R (recordable), where you can write data only once and then the CD becomes read-only.

CD-RW (rewriteable), where you can write and change data multiple times.

The speed ratings of a CD drive are expressed as an "x factor". Initially, CD drives transferred (read) data at a speed of 150 KBps, a speed now called 1x. The ratings of speed have now improved up to 10,800 KBps, which is approximately 72x faster than the speed of the first CD drives.

DVD Drives

Digital Video Discs (DVDs), now known as Digital Versatile Discs (DVDs), were initially introduced for storing and displaying video recordings, but now they are widely used for all types of data storage.

The speed ratings of a DVD drive are similar to those of CD drives, but the rotational speed of a 1x DVD drive is three times that of a 1x CD drive, so a 1x DVD drive provides a data transfer rate 9x faster than a CD drive.

However, there is a general rule for speed ratings on DVD drives; reads are the fastest, writes may be slower than reads, and rewrites are the slowest of all. DVD discs are of the same physical size and shape as CD discs but they have higher storage capacity and various other differences.

DVD ROM discs are read only discs that are used to distribute movies, computer applications, and software. You cannot change or modify the content of a DVD ROM. It has a maximum capacity of 15.9 GB of data.

SS DVD vs DS DVD

CDs store data on just one side of the disc, whereas DVDs come in two types: a conventional single-sided DVD (SS DVD) that stores data on one side and a dual-sided DVD (DS DVD) that stores data on both sides, but you have to turn the DVD over to read the second side.

Further, there are formats on each side of the DVD that may be either Single Layer (SL) or Dual Layer (DL), referred to as DVD SL or DVD DL, respectively. The SL format is the same as the CD format, which means there is only a single layer of pits, and the DL format has two pitted layers on both sides of the disc, with a different reflexive index at each layer.

The table given below, provides a comparison between the different types of DVDs:

Types	Sides	Layers	Capacity
SS DVD SL	Single	Single	4.7 GB of data
SS DVD DL	Single	Dual	8.54 GB of data
DS DVD SL	Double	Single	9.4 GB of data
DS DVD DL	Double	Dual	17.08 GB of data

Table 3-11: Comparison between SSD DVD and DS DVD

DVD-RW vs DVD-RW DL

Several standards for recordable DVD media come with "minus" (–) or "plus" (+). The DVD standards with a minus sign, DVD-R and DVD-RW, are an older standard than those with the plus and they are only compatible with old players. DVD-R and DVD+R media write data much like CD-Rs. Whereas, DVD-RW, DVD+RW, and DVD-RAM write and rewrite data much like CD-RWs.

The formats on each side of a DVD may be either Single Layer (SL) or Dual Layer (DL), known respectively as DVD-RW SL and DVD-RW DL. The SL format is the same as the CD format, which means that there is only a single layer of pits while the DL format has two pitted layers on both sides of the disc, with a different reflexive index at each layer.

Blu-ray

Blu-ray Disc (BD) technology is an enhancement of the storage capacity of DVD technology. It was developed by a consortium of electronics companies. BD drives are compatible with BD-ROM (read-only Blu-ray media), such as the media used for Blu-ray movies. To play Blu-ray movies, users must have a compatible player app installed.

There were two standards for Blu-ray: High-Definition DVD (HD-DVD) and Blu-ray Disc (BD). Standard DVD uses a red laser, whereas Blu-ray drives use a blue-violet laser to read the discs. The blue laser, combined with a special lens, provides a more focused laser and results in high density data storage.

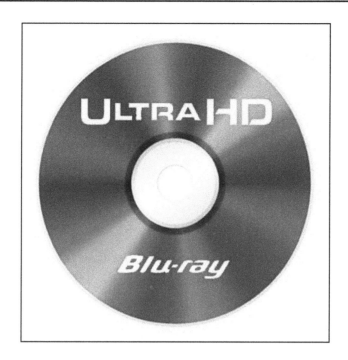

Figure 3-54: Blu-ray Disc

Blu-ray discs come in four different formats: single-, double-, triple-, and quadruple-layer versions. The following table shows the difference in different layers of Blu-ray, given below:

Types	Layers	Capacity
Blu-ray SL	Single	25 GB of data
Blu-ray DL	Dual	50 GB of data
Blu-ray TL	Triple	100 GB of data
Blu-ray QL	Quadruple	128 GB of data

Table 3-09: Comparison between Different Types of Blu-ray

Comparison between Different Data Rates of Optical Disks:

Optical Disk	Layers	Size of Data it Stores
CD	Single layer	700 MB
DVD	Single layer	4.7 GB per side
DVD DL	Double layer	8.5 GB per side
Blu-ray	Single layer	25 GB per side
Blue-ray DL	Double layer	50 GB per side

Table 3-12: Comparison between Different Data Rates of Optical Disks

BD-R

Blu-ray Disc Recordable (BD-R) can write to a disc once. BD-R is recordable not erasable, similar to CD-R, DVD+R, DVD-R. It has 25 GB capacity.

BD-RE

Blu-ray Disc Recordable Erasable (BD-RE) can be erased and re-recorded multiple times. BD-RE is recordable and rewritable; similar to CD-RW, DVD-RW, DVD+RW. It has 25 GB capacity.

Solid-State Drives

An SSD is a flash memory drive with no moving parts. Because the drive does not spin to retrieve data, it is much faster than a magnetic hard drive for storing and retrieving data. SSD is currently more expensive with less capacity than HDD, but SSD capacity is improving and costs are dropping.

The memory in most solid-state storage devices is actually a type of Electrically Erasable Programmable Read-Only Memory (EEPROM) but here, the data is written in blocks rather than bytes.

There are even smaller SSDs available for mobile devices. The Embedded Multimedia Controller (e-MMC) is a smaller SSD for embedded applications such as smartphones, tablets, digital cameras, and navigational systems. The e-MMC unit contains flash memory and an integrated controller on the same silicon die inside a Ball Grid Array (BGA) package.

M2 Drives

An M.2 drive is a form factor for Solid-State Drives. They are usually 80 x 22 mm in size. A typical SSD has a 2.5-inch form factor, but an optional 2.5-inch to 3.5-inch adapter allows it to be installed in desktop computers that lack 2.5-inch drive bays. While SSDs placed in drive bays are faster, they still connect via the hard drive cables to the motherboard.

The specification or form factor is also known as the Next-Generation Form Factor (NGFF). They are specially designed to allow high-performance storage in small, thin, and power-constrained devices, such as tablet and ultrabook computers. They are smaller than mSATA SSDs. The M.2 form factor can support applications such as Universal Serial Bus (USB), Wi-Fi, PCI Express (PCIe), and Serial ATA (SATA).

NVME

A Non Volatile Memory Express (NVME) connection allows a solid-state drive to read data directly from a PCI-E slot on the motherboard. It draws power through the motherboard and draws data from the motherboard at a much faster rate than SATA 3.

NVME is an open standard and it allows SSDs to read and write memory at the speed of flash memory. It fetches data directly through the PCIe interface rather than using SATA and is slower by SATA speeds. NVME drives are available in both M.2 or PCIe card form factors. With both form factors, the components are electrically connected to the PC through PCIe rather than SATA.

SATA 2.5

SATA 2.5 refers to an HDD with 2.5-inch form factor. These are usually found in laptops, and larger 3.5-inch HDDs are found in desktops. The 2.5 inches refers to the size of the spinning platters inside the HDDs. They are linked to the motherboard with a SATA cable.

Standard	Transfer Speed
SATA 1.0	150 MBps
SATA 2.0	300 MBps
SATA 3.0	600 MBps
SATA 3.2	1,969 MBps
eSATA	6 GBps

Table 3-13: Comparison between Different Versions of SATA

Magnetic Hard Drives

A magnetic hard drive is made up of a metal or magnetic disk that is coated with carbon metal oxide. It has an actuator arm along with an electromagnetic head, which is used to magnetize sections of the disk surface, resulting in reading and writing data onto the magnetic disk. Each disk contains an actuator and one spindle, which can hold several magnetic platters. One drive consists of multiple platters and surfaces, and they collectively store data on the drive. The disk rotates and operates at different speeds, which corresponds to the efficiency and performance of the magnetic drive.

The surface area of the magnetic disk is divided into blocks, made up of segments and sectors:

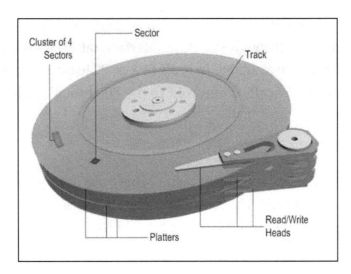

Figure 3-55: Magnetic Hard Drive with Basic Components

The rotational speed refers to how fast data can be accessed. For faster data access, users need higher speed. If the nature of the task does not really require high speeds, then go for 5400 RPM because high speed involves a cost factor. Drives with the higher RPMs access data faster but are costlier. However, lower RPMs introduce latency. Latency can be defined as the delay in time before a particular sector can be read. So, revolutions can be defined as how long it takes for the platter to revolve around for the read/write head to fetch the actual data and it is directly proportional to the rotational speed.

Hence, for a 7200 RPM drive, latency is about 4.2 milliseconds. But for a faster drive that runs at 10,000 or 15,000 RPMs, latency will be reduced up to 3 milliseconds.

Followings are the standard RPMs of magnetic disks:

- 5,400 rpm
- 7,200 rpm
- 10,000 rpm
- 15,000 rpm

5,400 rpm

The faster the revolution or rotation of the disk, the less the delay. A drive operating at 5,400 rpms will cause a latency of about 5.5 ms.

7,200 rpm

A typical 7,200 rpm hard drive provides a data transfer rate of up to 1,030 Mbps. Drives operating at 7,200 rpm can cause delay or latency of about 4.16 ms.

10,000 rpm

The disk rotating at 10,000 rpm reduces the delay or latency to about 3 ms. It also increases data transfer rates.

15,000 rpm

Drives operating at 15,000 rpm are higher-end drives and reduce latency to about only 2 ms. But these drives generate more heat and require more cooling components. They also provide faster data transfer rates for the same density.

Spin Rate	Typical Use	Desktop Drive Example	Laptop Drive Example
5400	"Green" power-saving drives	WD Blue Seagate 4TB Desktop HDD*	WD Blue Seagate Laptop HDD
7200	Midrange performance	WD Black Seagate Barracuda	WD Black Seagate Laptop Thin
10000	High Performance	WD VelociRatop	-
1500	Servers and enterprise	Servers	-

Table 3-14: Hard Disk Spin Rate Comparison

Sizes

Usually laptops use 2.5-inch hard drives or the 3.5-inch hard drives that are also used in desktop PCs. Small laptops use 1.8-inch hard disk drives.

2.5-inch hard disks are smaller in size compared to 3.5-inch hardware but they have less capacity and cache for storing data so they operate at low speed. The 1.8-inch drive is the smallest of all; it contains the least capacity and cache for data storage.

Hybrid Drives

A hybrid disk drive or solid-state hybrid drive (SSHD) is a blend of Hard Disk Drive (HDD) and Solid-State Drive (SDD). This ultimate solution provides users with improved storage performance and greater capacity at a low cost. It uses SDD to improve performance and speed and it uses HDD to improve the storage capacity and reliability of the disk drive.

SSHD uses adaptive memory technology. It stores frequently used data in NAND flash memory, which allows quick and easy access to required files.

SSDs were designed to replace HDDs in desktop and laptop PCs and they come in a range of form factors. Because SSDs are much costlier than HDD, manufacturers came up with a hybrid drive that

gives the advantages of SDD but costs less. A hybrid drive functions and looks like a normal HDD but it is comparatively faster and has some non-volatile memory, as does an SDD, where it stores the most frequently used data.

Flash Drives

Flash memory is memory that can retain its content, without electricity. It has no moving parts, so it is very durable. A flash drive, also called a thumb drive, jump drive, or USB drive, is a type of external SSD that is highly portable and inexpensive. Flash drives come in various sizes and capacities and can store up to hundreds of gigabytes of data. When a flash drive is plugged into a computer, it functions as a regular drive with a drive letter assigned to it.

Flash memory cards are widely used in various devices, such as smart phones, digital cameras, and navigation devices.

Solid-state memory is also used on tiny wafers of plastic called memory cards, which can be attached to and removed from the system with a reading device or card reader.

SD Cards

SD cards are technically the same device type as a USB flash drive. They are solid-state, use NAND memory, and have the same benefits and disadvantages as a USB flash drive. Secure Digital (SD) cards are small, high capacity, and high-speed data transfer SSD cards. They are widely used in portable devices such as digital cameras, digital video recorders, handheld computers, cell phones, and audio players.

SD cards are available in various capacities and come in three major form factors. The standard and most common form factor measures about 32 mm × 24 mm × 2.1 mm, the mini form factor measures about 21.5 mm × 20 mm × 1.4 mm, and the micro form factor measures about 15 mm × 11 mm × 1.0 mm in size.

Compact Flash

CompactFlash (CF) is a small sized removable mass storage device that is based on flash memory technology. This type of storage does not require power or battery to retain data.

CompactFlash (CF) was first introduced in 1994 and was one of the very earliest forms of SSD, but it is still popular today and its updated variations can still be found. CF is standardized with the CompactFlash Association.

Micro-SD Card

SD cards are available in various capacities. The microSD form factor measures about 15 mm × 11 mm.

Mini-SD Card

The miniSD form factor measures about 21.5 mm × 20 mm.

The xD-Picture Card

The xD-Picture Card is a flash memory card that was used in limited electronic devices, including digital cameras. Olympus and Fujifilm used xD-Picture Cards in digital cameras but they are no longer used in modern cameras. The original version had a data storage capacity of up to 512 MB and in advanced versions it went up to 2 GB.

The xD-Picture Card is smaller than the standard SD card, but bigger than miniSD and microSD form factors.

Memory Stick

The Memory Stick (MS) is a flash memory card introduced by Sony. It is roughly 5/8" × 1 3/4" in its original form factor with a data storage capacity of 4 MB and 128 MB. The Memory Stick Pro (MSP) followed it, with a data storage capacity of about 1 GB. Later came the smaller Memory Stick Duo (MSD), with a data storage capacity of about 128 MB. The advanced Memory Stick PRO DUO (MSPD) came with a data storage capacity of about 16 GB maximum, which was then followed by a version with a data capacity of about 32 GB maximum. Sony, in collaboration with Sandisk, came up with a more improved Memory Stick PRO Format for Extended High Capacity with a data capacity of 2 TB.

The following table compares the form factors of different memory cards:

Memory card	Abbreviation	Form Factor
Secure Digital card	SD	32 × 24 × 2.1 mm
mini-SD card	miniSD	21.5 × 20 × 1.4 mm
micro-SD card	microSD	15 × 11 × 1.0 mm
xD-Picture Card	xD	20 × 25 × 1.7 mm
XQD card	XQD	38.5 × 29.8 × 3.8 mm
Memory Stick	MS	50.0 × 21.5 × 2.8 mm

Table 3-15: Form Factors of Different Memory Cards

Configurations

RAID Arrays

Redundant Array of Independent Disks (RAIDs) or Redundant Array of Inexpensive Disks are sets of schemes specially designed to use multiple hard drives to store the same data at different locations (on different hard disks or storage devices) to provide better performance and fault-tolerant protection for data. RAID usually uses special hardware, known as a RAID controller, to achieve this, but it can also be achieved using special software. However, when using any of the RAID schemes, it is always necessary to configure multiple drives to work together. The set of disks is collectively known as a RAID array. The drives in the same set should be of equal size. The RAID scheme is identified by the word "RAID" followed by a number.

In RAID arrays, fault tolerance is the ability to prevent data from failing. This can be achieved by either using data redundancy or a special algorithm. Following are the different types of RAID schemes:

RAID 0

RAID 0, also known as disk striping, involves the process of dividing the data body into chunks or blocks and then distributing that data blocks across multiple storage devices in a RAID group. This improves the read and write speeds of the drive. Data is striped across various disks in an effort to improve efficiency.

RAID 0 distributes the striped data without parity. The data distributed among different drives is known as a stripe. A data slice or chunk or the data of an individual drive is referred to as a striped unit.

The operating system treats the separate drives in an array as a single hard drive, and when the data is to be written to the drive array, the RAID controller writes a portion of the data to the individual drive in the drive array. RAID 0 uses the total disk space for data storage in an array, but it does not provide any fault-tolerant protection of data in the event of drive failure. If any one of the drives in an array fails, all data will be lost.

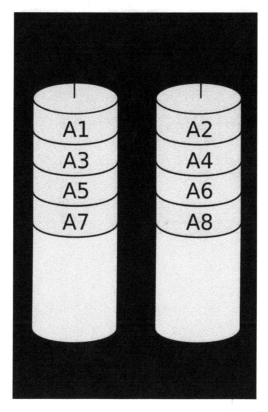

Figure 3-56: RAID 0 Array

RAID 1

RAID 1, also known as mirroring, writes data to the two drives simultaneously and provides fault tolerance through a mirrored set of data. If one of the two drives fails, the data is saved as it is also stored on the mirrored drive or surviving drive. RAID 1 improves the speed of reading data.

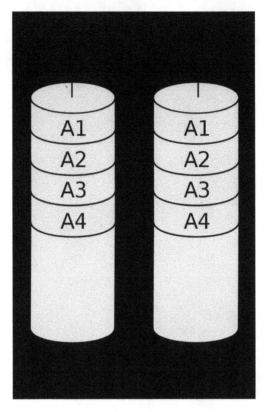

Figure 3-57: RAID 1 Array

RAID 5

RAID 5 is also known as striping with interleaved parity or striping with distributed parity. This configuration uses disk striping with parity. Data and parity are evenly striped among all the disks. Striping also allows users to reconstruct data in case of disk failure. It uses an algorithm to provide fault tolerance rather than data redundancy. It is considered one of the most commonly used RAID schemes as it allows more usable storage than RAID 1 AND 10, and it balances the read and write speeds.

One drawback of RAID 5 is that the speed of the reads from the striped set is slower because of the need to run the algorithm first.

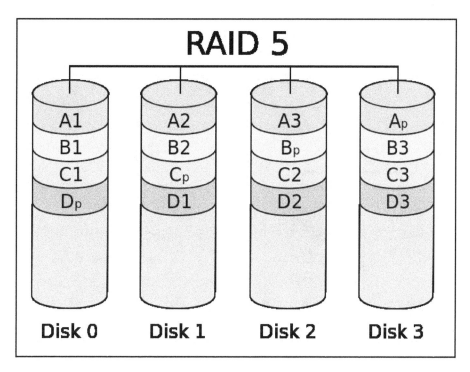

Figure 3-58: RAID 5 Array

RAID 10

RAID 10 configuration combines disk striping and disk mirroring to ensure data protection. It requires a minimum of four storage disks and stripes data among the mirrored pairs. Data is saved and can be retrieved as long as one disk in each pair (mirrored set) is functional. If both the disks in the same mirrored set fails, all the data will be lost because there is no use of parity in the striped sets.

A RAID 10 array is a stripe of mirrors. It provides the variety of fault tolerance of a mirror (of RAID 1) and the performance of RAID 0.

RAID 1 and RAID 10 use data redundancy to provide fault tolerance, and RAID 5 uses an algorithm to provide fault tolerance.

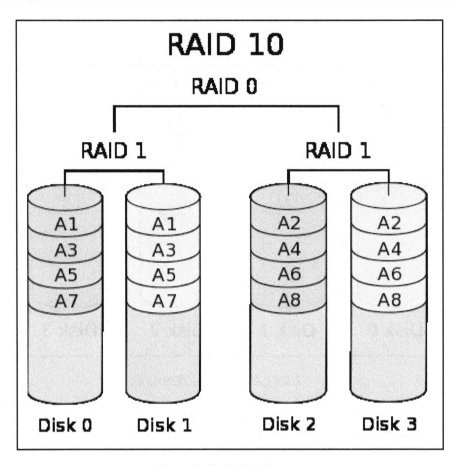

Figure 3-59: RAID 10 Array

Installing RAID Arrays

In the past, users had to install a special RAID controller adapter card to the system to get the benefits of RAID, but today many modern desktop and server motherboards come with a built-in RAID controller. Therefore, if users want to create a RAID array on a modern computer, they simply need to add the adequate number of hard drives.

The process of physically installing a RAID adapter is similar to installing any other bus adapter. After installing the adapter, install and connect each storage drive in the array, then boot the system, and then run the RAID controller setup program.

In the case of an integrated RAID controller on the motherboard, the setup program might be present on the BIOS Setup menu of the system, usually on an advanced menu. In the case of the separately installed RAID controller, look for prompts during boot up for a key to enter the RAID setup. Now, simply follow the menus from there and choose the RAID level.

Hot-swappable Drives

A hot-swappable drive, also known as a hot-pluggable drive, can be connected or disconnected to the system without turning the system off. Modern SATA and all external drive interfaces are hot-swappable.

However, that does not mean users can simply "pull the plug" of the drive anytime. In order to avoid the risk of data loss, first ensure that the disk is not currently in use before disconnecting it. Close all the applications or windows that rely on the drive, and then take the steps required by the operating system. In Windows, go to the notification area on the right side of the taskbar and then use the Safely Remove Hardware applet for safe ejection.

Disconnect External Storage Safely

To safely eject devices, users can follow these general steps to practice disconnecting a flash drive safely before ejecting it.

- Watch the notification area or system tray and look for a Safely Remove Hardware icon. It must be there if the OS is reading the flash drive
- Click the "Safely Remove Hardware" icon
- A menu will pop up. Click on the "Eject" option (which appears with the name of the flash drive, such as "Eject USB Drive" or "Eject Data Traveler")
- Wait until a message appears that prompts "It is now safe to remove the flash drive", and then eject it

---

Exam Note

Remember to securely remove USB flash drives in the operating system before physically disconnecting them. Keep in mind for the exam that most magnetic media is known as "disk" and optical media is known as "disc".

Mind Map of Installation and Configuration of Storage Devices

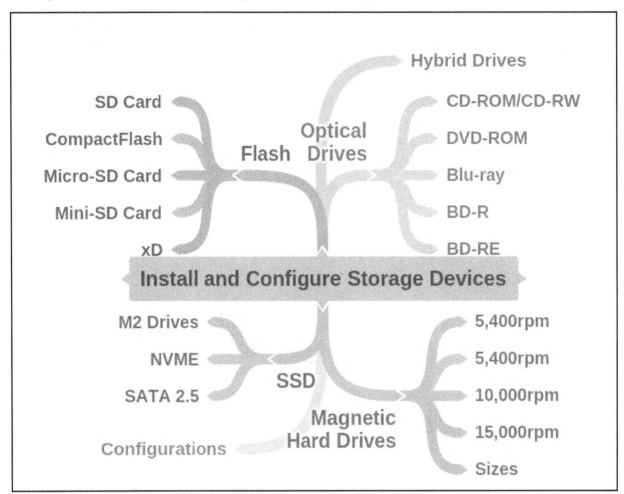

Figure 3-60 Mind Map of Installation and Configuration of Storage Devices

Install and Configure Motherboards, CPUs, and add-on Cards

This section deals with the motherboard, which is considered the fundamental block of every PC or laptop. A motherboard is basically a Printed Circuit Board (PCB) that includes electrical pathways, also known as buses, that interconnect electronic components. These components may be connected or soldered to the motherboard directly or can be added using expansion slots, sockets, and ports. Motherboards are considered the backbone of a computer. Each internal and external component of the PC links, directly or indirectly, to a single circuit, called the motherboard, which is also known as the system board, mainboard, or the planar board.

The following are some components added to the motherboard:

Central Processing Unit (CPU): At the heart of each computer is a special motherboard chip called a processor, which determines the power of the PC. The processor executes instructions, performs calculations, and coordinates input/output operations. Each motherboard has electronic chips that work with the CPU and are designed to exact specifications.

Random Access Memory (RAM): A motherboard contains special sockets or slots for the system's memory. These special sockets accept different types of RAM chips that are attached to small circuit boards called memory sticks or memory modules.

Expansion Slots: These slots provide a location for connecting additional components.

Chipset: A chipset is an integrated circuit on the motherboard. It controls how the motherboard and CPU interact with the system hardware. It also controls how much memory is to be added to a motherboard and decides the type of connectors to be connected on the motherboard.

Basic Input/Output System (BIOS) Chip and Unified Extensible Firmware Interface (UEFI) Chip: BIOS helps to boot the computer and manage the flow of data between the keyboard, hard drive, mouse, video card, and more. Now, the BIOS has advanced by UEFI. UEFI relies on BIOS for system configuration, setup, and Power-On-Self-Test (POST), but it defines a different software interface for boot and runtime.

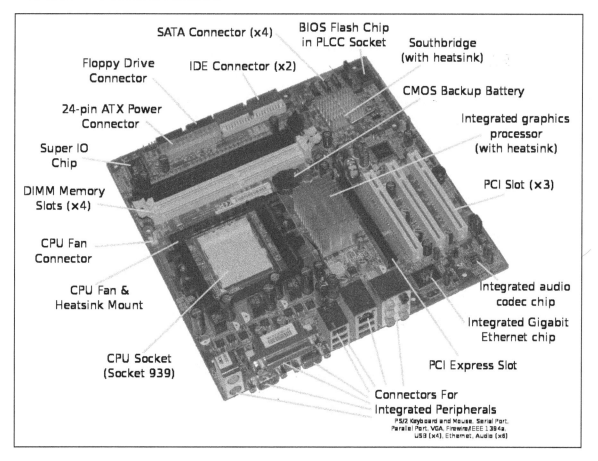

Figure 3-61: Motherboard with Add-on Components

The motherboard is made up of fiberglass, typically green or brown in color, with a meshwork of copper lines, referred to as traces. It provides pathways to the signals. Data, power, and control signals pass through all the connected components through these pathways. A group of wires with an assigned set of functions is collectively referred to a bus.

Motherboard Form Factors

A motherboard form factor refers to the size, shape, location, and type of components on the motherboard, for example, the size of the motherboard, the choice of power supply that is compatible with it, and the corresponding PC case that will adjust both the power supply and the corresponding components. There are various form factors of the motherboard, each with different components, layouts, and specifications.

Several form factors have been developed over the years, including the initial AT and NLX, ATX, and ITX form factors. These standards also have minor differences in things like their sizes, typical components, and some technology advancements. Following are some types of motherboard form factors:

ATX

The Advanced Technology eXtended (ATX) is a widely used standard for motherboards that was released by Intel Corporation and has been updated several times over the years. An ATX motherboard measures about 12" by 9.6" wide or 305 mm × 244 mm from front to back, which prevents it from interfering with the drive bays. This feature differentiates it from previous motherboards.

The first ATX motherboard accommodates integrated serial and parallel ports (I/O ports) and mini-DIN-6 (PS/2) keyboard connectors. The motherboard connects to the ATX power supply via a single 20-pin connector.

However, today's ATX motherboard includes memory slots for advanced RAM types, and supports a BIOS-controlled power management system. It supports multimedia, AMD or Intel CPU sockets, provides both SATA and PATA disk drive connectors, and supports USB and IEEE 1394, which is now referred to as FireWire.

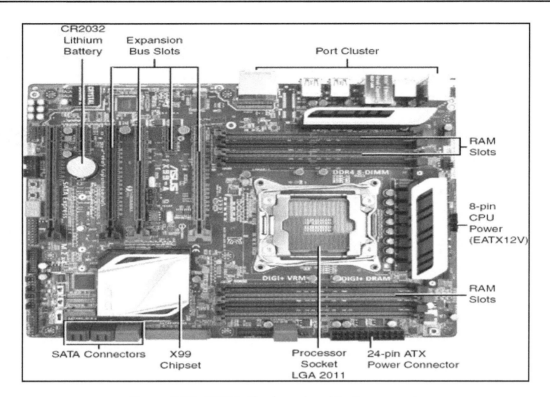

Figure 3-62: ATX Motherboard and its Components

Micro-ATX

Micro-ATX motherboards are much smaller in size than the regular ATX motherboard and have fewer expansion slots. Micro-ATX is a smaller form factor but it is backward-compatible with ATX. It uses the same shipsets (Northbridge and Southbridge) and the same power connectors as a full-size ATX board. Therefore, they can connect many of the same components. However, Micro-ATX is smaller in size; they can fit in standard ATX cases.

ITX

ITX, or EPIA, is a standard for motherboards released by the chipset-company VIA in 2001. It is smaller in size and is made to be used in low-power CPUs and cheaper chipsets. ITX is designed for very small desktop PCs for entertainment purposes, but ITX was never used in production. The ITX group includes Mini-ITX, Nano-ITX, Pico-ITX, and Mobile-ITX.

Mini ITX

Originally designed in 2001, Mini-ITX is a 6.7 × 6.7-inch (17 × 17 cm) motherboard that is slightly smaller than microATX, is screw-compatible, and can be used in microATX and ATX cases if desired. The original version used passive cooling to reduce noise and to conserve power, making it suitable for HTPCs; newer versions use active cooling due to the more powerful processors involved.

PCI is the first version of these boards to came with one expansion slot. The second version comes with a single PCIe ×16 slot. A computing device based on a Mini-ITX form factor is preferable for places where larger, therefore noisy, computers are not affordable.

Form Factors of Motherboard	Description
ATX	Most popular form factor 12 in by 9.6 in (305 mm by 244 mm) in size
Micro-ATX	Provides a smaller footprint than ATX Popular in desktop PCs and small form factor computers 9.6 in by 9.6 in (24.4 cm by 24.4 cm) in size
ITX	Comparable form factor to Micro-ATX 8.5 in by 7.5 in (21.5 cm by 19.1 cm) in size
Mini-ITX	Specially designed for thin clients and set top boxes 6.7 in by 6.7 in (17 cm by 17 cm) in size

Table 3-16: Comparison between Different Form Factors

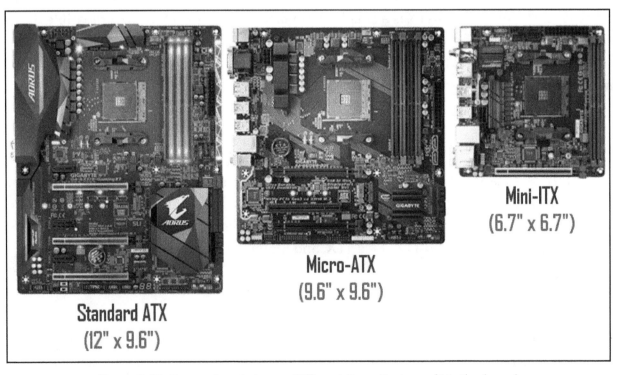

Figure 3-63: Comparison between Different Form Factors of Motherboard

NLX

New Low-Profile (NLX) or New Low-Profile extended was an Intel motherboard standard. NLX and LPX form factors had a riser board that connected to the smaller motherboard. Instead of slots into the motherboard, it used adapters go into the slots on the riser board. In order to install expansion boards, it used a riser card parallel to the motherboard.

Motherboard Connector Types

A motherboard is compatible with only certain types of memory and CPUs. This compatibility is based on the installed type of memory and processor sockets. Therefore, users must ensure that the CPU, memory, motherboard, power supply, and the case are compatible with each other.

PCI

A previously popular expansion slot is Peripheral Component Interconnect (PCI). PCI comes in four varieties: 32-bit 33 MHz, 32-bit 66 MHz, 64-bit 33 MHz, and 64-bit 66 MHz. There was also an upgrade to the PCI bus called PCI-X that was commonly found in servers.

Peripheral Component Interconnect (PCI) is an old expansion bus architecture but it can still be found on many new motherboards for backward compatibility. It is also referred to as conventional PCI to distinguish it from the modern PCIe.

The PCI uses a 32-bit or 64-bit parallel data bus for data transfer. Several variants of PCI have been developed over the years that vary the data transfer speeds and the bus width. The 32-bit bus is more popular, providing a data rate of up to 133 Mbps and running at 33.33 MHz.

Typically, PCI slots are 3 long white slots. Initially, PCI was developed for video. Advanced motherboards today only have one or two PCI slots but more PCIe slots.

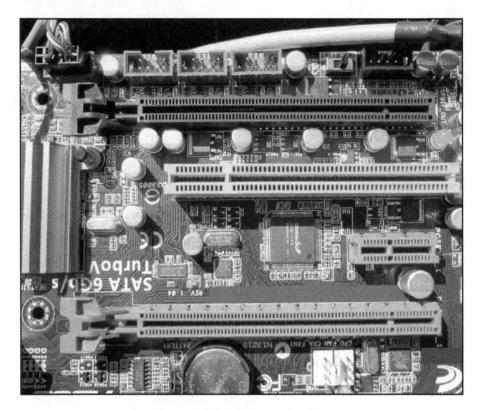

Figure 3-64: PCI Expansion Slot

Mini PCI

Mini PCI has a 32-bit data bus, the same as a conventional PCI but the Mini PCI is much smaller (both the card and the slot). Mini PCI cards are available in three form factors: Type I, Type II, and Type III. Types I and II each contain 100 pins in a stacking connector and Type III cards contain 124 pins on an edge connector.

PCIe

Peripheral Component Interconnect Express (PCIe), also referred to as PCI Express or PCI-E, is an advanced version of PCI that differs from it by using serial communications rather than parallel communications. It has different bus connectors and it is incompatible with conventional PCI adapter cards. PCIe bus is a group of serial channels. The PCIe connector label refers to the number of serial channels in a PCIe bus, where x1, x4, and x16 defines 1, 4, and 16 channels, respectively.

The following table shows the different PCIe connectors with thier channels and length:

PCIe Connector	Channels	Size
PCIe x1	1	1 ½ inches long
PCIe x4	4	2 inches long
PCIe x16	16	Approx. 4 inches long

Table 3-17: Comparison between Different PCIe Connectors

There are different versions of PCIe and the data transfer rate depends on which version of PCIe standard the bus installation supports.

PCIe Version	Channels	Data Transfer Rate
PCIe 1.0	16	250 MBps per channel or total of 4 GBps
PCIe 2.0	16	500 MBps per channel or 8 GBps
PCIe 3.0	16	1 GBps per channel or total of 12 GBps

Table 3-18: Comparison between Different Versions of PCIe

Mini PCI Express

Mini PCI Express, also known as PCI Express Mini Card, Mini PCI Express, Mini PCIe, or simply MiniCard, has replaced Mini PCI sockets in advanced laptops. This standard increases the throughput with a 64-bit data bus. It is 30 mm × 26.8 mm in size, which is much smaller than a Mini PCI card, and it contains a 52-pin edge connector.

Riser Cards

The riser card or riser board is an integrated circuit board that provides more slots for expansion cards in a motherboard. Riser cards are used in low profile or slim cases. Like motherboards, the riser card has expansion slots. This board is mounted in a special slot on a motherboard, and then the expansion cards are inserted in the riser card. Now the expansion cards are able to work parallel to the motherboard, allowing a smaller case size. The use of a riser card enables the use of more cards than the standard motherboard.

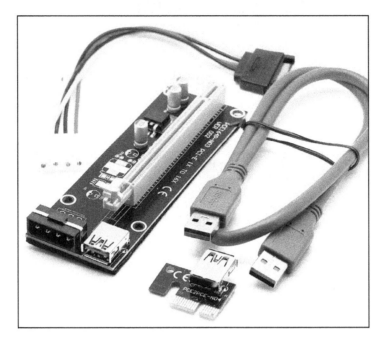

Figure 3-65: Riser Card

CPU Socket Types

CPU sockets connect the motherboard to the CPU. Almost every motherboard has at least one CPU socket, but the location varies from one motherboard standard to another. Older CPUs were installed by pressing the processor into the socket and it was retained in place by friction. Modern CPU sockets have a bracket or arm that raises up to accept the processor, which can easily be dropped in, and then lowers to hold the CPU in place. This socket is called a Zero Insertion Force (ZIF) socket.

PGA vs LGA

Pin Grid Array (PGA) sockets make use of ceramic or metallic pins to connect a processor to the motherboard. The underside of the processor's chip has a grid of pins that insert into the corresponding slots or holes on the motherboard. The packaging of a PGA CPU has varied for many years. One advancement of PGA is Pin Grid Array 2 (PGA2), which was used with Intel Pentium processors, followed later by the Staggered Pin Grid Array (SPGA), in which the pin rows are staggered to permit for a higher pin density than PGA.

Figure 3-66: LGA vs PGA

Intel later moved to the Land Grid Array (LGA) socket. An LGA CPU contains pads rather than pins although, pins continue to be used on motherboards. The pads on the processor contact with the pins in the socket on the motherboard and allow a higher density compared to PGA. In both PGA and LGA processors, the number that follows the word socket corresponds to the number of pins or pads in the array.

The following table shows the different types of Intel CPU sockets with the corresponding number of pins:

Socket	Number of Pins	Year Introduced
Socket T/775	775	2004
Socket B/1366	1366	2008
Socket H/1156	1156	2009
Socket H2/1155	1155	2011
Socket R/2011	2011	2011
Socket H3/1150	1150	2011

Table 3-19: Different Intel Processor Sockets with the Number of Pins

AMD manufacturers used LGA sockets. The following table shows the different types of AMD LGA sockets, with the corresponding number of pins:

Socket	Socket Type	Number of Pins	Year Introduced
AM3/940 OR 941	PGA	940 OR 941	2009
AM3+/942	PGA	942	2011
FM1/905	PGA	905	2011
FM2/904	PGA	904	2012
FM2+/906	PGA	906	2014

Table 3-20: Different AMD Processor Sockets with the Number of Pins

Comparison between LGA and PGA Sockets

	PGA	LGA
	Pin Grid Array	**Land Grid Array**
Durable	As the motherboard cannot be easily damaged by CPU misalignment, it is durable	Due to no fragile pins, the processors are less likely to be damaged by mishandling and drops. Here, the processor is durable
Pins	Pin Grid Array (PGA) sockets make use of ceramic or metallic pins to connect a processor to the motherboard	An LGA CPU contain pads rather than pins
Vendor	Mostly Intel	Mostly AMD

Table 3-21: Comparison between PGA and LGA

SATA

Serial ATA (SATA) is the most popular and widely used standard for connecting all internal drives such as Hard Disk Drives (HDD), Solid-State Drives (SDD), and optical drives (CD and DVD drives). Typically, a motherboard has at least four SATA connectors. SATA cables are thin and compact compared to the old ribbon cables that were bulky. SATA cables are approximately 39.4 inches long in size. Each SATA device is directly connected to the SATA controller, so it does not have to share

a bus with the data of other devices, resulting in greater throughput. Unlike PATA, SATA also allows hot swapping.

Figure 3-67: LGA vs PGA

eSATA

External SATA (eSATA) cables allow for external drives to be mounted at the same data rate. To protect the cable and the data, eSATA has better shielding. eSATA cables have a different connecter, to prevent the use of thinner SATA cables from being used outside the case.

eSATA can transfer information at 600 MB/s. Devices can connect at a maximum of approximately 6.6 feet (2 m). If the internal hard drive is damaged, an external drive linked to an eSATA or USB port can be used to boot and troubleshoot the system.

IDE

Integrated Drive Electronics (IDE) is popularly known as Advanced Technology Attachment (ATA) or parallel ATA (PATA). It is a standard electronic interface for IBM for connecting motherboards with hard drives and CD or DVD drives. IDE allows the drive to connect directly to the motherboard or controller. IDE and its advanced successor enhanced IDE (EIDE) are common drive interfaces.

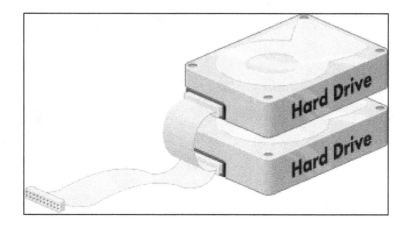

Figure 3-68: IDE Cable

Front Panel Connector

The front panel connector cables connect the motherboard to the front panel components. There are buttons on the computer's case to control the power of the motherboard and there are lights corresponding to different motherboard activities. These buttons and lights are connected to the motherboard with the cables from the front of the case.

The display of front panel contains hard disk drive activity lights, a reset button, a case speaker, a power on/off button, a key lock, and a computer power on light. They are connected to ensure that the function is running smoothly.

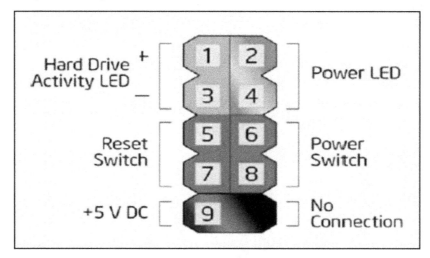

Figure 3-69: Front Panel Connector

Internal USB Connector

The Universal Serial Bus (USB) interface has made both the parallel and serial ports obsolete and become the interface of choice for PCs. It even replaced FireWire/1394 and SCSI. All the latest PCs contain at least one USB port located conveniently on the front, as well as on the back, of a desktop PC case. In laptops, these ports are located on the sides and back. Where users need more USB ports, they can attach a USB hub, a multiport connecting device for USB devices.

A USB is an external bus that connects with the PCI bus of the PC. Users can connect around 127 devices to a computer by using a USB. USB standard has several versions; the most popular are 1.0, 1.1, 2.0, and 3.0.

Figure 3-70: Different Types of USB Sockets

BIOS and UEFI Settings

A special type of chip is present on the main circuit board of almost all computing devices with some basic firmware that helps the device in booting up and communicating with the operating system and other hardware. This firmware is popularly called the Basic Input/Output System (BIOS). Traditionally, a PC's BIOS is on the motherboard and is referred to as the system BIOS. Each expansion card has its own BIOS chip that sends the device's play and plug settings to the motherboard's BIOS and to the operation system along with its regular functions.

The system BIOS is responsible for the following functions:

- Performing the Power-On Self-Test (POST)
- Performing a hardware test during startup
- Informing the processor what devices are present and how to communicate with them
- Translating the processor's request for a component into required instructions

Unified Extensible Firmware Interface (UEFI) has taken the place of traditional BIOS on newer and higher-end motherboards.

UEFI is a 32-bit or 64-bit BIOS that adds some benefits and features. The main advantages and features of UEFI are:

- It is not dependent on x86 firmware
- It supports file systems that allow booting up large drives up to 2.2 terabytes and more
- It supports 32-bit or 64-bit booting

The term BIOS or CMOS is used to indicate to both BIOS and UEFI firmware

Initially, the BIOS was placed and stored on a read-only memory (ROM) chip that was inaccessible for a user to make changes, whereas now it is found on the motherboard. To update a BIOS, replace the BIOS chip on the motherboard.

Motherboards contain another chip known as Complementary Metal-Oxide Semiconductor (CMOS). This is a special kind of Dynamic RAM (DRAM) chip that stores the exceptions to the BIOS settings. First the BIOS loads its basic settings and then the CMOS chip loads the default changes. A minimum amount of power or electricity is required by the CMOS chip to hold its data, and this power is supplied to the CMOS with a small battery on the motherboard. The utilities to the CMOS chip are known as CMOS setup or BIOS setup. CMOS chips are obsolete now and the battery and chip are no longer found on the motherboard.

Boot Options

Boot options, also known as BIOS boot order or device priority, allows users to select which media to boot: hard drive, USB, optical drive, over-the-network, and so on. This should normally be set to hard drive first. However, if users install an Operating System (OS) from removable media, they would want to configure that removable media first on the list of boot options.

Updating the Firmware

Motherboard manufacturers periodically release firmware updates for their motherboards. These updates may upgrade the performance, correct bugs in the code, and may add extra features like support for a new type of device.

The firmware update requires running a program to "flash" the BIOS or UEFI. What that really means in modern terms is updating the programming of the memory chip on the firmware-holding motherboard. Users can download a firmware update from the motherboard or PC manufacturer's website and follow the guide and utility to install it.

Therefore, when users buy a motherboard, a driver disc comes with it consisting of utilities to install specific operating systems to work with motherboard features like built-in sound, display, and networking adapters.

Firmware Settings

To access the computer's firmware settings, look carefully at the computer screen at startup. After the system hardware test, a message appears corresponding to the proper key sequence to enter the firmware setup program. Displaying "Setup" followed by a key or key sequence, typically F2, DELETE, or CTRL-ALT-ESC. This key or key combination varies among manufacturers and computers. The message displaying the key combination only appears for three to five seconds and users must use the required key combination within that allotted time.

On PCs with Windows 8 and higher, the Secure Boot feature sometimes does not prompt when the PC starts. It is enabled in the firmware settings. For such systems, there is another method of gaining access to the setup program through the Settings app.

Security Settings

Depending on the BIOS version, in the security section of firmware setup, users may have the option to configure up to three passwords: Supervisor/Admin, User/System, and Hard Disk Drive (HDD). All passwords are disabled by default.

- **Supervisor/Admin Password:** A Supervisor or Admin password controls access to the firmware-settings program itself
- **User/System Password:** The User or System password controls booting the PC
- **Hard Disk Drive Password:** In some systems, there is also a password for an HDD password, which should be given before a user can access the hard drive

BIOS Interface Configuration

Some systems come with an option that permits enabling the BIOS interface to connect to any paid service. Enabling this option involves the process of signing up for the service over the internet, where users can download additional software. Once they have enabled and subscribed to the service and connected the computer to the internet, the software installed in the operating system will contact the servers of the service and check for a theft report, as well as transmit system and GPS tracking information about the computer's location. A product name, such as Computrace or LoJack, may be attached to this service.

BIOS Security

A number of security features integrated into the BIOS of the system include BIOS passwords, drive encryption, Trusted Platform Module (TPM), and LoJack. The following section explains BIOS security features.

BIOS Passwords

Users can set a supervisor password for CMOS Setup programs, which enables CMOS settings to ask for a password in order to make any changes in the settings. A user password can also be set to restrict the PC from booting without entering the correct password.

In order to reset a forgotten password, remove or replace the CMOS battery to reset everything or use a Reset Jumper on the motherboard.

Drive Encryption

Newer versions of Windows make use of a certificate stored in the UEFI that verifies the boot loader for authenticity, that is, checking it has been digitally signed by Microsoft. If the hard drive's boot loader is not authentic, then the computer will not boot to that hard drive.

Drive encryption is one of the most popular ways of protecting our data with full-disk encryption. Here, every single bit of data will be encrypted on a storage device. The downside of drive encryption is that it is complicated to work out how to boot an operating system that is already encrypted.

This encryption can also be done by using software. In some Windows editions, this software is called Windows BitLocker. This provides full-disk encryption when you are using Windows. It integrates with the Trusted Platform Module (TPM) the part of the BIOS that provides hardware cryptographic functionality.

TPM

Replacing and formatting the existing hard drive is not enough for proper security. It is better to take advantage of the built-in Trusted Platform Module (TPM), an embedded security chip that stores encrypted keys, passwords, and digital certificates. Different services can use the TPM chip, without cost. When you use the TPM with a BIOS-level Administrator password and a User password required at power-on, the system becomes virtually useless to a thief.

In some devices there is a TPM chip on the motherboard. The chip contains the keys to unlock the drive. When the system boots, the TPM chip compares hashes of the drive with previously taken snapshots of the drive and only unlocks the drive if the results are satisfactory. If any changes or tampering of the Windows installation is found, the TPM chip will not unlock the drive.

Real-world Scenario

Background

The Trusted Platform Module (TPM) is an international standard for a cryptoprocessor that comes with many of today's motherboards. When customers encrypt their Windows computers, the keys are placed in the TPM, which the OS does not have direct access to so no Windows malware can extract them. Only BIOS/UEFI can access the TPM.

Challenges

Infineon Technology, a German semiconductor firm, announced that its TPMs were generating insecure RSA keys. The primary manufacturers that seemed to have been affected by this were Lenovo, HP, and Fujitsu.

Infineon stated that a vulnerability existed in its TPM firmware that led to the creation of RSA public keys for non-secure applications. This implied that all software programs that may have used those TPM RSA keys were now vulnerable to attack.

Solution

Users need to update the latest Infineon firmware or get the latest Windows patches. In the latest Windows patch bundle, updated firmware has already been released, but users will need to regenerate their keys in UEFI settings to substitute the insecure keys with secure ones. Users will need to manually clear their old TPM keys in BIOS/UEFI after updating the firmware.

Conclusion

TPMs can also store biometric and other authentication information that cannot be stolen by remote hackers or even through physical attacks (someone stealing the laptop and extracting the keys), although this may require additional anti-tampering enhancements from device manufacturers.

LoJack

LoJack is a solution introduced by Absolute Software that enables users to remotely locate, lock, and delete data on a device in the event it is stolen. LoJack is a small piece of software embedded on the computer and is very difficult to detect. It not only protects data from being misused but it also gathers forensic data that can help to locate the device and aid its recovery.

Secure Boot

Secure Boot prevents malware that tries to replace the Windows boot loader, such as rootkit, from entering or modifying the system. It also prevents an unauthorized OSS from loading during the original system boot. The Secure Boot feature can be enabled or disabled in firmware setup, but this depends upon the operation system's version, which should be Windows 8 or later. By default, Secure Boot is enabled on computers where it is available.

The Secure Boot feature may be modified or controlled from the Security section or the Boot section in the firmware setup, depending on the firmware make and version.

CMOS Battery

Like a PC, earlier laptops have a small battery on the motherboard that supplies power to the CMOS chip that holds the system's BIOS settings. Advanced models use flash memory rather than CMOS. If there is a CMOS battery failure, for example, losing time and date when the computer is off or when not connected to main battery power, then users need to replace the CMOS chip or battery. Find out the location and type of battery used in the laptop and refer to the manufacturer's documentation to ensure that the correct steps are taken to open the laptop and replace the CMOS battery. A CMOS battery will work properly for about three years before it needs to be replaced.

Figure 3-71: CMOS Battery

Mind Map of Installing and Configuring Motherboards, CPUs, and add-on Cards

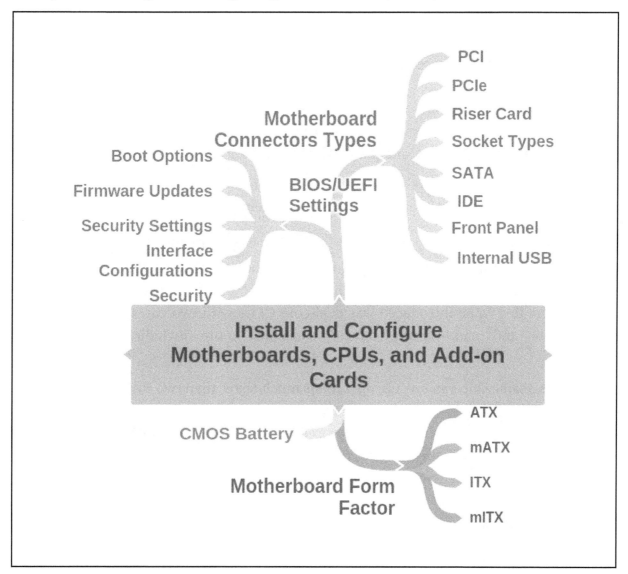

Figure 3-72: Mind Map of Installing and Configuring Motherboards

CPU Technology and Features

A CPU employs a number of technologies based on standards and proprietary designs, which are constantly evolving. This section deals with the introduction of common CPU technologies and their features.

Architecture

A CPU supports a particular size, which is the size of the permitted chunk of data that can enter and exit the processing unit during operation. This is also called the architecture of the chip and is either 32 bits or 64 bits on modern PC CPUs. The architecture is important because it determines

which operating system version the PC can support. Users are limited to the 32-bit Windows version on a 32-bit CPU, which supports up to 4 GB of RAM. A 64-bit CPU is capable of handling either 64-bit or 32-bit Windows.

Single Core

The core of a processor is a processing unit that reads specific actions to perform in instructions. Single, dual, quad, and octa cores corresponds to 1, 2, 4, and 8 cores, respectively. A single core processor performs the complete instruction cycle of all instructions, consisting of executing, fetching, decoding, accessing memory, and writing back. Multicore processors are designed to simultaneously perform multi-task and parallel processing.

Single core CPUs can only be found on low-power solutions, but the minimum processor seems to be 2 cores, one for the task and one for the operating system.

Multicore

In recent years, the most prominent change in CPUs has been the introduction of multicore CPUs on the same integrated circuit. In essence, each core is a CPU with its own set of control units, ALUs, and records. The first to be introduced was dual-core CPUs with two cores. Quad-core CPUs are widely available, and manufacturers offer 6 cores and more, including 128-core superchip processors.

Two cores on the same chip can execute operations much faster than two single-core processors. In true parallel execution, a dual-core CPU can process two threads simultaneously, and each core has its own L1 cache; three-core CPUs can process three threads simultaneously, and so on. Manufacturers have made other changes to the CPU architecture as well as using multiple cores to make them faster and more energy saving.

Virtualization Support

Most modern CPUs include support for virtualization, i.e., the processor is capable of managing multiple operating systems running simultaneously via BIOS-enabled virtual machines. Virtualization Technology (VT) is the name of the technology group involved in Intel CPUs. AMD's technology for virtualization is AMD-V.

Hyperthreading

Hyperthreading enables a single processor to manage two separate sets of instructions simultaneously. To the operating system, hyperthreading makes the system appear as if it has several processors. Intel argues that this can lead to a 30% increase in efficiency, but studies have shown that the increase is application dependent.

Hyperthreading, also called Simultaneous Multi-Threading (SMT), is a CPU technology that allows two or more threads to run simultaneously within a single execution core. This is considered to be

partially execution in parallel. Intel introduced Pentium 4 Xeon CPU hyperthreading, which is referred to as Hyperthreading Technology (HT Technology).

Real-world Scenario

Background

Hyperthreading is Intel's implementation of Simultaneous Multi-Threading (SMT), a technique used to divide a single physical processor core into two virtual cores known as hardware threads. Hyperthreading reduces the amount of time required to perform parallel computing tasks in which a large number of calculations or executions are performed at the same time. The performance boost is the result of two logical processor cores sharing the hardware of a single physical processor. The added logical cores make it simpler to divide large tasks into smaller ones that can be accomplished faster.

Challenge

A team of security researchers found serious side-channel vulnerability in Intel CPUs that could enable an attacker to sniff out sensitive protected information, like passwords and cryptographic keys, from other processes operating in the same CPU core simultaneously with the multi-threading feature enabled.

The new side-channel vulnerability lies in Intel's hyperthreading technology, the company's implementation of SMT. Since SMT operates two threads in two independent processes alongside each other in the same physical core to increase efficiency, it is possible for one process to see a surprising amount of what the other is doing. Thus, an attacker can operate a malicious PortSmash process alongside a selected victim process on the same CPU core, enabling the PortSmash code to snoop on the operations performed by the other process by measuring the exact time taken for each operation.

The vulnerability, codenamed PortSmash (CVE-2018-5407), entered the list of other dangerous side-channel vulnerabilities, including Meltdown and Spectre, TLBleed, and Foreshadow. PortSmash is the second processor attack to targets hyperthreading.

Solution

The easy fix to the vulnerability of the PortSmash is to disable SMT/hyperthreading in the CPU chips. Disabling Intel's hyperthreading helps to prevent previously disclosed Spectre-class attacks, as well as future timing attacks.

Conclusion

PortSmash presently poses a threat mainly to people using PCs or services that enable untrusted individuals to use the same physical processor. These consumers should pay

close attention to the research and carefully consider the suggestions. For the time being, the danger to others is likely low, but that could alter with more research.

Speed

A CPU's clock speed is the speed at which the instructions can potentially be executed. The speed of the CPU clock is measured in billions of cycles per second or gigahertz (GHz). CPUs of different types and models are available, with a range of clock speeds.

All other characteristics being equal, the CPU with the faster clock speed will be costlier. However, the fastest clock speed alone will not correspond to the fastest CPU. Manufacturers make use of various technologies to speed up CPUs.

Overclocking

The process of overclocking is to force a CPU or other computer component to operate at a higher clock rate than they are supposed to. This can be done by increasing the motherboard's clock speed. A CPU has no speed of its own, so users can vary the speed of the CPU according to requirements; it only has a maximum speed for which it is rated. The actual measurement of the PC's operation depends on the system clock of the motherboard. Gamers and PC hobbyists often overclock their CPUs, chipsets, video cards, and RAM. The disadvantage of overclocking is that it generates more heat and can damage the motherboard, CPU, and other chips, which can explode and/or burst into flames.

Integrated GPU

Computer users who want better video performance can purchase a separate video adapter with a GPU. Both Intel and AMD have a Graphics Processing Unit (GPU) inside the CPU on some of their processor models.

With an integrated GPU (iGPU), sometimes called an Integrated Graphics Processor (IGP), an external video card with a GPU is not needed, and graphical information is processed quickly, with reduced power consumption. Today's CPUs have multicore processors, and GPUs have hundreds of smaller core processors. GPUs can also be used for other reasons that are not directly linked to graphics but that increase system performance. These GPUs are sometimes referred to as General Purpose GPUs (GPGPUs).

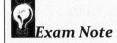
Exam Note

> Understand the differences between hyperthreading and multicore technologies. Hyperthreading allows a single-core CPU to calculate two instruction sets simultaneously, whereas multicore CPUs calculate two or more instruction sets simultaneously–one instruction set per core.

Compatibility

Intel

Intel Corporation has released a great number of CPU models, from the Intel 8086 in 1978 to the new generation of processors, which come with a diversity of model names. Years back, Intel released a variety of processors such as Pentium, Pentium II, Pentium 3, and Pentium 4 for standard usage, Celeron for economy models (cost effective with limited features), and Itanium or Xeon for high-end server models. In the modern world, Intel classifies a generation of CPUs by its microarchitecture, which is represented in the form of a code name, for example, Haswell (2013), Broadwell (2014), and Skylake. Inside a microarchitecture family, these models are classified as low-end, mid-range, and high-end models. Pentium and Celeron are classified as low-end CPUs, i3 and i5 are classified as mid-range models, and i7 and i7 Extreme are classified as high-end models.

There are various models of processor and each and every model is categorized by the purpose for which it was specifically designed, for example, for server, desktop, workstation, notebooks, or internet devices. Furthermore, Intel designed a separate category of CPUs for embedded and communication device markets.

AMDs

Advanced Micro Devices (AMDs) are one of the Intel's biggest competitor in the processor range. They have released a wide variety of products based on integrated circuits. Like Intel, they categorize their processors by design purpose, for example, server, desktop, workstation, notebook, and embedded devices. They also compete with Intel by offering each model with a variety of multicore configurations. They specify the AMD Opteron CPU brand for use in servers, whereas the AMD FX brand is for use in graphics workstations and high-end desktops.

Several AMD ranges specify different levels of laptop use. For example, A-Series CPUs with integrated GPU on laptops are dedicated for use in the home market. AMD dedicates some Athlon and Sempron CPU models to desktop computers and so on.

Cooling Mechanism

The more powerful a PC is the more heat it will generate within the case. Heat is the enemy of the PC. An overheated CPU will fail. Rather than allow heat to cause damage, several techniques are employed to maintain an optimum operating temperature, both passive and active. Some components will even slow down before any damage occurs, so they produce less heat. Manufacturers have come up with different methods for providing sufficient cooling for the whole system. These methods include heat sinks, fans, thermal compounds, and liquid cooling systems.

Case Fans

Initially PCs depended on a power supply fan to provide all the cooling for the interior of the computer. In modern PCs, the power supply fan sucks in cool air and sends the heated air out through the back. Additional methods are used today, but the power supply fan still plays an important role in keeping the PC cool. Seeing a fan mounted directly over the CPU is very common.

A power supply fan can also be supplemented by one or more case fans. In contrast to a power supply fan inside the power supply, a case fan is a fan mounted directly on the case. Systems not accompanied by a case fan may have mounting brackets to add one or more case fans.

Heat Sinks (Passive Cooling)

A heat sink is a metal block, metal bars, or metal fins that connect to the top of the processor or other parts of the motherboard. Heat from the processor is transmitted to the heat sink and then blown away by the air flow throughout the computer case.

Older CPUs use standard heat sinks to cool the system, which worked well enough because those CPUs did not produce excessive amount of heat. However, in modern systems, standard passive heat sinks cannot extract all the heat from a system; powerful fans are required to effectively expel the heat. For other chips, for example the Northbridge chip or GPU but not the CPU itself, motherboards still use passive heat sinks.

Liquid Cooling Systems

Many of the modern systems feature one or more liquid cooling system, providing sealed a liquid cooling system that transfers heat from multiple components through conduction, to active systems that use tiny cooling units. Generally, liquid cooling is more effective than standard cooling, so it is sometimes used in overclocked systems to help keep the CPU cool enough to work at a higher speed. However, it is also more expensive, more difficult to install, and in the event of a leak, it can cause serious system damage with short-circuiting.

Thermal Compounds

Thermal paste is a heat-conductive, electrically insulating paste that helps to increase heat transfer between a hot chip and a heat-dissipating fan or sink. It is also known as a heat sink compound or

thermal grease. Users apply a thin layer between components. Depending on the type, it may or may not have adhesive characteristics – it is usually called thermal adhesive when it helps to adhere.

Case Design

CPU case design allows maximum airflow over the components. An integral part of this design is the placement of vents, positioned either to pull in fresh air or expel hot air. If this airflow is altered, even by adding openings, the system may overheat. Therefore, make sure to cover all expansion slot openings on the back of a PC. The bracket of the expansion card covers every opening that matches a busy expansion slot. To preserve the correct airflow, a metal slot shield covers and protects an empty slot.

Expansion Cards

An expansion card is an electronic card or board that is used to add extra computer functionality. It is inserted into a computer's motherboard expansion slot. Expansion cards have edge connectors to establish an electronic connection between the card and the motherboard, allowing these two to communicate. There are many different categories of expansion, such as network cards, sound cards, video graphics cards, etc. All expansion cards are used to improve the quality of their specific function. For example, video graphics cards, are used to improve the quality of video.

Video Cards

Video cards are also known as graphics cards, display adapters, video adapters, video controllers or video boards. It is the most widely used expansion card and is inserted into the computer's motherboard. It is this that creates a picture on the display screen. Without a video card, users would not be able to see the graphical content on the display. The video card is basically a piece of hardware inside the computing device that handles the processing of images and video. Gamers prefer video cards to integrated graphics because integrated graphics consume extra processing power and video RAM.

Video cards can be installed in the PCI, PCIe, and AGP slots – the AGP slot is recommended. However, the newer PCIe slots supports more bandwidth. AGP is parallel and provides a wider data path, whereas PCIe is serial and provides comparatively less bandwidth. Nonetheless, modern PCIe provides a bandwidth of up to 16,000 MBps compared to AGP, which is 2,000 MBps.

Onboard

The term onboard or integrated is used to refer to hardware components located on a circuit board, for example, integrated network cards, sound cards, video cards, or WLAN. Users cannot remove these integrated or onboard components from the system as they can with expansion cards.

However, they can be enabled or disabled by using software or a CMOS setup or they can be automatically disabled when an expansion card is added to the system.

<u>Add-on card</u>

If a motherboard does not have a required integrated component, users can add an expansion card to a PCIe slot. During the planning stage, users should make sure the desired card is available and then determine the card's requirements: version of PCIe, bus width, and so on.

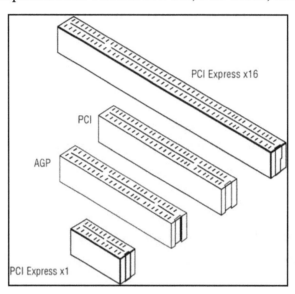

Figure 3-74: AGP and PCI slots

Sound Cards

Sound cards, also called audio adapters, are used to convert digital information from computer programs into analog sound that comes out of the speakers. This is called a Digital-to-Analog Converter (DAC). Sound cards also convert analog information into digital data for processing, for example capturing analog input from microphones and converting it into digital samples that can be stored on a PC. This is called an Analog-to-Digital Converter (ADC). Sound cards can also process digital-to-digital input and output.

Sound cards can be either internal or external. Internal sound cards require opening the case for installing the card in its slot. External sound cards can be simply plugged into a USB socket.

Network Interface Cards

Network cards, network adaptors, PC cards, or network interface cards connect the PC to a network, either wired or wireless. Generally, network interface cards (NICs) are connected to the system via an expansion slot or they might be integrated into the motherboard, but they can also be added through a PCMCIA or USB port/slot. Network interface cards are made for fiber optics, Ethernet, token ring (almost obsolete now), and 802.11 (wireless) connections. The Ethernet, fibre optics, and

token ring accept the appropriate cable along with the connector, while the wireless cards contain the antennas and radio transmitters.

Network cards perform autosensing, which means the card can sense whether the connection is capable of either half duplex or full duplex and auto negotiate with no action required.

Many systems also contain a wireless NIC, which can be either Wi-Fi or another wireless type, such as Bluetooth, cellular, or Near Field Communication (NFC).

USB Expansion Card

A USB expansion card provides additional USB ports to the system, allowing more USB devices to be connected simultaneously. They contain a controller card and operate as a USB switch, making several port connections using the same USB header. They can support up to 127 devices on a single cable. USB 1 provides speed up to 1.5 Mbps with a full speed of 12 Mbps. USB 2 transfers data at a rate of 280 Mbps and provides a full speed of 480 Mbps, and USB 3 typically transfers data at the rate of 4 Gbps with a full speed of 5 Gbps.

USB 3.1 is also under consideration, with speed rates of up to 10 Gbps, it will be backward compatible with both USB 2 and 3.

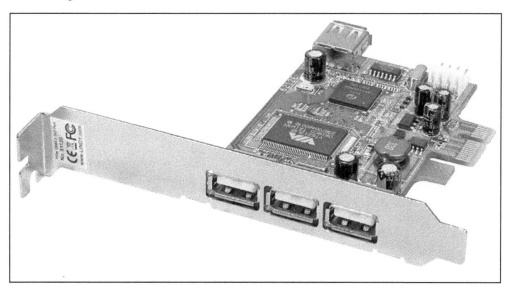

Figure 3-75: USB Expansion Card

eSATA Cards

Storage cards such as eSATA cards, which can be plugged into a slot (typically PCIe), contain storage devices. These cards are Solid-State Drives (SSDs). This is more like adding an external drive except, it is added by inserting the card in a slot inside the box rather than an actual hard drive.

The following are other ways these cards may be connected to the PC:

- (Parallel) SCSI
- Parallel ATA (IDE) interface (mostly replaced by SATA)
- USB
- Serial ATA SATA
- PCIe
- Serial-attached SCSI (generally found on servers)
- Fiber Channel (almost exclusively found on servers)

Exam Note

Compatibility is key! Find the correlation between sockets, chipsets, and CPUs by analyzing the motherboard and CPU documentation. Reapply thermal compound whenever removing and reinstalling a heat sink.

Mind Map of Installing and Configuring Motherboards, CPUs, and add-on Cards

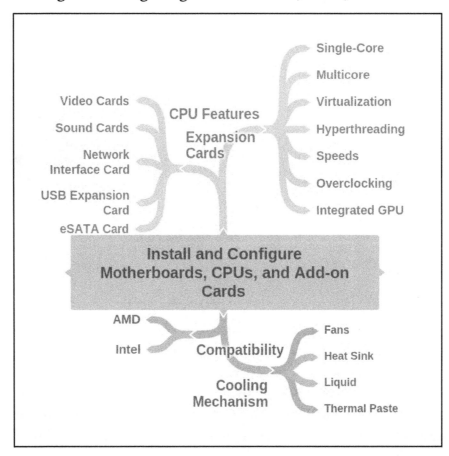

Figure 3-76: Mind Map of Installing and Configuring Motherboards

The Purposes and Uses of Various Peripheral Types

A peripheral or computer peripheral includes all the elements and devices that are externally connected to the system but are not part of the core architecture of the computer. The core elements of a computer include the central processing unit, power supply, motherboard, and the case of the computer. Technically, all other things outside the CPU's case are considered peripheral devices. Users can connect peripheral devices to the computer to expand the overall functionality of the system.

Types of Peripheral Device

Peripheral devices are mainly divided into three categories:

Input Devices: Devices used to take input, such as a mouse and a keyboard.

Output Devices: Devices used to present the output, such as a monitor and a printer.

Storage Devices: Devices used to store information, such as a hard drive or flash drive.

Some peripheral devices fall into more than one category, for example, a CD-ROM drive, which is both an input device, as users can read data or music a CD, and output device, as users can write data to a CD.

Peripheral devices can be either external or internal. Internal peripherals are also called integrated peripherals. Mostly, when people say "peripherals", they typically mean external peripherals.

This section deals with different types of input device, output device, devices that are both input and output, and some storage devices.

Printers

A printer is the hardware or machine used to convert soft copy data into a hard physical copy (on paper). A printer accepts textual and graphical data from a computer and prints that information on paper, usually to standard size sheets. Printers come in various size, speed, sophistication, and cost. Higher resolution color printers are more expensive than regular printers.

Types of Printer

PC printers can be categorized as either impact or non-impact printers.

Impact Printers

Impact printers were the old printers and their working pattern resembled an automatic typewriter, with a key leaving an inked impression (a letter) on paper for each printed character.

Dot-Matrix Printers

The dot-matrix printer is also an impact printer and is one of the popular and low-cost PC printers. It strikes or leaves an inked line at a time on the paper.

Inkjet Printers

An inkjet printer is a popular non-impact printer. It works by spraying ink from an ink cartridge at very close range as the paper rolls over the drum. An inkjet printer prints one line rather than a letter at a time.

Laser Printers

Another type of non-impact printer is a laser printer. The laser printer operates by using a beam of laser that is reflected from a mirror to attract ink (known as toner) to the selected areas of paper, as the paper rolls over a drum. It prints one third of A4 at a time, so it requires three turns to print a full sheet of A4.

LaserJet Printers

A LaserJet printer uses a toner of wax and ionized carbon, which is covered on a photosensitive drum. Static charging is used to attract toner from the drum to the paper as the paper passes over a heated roller, warming the toner. As it dries it sticks to the sheet of paper.

Scanners

Scanners are devices used to take a digitized image (soft copy) of a hard copy document. They are mostly used to store or archive documents, letters, or forms, etc. in electronic format. Document storing and archiving companies process thousands of documents, digitizing, encoding, and storing them in storage devices, on disk, or on a network.

Scanners require a TWAIN driver to be capable of converting data into a format understandable for PCs. They also require different applications to control the scanner itself.

ADF Scanner

Automatic Document Feeder (ADF) scanners pull the paper/image from the top and return it at the bottom.

ADF technology is used in scanners and copiers to feed pages into the machine. It permits multiple pages to be scanned or copied in just one go. There is no need to place each and every individual page in the scanner or copier for scanning.

Flatbed Scanners

Flatbed scanners require a user to manually place the document flat on a glass surface. This method of scanning is convenient where users have to scan a single page or few pages, but where multiple pages require scanning, ADF is preferred. Modern scanners include both an Automatic Document Feeder (ADF) and a flatbed scanning surface so that the user can choose according to the requirements.

Barcode Scanners

A barcode is a small rectangular image with a unique pattern of vertical black bars and white spaces. A bar code contains information referring to the type of use, and they can be scanned and interpreted by computer software. There is a bar code on the packaging of almost every product, and it includes the product's vendor, inventory, and pricing information.

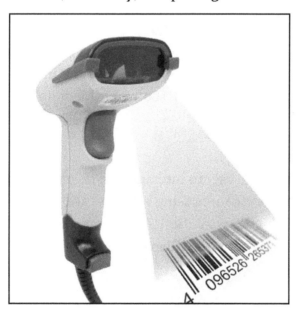

Figure 3-77: Barcode Scanner

A barcode reader is a device, or a USB device, that is used to scan barcodes. It interprets the barcode by sending serial data in the form of an ISBN. It uses a laser beam to estimate the thickness of lines and this line thickness is then translated into a code sequence. The code is then transferred to the computer application, which then stores the sequence number in a database record.

QR Readers

A Quick Response (QR) code is a kind of barcode that consists of a matrix of dots. This code can be scanned using a QR scanner or a smartphone. The process of scanning requires software to be

loaded on the device. The software translates the dots of the code into numbers or a string of characters. The diagram below shows a QR code being scanned with smartphone.

Figure 3-78: Scanning a QR Code

Almost all QR codes are square in shape and contain three square outlines in the top-left, bottom-left, and top-right corners. These square outlines correspond to the orientation of the code. The dots within the QR code contain content, format, and version information. QR codes also provide a certain level of error correction, defined as L (Low), M (Medium), or H (High).

Monitors

A monitor is a screen that allows the user to interact with the display of every processing. It displays the text, video, and graphics information using a video card inside the computer case. Monitors display information at a much higher resolution. A monitor is also known as a screen, display, video screen, video display, video display unit, or video display terminal.

Modern monitors consist of LCD (Liquid Crystal Display) or LED (Light-Emitting Diode) displays. These monitors are very thin and are known as flat-panel displays. They contain control buttons that enable users to change the setting of the monitor's display.

Earlier monitors consist of CRT (Cathode Ray Tube) displays. CRT monitors are larger and heavier and occupy more desk space.

VR Headsets

A Virtual Reality (VR) headset is apparatus worn over the head that completely covers the ears and eyes to create an immersive 3D experience of an image or video. VR headsets combine a gyroscope, accelerometer, magnetometer, and proximity sensor. They are also known as "VR goggles". These headsets are expensive and require a very robust computer to handle the animation.

Optical Drive Types

An optical drive or optical disc drive is a drive that is used to accept, read, and write data to Compact Discs (CDs), Digital Versatile Discs (DVDs), or Blu-ray discs.

The music, video, or data is stored on the disc using microscopic raised and depressed areas called pits and lands, respectively, which are shielded by a protective transparent layer. Pits and lands are used to represent binary 1 and 0. A light sensor and a laser beam are used to read the data from the disc.

Most laptops do not have optical drives, for example, CD/DVD/BD drives. When one is necessary, external optical drives are a good solution. They connect via USB and generally self-load the drivers. This option enables PCs to share drives that are not as necessary as they were just a couple of years ago and helps to keep down the weight of laptops.

Mice

A computer mouse is a wireless or wired device that moves the cursor on the display screen, enabling the user to interact with the computer. There are several features on some mice that enable for scrolling and browsing the Web. Wireless mice use Bluetooth to connect to the computer.

Windows, MacOS, and Linux include mouse drivers. To install a USB mouse, just plug it in, and install the drivers required by the operating system. Mice are part of the Human Interface Device (HID) category in Device Manager, and after the mouse is connected, Windows installs HID drivers.

To install a wireless mouse, plug the receiver into a USB port and follow the instructions to pair the mouse and receiver. Receivers that can control multiple devices, such as Logitech's Unifying receiver, might require installation of additional software to allow pairing of multiple devices with a single receiver.

Keyboards

The most common way to interact with a computer is to use a keyboard. Like a mouse, it can be wired or wireless Bluetooth. There are many types of keyboard designed for use in various environments and for use on different devices. There are keyboard drivers for Windows, macOS, and Linux. To install a USB keyboard, just plug it in and the operating system will install the drivers needed.

Keyboards require specific drivers to access additional buttons and media functionality other than the regular driver of the keyboard. Refer to the manufacturer's manual to determine which keys correspond to which symbols.

Touchpads

Touchpads (also known as trackpads) are available as externally connected devices, allowing users to experience the same interaction on a computer as is available with some laptops. They perform most of the functions of a mouse, with finger movement across the pad guiding the cursor. Some touchpads enable multi-touch actions for resizing images and other functions. Touchpads connect via USB and self-install the drivers.

Touchpads are built into nearly all laptops and the keyboards of many tablets. Touchpads are also available as standalone devices or integrated into keyboards. Touchpads and keyboards that include touchpads plug in through a USB port and are recognized as mice by the built-in Windows drivers.

Touchpads use the same mouse driver and is capable of providing the same functionality as a mouse. Laptops use touchpads more commonly. Touchpads can be enabled or disabled according to requirements.

Digitizers

A digitizer is a graphics pen that is used when users need to draw a signature or trace out the shape of something on the screen. To make use of a digitizer, the device first requires the driver to be installed. Digitizer pads can also be used in order to get more precise and fine detail of an object.

Digitizer also refers to the electrical force within a laptop screen that is touch sensitive. It is located just under the glass of the laptop screen. It senses and responds to touch.

Signature Pads

This is a device used to capture handwritten signatures on an LCD pad using a graphics pen or stylus. A sensor in the signature pad "reads" the pressure from the tip of the stylus and transfers the signature data to the computer.

Signature pads are used where signature verification is needed in banking, medical, retail, and other environments. The signature, captured via Optical Character Recognition (OCR), creates a legal document. Some have touchpad overlays that enable signature with a finger. Most signature pads use a USB interface.

These captured digital signatures can then be imported into ID software programs, legal documents, official data, and into security programs. Digital signatures can also be stored for future use.

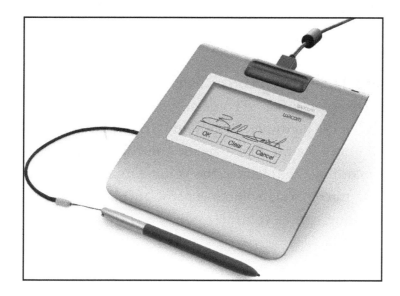

Figure 3-79: Signature Pad

Game Controllers

A game controller, gamepad, or joypad is an input device used for playing or controlling games. It has multiple buttons and pointing devices that are pressed with thumbs and fingers. Gamepads were first introduced with gaming console systems as a peripheral device to connect the user with the system.

Game pads and joysticks are connected to a computer USB port. In most cases, when a game pad or joystick is plugged in, Windows automatically installs compatible drivers. If a controller does not work, however, it may be necessary to select the correct driver manually from the Device Manager properties sheet of the controller. If a controller uses Bluetooth, pair it with the receiver in the system.

MacOS has varied support for game pads and joysticks. With some controllers, users can install vendor-supplied MacOS drivers. If a controller uses Bluetooth, pair it with the system. Game pads and joysticks on Linux are supported by the "Joystick" interface and the newer "evdev" interface.

Camera/Webcams

A digital camera is designed to capture photos of anything, anytime, anywhere. Typically, cameras consist of a media SD storage card, where pictures and videos are saved, and it can be used to transfer these saved files onto a PC for further processing and editing.

In modern laptops, smartphones, and microphones there is a webcam mounted on the top of the display to stream live pictures or video. However, this feature is only enabled when needed by an application, for example Skype on a PC or laptop, WhatsApp video on an Android smartphone, or live streaming on Facebook, etc.

Micropones

3.5 mm-jack or USB microphones depend on audio card drivers and editing software to allow the device to record an audio file such as Sound Forge or Audacity. Modern laptops and phones contain an embedded microphone in the hardware, supported by the OS. In Windows, microphone volume is controlled by the Windows Sound applet mixer control. To mute or unmute or adjust the microphone, go to the recording tab to adjust the volume. In MacOS, go to System Preferences > Sound > Input to find the microphone volume control. In Linux, go to System Settings > Sound >Input to find the microphone volume control.

Speakers

Speakers connect to the system using the 3.5 mm mini-jack ports or RCA on the audio card. Today, USB speakers are available and are very common. Speakers are made up of a cone with an electromagnet at its base, which produces vibrations and generates sound.

Headsets

A headset, also known as earphones, headphones, or hands-free, is an output device that plugs into the laptop, computer, or smartphone . It enables you to listen to music, any other audio, or watch a movie without disturbing people. There are headsets that also include a microphone (to input audio or voice), which is a popular option for video conferencing, Skype communication, computer gaming, and much more.

Projectors

The LED and LCD projectors are used to project the computer display onto a wall or another screen. It magnifies the image and therefore results in a much larger display than possible from a regular laptop or computer screen. The disadvantage with LCD display is that it depends on high-watt bulbs, which produce a great amount of heat and are susceptible to burn out. The high watt bulbs are also prone to failure, so in LCDs, bulb replacement takes place periodically.

LED projectors, however, use light-emitting diodes, so there is no dependency on bulbs. An LED unit can work for many hundreds of hours but is comparatively costly.

Brightness/Lumens

Lumens refers to the measure of light that is provided by the screen. In a dark room, three thousand lumens might be the visible lightness of a monitor. Whereas in a lit room, six thousand lumens are the visible light of a monitor.

Brightness corresponds to the luminance of the display and it can be adjusted according to the user needs. The measurement brightness is candela per square meter.

The contrast ratio refers to the measurement of the difference between the darkest possible pixel (black) and the brightest possible pixel (white). This is different from the brightness.

Monitor screens and graphics cards should be calibrated so that the image is correctly supplied by the system and correctly interpreted by the monitor display. To deal with this, the monitor drivers and graphics cards contain calibration data to make sure that files remain consistent if switched to another PC with different hardware.

External Storage Drives

There are various types of external storage devices, some of which have already been discussed in this chapter, for example, optical drives such as CDs, DVDs and Blu-rays, which are widely used to store and transfer data from one place to another. There are other external storage types, such as flash drives, which include SD cards, compact flash drives, micro-SD cards, mini-SD cards, and Xd cards. They are also used to store and transfer data from one device to another.

For example, a digital camera is used independently of the PC and files are uploaded separately. Modern camcorders can also store data to external storage.

KVMs

A Keyboard, Video, and Mouse (KVM) is a device that is used where there is limited space. A keyboard, video monitor, and mouse are attached to two PC cases. The KVM reduces hardware requirements and can control two active systems simultaneously. To switch between the two active systems, a special key combination is used. A common application of KVM is in server rooms and small offices.

In a server room, it is common to find almost 10 servers in a rack with a workspace controlling and monitoring these servers in the center of the rack. This is a designated area set for administrators, from which they can monitor and control the servers. There is a monitor along with a mouse and keyboard. KVM hardware is connected through a KVM box to all of the servers, and a special key combination is used to switch control from one server to another.

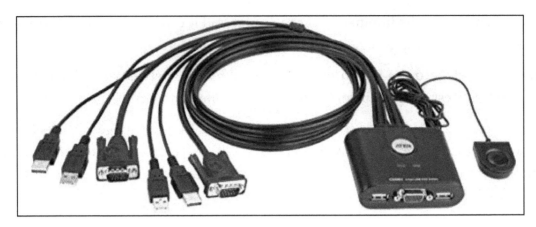

Figure 3-80: KVM

Magnetic Readers/Chip Readers

The magnetic strip on the back of debit, credit, gift, and other smart cards distinguishes between different customer and banking information. Magnetic card readers are popularly used to decipher the different tracks on the magnetic strip by using electronic technology.

NFC/Tap Pay Devices

Near-Field Communication (NFC) is low power, low-range RF signal communicating between devices. Common applications of NFC include direct printing and easily paying for goods and services in a retail store with smartphones and smart cards. The Apple iPhone6 and some smartphones with installed Google Wallet support NFC payments at a Point of Sale (POS) or wireless-enabled terminal.

It works by simply holding the phone near to the terminal until an approval message is noted on the POS or terminal.

Smart Card Readers

A smart card is a plastic card that looks like a credit card or an ID badge that includes a built-in microprocessor or memory used for storing the user's personal identification, financial transactions, or other important data. Many credit cards also have special chips on them that make them "smart cards".

A smart card reader is used to access data from a smart card. These readers can be either contact or touch readers for example, they can be machines where users swipe or insert cards, or they can be contactless readers that sense the presence of smart cards nearby and read its data. Card readers are

also available to interface with systems to process data from smart cards. These card readers have their own application setup and some models directly plug into a USB port.

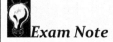

Exam Note

Install devices that are both input and output. These include but are not limited to touchscreen devices, KVMs, smart TVs, and set-top boxes.

Mind Map of the Purposes of Various Peripheral Types

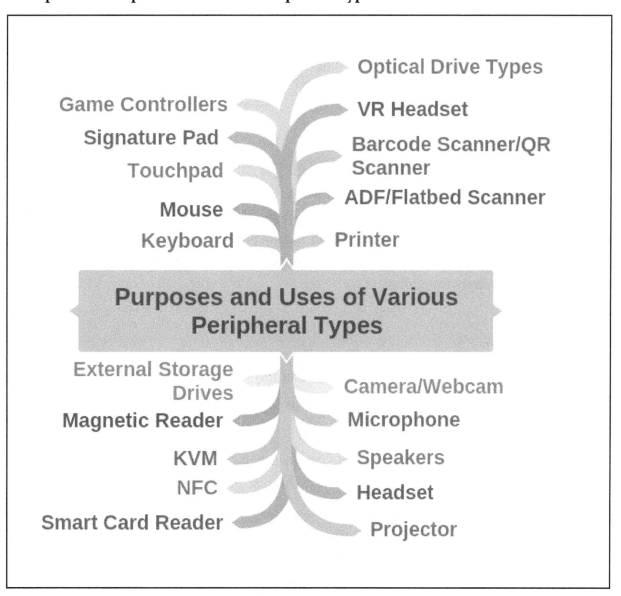

Figure 3-81: Mind Map of the Purposes of Various Peripheral Types

Summarize Power Supply Types and Features

The power supply is an electrical device that is used to provide electrical power to the electrical loads (electronic devices). The primary function of the power supply is to change the electrical current from the power outlet into usable power (such as required voltage, frequency and current for the load) that is required by attached devices. These power supplies are also known as electric power converters. Some types of supplies are separate hardware units whereas others are built into the electrical appliances to which they supply the required power.

A power supply drives energy from different types of energy sources, such as electrical energy transmission systems or electromechanical systems, which include generators and alternators, solar power converters, andother energy storage devices such as rechargable batteries, fuel cells, or other power supplies. Typically, there are two types of power supply:

- AC power supply
- DC power supply

Terminology Used in Power Supply

In a desktop computer, a power supply, also known as a Power Supply Unit (PSU), is the device that supplies power for all the components on the motherboard and is located inside the PC case at the back. Each component receives the exact amount and type of power it requires, but the power supply itself has its own requirements. Therefore, users need to understand some basic terminology related to the power supply functions.

115V vs. 220V of Input

The first thing users must ensure is that the power supply is compatible with the AC voltage that is used in their region. The widely used AC voltages are around "110 V", (usually 115 V and 127 V), and "220 V" (usually, 230 V and 240 V).

For example, in North America, power outlets supply about 110 to 120 volts AC at a frequency of 60 Hertz (U.S. standard) and the standard power for the rest of the world (International standard) is 220 to 240 VAC at 50 Hz.

Manufacturers have produced power supplies with dual voltage capability. Power supplies can either automatically switch or can be manually switched between dual voltages according to compatibility with the states. In a fixed input power supply, there is a switch at the back for selecting the required input voltage but an auto-switching power supply can analyze the incoming voltage and switch to accept either 120 or 240 VAC.

5V vs. 12V Output

The power supply works by converting the AC voltage from wall outlets into the DC voltage that the electronic device requires; usually desktop computers require: ±12 VDC, ±5 VDC, or ±3.3 VDC (volts DC). The power supply achieves these voltages by using a series of switching transistors, which led to the term switching-mode power supply.

The supplied power enables the computer's components to perform their function. A power supply converts the incoming 115VAC current into the four voltages that a computer needs to be operational. These voltages are +5 volts DC, –5 volts DC (ground), +12 volts DC, and –12 volts DC (ground).

Devices such as cathode-ray tubes or laser printers have their own high-voltage power supply (HVPS) because they require high voltages to be operational.

24-PIN Motherboard Adapters

A power connector enables the motherboard to be linked to the power supply. There is a single power connector consisting of a block of 20 holes (in two rows) on an ATX. There is a block on an AT consisting of 12 upright pins; two connectors with six holes each cover these pins.

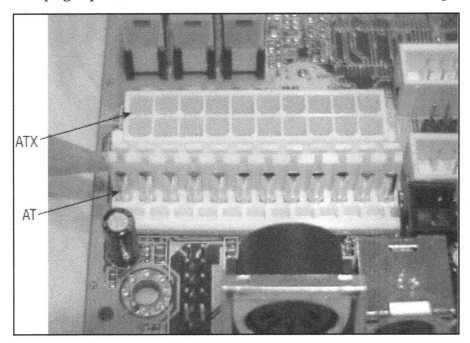

Figure 3-82: Power Connectors on a Motherboard

When using an AT power connector, the power cable coming from the power supply has two distinct connectors labelled P8 and P9. For proper function, when attaching the two parts to the motherboard, the black wires on one should be next to the black wires on the other.

Wattage

A power supply output capacity is measured in watts, and when users connect power-hungry devices to the system, they must ensure that maximum capacity of the power supply will not exceed the available capacity of power supply. The required power supply wattage can be estimated by adding the wattage needs of each component, the motherboard and the CPU. If the proper wattage is not supplied, problems such as lockups or spontaneous reboots may occur. Usually power supplies provide between 250 watts and 1,200 watts of power. It is good practice to have more power than required for the current system so that further devices can be added in the future.

The Number of Devices/Types of Devices to be Powered

Users need to consider a few things before purchasing a power supply, for example, the total wattage required by all the components, the PC's motherboard, and the appropriate connector types required by the devices. This section deals with the different connector types and the respective voltage requirements.

SATA

The SATA power connector consists of 15 pins, where 3 pins are designated for 3.3 V, 5 V, and 12 V respectively and each pin carries 1.5 amps of current. As a result, it draws 4.95 watts + 7.5 watts + 18 watts, or a total of about 30 watts of power.

Molex

A Molex connector is used to supply power to several types of drive. It consists of four pins, two with 12 V and two with 5 V. They are standard for older SCSI drives or for IDE (PATA). The total power drawn is about 10 to 40 watts for SCSI and from 5 to 15 watts for IDE.

Four/Eight-Pin 12 V

When Pentium 4 was introduced, the motherboard's power requirement increased. Additional power connections were given to the motherboard in 4-, 6-, or 8-pin formats.

A mini four-pin square version of the ATX connector supplies 12V with its two pins, and an eight-pin version, with pins arranged in two rows, contains four 12 V leads. They connect to other components, such as the processor, or to a network card that may require power.

Figure 3-83: 4-8 Pin 12Volt Power Connector

PCIe Six/Eight-Pin

PCIe slots require more power and draw power to the main 20-pin connector. The PCIe connectors can consist of six pins and may contain a further two-pins on the side for cases where an eight pin connection is required.

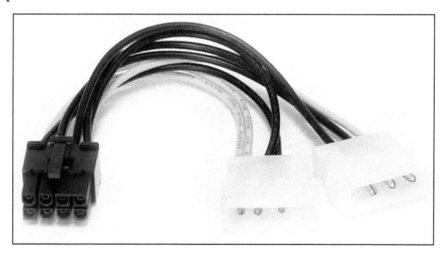

Figure 3-84: 6-8 Pin Power Connector

20-Pin

A 20-pin connector is the main ATX connector. Four of its pins carry +3.3 V, -3.3 V, +5 V, and -5 V of power. This means the motherboard can draw about 20 to 30 watts of power.

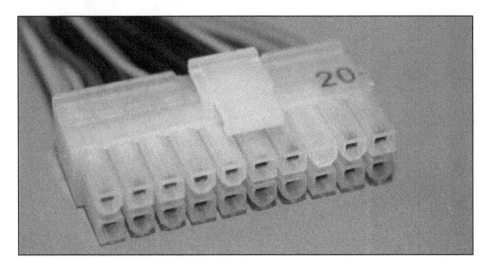

Figure 3-85: 20-Pin Power Connector

24-Pin

The 24-pin ATX connector is simply the same 20-pin connector discussed above, but with a 4 extra pin connector on the side. The additional 4 pins provide 5 V standby, +12 V, -12 V, and 3.3 along with the power drawn by the regular 20-pin connector.

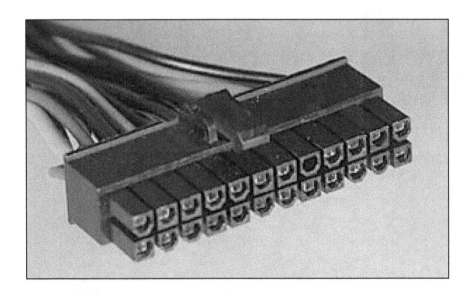

Figure 3-86: 24-Pin Power Connector

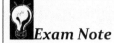**Exam Note**

Be able to identify SATA, Molex, and PCIe power connectors, know their associated voltages, and know their number of pins.

Mind Map of Power Supply Types and Features

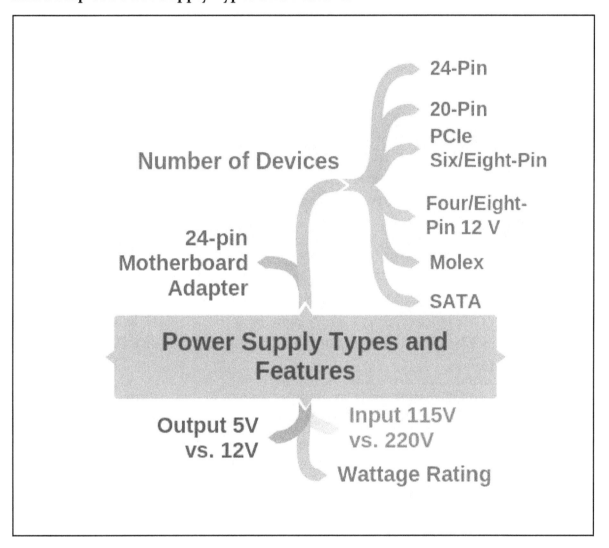

Figure 3-87: Mind Map of Power Supply Types and Features

Select and Configure Appropriate Components for a Custom PC Configuration to Meet Customer Specifications or Needs

Users will need to be able to work on custom PC configurations for some clients either as new builds or as upgrades to existing computers. Desktop computers require an amazing number of decisions, from selecting the right motherboard, CPU, and memory size to choosing the right peripherals, power supply, and display. The A+ 220-1001 exam objectives offer guidelines for seven configurations for graphics, A/V editing, virtualization, gaming, network-attached storage devices, thick clients, and thin clients. This section covers the requirements for these systems as well as how to choose the correct options for each one.

Graphics/CAD/CAM Design Workstation

High-end graphics PCs are required to provide high-resolution graphics as quickly as possible. Therefore, the most important requirement for a high-end system is a multicore processor with efficient and fast logic-processing capabilities. A load of processing can be shared by the Graphics Processing Unit (GPU), a specialized chip that is present on high-end graphics adapter cards, which reduces some of the load from the CPU.

Engineers, designers, and architects require systems or software capable of creating very complex graphics rendering for design and manufacturing. One popular category of software used by concerned authorities is Computer-Aided Design (CAD), which enables the design of a wide variety of substances, from basic machine parts to extremely complex products such as cars, aircraft, or boats. The CAD software enables you to view the design of an object in 2-D or 3-D image, from all angles and from different distances.

Another type of software for this purpose is Computer-Aided Manufacturing (CAM), which sometimes works in collaboration with CAD. A CAM system can control the machines used to manufacture an object. A combined Computer-Aided Design/Computer-Aided Manufacturing (CAD/CAM) system enables designers to go from design directly to manufacturing a product.

A design workstation requires a powerful processor of 64-bit four-, six-, or eight-core processor or two four-core processors to deal with all the required computation, a high-end video card driving a high-quality output or certified graphics display, a great amount of disk space, and a lot of RAM – 16 GB or 32 GB (good) to 128 GB (great). Users also require fault-tolerant RAID 1, 5, or 10 in order to minimize the risk of losing valuable design data.

In a workstation, a designer also requires a pointing device such as a stylus, light pen, or digitizing tablet with finer control than an ordinary mouse. Users will also require an appropriate printer for rendering images and detailed specifications, such as a large format printer or plotter. A plotter is a dedicated high-precision device used by the designers to create images in black and white or in color using specialized pens rather than ink cartridges.

SSD

SSD with a multicore processor has the benefit of fast rendering 3D or 2D graphics. Examples of SSD are Intel Core i97 Extreme Edition and AMD Ryzen 7 with processor 4.0 GHz or faster, six cores or more, large cache (8 MB or more total cache), and 64-bit support.

High-end Video

The final graphics output can be an animation or post-production effects added to a digital film file. Here, rendering is done in high-end output across multiple frames with the standard framerate for a film of 24 frames per second. For gaming purposes, this rate can be as high as 120 fps, or even higher.

A graphics card is used to render images or video very quickly. The monitor must be able to display the images with an average refresh speed so that all of the images can be displayed. Hence, the two key metrics are the refresh rate and the resolution for this purpose.

Maximum RAM

Graphics cards contain a buffer cache for storing images that have already been provided and stored in memory before they are issued to some other component, for example, to the monitor display. The rendered images will contain various polygonal shapes within 3D space, so a large amount of memory is required to render and rasterize the eventual image, and to send it to the monitor as one frame.

Features	Benefits	Recommendations and Examples	Notes
SSD with multicore processor	Fast rendering of 3D or 2D graphics	4.0 GHZ or faster, six cores or more, large cache (8 MB or more total cache), 64-bit support Intel Core i97 Extreme Edition AMD Ryzen 7	Fastest multicore CPUs available from Intel or AMD
High-end Video	Faster rendering of 3D or 2D graphics on applications that support GPU acceleration (AutoCAD, Photoshop CC, and other)	PCIe CAD/CAM or 3D cards with 2 GB or more RAM optimized for OpenGL 4.x, DirectX 11 or 12, support for two or more displays	Fastest GPUs available from AMD or NVIDIA More GPU RAM offers faster performance when rendering large 3D objects

		AMD RadeonPro (CAD, CAM, CGI, Photoshop) NVIDIA Quadro series (CAD, CAM, CGI)	FirePro and Quadro cards use drivers optimized for CAD/CAM/CGI
Maximum RAM	Reduces swapping to disk during editing or rendering	16 GB or more DDR3 or DDR4 Use matched memory modules running in multichannel configurations	System should be running a 64-bit version of the operating system

Table 3-22: Graphic/CAD/CAM Design Workstation Features

Audio/Video Editing Workstation

An audio/video editing or multimedia workstation demands a specially designed audio and video card for getting the highest accuracy possible during editing. A large screen monitor (preferably two) is required, along with large and very fast SATA hard drives. In an effective configuration, three hard drives are required: one for the system and application programs, one for the video streaming, and one for storing the processed or edited video. The movement of vast amounts of data on and off disks can create difficulties (bottlenecks) for an editing workstation. The hard drives, which a user chooses for this purpose should be very fast; standard 7200 rpm drives are good, whereas 10,000 rpm drives work much better. Users also require a high-wattage power supply to feed all these components. They can also add specialized equipment such as real time effects, stereo 3-D capture and editing capability.

Multimedia editing in real time requires serious processing power. Dedicated systems are there, such as Media 100 or SADiE, with their own hard drives and processors that do not use the PC's drives and processors. With a multimedia editing workstation, edits need to take place in real time.

Specialized Audio and Video Card

Specialized audio and video or multimedia cards are considered one of the biggest requirements of a multimedia workstation. Ensure that the card is able to handle higher data transfer speeds, high-definition resolutions, and larger frame rates of 25 frames per second as a minimum.

Large, Fast Hard Drive

As discussed earlier, a minimum of three hard drives are required by a multimedia workstation. However, Redundant Array of Independent Disks (RAIDs) can also be used for better performance, as RAID 10 provides a higher data transfer speed at the block level, along with fault tolerance ability. The physical drives are typically solid state, because they allow extremely fast data access speeds.

Dual Monitors

By having multiple displays such as dual or triple monitors, the editor has a separate preview of different functions at the same time such as the timeline, and the bin of storage materials. The process of editing a video can be made easier by simply dragging and dropping material from the bin to the timeline. The media clip has a start and end point on the timeline and they can be modified by moving the drag handles to begin a new start and end point.

Features	Benefits	Recommendations	Notes
Multicore processor	Fast rendering of 3D or 2D graphics	4.0 GHZ or faster, six cores or more, large cache (8 MB or more total cache), 64-bit support Intel Core i97 Extreme Edition AMD Radeon series	Fastest multicore CPUs available from Intel of AMD
Maximum RAM	Reduces swapping to disk during editing or rendering	16 GB or more DDR3 or DDR4 Use matched memory modules running in multichannel configurations	
Specialized audio card	Higher sampling rated and higher signal-to-noise ratios for better audio quality	24-bit, 192 KHZ or better audio performance; upgrading Op-amp (operational amplifier) sockets; PCIe interface Sound Blaster ZxR ASUS, Xonar H6, Essence ST, Essence STX	PCIe interface is preferred because it is faster than PCI Upgradable Op-amp sockets allow customization of audio characteristics
Specialized video card	Faster performance when rendering video	AMD FirePro W-series, AMD Radeon R9 NVIDIA Quadro M series	Fastest GPUs on market HDMI, DisplayPort or DVI interface
Large, fast hard drive, SSD if possible	Faster writes during saves, faster retrieval of source material during media editing and creation	Maximum performance: SATA Express or M.2 SSD drive Good performance: SSD SATA 6 Gbps large enough for windows and applications (128 GB-512 GB) and separate SATA 6 Gbps or USB 3.0 data drive or SATA hybrid drive	If an SSD is used as the main drive use a fast hard disk drive for temporary files

		4 TB or larger SATA 6 Gbps or USB 3.0 drives from Seagate, WD, Toshiba, HGTS	
Dual monitors	Editing software menus and playback can be on separate screen Can render and edit while using secondary display for other applications	27-inch or larger from many vendors	HDMI or DisplayPort interfaces recommended: DVI acceptable avoid VGA-only displays

Table 3-23: Dual Monitors Features

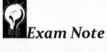**Exam Note**

Do not forget, graphic/CAD/CAM design workstations need powerful high-end video cards, solid-state drives (SATA and/or M.2), and as much RAM as possible. Remember that audio/video workstations require specialized A/V cards; large, fast hard drives; and multiple monitors.

Virtualization Workstation

A virtualization workstation is simply a computer that is used to gain a preview of the on-screen simulation of a computing environment. It allows users to run different OS and applications simultaneously on a computer isolated from the running OS and hardware of the computer. It can run a simulation of an entire computer including operating system, hardware, desktop, server's operating system and different applications. It may also run the simulation or virtualization of an application along with all the supporting software. A virtual machine is a single instance of such a simulation, and multiple virtual machines can run on the same workstation, if it contains sufficient memory, computing power, and disk space to support them.

A virtualization workstation requires a very fast multicore CPU, and both the processor and BIOS/UEFI must support virtualization. The term Virtual Technology (VT) is used in Intel CPUs and chipsets for indicating compatibility, and the term AMD-V is used in AMD CPUs and chipsets.

There is also Hyper-V, which allows prioritizing one VM over another for system resources.

Maximum RAM and CPU Cores

A virtualization workstation requires a lot of RAM to handle the virtualization process and to allow for real time processing. In order to run the virtualization process smoothly, users must figure out how much RAM and hard drive space they need, and how many cores or even additional processors they require.

If the desired workstation will run many virtual machines, users will require more CPU power, more RAM, and more disk space; they can also use high-speed data busses as well. In the case of server virtualization, users need to connect Network Interface Cards (NICs) to a high-speed network.

Therefore, the key to virtualized systems is based on how the resources (RAM, processor, hard disks and the required buses) are shared.

Gaming PC

A gaming PC consists of specialized, expensive and high-ability hardware. They are high-end PCs and use a high-RAM graphics card for fast data rendering. Gaming requires high quality and extremely fast feedback. For this purpose, vision and sound are paramount.

Along with the keyboard and mouse, gaming also requires appropriate peripherals, such as gamepads, joysticks, and wheels. A multichannel sound of up to 7.1 channel high-definition (HD) surround sound is also required, which provides the consumers with a realistic experience through a subwoofer and six surround speakers.

SSD and Multicore Processor

Gaming is processor heavy, so a gaming PC must contain a powerful processor to deal with all the graphics calculations, with at least 16 GB of installed RAM, a motherboard that allows SATA3, preferably a solid-state hard drive of 1 TB or 2 TB, which must be 7200 rpm or an even faster.

High-end Video/Specialized GPU

Gaming PCs also require a specialized high-end video GPU card along with at least 1 GB of graphics RAM. These specialized GPUs assist the processor by rendering the video using graphics RAM rather than conveying this task to the CPU. This frees up CPU resources to perform its regular processing.

High-Definition Sound Card

High definition sound cards are used in most of games and movies to provide clear and quality sound. Gamers want to be immersed in the experience of gaming and to imagine that they are actually a part of the game; for this purpose, high-end stereo and surround sound are used.

The audio card contains a processor capable of decoding audio and transmitting it to the sound bars or speakers. Usually, digital output such as HDMI, Optical, or RCA digital is used to allow crystal-clear audio.

High-end Cooling

Sometimes, gamers overwork the processor by playing too many games. This increases the power requirements along with the generation of heat and fan noise. To avoid this, thermal-pipe cooling and ultra-quiet fans are required to provide sufficient cooling.

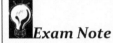**Exam Note**

Remember that virtualization systems rely heavily on CPU and RAM. These systems need maximum RAM and CPU cores. A gaming PC needs a high-end video with specialized GPU, a high-definition sound card, an SSD, and high-end cooling.

Mind Map of PC Configuration to Meet Customer Specifications or Needs

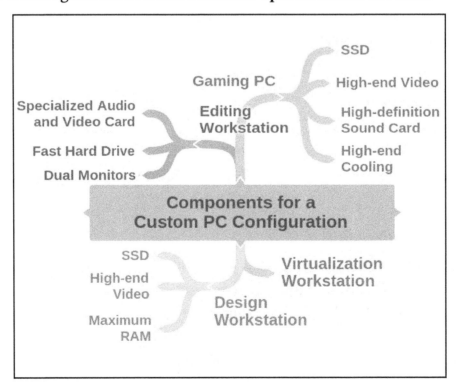

Figure 3-88: Mind Map of PC Configuration to Meet Customer Specification or Needs

Network Attached Storage Devices

Data storage demands are now typically greater than a workstation can manage. Network-Attached Storage (NAS) is an in-house backup and storage solution that consists of a multiple-drive bays storage server that can hold large hard drives that are accessible on a network. A NAS device can store data from all the devices for access or backup.

The following section deals with different types of data storage options.

Media Streaming

Media streaming involves the process of sending audio or video content in compressed form over the internet to be played immediately, rather than being saved first to the hard drive. A common example is to access media files from a file server. The data is not actually sent, but is streamed to the presentation device. Devices involved in the transmission or streaming of data are referred to as media streaming devices.

File Sharing

A common access point for all files across the network is typically a file server. File sharing can be done by sharing a file across the network using a Universal Naming Convention path in a format given below:

\\<Computer Name>\<Shared Folder>

For example: \\MyComputer\SharedFile

Permission is granted for sharing, and the files or folders on the volume contain separate security permission (NTFS permissions). The cumulative permissions secure the overall communication, with the most restrictive taking effect.

Gigabit NIC

A Gigabit Network Interface Card (NIC) has the bandwidth to provide a data rate of up to 1000+ Mbps, making it an excellent choice for gaming, movies, and high definition file transfer, increasing its quality for transferring from where the file is stored to where it has to be played or presented.

Raid Array

RAID can be a significant feature with a NAS and is considered important on business-class systems. However, remember that RAID was designed for mechanical hard drives and may not be necessary if information is simply being backed up for personal use.

Hard Drive

Hard Disk Drives (HDD) have been considered the default storage component in desktop and laptop PCs for decades. Modern hard disk drives are far more efficient and higher-performing than

ever, but the basic underlying technology is still the same. Hard disk drives consist of rotating magnetic platters paired with read/write heads that move over the platters' surfaces to record or retrieve data. As the speed of platter rotation increases, the faster the hard drive performs. A hard drive connects to a system via the SATA or Serial ATA interface. Today's laptop computers have hard drives that consist of hundreds of gigabytes of storage space.

Standard Thick Client

A **client** is software that is connected to the server software over a network. For example, a client can access a print server as well as the file server for a printing job while simultaneously saving and retrieving a file. Or, it can be an email client who connects to an email server. The operating system running underneath these clients is also referred to as the client.

A **thick client** is simply another name for a desktop PC that is connected to the network with several applications installed. The term "client" implies that the computer behaves as a client in a connected network, to various servers or services for network browsing, email, file sharing, and more. There are recommended requirements for CPU, memory, disk storage and all installed desktop applications for a thick client. A fast internet connection is also required, along with one or more internet browsers and other applications.

The drawback of the thick image is that it is quite overloaded or bloated and therefore consumes a long time to deploy.

Desktop Applications

A thick client contains all the necessary applications required by the organization. However, they are used on an as-and-when basis. For more applications, licenses are required, and companies may purchase only a limited number of licenses per computer and not per user.

Meets Recommended Requirements for Selected OS

Users have to ensure that the software installed on the thick image must be compatible with the hardware systems it is installed on. For example, 64-bit hardware will be required for running a 64-bit application. Users can run 32-bit applications on 64-bit hardware (image) where the OS is also 64-bit.

Thin Client

A thin client is a scaled-down and low costing PC used primarily for accessing the internet and does not require a whole package of local applications. A PC configured as a thin client therefore has minimum requirements of the Windows version installed because it assumes that all tasks are properly done and stored on the network (private or internet). However, a user requires a fast internet connection to gain access to applications such as an internet browser, an email client (unless the user accesses email solely via the internet browser), and web applications for basic word

processing. Thin clients are not so popular in the field because they have been replaced and overshadowed by netbooks and tablet PCs, with similar cost and better performance.

There is a hybrid image, which is basically a thin image that is partly configured with the most common apps but not all of the departments.

Basic Applications

The thin image usually does not contain applications, but it sometimes contains applications that are common across the organization and are centrally licensed for use by all staff members such as Adobe Acrobat Reader and Google Chrome.

Meets Minimum Requirements for Selected OS

A thin image is configured for minimum hardware requirements and can be applied to all machines. If required, a DISM command can be run to transform the requirements for higher-specification machines, or a separate image can be used for higher-specification machines.

The following are the minimum requirements for Windows 10:

- *RAM*: 1 GB (32-bit) or 2 GB (64-bit)
- *Free Hard Disk Space*: 16 GB
- *Processor*: 1 GHz or faster
- *Graphics Card*: Microsoft DirectX 9 graphics device with WDDM driver
- A Microsoft account along with internet access

Network Connectivity

A network card is required for the process of receiving an image through deployment. If it is configured to boot from the NIC, then the process begins by acquiring an IP address from a local DHCP server. Once the IP address has been assigned, then a boot image will be required. The boot image will be provided by a Windows Deployment Server if the hardware is not able to load a complete image. The boot image comprises additional hard disk drivers and network maps to obtain the full image.

It is possible to re-image several hundred PCs in deployment to a working state within a matter of minutes.

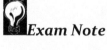

Exam Note

Network-attached storage (NAS) devices usually require a RAID array, gigabit NIC, file sharing, and the capability for media sharing. Viruses have a hard time sticking around a thin client because the RAM is completely cleared every time it is turned off.

Mind Map of PC Configuration to Meet Customer Specifications or Needs

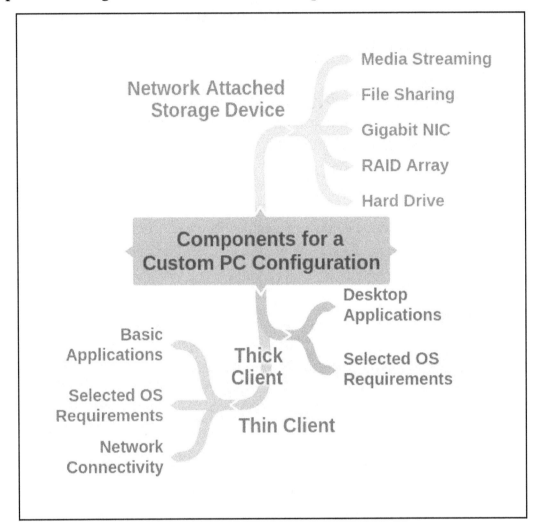

Figure 3-89: Mind Map of PC Configuration to Meet Customer Specification or Needs

Install and Configure Common Devices

Installing a laptop or desktop system is not all that difficult once the operating system is installed. Some settings may require to be set to certain components, and user accounts must be prepared to assist the users. This section also covers configurations for touchpads, touchscreens, and common application and device settings. The topics in this section include the following:

- Desktop
- Laptop/common mobile devices

Desktop

Both thin and thick clients require network configuration to operate on the network, and user accounts must be established and secured.

Thin Client

The thin client must have a network setup. In most cases, clients should use DHCP for this. If users have a wireless router, these configurations can be issued. However, for better performance, plug the thin client into the Ethernet ports that typically come with ISP-provided routers. If DHCP is not in use, make sure the thin client has an IP configuration that will enable it to connect to the server and to other required resources including the internet.

Thick Client

Users should treat the installation of a thick client in the same manner they would a thin client. If users have a wireless router, these configurations can be issued. However, for better performance, plug the thick client into the Ethernet ports that typically come with ISP-provided routers. If DHCP is not in use, make sure the thick client has an IP configuration that will enable it to connect to required resources including the internet.

Account Setup/Settings

You need to generate user accounts and passwords for those who use the device on both thin and thick clients. Ensure accountability by using no shared accounts. Every user should have a distinctive combination of username/password.

Latop/Common Mobile Devices

Optimizing features on a laptop makes it possible for a user to have an improved and often customized experience. While the default settings on the following features will work, a better computing experience may be provided by customization.

Touchpad Configuration

Touchpads or trackpads are built into almost all laptops and the keyboards on several tablets. Touchpads and keyboards that include touchpads plugged in via the USB port and are identified as mice by the built-in Windows drivers. If a touchpad or keyboard with integrated touchpad is wireless, it is usually recognized automatically. If a touchpad or keyboard has extra keys or buttons, it might be necessary to install proprietary drivers to allow the additional keys or buttons. Proprietary drivers are also essential to allow multi-touch gestures (using two or more fingers).

To customize the settings on a touchpad in Windows 10, open Windows "Settings" and tap on the Devices icon to open the "Bluetooth & Other Devices" window.

On a Mac, access the settings by taping the Apple icon in the top-left corner of the screen and choosing "System Preferences". The Apple touchpad opens with different settings and customization options for pointing and clicking, scroll and zoom options, and other gestures.

Touchscreen Configuration

During device configuration, touch screens often require a calibration algorithm to be run. This allows the device and user to learn to communicate; a user must understand how sensitive the touchscreen is to their touch. If it does not respond correctly, a touchscreen can easily be recalibrated. To do this:

- Open "Control Panel" and choose the "Tablet PC Settings" option (If this option is not available, check whether the drivers are present)
- Click the Calibrate button and then select the option for calibrating the screen for pen or touch input
- Follow the instructions to perform the calibration
- Tap "Yes" to save the settings

Application Installations/Configurations

To ensure the application is securely installed and can operate fully, minor housekeeping must always be done when installing and configuring applications. Different types of applications have different requirements and procedures. However, a few basic steps apply to all applications:

- Determine whether the computer has sufficient resources to efficiently operate the application. If so, download the installation file from a reliable source. Use common sense and be careful of potential virus-infected applications from unknown sources
- Find the .exe file for the downloaded application (typically in the Downloads folder)
- To run the Setup program, double-click the .exe file and look for a dialog box asking for storage and shortcut preferences. If prompted to choose between an automatic install and a custom install, it is generally recommended you opt for auto installation, unless there are particular settings to be altered
- Follow the directions to complete the installation and then reboot if necessary

Synchronization Settings

Synchronization is the matching up of documents, email, and other types of data between one computer and another, using mobile devices or with cloud storage and cloud applications. Synchronization is used to bring files in line with each other and to force devices to coordinate their information.

Account Setup/Settings

Setup and settings issues include updating passwords and other account settings, when installing applications, such as payment information for subscription services, depending on the application's

functionality. For example, applications for financial management may also need to change settings with other vendor accounts.

Wireless Settings

Account and setting configuration may also be applicable to wireless settings. Some applications may require the transfer of significant personal or payment information, and it is essential to ensure that information is securely sent and obtained. In addition, wireless settings such as those for firewalls or access controls may need to be configured.

*Exam Note*

Identify the difference between a thick and a thin client. A thick client runs the operating system and applications from the local hard drive, whereas a thin client runs these components from a remote server.

Mind Map of Installing and Configuring Common Devices

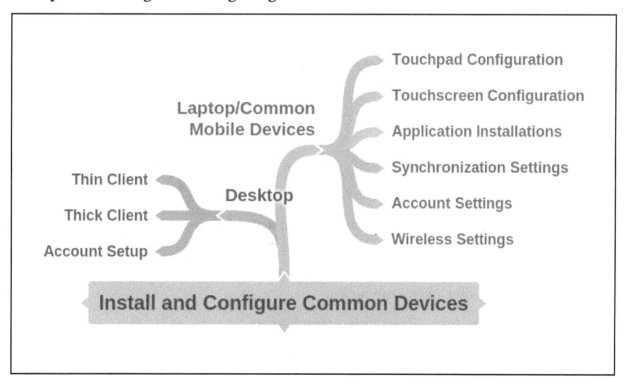

Figure 3-90: Mind Map of Installing and Configuring Common Devices

Configure SOHO Multifunction Devices/Printers and Settings

In any computing environment, printers are one of the most popular components, from home to office. The variety they cover is phenomenal, from a cheap free model included in the purchase of a PC to a monolith in a big office churning hundreds of pages a minute.

Regardless of where a printer falls in that spectrum, they are all the same because they need to be installed and properly configured for use. In addition, most printing devices today are multifunction devices. They print, scan, and fax in various combinations.

Memory

The memory of a printer is used to hold and process the print jobs in the printer queue. The more memory a printer has, the better will be the performance. You will require more memory if there are more users and larger print jobs. Dot-matrix and inkjet printers have little memory, the older printers only used a buffer to hold a few characters.

Drivers

These are printer software components that enable the device to communicate with the operating system. For greater efficiency, it is important to install the correct and most recent driver in your

printer. The printer driver may vary depending on the operating system running on the client computer, and if a printer is connected to more than one client computer or operating system, then you must ensure that you have the appropriate driver installed for each operating system running.

Firmware

Firmware can be considered the operating system for the printer. It is installed on the printer. Drivers can be updated periodically but firmware rarely is.

Consumable items for printers are those that you must keep changing as you use the printer. These variable items get consumed easily and must be refilled. They include toner or ink and paper. Always use recommended consumables for your machine. For example, do not use an inkjet media in a laser printer as a laser printer's fuser can melt it.

Use Appropriate Drivers for a Given Operating System

The driver software installed in the printer controls how the print job will be processed. An appropriate installed driver enables the computer to print to that printer correctly. Also, remember that drivers are operating system specific, so wisely choose the one that is appropriate for both the printer and the operating system.

An interface refers to the set of hardware and software that enables the device to communicate with a computer. Each printer, contains at least one interface, but some printers contain several interfaces to make them more efficient and flexible in a multiplatform environment. A printer with several interfaces usually switches between the different interfaces, so that many computers can print at the same time.

Configuration Settings

In order to configure the printer, you must be aware of various settings that are present and what purpose they serve. The succeeding section deals with the configuration of common settings, features, and characteristics of printers.

Duplex

In the context of printers, duplex or data duplexing refers to the capability of a printer to perform double-sided printing. The duplexer is an optional item that can be added to the printers, usually added to the laser and inkjet printers. This feature can be built-in to the printer and sometimes it can be an optional assembly added to the printer. But the main purpose of duplexing is to allow printing on both sides of the paper by turning the printed sheet over so it can print on the back through the printer.

Collate

Collating refers to the process of arranging the printed pages of a print job in their respective order so that multiple sets of the output are in proper sequence. A collator unit is a series of trays – each page of the output is stored on a separate tray in the collator, beginning with the first page.

That is how collator aligns the document consisting of several pages. It compiles the document by stapling it (it has a staple with it), professionally this is called stitching.

Orientation

The orientation of data or document refers to the direction of the printed matter on the page. The orientation can be landscape or portrait. In the landscape orientation (long width), the printing is done across the paper turned on its long side, whereas in portrait (thin width) the paper is turned up vertically and printed top to bottom.

Quality

The term quality includes the quality of paper, the description of sharpness, depth of the color on the paper, the speed of the printing process, and resolution settings. Refer to the DPI settings to control all these features. The respective settings control the size of objects on display and therefore their quality. If users increase the size of an object, its quality will decrease.

Device Sharing

Device sharing involves the techniques and hardware technology to get information to and from the computer. There are many types that can be divided into two main types: wired and wireless.

Wired

The following section deals with the different types of wired technologies to enable device sharing on printers.

USBs

A USB is one of the most popular choices of interface for almost every peripheral. The advantage of this interface for printers is that it provides a higher data transfer rate than either serial or parallel and it auto negotiates the new devices and connections. A USB is a Plug and Play device, and it allows various printers to be connected simultaneously, without adding extra ports or system resources.

Serial

The serial connector is the traditional RS-232 serial port found on almost all PCs. It provides a direct connection between two PCs. It is used to copy and transfer files from one system to another. Typically, a COM2 or DB25 cable is used for this purpose.

It is the original printer interface on older computers and is no longer used for printing because it is very slow.

Ethernet

In most large-environment printers, such as laser and LED printers, a special interface allows them to be connected directly to a network. These printers contain a ROM or NIC-based software that enables the printer to communicate with networks, servers, and workstations.

Wireless

The following section deals with wireless methods of device sharing for printers that include Bluetooth, 802.11x, and Infrared (IR).

Bluetooth

Bluetooth is an infrared technology that connects a printer to a computer within a short range. The maximum range is about 100 meters or 330 feet, but it is recommended that devices are placed within 10 meters or 33 feet.

Most Bluetooth-based printers are portable or receipt printers. Printers lacking Bluetooth support can use special Bluetooth adapters to connect with PCs or mobile devices that use Bluetooth.

Bluetooth is one of the simplest and secure wireless technologies, as most computing devices are Bluetooth enabled. An exchange of PIN code is required by both the devices to be paired with each other. Once paired, files can easily be shared. Bluetooth is a simple, fast, and efficient solution for data sharing.

802.11 (a, b, g, n, ac)

Most new printers and multifunction devices include some level of 802.11 (Wi-Fi) support. The configuration method is typically similar to that used for wired Ethernet, with the additional step of specifying the wireless network's SSID and encryption key (if used). When this configuration is finished, all devices on the network with the proper print driver can use the multifunction device.

A printer that is network-enabled and contains a wireless adaptor can become a part of wireless Ethernet i.e. IEEE 802.11b, a, g, n, or ac network, just as it is a wired network client. In order to gain secure wireless access to printers, the following protocols can be used:

Wired Equivalent Privacy (WEP)
WEP is an encryption protocol, introduced in 802.11b. It is used to encrypt data packets using an augmenting seed, but WEP can be easily cracked so it should not be the only option.

Wi-Fi Protected Access
This authentication system is used to connect and establish a session between devices, where a password known by both parties is required.

For larger network environments where security is a problem, use 802.1x certificate management, where a certificate file is used to either encrypt or authenticate the user. The same certificate needs to be on the sending and receiving computers.

Infrastructure vs. Ad Hoc

The architecture of the printer refers to the way users set up a wireless printer. There are two modes of architecture for printers: Infrastructure and Ad Hoc.

In the ad hoc mode, all devices can communicate with each other directly in a peer-to-peer arrangement. Each user who wants to access the wireless printer has to build their own connection to the wireless printer, and they need to be in the same IP network and the same WLAN as the printer.

In infrastructure mode, an access point (AP) is used by the wireless network and all the data communication takes place through the AP. Here, the printer needs to be configured to automatically connect to the AP, but wireless clients and the printer need to be on the same network.

Ad Hoc Wireless Network Support in Windows

Wireless Ad Hoc networking is endorsed via the Network and Sharing Center in Windows 8/8.1. It is also accessible from the command line in Windows 8/8.1 using Netsh, but in Windows 10 it was deleted.

Ad Hoc wireless networking is supported through the Network and Sharing Center in Windows 8/8.1. It is also available from the command line in Windows 8/8.1 using Netsh, but it has been removed from Windows 10.

Ad Hoc Wireless Network Support in MacOS

MacOS supports Ad Hoc wireless networking on the Finder menu through the Wi-Fi Status icon. MacOS refers to this feature as "computer-to-computer" networking. When this feature is enabled, the computer cannot connect simultaneously to other Wi-Fi networks.

Ad Hoc Wireless Networking Support in Linux

Ad Hoc wireless networking in Linux is sometimes referred to as an Independent Basic Service Set (IBSS) network. Depending on the distro, this can be configured by switching on the wireless hotspot service in the network settings or by using the iw and ip command line tools.

Integrated Print Server (Hardware)

Connecting the print server to the printing device either directly or through a network using an IP address, enables the printing device to manage all print jobs through the server. This eliminates the need to install the printer driver on individual machines; the print request is managed and rendered by the print server.

A print server is a handy option for adding a printer to the network rather than connecting individual host computers directly to the printers. There is a dedicated NIC in the printer for this purpose, which differs from computer's NIC in the sense that it has a processor in it to perform the management of the NIC interface. This NIC is solely dedicated for receiving print jobs and sending the status of the printer to the users. This increases the printing capability, makes it faster and more efficient. The NIC is dedicated to receiving print jobs and sending printer status to clients.

Cloud Printing/Remote Printing

The facility of printing remotely over the internet has been available for several years. Cloud printing, however, is a new service being offered by cloud vendors. With cloud printing, users no longer need to be at the office or home office to make a printout. Cloud vendors also introduced cloud-ready printers in a sequence that does not require the PC to be connected to the internet. It makes the process of connecting end devices to the cloud print server much easier. With remote printing, users can print a document stored on the host with the remote printer.

Another option for the print server is to create a VPN connection to the network. Once it is connected to the network over the VPN, users are able to connect to and print to the printer wherever they are and whenever they need.

Exam Note

Know the four printer configuration settings: duplex, collate, orientation, and quality. Be familiar with the possible interfaces that can be used for printing. The types generally fall into two categories: wired (USB, parallel, Ethernet) and wireless (Bluetooth and 802.11x).

Public/Shared Devices

Previously, sharing printers on a network used to require both the printer and the user to be on the same local network, but recent technologies for print sharing have made shared printing available beyond physical access to a printer.

Public cloud printing devices are available in some office supply stores, schools, and other business centers located in hotels and airports. The clients can submit print jobs via email, web interfacing, mobile apps, or special print drivers. Thus, public cloud printing is available to any sort of computer or device that has internet access.

All operating systems permit users to share a local printer among various end users or connect the printer over the to the network or internet. In Windows 8, to connect to a printer, go to the "Control Panel", select "Devices and Printers", and it will present the list of recognized printers. It also allows users to add new ones according to requirements. Users can add other printers by clicking the option "Add a printer".

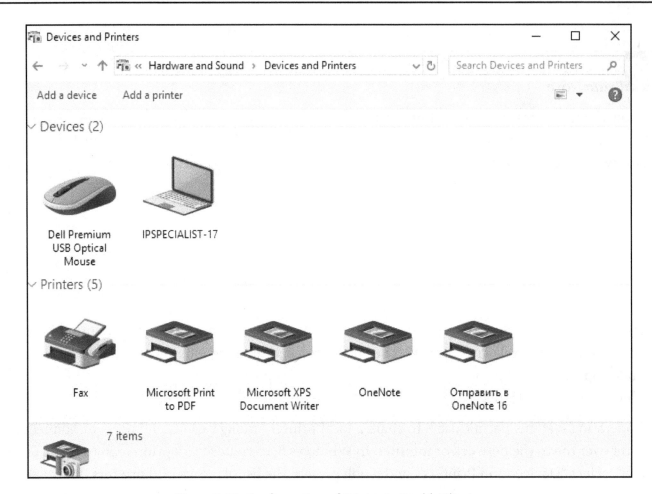

Figure 3-91: Configuration of Printer to Enable Sharing

Sharing Local/Networked Device via Operating System Settings

In order to share a local or networked printer by using Windows operating systems, right-click the printer's icon and select "Printer properties".

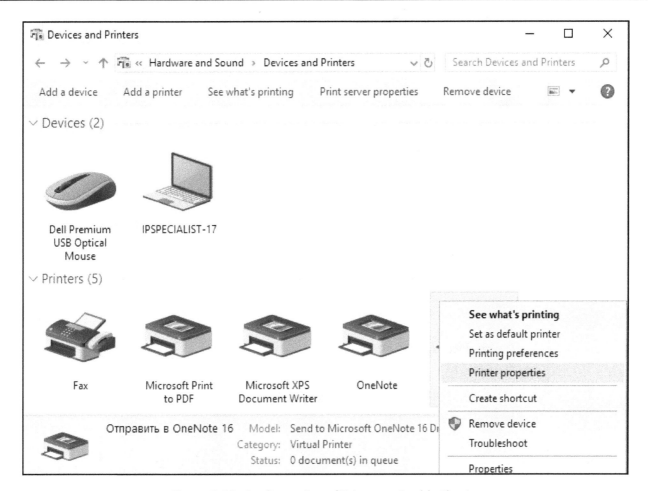

Figure 3-92: Configuration of Printer to Enable Sharing

Click "Next" and then click the "Sharing" tab.

Figure 3-93: Configuration of a Printer to Enable Sharing

Select "Share This Printer" and provide a relevant name for the printer, so that the printer will be known by it on the network. The printer will appear with this name when adding a new network printer on a client.

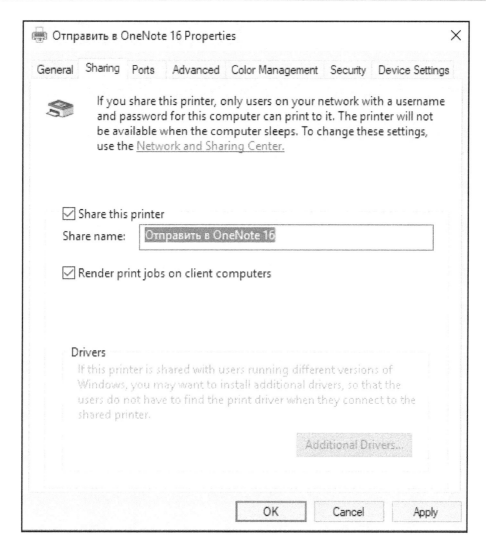

Figure 3-94: Configuration of a Printer to Enable Sharing

Now, click on "Network and Sharing Center" in the prompted Windows as shown above. The following window will pop up:

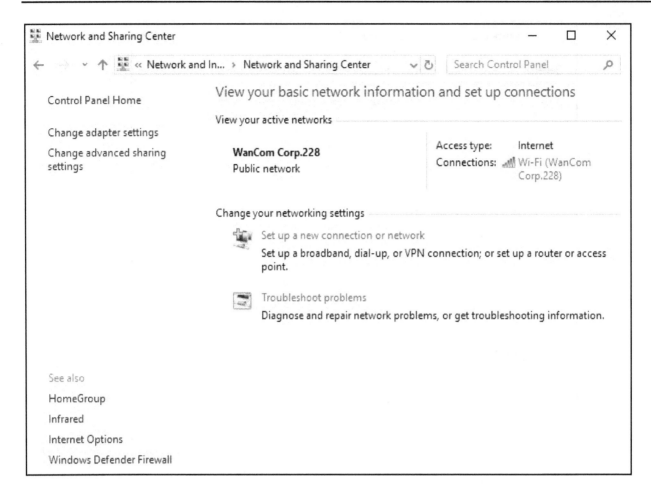

Figure 3-95: Configuration of a Printer to Enable Sharing

Go to "Change advanced sharing settings". The following windows will pop up. Select "turn on file and printer sharing" and save the settings.

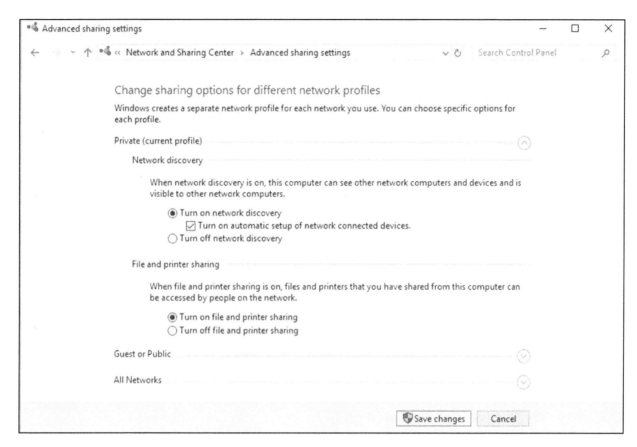

Figure 3-96: Configuration of a Printer to Enable Sharing

Now, the printer will become sharable for all.

Verification:

In order to verify printer sharing, go to the "Devices and Printers" tab from another PC in the network or vicinity:

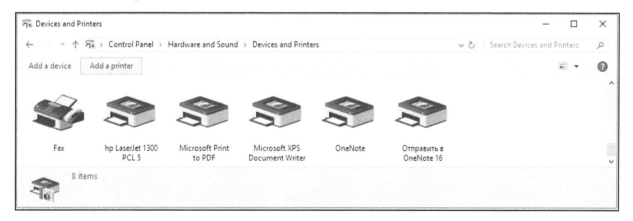

Figure 3-97: Configuration of a Printer to Enable Sharing

The following window will pop up with the name of shared printer, as shown below:

Figure 3-98: Configuration of a Printer to Enable Sharing

Click "Next" to install the driver for the shared printer:

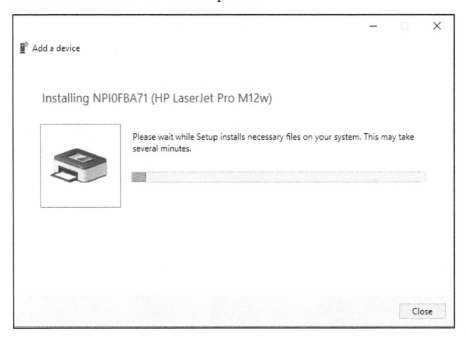

Figure 3-99: Configuration of a Printer to Enable Sharing

On successful installation, the following window will pop up:

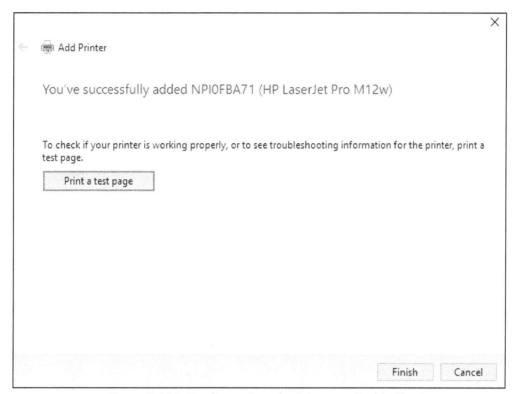

Figure 3-100: Configuration of a Printer to Enable Sharing

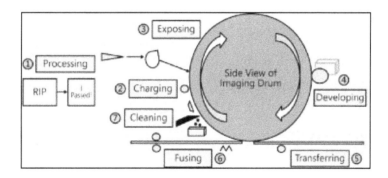

Figure 3-101: Configuration of a Printer to Enable Sharing

Now, users can print documents by just clicking the print option in the file.

TCP

Users usually depend on direct TCP/IP connections if a network printer is being controlled by Windows. However, printers that are controlled by MacOS might also make use of the Bonjour networking service, and use AirPrint to automatically locate and download printer drivers.

A TCP printer is one that cannot be shared by a computer, but with its own IP address and network card. Transmission Control Protocol (TCP) depends on a DNS server to discover the IP addresses of devices inside the network.

Bonjour

An apple technology, Bonjour is used to discover devices inside a network that are not listed (not connected but are present in the neighbourhood). It relies on multicast Domain Name System to find the proximity of the IP address and name of the devices that are in its neighborhood. It also facilitates the sharing of a printer across the network. It is common for Apple OS or for Mac, but can also work with Windows.

AirPrint

Another Apple technology, AirPrint enables a user to discover an AirPrint-enabled printer and print documents or pictures without setting up a local network. AirPrint creates full-quality printed output without the need to download or install drivers. Many printers that are available today are ready to support AirPrint. Whereas, AirPrint uses an Access Point (AP) to print to the wireless printer and does not support direct printing to the wireless printer. This means an Airprint relies on an AP and this technology can only be used in a WLAN where an access point is present.

Data Privacy

In cases where users are sharing a single device, data privacy is a problem. There are many precautions that need to be taken to ensure the privacy of data sent to the printer.

- Make sure that all users trying to access the printer are authenticated to the device
- Make sure that users are given particular rights to the devices they need to perform their job
- Make use of Data Loss Prevention (DLP) that controls the printing, sharing, emailing, or deleting of data or documents
- Make use of the accounting and auditing features to keep the track of who accessed certain resources and when

When a file is sent to a printer, the print spooler creates a unique print file. To avoid unauthorized users from opening the print file and extracting data from it, two methods can be used: user authentication and hard drive caching.

User Authentication on the Device

In larger organizations, it is difficult to keep a track of all users using a specific resource. Therefore, user authentication helps to ensure that only authorized users can access the resource. Extensible Authentication Protocol (EAP) technologies are used to authenticate a user by authenticating their finger prints or retina pattern or by using a username and password stored on the local database or in AD, or by using a pin code or pattern swipe.

Hard Drive Caching

The data stored on the hard drive is cached to make it easily and quickly accessible by the running application. This means that the required data is temporarily written to another area of the hard drive for easy access.

In most enterprises, multifunctioning devices have hard drives and they cache information on those hard drives. Users must take precautionary steps to protect the data on hard drives, which can be stolen from the hard drive, either by extracting the data from replaced hard drive or by having a remote access of that data.

Following are techniques for securing data on the hard drive of a device:

Encryption

Encryption encodes the stored data on the hard drive and makes it un-understandable for others, so that it cannot be retrieved easily even if the hard drive is removed from the machine.

Overwriting

Overwriting manipulates the values of the bits on the disk that can be done by overwriting existing data of the file with random characters. By overwriting the occupied disk space of the file, its traces are removed, so the file cannot be easily reconstructed.

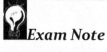
Exam Note

Know how to install printers. The manufacturer is the best source of information about installing printers. However, users should know about the wizards available in Windows as well.

Mind Map of Configuring SOHO Multifunction Devices/Printers and Settings

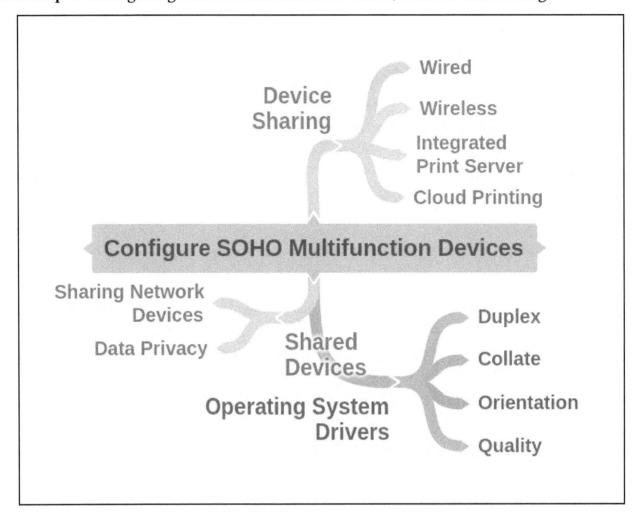

Figure 3-102: Mind Map of Configuring SOHO Multifunction Devices/Printers and Settings

Install and Maintain Various Print Technologies

Printers are considered one of the most widely used elements in any computing environment, from home to office. There is a phenomenally wide range of printers available, from a free printer provided by a vendor with the purchase of a PC up to a monolith in a large office, churning out hundreds of pages a minute. Regardless of the category in which a printer comes, they are all the same in the sense that they must be installed and configured properly. Further, most printing devices are multifunction devices today, i.e., they scan and fax as well as print.

Apart from the physical body of the printer, there are also components and consumables that are associated with it. Following are the main components printers:

Laser Printer

Laser printers are also referred to as Electrophotographic (EP) printers or page printers because they perform their print job one page at a time. Laser printers are non-impact and sheet-fed.

A laser printer works by using a laser beam shone onto a rotating mirror, which then directs the beam at specific areas of a photosensitive drum. These photosensitive areas attract an ionized carbon/wax composite commonly known as toner, which is then attracted to the paper as it rolls over the drum. Pressure and heat is then applied to the paper to seal the toner.

It processes an A4 paper in a short span of seconds. It is a cost effective and economical solution because it can process several thousand sheets per toner cartridge.

Following are the major components of an EP (laser) printer:

Printer Controller

Printer controller is a large circuit board that behaves like a motherboard for the printer. It contains the RAM and processor to convert data coming from the computer onto a page to be printed.

Imaging Drum

The imaging drum applies the page image to the transfer belt or roller; frequently combined with the toner supply in a toner cartridge. It is a photosensitive drum; one strike by the laser light causes the toner to attract to those parts of the drum, as the drum rolls over the toner reservoir. The imaging drum and toner cartridge are typically packaged together as a consumable product.

Figure 3-103: Imaging Dru

Fuser Assembly

The fuser assembly fuses the page image to the paper. It consists of a fusing roller, and as a paper passes through the hot fusing rollers, it melts the toner onto the paper. The fuser unit or heat lamps provide heat of up to of 200 °C to seal the unbounded toner onto the paper.

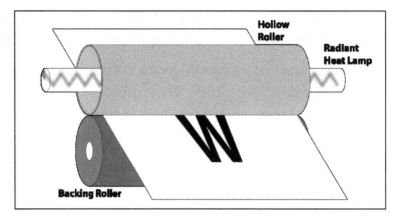

Figure 3-104: Fuser Assembly

Transfer Belt

The transfer belt transfers the page image from the drum to the page. Most color laser printers use a transfer belt, which moves the paper sheet through the assembly and ensures there is no misalignment during transit. The paper passes through the toner cartridges in turn and are perfectly aligned because of the rubber belt that holds the sheet in its proper position, with the help of friction or static electricity, in order to apply toner uniformly.

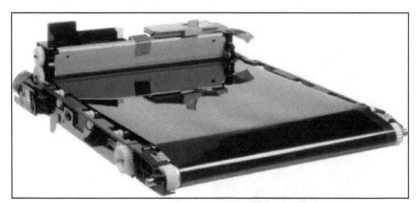

Figure 3-105: Transfer Belt

Transfer Roller

The transfer roller transfers the toner on to the sheet of paper. It has an opposing electrical charge to the drum. The unused toner is also accumulated by this roller and returned to the toner cartridge.

Pickup Rollers

The pickup roller picks up the paper. It is a large rubber roller (also known as the finger or foot) used for making contact, using a high degree of friction, with the paper. Hence, the top sheet of the ream is pulled forward and passed to the further pinch rollers or registration rollers, which then convey the sheet uniformly into the assembly.

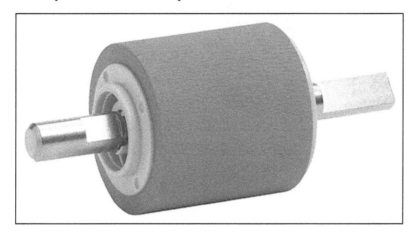

Figure 3-106: Pickup Rollers

Separator Pads

The separation pad or stationary pad enables pickup rollers to pick up only one sheet of paper at a time. It is located underneath the pickup roller and is used to separate the sheets so that only the first sheet of the bundle is conveyed into the assembly. The pad is made of board or cork, and provides a surface for the pickup roller. The pickup roller and the pad are common items that need periodic replacement.

Figure 3-107: Separator Pa

Duplexing Assembly

The duplexing assembly switches paper from the front to the back side so that the printer can print on both sides of the paper. It is used to turn over or flip the sheet so that the back of the paper can be printed as well.

Figure 3-108: Duplexing Assembly

Imaging Process

The laser imaging process of the printer consists of the following steps:

Processing

The image or text to be printed is sent to the printer, where it is recalculated and stored in RAM while the printer readies itself for the laser printing. This data has been sent at a speed accepted by the printing device.

Charging or Conditioning

A negative charge is applied to the drum by the primary corona or charge corona, which is typically powered by a high-voltage power supply within the printer, 600 V DC. This allows the drum to attract and stick the toner to itself.

Exposing or Writing

In this process, areas of the drum are exposed to laser beams, where the image will be produced, making these parts of the drum sensitive. The electrostatic charge will be applied only to the affected parts.

Developing

The surface of the drum holds an electrical representation of the image to be printed. These discrete electrical representations first need to be converted into a format that can be transferred to the paper. The toner is transferred to the sensitive areas of the drum that were exposed during the writing step and as the drum rolls over, the toner is applied to the painted area of the drum.

Transferring

In this step of the process, the developed image is rotated into position. The controller reports the registration rollers that the paper should be fed through. The registration rollers pass the paper underneath the photosensitive drum, and the process of transferring the image begins.

The transfer corona wire applies the positive charge to the paper. The toner is attracted to the paper because the paper now has a positive charge and there is a negative charge on the toner particles on the drum. In numerous printers, the paper passes by a static elimination device (often a strip), which removes excess charge from the paper. To apply the different layers of colors to the paper, some color laser printers use a transfer belt. Some printers use a duplexing assembly that enables the paper to be printed on both sides.

Fusing

In this step of the process, the fusing setup makes the toner image permanent. Here, the sheet passes through a fuser roller or heat roller assembly, which fuses or bonds the toner onto the page.

Cleaning

In the final step of this process, a rubber blade removes excess toner from the drum as it spins. The blade is used to wipe off or collect any toner left on the drum and replace it in the EP toner cartridge.

Maintenance of a Laser Printer

To keep laser printers working efficiently and to upgrade their life as much as possible, ensure that the printer's maintenance is done periodically, as outlined by the manufacturer's guidelines. In many printers, scheduled maintenance involves installing a maintenance kit, which includes pickup rollers (for the trays), a fuser, transfer roller, separation rollers, and feed rollers.

Replacing Toner

Toner is the main consumable item in the laser printers and must be replaced regularly. Toner cartridges are used to store toner in laser printers. Use the recommended toner for the printer. Inappropriate or bad supplies could ruin the printer and break the warranty. Reattach the toner cartridge to avoid spills before moving or shipping a printer from one place to another.

Applying a Maintenance Kit

There are different maintenance kits for different printers that are marketed by the manufacturer. The kit typically contains a transfer roller, fuser, and feed/separation rollers. A counter present on the laser printer identifies the requirement of a maintenance kit. Apply the new maintenance kit and then reset the counter.

Calibration

Calibration is the process of comparing the output with the reference standards or expected output. All the hardware, including the scanner, monitor, and printer, should match in color, margins, and so forth. Laser and inkjet printers often a need to calibrate.

The process of calibration varies for each manufacturer. The following are the general steps for calibration:

- During software installation, a window will prompt the installation wizard and ask "if you want to calibrate now" click "Yes"
- The printer then prints various sets of numbered lines. Each set of lines corresponds to an alignment instance. Then the wizard will ask you to choose the set that looks the best
- Enter the set number and then click "OK". The process of alignment ends here. But in some cases, an aligned page is printed to verify the desired setting, and users are given a chance to modify the settings if required

Cleaning

Make sure that the printer and the area around the printer is clean. Wipe it down after replacing the toner or carrying out any maintenance. Make sure to clean the debris properly, as a dirty printer and dirty components can affect the printed output.

Advantages of Laser Printers over Other Printers

Speed

Laser printers can print anywhere from 10 to 100 pages per minute (ppm), depending on the model and whether it is a black-and-white or color laser printer.

Print Quality

The laser printer commonly prints at 600 dots per inch (DPI), which is considered letter quality, but 1200 DPI and 2400 DPI resolution printers are available.

Inkjet Printers

Inkjet printers are one of the most popular type of printers in use today. Inkjet printers spray ink to print text or graphics on to the page. Inkjet printers provide a high-quality and low-production solution that is ideal for images and photographs.

There are two main types of inkjet printer: thermal and piezoelectric. The differences between them is how the ink is sprayed onto the paper. A thermal inkjet printer works by heating the ink to about 400 degrees Fahrenheit, producing vapor bubbles that push the ink out of the cartridge – thermal

inkjets are also referred to as bubble jets. Whereas, a piezoelectric printer uses electricity rather than heat.

Inkjet printers are more popular because they are comparatively cheaper and can print in color. However, they are slower than laser printers and the cost of ink per page can be higher than it is for a laser printer. Therefore, most enterprises prefer laser printers for their main printing needs and have inkjet printers for color printing. The main components of an inkjet printer will be discussed in the following section.

Ink Cartridge

The ink cartridges contain the ink for printing. Some cartridges have the print head along with it for that color of ink. Sometimes, users get a new print head when they replace the cartridge. In some other printer models, the ink cartridge is just an ink reservoir, and the arm heads are not actually attached to it and do not need replacement. But where the ink reservoir and print head are the same unit, they are held in place by an actuator arm that moves the arm head left to right across the page.

Print Head

The print head sprays small drops of ink onto the sheet of paper. Different amounts of basic color inks such as magenta, cyan, yellow, and black form the specific color as the jet points at the same point on the page. The print head also has a chip that contains information on to how full the ink reservoir is, from the time of its original purchase.

Roller

A platen roller lies behind the paper. This roller rolls the paper into a C-shape and holds it in tension during the application of ink.

Feeder

Usually a plastic back plate is used at the top of the printer to keep the paper in position. The feeder roller and separation pad are located at the base of this plate, sending one sheet at a time into the assembly.

Duplexing Assembly

As with the laser printer, the duplexing assembly is used to turn over or flip the sheet so that the back of the paper can also be printed.

Carriage

The carriage is a plastic assembly that retains the print head in place. The carriage assembly enables the print head to move from left to right in front of the paper. The carriage return is basically a motorized belt mounted around two metal runners.

<u>Belt</u>

A rubber belt is a part of the carriage return, which rotates the belt clockwise or anticlockwise to move the carriage left to right along with the track. It is driven by the motor.

Calibration

Calibration is the process that ensures the proper alignment of the cartridges to one another and to the paper to maintain high quality printing. On an inkjet printer, calibration refers to the head alignment. The printer aligns the ink cartridges automatically each time they are replaced or installed.

Maintenance of an Inkjet Printer

While inkjet printers use a different technology for printing data, meaning a different maintenance schedule, they have some of the same maintenance procedures. The maintenance of inkjet printers involves the following:

<u>Clean Heads</u>

The print heads play a vital role during printing so their maintenance cannot be neglected. There are two maintenance activities to be applied to the print heads. If the colors do not print the same for example, blacks have a bronze look, users need to wipe off or clean the nozzles. The head cleaning cycle is typically used to clear out the nozzles.

The second maintenance activity is head alignment. If the printing head is misaligned, users will find white repeating lines or a grid-like pattern on the printing paper. In modern printers, there is an automatic alignment and cleaning function; you just need to perform these manually by referring to the printer documentation.

<u>Replace Cartridges</u>

When ink gets low, you need to remove the old cartridge and replace it with a new one. You can follow these general steps for cartridge replacement:

- Uncover the printer and locate the position of the button that is used to hold the cartridge in position
- Remove the cover that is over the cartridge
- Pull and remove the old empty cartridge
- Now, place the new cartridge in its position. It will "click" into the place
- Replace the cartridge cover
- Use the same button to hold it in its home position that is used to place the cartridge into the replacement positon

Calibration

Calibration of the printer can be performed by accessing the properties of the printer and the calibration function on the General Tab or the Advanced Tab. Select the calibration function and the printer will automatically perform the calibration process. In some cases, you need to calibrate whenever you replace the cartridges.

Clear Jam

Paper jams can be caused by using a poor quality paper, but sometimes jams occur with good paper. Follow these general steps solve paper jams:

- Check the paper tray. If you see a piece of paper sticking out or protruding from where the paper is picked up, pull it out gently
- If the jam still exists, open the rear access door and check inside the printer. If there is any paper stuck inside, pull it out gently; make sure to remove all the pieces
- Now, check the front door of the printer and look for any pieces that might be stuck in this area; if present, gently pull them out
- Select the resume button in order to resume the print process when the jam is cleared

Exam Note

Know that laser printer components include the imaging drum, fuser assembly, transfer belt, transfer roller, pickup rollers, separation pads, and duplexing assembly. Describe the function of the components of an inkjet printer. These include the ink cartridge, print head, roller, feeder, duplexing assembly, carriage, and belt.

Thermal

Thermal printing is considered an old technology today and can be found in older fax machines. It works by printing on a waxy paper that comes on a roll; when the heat passes over the roll, the paper turns black. This technology can also be found on many handheld package tracking and Point-of-Sale (POS) devices such as credit card terminals.

Thermal printers consist of the following parts:

- **Thermal Head:** This produces the heat and prints to the paper
- **Platen:** This is a rubber roller that feeds the paper to the print head
- **Spring:** This applies pressure to the print head, which connects the print head to the paper
- **Circuit Board:** This regulates the mechanism that moves the print head

Thermal printers use a print head for printing, i.e., when it needs to print, the print head heats and cools spots on the print head. The paper underneath the heated print head turns black on those spots. As the paper passes through the printer, the pattern of black spots produces an image on the page of what is being printed.

There are some variations of thermal printing that are available today. They are especially designed for professional usage and are high-end color graphics printers.

Thermal Wax Transfer Printers

Another type of thermal printer uses a heat-sensitive ribbon instead of heat-sensitive paper. The print head of the thermal printer melts wax-based ink from the ribbon onto the paper. These printers are also referred to as thermal transfer or thermal wax-transfer printers. This is a color, non-impact printer that is high quality but usually expensive.

Dye Sublimation

Dye sublimation is another non-impact, color line printer. It works by converting solid ink into a gas, which is then applied to the sheet of paper. It applies the color in a continuous tone, instead of individual dots, and the colors are applied to the paper one by one. The ink is available in the form of film rolls. The ink and the paper for this printer is expensive and the print speed is slow, but the quality of print is extremely high.

Following are the key components of the thermal assembly:

Feed Assembly

Feed assemblies or feeders allow users to feed input they are printing on paper, cards, and so on. Some feed assemblies allow users to swap between multiple inputs or feeds, which is useful where users require alternate printing on different types of materials.

A pinch roller is used to pull the paper from the reel onto the feed assembly.

Heating Element

The heating element is used to heat specific parts of the paper, which react chemically and change color (sublime). The heating element generates the heat and performs the actual printing. It is one of the most expensive components of the printer. Printers that use ribbons are thermal transfer printers, and printers that use thermal paper are known as direct thermal printers.

Special Thermal Paper

The areas of the thermal paper exposed to heat from the heating element react. Here, the dye is visible on the page. In order to print with a thermal printer, use heat-sensitive paper specially designed for the printer as it is different from paper used in other types of printer. Rolls of thermal paper come in a variety of sizes and colors.

Maintenance of a Thermal Process

Unlike laser printers, thermal printers have no moving parts, so they require less maintenance than other printers. Maintenance includes inspecting the paper tray and replacing the paper, cleaning the heating element, and removing any debris that may be left behind. The following sections deal with the maintenance of thermal printers.

Replace Paper

Replace thermal paper when needed. Ensure the feed area is kept clean from slivers of paper and other debris.

Clean the Heating Element

The heating element in a thermal printer is the equivalent of the print head in laser and ink jet printers. It must therefore be kept clean to ensure maximum print quality. After each roll of thermal transfer ribbon, many vendors suggest cleaning the print head. Users can also use isopropyl alcohol to clean the print heads. It is available in wipes, pens, pads, and swabs from various vendors.

Always unplug the printer before approaching the heating elements of the printer. Let the heating elements cool down first. Refer to the manufacturer's manual to clean the thermal elements. There are recommended cleaning cards, cleaning pens, and kits that are available for cleaning the thermal element.

Remove Debris

Ensure that the printer is always free of dust and debris. Any type of particle that enters the printer can interfere with the paper feeding properly or can badly affect the print quality. To clean up debris for better print quality and longer print life, use isopropyl alcohol wipes or other cleaning materials as recommended by the printer vendor.

Impact Printer

An impact printer uses force to transfer ink to paper to print characters and graphics. Impact printers are the oldest printer technology and are used mainly in industrial and point-of-sale applications.

They consist of a print head, which is made up of a block of metal pins that extend and retract the head. These pins are designed to trigger and extend in patterns that form the letters and numbers, transferred by moving across the paper. Older models, known as Near Letter-Quality (NLQ) print, used nine pins. Later models gave better Letter-Quality (LQ) output and used 24 pins.

The most common form of impact printers are dot-matrix printers, so called because they generate the appearance of completely formed characters from dots placed on the page. Non-impact printers are unable to do that. Dot-matrix printers are not commonly found in modern offices because of their drawbacks, including slow speed, noise, and poor print quality.

Print Head

The common term "Impact" is used to describe daisy wheel and dot-matrix printers, which have a series of pins known as solenoid fires, used in a pattern to form a letter or number. The daisy wheel involves the same process, but a slug is used instead of solenoid fires, where a slug is a metal hammer with the embossed font on the hammer head that is swung forward, making contact with the paper and leaving an impression. The print processes character by character and works across the line.

The most common types of print heads are 9 pins, 18 pins (two columns of 9 pins each), and 24 pins (which provides near letter quality, or NLQ, printing when used in best quality mode).

Ribbon

The ink ribbon is located in front of the paper. The printer presses the inked ribbon onto the paper to leave an impression. The platen gap is the key factor here. This is the distance between the platen roller and the print head. If they are placed too close, the paper may be torn, but if the print head is placed too far away, a light, faint or no impression may occur on the paper.

Tractor Feed

Impact printers use simple uncoated paper or labels in different widths and sizes. Impact printers intended for point-of-sale receipt printing might use roll paper or larger paper sizes. When larger sizes of paper are used, these printers usually use a tractor feed mechanism to pull or push the paper past the print head. Tractor-fed printer paper and labels have fixed or removable sprocket holes on both sides of the paper. The paper used for printing is stored as concertina-fashion in a box.

This form of media is often called "impact", "dot-matrix", "continuous feed", or "pin-feed" paper or labels.

Impact Paper

Impact paper can be sheet-fed using the registration rollers. The extremes of where the print head can move to is considered the printable area. Consideration of the printable area is important, to make the paper aligned and calibrated from character position 1, so that a margin is left. The paper feed section contains two metal fingers on either side of the sheet, which is specialized to keep the sheet central with respect to the platen roller and assembly, and to ensure that the paper is fed in the proper position.

Maintenance of an Impact Printer

The print head of the dot matrix printer reaches high temperatures, so avoid touching it and getting burned. Most dot-matrix printers contain a temperature sensor to indicate the temperature of the

print head. The sensor interrupts the process of printing to let the print head cool down and then allows the process of printing to begin again. A faulty sensor can cause the printer to print a few lines and then stop for a while, print more, then stop, and so on. The following sections deal with the maintenance of different parts of an impact printer.

Replace the Ribbon

Keeping the ribbon fresh is essential because when the ribbon is worn, the quality of printing goes down. It is also essential because the ribbon on an impact dot-matrix printer lubricates the pins in the print head and protects the print head from impact damage.

In addition to replacing the ribbon when print quality is no longer acceptable, be sure to discard any ribbon that creates cuts or snags, as these may snag a print head pin and crack or bend the pin.

Replace the Print Head

If users replace ribbons when required, they minimize the chances of needing to replace the print head. However, if a print head suffers damage to one or more pins, it will need to be replaced. Damaged pins might snag the ribbon, and if a pin breaks, it will leave a gap in the printer's output characters.

The print head and the debris should be cleaned off with a cotton swab or denatured alcohol, but it should never be lubricated.

Replace the Paper

Preventive measurements not only deal with keeping the print head clean and dry but also with vacuuming shreds of paper from inside the machine. This vacuuming should be done on a regular basis when needed, but it is mandatory when replacing the paper.

Virtual Printers

The term virtual printer applies to any utility that is used as a printer by an application but generates a file rather than a printout. A virtual printer is not an actual or physical printer; it is a driver or a piece of software installed on the computer. The user interface of a virtual printer is similar to a printer driver, but the virtual printer is not physically or virtually connected to an actual printer. The virtual printer is commonly used to create and protect the format of a document, for example, creating a PDF file (Portable Document Format), which looks exactly the same as the printed document when viewed on a computer screen.

The resulting output from a virtual printer is a formatted file to be used by the end user or can be used attached to an email. Since Office 2010 introduced supports XML and PDF printouts for editing, the need for virtual printers has reduced, but they are still in use today.

Printing to File

Not all print devices print to actual paper. A virtual printer is a driver or print object inside the OS that is used to convert a file into another format, which is then used by another program. This enables the files to be converted from a proprietary format to a more generic format.

All virtual printers print to a file of some kind. Some virtual printer drivers print to a certain type of file for an application associated with it.

To print to a file in Microsoft Windows:

- Open the Print dialog
- Select the printer
- Check the "Print to File" box
- Click "Print"
- You should be prompted for a file location. If not, check the Documents folder to locate the file. The file is stored with the .prn file extension

With MacOS, use the Print dialog and select "PostScript" for output to a PostScript printer.

Printing to PDF

This virtual printer driver creates an Adobe PDF file, which is a platform-independent page or document description. The resulting file can be easily sent via email to any platform that has a PDF reader application installed in it, and it will look exactly the same as it did originally.

The PDF is the most common document format introduced by Adobe. This contains metadata about the file and security information restricting access to the file to certain users.

When users print to PDF in Windows using a Windows app, they are prompted to specify the destination of the file. However, most other PDF options (compression, metadata support, and others) are not available. Uses can use the "Save to PDF" option, when offered, to control these settings.

With MacOS, use the Print dialog and open the PDF menu to select the type and destination for the PDF file. Users can add title, author, subject, and keywords metadata. Use the "Security Options" button to set up password restrictions for opening, copying content, or printing the document.

To print to PDF in Linux, install CUPS-PDF (the CUPS printer driver for PDF). Restart your system (if necessary), and PDF will show up in the list of printers.

Printing to XPS

XML Paper Specification (XPS) is Microsoft's equivalent of PDF. XPS does not rely on the PostScript language, as this is commonly used for sending management information and true-type fonts.

The XPS viewer can be added as a feature to a server. The respective driver creates a Microsoft XPS document, a page description layout that looks like PDF but is Microsoft's product. The driver for this purpose is also called Microsoft XPS Document Writer.

Current versions of Windows include the Microsoft XPS Document Writer virtual printer. Select this printer to create an XPS (XML Paper Specification) document. When users select this option, they can optionally enable the opening of the XPS file after it is saved.

Printing to Image

This is a specialized driver that outputs print to an image and creates a bitmap image file out of the page to be printed. However, this is no longer very popular because the quality of PDF files has made it the most popular format for printing a file to an image. The PDF is good on any platform and does not distort when modified or resized.

One way of printing to an image is to use Microsoft's **Snipping Tool**, which allows users to choose an area of the screen then create and save it as a new image.

3D printers

3D printing is the common term given to what is technically known as additive manufacturing (AM). There are two basic types of 3D printing:

Fused Deposition Modeling (FDM)

FDM is an additive method in which materials are fed into an extruder, superheated, and then applied layer by layer on top of a substratum to produce 3D shapes that instantly harden.

Stereolithography

This is a more industrial process involving photopolymer resins and lasers that is beyond the scope of the A+ exam.

Many companies make 3D printers. Some use proprietary processes and file types, while others use standardized processes and files. The device generally has a cuboid shape with one or more glass wall that allows the user to view the production process.

Many 3D printers can be linked via USB, Wi-Fi, and Ethernet. A computer running an operating system such as Windows 7 and higher or OS X 10.9 and higher can control these printers.

Plastic Filament

This is the plastic material that is fed from a spool, although it is possible to use many different materials. Polylactic Acid (PLA) and Acrylonitrile Butadiene (ABS) are the two most prevalent filament kinds. The filament is the "ink" of an FDM printer and is available in different colors.

Comparison between Various Printers

There are various types of printers available today that differ from each other in many ways. The following are some of the common differences:

Continuous Feed vs. Sheet Fed

Continuous-feed printers feed paper using a system of tractors and sprockets. The dot matrix is an example of a continuous feed. Sheet-fed printers use a paper tray to accept plain paper.

Impact vs. Non-impact

Impact printers actually strike an inked ribbon on the paper and therefore can print multipart forms, whereas a non-impact printer does not strike the paper for delivering ink onto the page. Dot matrix is an example of impact printers; all other printers covered in this chapter are non-impact.

Line vs. Page

A line printer prints on the paper one line at a time; whereas page printer prepares the entire page in memory and then prints it all at once. Dot matrix and inkjets are examples of line printers; laser printer is an example of a page printer.

Exam Note

Identify examples of using a virtual printer. These include print to file, print to PDF, print to XPS, and print to image.

Mind Map of Various Types of Printers

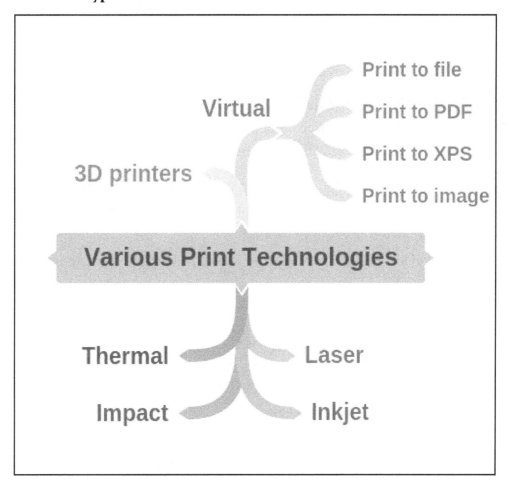

Figure 3-109: Mind Map of Various Types of Printers

Summary

Explain Basic Cable Types, Features, and Their Purposes

- The most popular method for adding devices to desktops, laptops, and tablets is to use a USB port
- Adapters are available to convert between different kinds of display ports, such as DVI and VGA or DVI and HDMI
- Converters are available for USB ports, such as USB Type-A to mini-Type-A, or USB to Ethernet
- Ethernet ports have RJ-45 connectors. RJ-11 ports are found on internal and external modems

- Fiber cabling is used to carry information over longer distances, and coaxial cabling is used for video networks

Identify Common Connector Types

- Cable internet connections use RG-6 coaxial cable with an F-connector on the end
- BNC is an older connector form used by coaxial networks
- RJ45 is the connector used on patch cables with twisted-pair
- DB-9 is a serial connector used with RS-232 connections

Install RAM Types

- DDR3 is a 240-pin architecture. 288-pin is DDR4, 184-pin is the first version of DDR (DDR1)
- SODIMMs is 200-pin architecture in laptops
- DDR2 is a type of DRAM that, for the most part, was used in either single-channel or dual-channel environments

Select, Install and Configure Storage Devices

- Blu-ray, at a typical maximum of 50 GB, has the largest storage capacity
- Non-Volatile Memory Express (NVMe) is a specification for accessing storage while using PCI Express
- The 3.5-inch drive is used in desktop computers. The 2.5-inch drive is used in laptops and other smaller devices

Install and Configure Motherboards, CPUs, and Add-on Cards

- Important motherboard parts are processor, RAM slots, RAM, expansion slots (PCI, PCIe, and AGP), and cooling devices
- Processors can be multicore and can have very fast cache memory
- The clock speed refers to the internal clock of the processor. This is not the same as the bus speed
- PCI is a 32- and 64-bit parallel bus

Explain the Purposes and Uses of Various Peripheral Types

- A KVM connects various PCs to a single keyboard, mouse, and monitor
- The mouse, printer, and LED display all deal with resolution
- Video projector's light output is measured in lumens

Summarize Power Supply Types and Features

- Power supplies are usually rated in watts
- Molex connectors offers 12 volts and 5 volts
- PCIe power can be 8-pin or 6-pin

Select and Configure Appropriate Components for a Custom PC Configuration

- A virtualization workstation is a PC that operates one or more virtual operating systems
- Network-Attached Storage (NAS) is when one or more hard drives are installed into a device known as a NAS box or NAS server that connects directly to the network

Install and Configure Common Devices

- The setups of thin and thick clients can differ from a hardware and connectivity standpoint
- Thin clients are meant to use an OS that is embedded in RAM
- Thick clients have a hard drive
- Chrome OS is a fairly simple system compared to Windows and other operating systems

Configure SOHO Multifunction Devices/Printers and Settings

- Duplexing (as it relates to printers) means to print to both sides
- Bonjour is a MacOS service that allows automatic discovery of devices on the LAN; it can also be run on Windows
- AirPrint is an Apple technology for MacOS and iOS used to automatically locate and download drivers for printers
- Mobile devices can use Bluetooth ad hoc mode network printing where no wireless access point exists

Install and Maintain Various Print Technologies

- The proper order of the laser printing/imaging process is processing, charging, exposing, developing, transferring, fusing, cleaning
- Feed assembly, thermal heating unit, and thermal paper are associated with thermal printers
- Print head, ribbon, tractor feed, and impact paper are associated with impact printers
- Inkjet is the type of printer that applies wet ink to paper

Practice Questions

1. Which connector is used for cable internet?
   A. DE-9
   B. RJ-45
   C. BNC
   D. LC
   E. F-connector

2. Which sort of cable can connect a PC to another PC directly?
   A. T568A
   B. SATA
   C. Crossover
   D. T568B
   E. Straight-through

3. Which of the following would be suitable for 1000-Mbps networks? (Select all that apply)
   A. Category 3
   B. Category 5
   C. Category 5e
   D. Category 6

4. Which connector is used for telephone cord?
   A. RJ-45
   B. RJ-11
   C. BNC
   D. RS-232

5. Which type of RAM is not compatible with any earlier type of random-access memory?
   A. DDR2
   B. DDR3
   C. DDR4
   D. DDR5

6. How many pins are on memory module of a DDR3?
   A. 184
   B. 200
   C. 240
   D. 288

7. How much data can an SATA Revision 3.0 drive transfer per second?
   A. 6 Gb/s
   B. 50 MB/s
   C. 90 MB/s
   D. 16 Gb/s

8. Which level of RAID stripes information and parity across three or more disks?
   A. RAID 0
   B. RAID 1
   C. RAID 5
   D. RAID 10

9. Which of the following has the biggest potential for storage capacity?
   A. Blu-ray
   B. CD-R
   C. CD-RW
   D. DVD-RW

10. Which component provides power to the CMOS when the PC is turned off?
    A. Lithium Battery
    B. POST
    C. BIOS
    D. Power Supply

11. Which of the following connectors is used to power a video card?
    A. 24-pin power
    B. 6-pin PCIe
    C. Molex
    D. 3.5-mm TRS

12. Which of the following is a chip that stores encryption keys?
    A. Secure Boot
    B. Firmware
    C. TPM
    D. Intel TV

13. What does Hyper-Threading do?
    A. It provides a high-speed connection from the CPU to RAM
    B. It allows four simultaneous threads to be processed by one CPU core
    C. It allows two simultaneous threads to be processed by one CPU core

D. It gives multiple cores within the CPU

14. Which of the following is a description of light output?
    A. KVM
    B. Lumens
    C. Contrast
    D. CHS

15. Which of the following are considered as both input and output devices?
    A. Smart card reader, motion sensor, biometric device
    B. Keyboard, mouse, touchpad
    C. Printer, speakers
    D. Smart TV, touchscreen, KVM, headsets

16. How many pins do the SATA power connector has?
    A. 8
    B. 12
    C. 15
    D. 18

17. Which of the following is a desktop computer system?
    A. Thick Client
    B. Thin Client
    C. SAN
    D. NAS

18. Which voltages do a Molex power connector supply?
    A. 3.3 V and 1.5 V
    B. 5 V and 3.3 V
    C. 12 V and 5 V
    D. 24 V and 12 V

19. Which of the following would include a gigabit NIC and a RAID array?
    A. Gaming PC

B. Thin Client

C. NAS

D. Audio/video editing workstation

20. Which stage of the laser printing/imaging process involves extreme heat?
    A. Transferring
    B. Exposing
    C. Writing
    D. Fusing

21. What kind of printer is the most often-used shared network printer in businesses?
    A. Laser
    B. Impact
    C. Thermal
    D. Inkjet

22. What type of printer applies wet ink to paper?
    A. Laser
    B. Impact
    C. Thermal
    D. Inkjet

Chapter 04: Virtualization & Cloud Computing

Cloud Computing is a new operational model and a set of technologies for managing shared pools of computing resources. Cloud computing is the practice of using a network of remote servers hosted on the internet to store, manage, and process data rather than using a local server or personal computer. It is the on-demand delivery of computing resources through a cloud services platform with pay-as-you-go pricing. It is the distributive technology of cloud computing that makes it a powerful means for an organization to grow its business in terms of time and cost efficiency, profitability, and scalability. Cloud computing provides a lot of advantages to the users and makes their work much easier.

Some of the advantages are:

The Benefits of Massive Economies of Scale

With cloud computing, users can achieve lower variable costs than they can get on their own. Cloud computing providers such as Amazon build their own data centers and achieve higher economies of scale, which results in lower prices.

Stop Guessing Capacity

Users can access as much or as little resources they need instead of having to guess their needs and buying too much or too few resources. They can scale up and down as required with no long-term contracts.

Increased Speed and Agility

New IT resources are readily available on the cloud. Hence, their functionality can be tuned according to demand. The result is a dramatic increase in agility for organizations.

Stop Spending Money on Running and Maintaining Data Centers

Cloud computing eliminates the traditional need for spending money on running and maintaining data centers.

Go Global in Minutes

Organizations can enjoy lower latency at minimal cost by efficiently deploying the application in multiple regions around the world.

Trade Capital Expense for Variable Expense

Pay only for the resources consumed instead of having to invest heavily in data centers and servers before knowing the requirements.

Virtualization

Virtualization is the technique of deploying multiple machines on a single on-premises or remote hardware. Physical hardware hosting a dedicate machine for a service can also be migrated on powerful hardware running multiple virtual machines, both in isolated and shared environments. Virtualizing on the cloud offers much more scalability and ease of management compared to on-premises virtualization.

The fundamental concept of virtualization is to deal with the burden of workload by transforming traditional computing into modern computing, making it more scalable, efficient, and economical.

Virtualization can be classified as:

- Hardware-level Virtualization

- Operating System Virtualization

- Server Virtualization

Innovation of virtualization technology is an antidote to the need for multiple hardware. It is cost and energy saving, providing speedy management of computing and networking.

Cloud computing depends on the concepts of virtualization. In cloud computing, computational resources like space/memory and processors that require a host (either an operating system or the hypervisor) are allotted to users.

The virtualization model consists of cloud users, service providers, virtualized models, and its host software. Virtualization models make it conceivable to run numerous operating systems and different applications on the same server at the same time.

Advantages of Virtualization Technology

The advantages of virtualization technology are as follows:

- It is a big step toward new technology that makes life easier and better

- It helps to make cloud computing more efficient and eco-friendly

- It is one of the most cost-saving, hardware-reducing, and energy-saving techniques

- It provides isolation

- It is resource sharing

- It provides an aggregation of resources

- It provides dynamic resources

Comparison and Contrast of Cloud Computing Concepts

Common Cloud Models

Choosing the right service model is a critical success factor for delivering cloud-based solutions. In order to choose the right service model or combination of service models, one must fully understand what each service model is and what responsibilities the cloud service providers assume versus the responsibilities the cloud service consumer assumes.

"A cloud service model is what our customers are asking for to take them to the next level and free them from the bondage of mainframe and client-server software."

—Marc Benioff, CEO, Salesforce.com

In this section, we will discuss the common cloud models: Infrastructure as a Service (IaaS), Software as a Service (SaaS), and Platform as a Service (PaaS).

Infrastructure as a Service (IaaS)

- This is a category of cloud services that gives the customer with processing, storage, networks, and other fundamental computing resources

- The customer is able to deploy and run subjective software, which can incorporate operating systems and applications

- The customer does not manage or control the fundamental cloud infrastructure but has control over operating systems, storage, deployed applications, and possibly limited control of select networking components (e.g., host firewalls)

- Providers include Amazon EC2, Rackspace Cloud servers

Software as a Service (SaaS)

- This is a software model that enables the customer to use the provider's application running on a cloud infrastructure

- The applications are available from different client devices such as a web browser (e.g. web-based email)

- The customer does not manage or control the hidden cloud infrastructure including networks, servers, operating systems, and storage

- Providers include Google Apps, Caspio, Nivio

Platform as a Service (PaaS)

- This is a category of cloud services that enables customers to deploy onto customer created cloud infrastructure or obtain applications created using programming languages and tools supported by the provider

- The customer does not manage or control the hidden cloud infrastructure

- The customer has control over applications

- Providers include Windows Azure, Google App

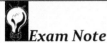
Exam Note

CompTIA A+ Exam (220-1001) may include questions regarding the acronyms IaaS, SaaS, PaaS and the differences in their services.

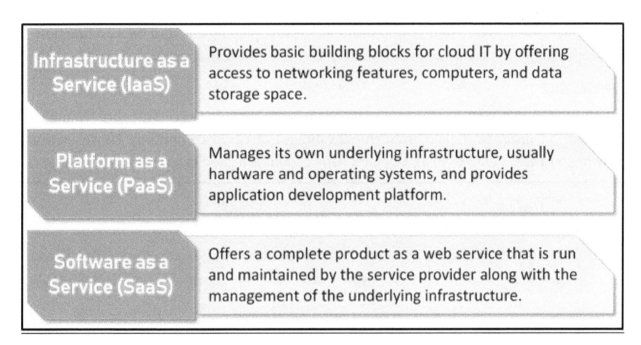

Figure 4-1: Common Cloud Service Categories

Public vs. Private vs. Hybrid vs. Community

Public Cloud

The Public Cloud is one of the most vital models in which service providers create resources, such as storage and applications, which are available to the overall public over the internet or web applications/web services. Usually, public cloud services are free or offered on a "pay-as-you-go" display.

In public cloud, hardware, application, and bandwidth costs are secured by the service provider, so it is a simple and economical set-up for the user. Google AppEngine, Windows Azure Services Platform, Amazon Elastic Compute Cloud (EC2) are examples of public clouds.

Private Cloud

A virtual Private Cloud is an on-demand configurable pool of shared computing resources allocated within a public cloud environment, providing a certain level of isolation between the different

organizations using the resources. Amazon's Elastic Compute Cloud (EC2) or Simple Storage Service (S3) are examples of private clouds.

Hybrid Cloud

A Hybrid Cloud is a combination of public and private clouds where the infrastructure is partially hosted inside the organization and is remotely in a public cloud. For example, an association may use Amazon Simple Storage Service (Amazon S3) as a public cloud service to record their data but at the same time continue their in-house storage for instant access to operational customer data. Hybrid storage clouds are extremely important for record keeping and as a backup function. It is a decent methodology for a business to exploit for cost effectiveness and scalability.

Community Cloud

A Community Cloud is where various associations with comparable necessities are willing to share infrastructure in order to benefit from the advantages of cloud computing. However, costs are typically higher than a public cloud. Google's "Gov Cloud" is a good example of community cloud.

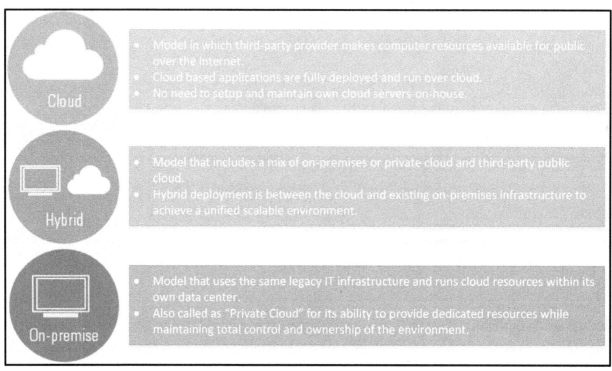

Figure 4-2: Common Cloud Models

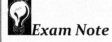**Exam Note**

Understand the purposes of public, private, hybrid, and community clouds.

Real World Scenario

> *Background*
>
> The online auction company Acme eAuctions (AEA) built its entire infrastructure on-premises before cloud computing was a marketing buzzword. AEA's management believes that moving to the cloud can give the company a competitive advantage in the following areas:
>
> - Speed to market
>
> - Flexibility
>
> - Scalability
>
> - Cost
>
> *Challenges*
>
> AEA already has a huge investment in physical infrastructure, so its shift to the cloud will have to occur one piece of infrastructure and one application domain at a time. Since AEA already has a mature data center, it may choose to keep certain pieces of its architecture on-premises in a private cloud (for example, payment processing) and others in the public cloud.
>
> *Solutions*
>
> AEA is a prime candidate for leveraging a hybrid cloud solution. If AEA were a start-up and building a solution from scratch, it would likely build its solution 100 percent in the public cloud to eliminate the need to raise capital for building or leasing multiple data centers. For parts of its application, such as payment processing, that it deems too critical to put in a public cloud, it could leverage a SaaS solution that is certified for regulatory controls, such as PCI DSS.
>
> *Conclusion*
>
> The point here is that there is no one right answer to any problem. Companies have many options when it comes to cloud computing, which is why it is critical that managers, architects, product managers, and developers understand the different deployment models as well as the service models.

Shared Resources

Shared resources are served to multiple customers using a multi-tenant model where various physical and virtual resources are progressively assigned and reassigned according to the costumer's

request. Data of multiple tenants are completely isolated from each other. There are two main ways to share resources over the internet, either using an internal cloud or an external cloud.

Internal Vs. External Cloud

Internal and external clouds are defined by the ownership of the cloud's resources. With an internal cloud, a company may need the flexibility of cloud services but also have security and guaranteed availability requirements that prevent the company from accessing cloud services outside its own network. An internal cloud is similar to a private cloud, but is built and owned inside the organization. With an internal cloud, the company gets the virtualization services and flexibility of a commercial cloud but with the security and reliability that comes from within the company's network infrastructure. While the cost of an internal cloud may be higher than outsourcing to commercial services, there is still reduced cost in sharing resources internally.

An external cloud is a cloud solution that exists outside an organization's physical boundaries. It can be private-, public-, or community-based, as long as it is not located on an organization's property.

Rapid Elasticity

Systems need to be designed in a way that makes them capable of growing and expanding over time without a drop in performance. Cloud-based architecture can either be manually scaled up or down (on-demand scaling) or set up for auto-scaling to expand or shrink resources to keep them instantly available with optimum cost per traffic.

On-Demand

Cloud service customers can customize their computing resource requirements such as the number of instances, amount of storage or computation power without requiring the involvement of IT staff.

Resource Pooling

The Resource Pooling feature allows cloud service providers to manage a large pool of physical and virtual resources such as storage, CPUs, memory, network bandwidth, and much more in order to serve customers or end-users. These resources can be allocated dynamically (assignment and re-assignment of resources) from the resource pool as per customer's demand using a multi-tenant model.

Exam Note

Get familiar with the terms rapid elasticity, on-demand service, and resource pooling.

Measured Service

Measured Service refers to how cloud services are monitored for quality and effectiveness. Metrics for measuring services can help with decision making about what services to adopt and how to calculate service prices.

Metered Service

Cloud computing services are purchased by organizations much like they purchase utilities such as gas and water: costs are based on usage. Cloud computing services are usually calculated on an hourly basis. Outsourcing by the hour can mean immense savings for customers and it is this feature that has driven the growth of cloud services.

Exam Note

Understand the difference between measured and metered services.

Off-site Email Applications

Today's cloud-based options are a more efficient alternative to server-based emails and provide better scalability and flexibility. There are several advantages of switching to cloud-based emails for business, for example:

- Cost Saving

- Flexibility and Scalability

- Improved Security

- Remote Access

- No Maintenance Cost

Server Space

When you are running your website and email on the same server, it normally has 1gb or below of storage space. In a scenario where you have 5 employees, they would have to share that 1 Gb of storage space, each getting an account of 200 Mb – which in this day and age, is quite insufficient. Cloud-based email solutions come with huge quantities of storage, (often 10 Gb+) so you will never have to worry about deleting an email ever again.

Secure

No one can change or interfere with any email inside the cloud, either for audits or litigation.

Access Anywhere

Users can access their records using any device, anywhere, anytime as long as they have an internet connection.

- Email access is instantly available from a home computer, tablet, or even from a smartphone

- Workers' productivity levels increase, especially for remote workers

- Cloud-based email accounts sync up immediately and automatically, so data is available from multiple devices

Unlimited Backup

Unlike in-house email archiving, the cloud-based email record solution does not limit space. It develops as the volume of emails develops.

Iron-Clad Security

Data security for cloud-based solutions is more secure and advanced than local solutions. When it comes to setting up the email account, think about moving to cloud-based email service. It is a cost effective, secure, and flexible solution for storing emails.

Collaboration

Cloud-based environments have a number of benefits including efficient collective and collaborative team work, which improves productivity.

The following are the benefits of cloud collaboration:

- Real-time project collaboration

- Document editing

- Video and voice conferences

- Instant project updates

- High storage capacity for sending and storing multimedia-rich emails, including video messages

Cloud-based email is automatic, dependable, and constantly active, permitting companies to focus on the daily work process instead.

Real World Scenario

> **Background**
>
> National Oceanic and Atmospheric Administration (NOAA) is a federal agency with over 25,000 employees whose mission is to understand and predict change in climate, weather, oceans, and coasts.
>
> **Challenges**
>
> NOAA has employees working in all environments, for example, the air, on land, and on the sea. Employees rely heavily on internet-connected devices and collaboration with

team members and other agencies. NOAA needed a cost effective way of providing a reliable collaboration between team members.

Solutions

To enable efficient email and collaboration capabilities, NOAA chose a cloud-based solution that includes email, instant messaging, video conferencing, shared calendars, and shared documents. Migrating to these cloud services cut NOAA's costs in half and removed the burden of managing software and hardware updates in a highly distributed and device-heavy environment. NOAA's management staff claims that the cloud-based email and collaboration tools are faster and easier to deploy than the on-premises solutions and the services themselves were more modern.

Conclusion

NOAA moved to a cloud-based email solution—Google's Gmail—at the beginning of 2012. Moving its email and collaboration services to the cloud created great business value by delivering a better overall service at half the price with less effort.

Cloud File Storage Services

The concept of cloud file storage involves storing data in the cloud. File storage services provide accessibility to servers and applications over this shared file system. This ease of accessibility makes cloud file storage a model for workloads that depend on shared file systems and deliver simple integration without code changes.

The cloud is a classified storage system that provides shared access to file data. Users can create, delete, adjust, read, and write files and can organize them efficiently in directory trees for intuitive access.

Cloud file sharing is a service that provides synchronized access for various users to a common set of file data. For security, file sharing over the cloud is carried out with user and group permissions giving administrators full control of access to the shared file data. The advantages of cloud file storage are ease of use, scalability, low cost, and interoperability.

In the following section, we will discuss cloud file storage services.

Synchronization Apps

With cloud-based synchronization, apps on a mobile device send data to the cloud, where it is downloaded by other mobile apps, web browsers, or programs running on Windows or MacOS computers.

Data that is synced via cloud-based synchronization is encrypted and secured by passwords and usernames. Mutual authentication is used by each side of the connection to verify its identity to the other side.

There are many cloud file storage services such as IDrive, pCloud, Mega, One drive, iCloud, Google Drive, Box, Next cloud, and Spider Oak.

<u>IDrive</u>

IDrive provides continuous syncing of your files, even those on network drives. The web interface keeps sharing files by email, Facebook, and Twitter. It is easy to use, fast, and has no two-factor authentication.

The following are the features of IDrive:

- Online File sync
- Multiple Device Backup
- Snapshots and Versioning
- IDrive Express
- Manage Computers
- Disk Image Backup
- Security and Privacy
- Continuous Data Protection
- Go Mobile
- Retrieve Data
- True Archiving
- Stay Informed

<u>pCloud</u>

pCloud is one of the best storage services for storing large media files. Although some bandwidth limits apply, there appears to be no limit to the size of files you can upload, allowing you to sync large media files. The service is accessible for all desktop and mobile platforms and users can log in through the website. It is elegant, easy to use, affordable, and no collaboration tools are needed.

The following are the features of pCloud:

- **Collaboration:** Share download and upload links, brand your download links and invite users to a shared folder
- **Security:** Includes TLS/SSL channel protection, and 256-bit AES encryptions for all files

- **File Management:** Great for file versioning, remote upload, data recovery, and online document preview

- **Backup Form:** Includes Dropbox, Facebook, Instagram, OneDrive, and Google Drive

- **Media and Usability:** Video streaming, built-in video player, and unlimited file size and speed

- **Access and Synchronization:** Automatic sync across multiple devices, automatic upload of your camera roll, etc.

Mega

Mega is one of the best cloud storage services. Mega offers a web interface and mobile apps that enable users to upload files or photos and sync clients with desktop machines.

Mega ensures that all data stored in its cloud is encrypted on the device before it reaches the firm's servers.

The features of Mega are as follows:

- **Mobile App:** Access and stream files on a smartphone or tablet. Upload and sync videos and photos. Secure end-to-end encrypted chats with contacts

- **MEGA Sync:** Easy automated synchronization between computer and MEGA that permits users to access and work with data securely across different locations and devices

- **Browser Extensions:** Extensions for Chrome and Firefox for improved security, improved file transfer performance and reduced loading times

- **Business Account:** An easy and secured collaboration with chat, audio/video calls, and file sharing, all using advanced end-to-end encryption.

OneDrive

OneDrive is supported by Microsoft and is ideal for window users. The available file storage is only 5 GB. Microsoft's Photos app can use OneDrive to sync pictures across all your devices. There is an app for Android, iOS, and App Store for Mac users.

The followings are the features of OneDrive:

- **Files on Demand:** Users can access all OneDrive files in Windows 10 without taking up PC space

- **Document Scanning:** Users can scan on their mobile and store their documents, business cards, receipts, or whiteboard notes in OneDrive

- **Expiring Links: Users can increase OneDrive security** with office 365 by setting an expiry date for the links to files and photos they share

iCloud

iCloud is a cloud storage service from Apple Inc. This application is built into every Apple device offering cloud storage. It allows users to store up to 5 GB of photos, files, notes, audios, videos, and more for free. If users need to back up their iPhone to iCloud, they will want more than the free 5 GB allowance Apple gives. But compared to rivals, iCloud prices are very reasonable.

The Mac Finder app incorporates iCloud Drive, where users can store any files they want. Documents generated in the iWork office suite are also saved to iCloud and can sync across devices. Windows users can sync their files with iCloud Drive using the official user and access the iWork apps on the iCloud website.

Google Drive

Google Drive is one of the most popular choices, fullest-featured, and most generous cloud storage and syncing services, with admirable productivity suite collaboration capabilities. Google Drive offers a generous amount of free file storage. Users can also store high classification photos on their mobile phone with the companion app Google Photos, and make use of Google's own office suite (now known as G Suite). Also, improvement to paid Google Drive plans is now called Google One.

The downside is the fact that the web interface is not very easy to use, while Mac and Windows consumers can download a desktop app to drop-and-drag files simply.

Box

The syncing and storage tool Box is easy to use, faster, more responsive and greatly customizable, allowing users to incorporate their account with a vast range of apps and services. It is supported by many apps such as Google Docs and Office 365 and has a free account file upload with a limit of 250 MB.

It is also incorporated with G-Suite, which means Docs, Sheets, and Slides are automatically saved and managed in Box.

Next Cloud

Next Cloud is not an online cloud storage provider itself but provides free software to download and install a cloud storage service on a specific server. Using a server on a home network for cloud storage is quicker. Users can also allow encryption and make sure the data never leaves their home network, which is far safer. It is an innovative self-hosting solution.

Virtual Application Streaming

Virtual application streaming is a technology where an application is isolated from its fundamental operating system and is streamed to an isolated environment on a targeted device, but is implemented on the server. Registry keys and files are printed at an isolated location and are recalled from that location when the application is implemented.

Subsequently, the application now works with one file instead of many files spread during the system. It develops easy-to-run applications on different computers and previously mismatched applications can be run side by side. This technology for the Windows platform includes:

- Ceedo

- Cameyo

- Critix XenApp

- Microsoft App-V

- Numecent

- Oracle Secure Global Desktop

- Symantec Workspace Virtualization

- VMware ThinApp

- Turbo

The Benefits of Application Virtualization:

- Allows mismatched applications to run on a local machine simultaneously

- Lacks fewer resources compared to using a separate virtual machine

- Facilitates faster application deployment

- Maintains a standard, more active, and cost-effective OS configuration across multiple machines in a given association, independent of the applications being used

- Facilitates security by separating applications from the local OS

- Allows applications to be copied to convenient media and be used by other user computers, with no necessity for local installation

- Allows easier tracing of license usage, which may save on license costs

- Increases the capability of handling high and diverse/variable work volume

Application virtualization is popularly used in banking, business scenario simulations, e-commerce, stock trading, and insurance sales and marketing. Application virtualization allows applications to run in environments that do not suit the native application. For example, Wine allows some Microsoft Windows applications to run on Linux. Wine is a free and open-source compatibility layer that aims to allow computer programs developed for Microsoft Windows to run on Unix-like operating systems.

Another form of virtualization is Application Streaming where only sections of application code, settings, and data are provided when they are first required. Applications run openly from a virtual machine on a central server that is totally separate from the local system. By comparison, application streaming runs the program locally but still includes the centralized storage of application code.

The concept of application streaming carries some major advantages over traditional software distribution. Given the difficulty of modern applications, numerous functions are never or rarely used, and pulling the application on demand is more capable in terms of server, user, and network usage. Streaming also permits applications to be reserved on the local system and still run in a traditional way. Updates can also be organized automatically to the cached application files.

Cloud-based Applications

A cloud-based application is an application that is hosted in cloud instead of being hosted on a local server. It can also be considered a mixture of standard web applications and traditional desktop applications. Cloud-based applications can also be operated in the offline mode, just like desktop applications. It provides a great and rich experience to users and gives instant response to user's actions. It is really easy to update cloud applications, as the developers just need to upload the newer version of the cloud application to the web server. Cloud-based applications cannot be installed on a computer; they can only be operated either online or offline.

The followings are the features of cloud-based applications:

- They can be operated from the web browser and/or can be installed on desktops, smartphones, etc.

- They provide multi-tenancy solutions

- Data in cloud-based applications can be cached locally for a full offline mode

- Data of cloud-based applications is stored in a cloud or cloud-like infrastructure

- They can be used across a wide range of services such as application development platforms, storage, computing cycle, etc.

- User data and business-related data can be stored at multiple data centers

Virtual Desktop

A user's desktop environment (the wallpaper, icons, folders, windows, widgets, toolbars, etc.) is stored remotely on a server, called a Virtual Desktop. Desktop virtualization software splits the desktop operating systems, applications, and data from the hardware user, storing this "virtual desktop" on a remote server. Desktop virtualization is a desktop computer that hosts a single guest virtual machine. The virtual machine can be a Linux system, a Windows desktop or server, a

FreeBSD system, a DOS virtual machine, a Novell server, a Mac OS X or another operating system. Virtual Desktop Infrastructure (VDI) is a data center technology that supplies hosted desktop images to remote workers.

The remote server that runs and supports virtual desktops uses software called a <u>hypervisor</u> to build a "virtual machine" that pretends the user's desktop environment and abilities. In a Virtual Desktop Environment, employers access their personal desktop remotely, over the internet, from any user device. Critix, VMware, and Microsoft are the three major virtual desktop providers.

Virtual desktops offer greater security to an organization, since workers are not carrying around confidential company data on a personal device that could be lost, taken, or tampered with. Desktop virtualization provides many data integrity benefits.

Virtual NIC

A NIC is the physical network interface controller for hosts. A VNIC is a Virtual NIC based on physical NICs. Virtual NIC can be treated as a NIC working in a virtual machine. Visualizing a physical NIC into a visual NIC can allow a VM to connect to the internet or bridge to different network segments.

For constructing different network segments, a Virtualization Station provides five different NIC modules for adding virtual Network Interface Controllers (NICs) to virtual machines, including Intel Gigabit Ethernet, NE2000, PCnet32, Realtek Fast Ethernet and Virtual Gigabit Ethernet.

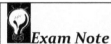
Exam Note

Understand the Virtual Desktop service and the working mechanism of Virtual NIC.

Mind Map of Cloud Computing Concepts

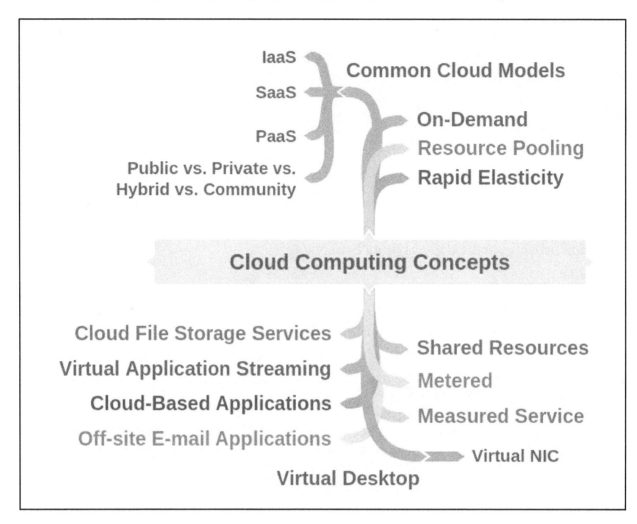

Figure 4-3: Mind Map of Cloud Computing Concepts

Set up and Configure Client-side Virtualization

There are many advantages related to client-side virtualization. Of note is that this facility helps in tightening up security, which helps to secure all the data as well as give control of data management. The traveling data can be more secure and therefore one can feel in control of the system. There are several features that client-sided virtualization has, some of which are described below.

The Purpose of Virtual Machines

Virtual machines work like a complete computer system but not another computer hardware, it has the unique ability to operate two Operating Systems (OS) on the same computer hardware at the same time. This feature is not in any sense insecure as there is no data loss on the host computer when a file runs on the virtual machine system. If the primary computer operating software is wiped out by viruses, it can easily be exchanged with a fresh one. The Virtual Machine interface has the facility to install the operating system on the host computer using its own interface.

So we can say that the main objective of Virtual Machines is that we have a software version of hardware that actually does not exist. Also, the employer can save his/her valuable time by working on a single computer instead of separate computers. It saves on electricity costs as only a single computer is being used. There are many more advantages. Crucially, users can install the kind of programs and software that they had never thought of running on the host computer operating software.

Virtual machine can be classified into two types: System Virtual Machines and Process Virtual Machines.

System Virtual Machines offer the computer-supported interface to perform functions and commands as the real operating system. This system can be used where no physical hardware exists for many uses and delivers an opportunity to use same computer architecture; however with two operating systems that are used at the same time. Virtual machine software is connected to the hard drive of the host computer system, separated by virtual patrician and can use for the fax, printing, and other applications of the host computer. Therefore, creating time and energy savings.

Resource Requirements

We know that any software requires a certain amount of space to be available to run and perform well. Where there is not enough space, the software and operating system will take extra time to processing and there may be delays. Virtual Server 2005 serves as a virtual machine system resource. Users can assign the memory required to be assigned to the virtual machine is in accumulation to the control settings on how much the host computer's CPU resources will be assigned to the Virtual Machines. We previously discussed the types of virtual machines. Here, we look at resource allocation.

Allocation of Memory: This is the main part of its configuration. When we generate a virtual machine, it is essential to identify the memory requirement. This will be the total memory in GBs or MBs that the virtual server assigns to the virtual machine. There is a maximum memory limit of 3.6 GB, which is also based on the convenience of space in the physical memory and this can be further modified when the virtual server is off. It is essential to refer to the memory setting's page that automatically shows the calculation after considering the availability of physical memory to how much memory you can assign. However, the virtual machine requires at least 32 MB space more than the quiet maximum to run Video RAM (VRAM). **Allocation of Other Resources:** This is the maximum and minimum allocation of resources the host computer has obtained to the virtual machine along with the other level of controls. The resource allocation page shows what resources are identified. This is called Resource Allocation by Capability. Users can allocate the number ranging from 1 to 10,000 to a virtual machine indicating how much it is significant to allocate resources to that specific virtual machine over others. The "1" denotes the minimum and "10,000" denotes the maximum weight. This is called Resource Allocation by Weight.

Emulator Requirements

There is a little difference between virtualization and emulation. The concept of **emulation** is the complete process and mandatory requirements for a virtual machine to work like a physical/host computer. All the operations are virtual in software where the virtualization requires hardware like CPU of the host computer. This duration was first used by IBM in 1957 and was mentioned to the hardware only, but today in the modern age, it is used for both the hardware and software configurations. Emulators were created to run a program designed to usually run on different computer architecture. The video games in Playstation2, for example, can be played in PC or Xbox 360 by providing an ideal environment. There are numerous types of emulators written in C-Language and some of them in Java such as Commodore 64, Atari, Nintendo, etc. However, most were written in C-Language and were difficult to use. Java emulators are easier. The Java PC project (JPC) is a Java emulator for the X 86 platforms, for use when connected to a Java Virtual Machine. This program connects to the primary operating system of the host computer and builds a virtual layer, allowing you to install another favorite operating system reliably and quickly. The JPC is installed on Linux, Windows, etc. operating systems, providing a dual security system. It will not damage data on the primary computer because of the various security layers. It runs at about 20% of the speed of the host computer, making it the fastest emulator software. The emulation process involves the availability of an advanced computer architecture to give users the possibility of using many restricted consoles on the PC.

Security Requirements

It was once assumed that virtual machines could not be attacked and that they are mostly harmless when running computer operations. The actions of attackers have proved this to be untrue. The first Trojan virus, in 2012, was called "Morcut". Software companies participated in the virtualization with the purpose of developing a safe working environment that that would save costs, but this was completely unsuccessful. Also, users want the security of registered antivirus software. Most security concerns arise from the operations, not from the virtual machine itself.

Several approaches and techniques are needed for good security. The first technique is to use a safe and secure network for data sharing and to always connect a registered anti-virus program on the host computer. Viruses may attack the data center of a virtual machine when allocating data from the network of the host computer using a Network Interface Card (NIC). We can use the trusted share of the hard disk of the host computer as patrician for several operations of the virtual machine. Also, users can put an anti-virus program in the virtual machine and save on scanning the data as a predictable task and save from malware. To make virtual machine a secure one, users must use the anti-virus program, patching and cloning and host-based detection of errors and viruses. Furthermore, severely control the unsecure network availability on the host computer will lead to the security of data on the virtual machine to much scope.

Kaspersky identifies three approaches to safe data and other operations on virtual machines:

The **Agent-Based Approach:** An anti-virus program is installed on each virtual machine used on the host computer. This process will, however, provide security to virtualized data, but it can still be compromised using this approach.

The **Agent-Less Approach:** Despite consuming the traditionally used antivirus programs, virtual machines must have a built-in anti-malware that will preserve it from attacks from network integration, etc. It allows the virtual machine to update and it takes much less space. However, because of unavailability of scanning, processing and other possibilities as to full anti-virus program, the agent-less approach limits itself from whole security. This approach requires more space because it needs a separate system manager. This approach is much more effective where the virtual machines are used for data storage.

The **Light-Agent Approach:** This is a mixture of the agent-less and agent-based approaches and involves a special toolbox to control numerous malware activities. Malicious websites can be blocked by an alarm alert sound system. This is the most often used approach as it provides the best fit between performance and safety.

Network Requirements

Users need to follow some steps to connect their virtual machine to a network. A single IP Block is necessary for a public or private network. Whether you use a public or private network will depend on you interests and operations. If users have not connected a virtual machine, this can be done from the Public Network IP Manager. Users should find some links for such information.

Exam Note

Understand the resource requirements, emulator requirements, security requirements, and network requirements and working mechanisms in detail to answer questions regarding configuration of client-side virtualization.

Hypervisors

Hypervisors are also called "Virtual Machine Monitors (VMM)" and are used to run virtual machine operations. There may be more than one VMM running on a particular computer, allowing it to run and control more than one virtual machine. The hypervisor assigns the CPU resources to all the virtual machines installed on the host computer with the memory and disk allocation.

There are two types of hypervisor:

TYPE-1: This is directly installed on the host computer hardware and directly managed by the virtual machine manager. It is also known as the bare-metal, which means a computer with no hardware

or operating system. If users are using the Microsoft Hyper-V hypervisor, Citrix XenServer, or VMware Oracle VM Server for x86, KVM, they all are the first type of hypervisor where they are occupied on.

TYPE-2: These are also known as hosted hypervisors. The native/bare-metal hypervisors need hardware while the type-2 needs an operating system to run.

Now, a problem that may arise is deciding which type to use; this totally depends on users and the resources available. However, type 1 is the most dependable and secured hypervisor as it does not require an operating system to run. This feature also makes it the faster hypervisor. There might be some limitations in operating the type 2 because of the necessity of an operating system.

The hypervisor creates duplication of data allowing a better backup. The hyper version technique is also cost effective and less complex than other current techniques for data duplicating.

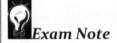*Exam Note*

Understand the difference between Hypervisor Type -1 and Type 2.

Mind Map of Client-side Virtualization

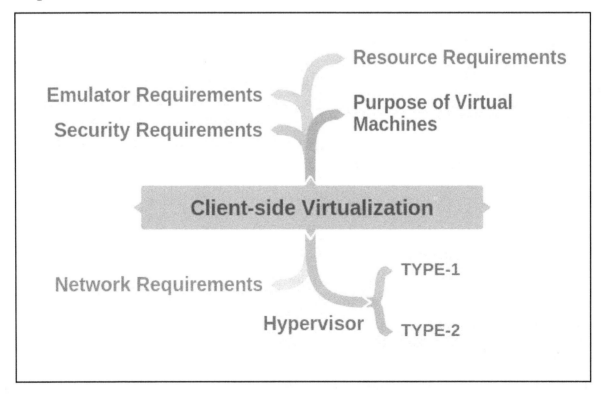

Figure 4-4: *Mind Map of Client-side Virtualization*

Summary

Compare and Contrast Cloud Computing Concepts

- Cloud computing is the practice of using a network of remote servers hosted on the internet to store, manage, and process data rather than using a local server or personal computer

- Cloud computing is the on-demand delivery of computing resources through a cloud services platform with pay-as-you-go pricing. It is the distributive technology of cloud computing that is a powerful means for an organization to grow its business in terms of time and cost efficiency, profitability and scalability

- Public and private clouds both make use of common technology solutions such as virtualization

- The difference between the various cloud solution services is who is responsible for what pieces of infrastructure

Set up and Configure Client-side Virtualization

- Virtualization solutions allow for better utilization of underlying hardware

- "Process Virtual Machines" are also called "Application Virtual Machines" and "Managed Runtime Environment" because of the feature that this software installs within a computer system's primary operating system

- Client-side virtualization has several features, some of which are described in resource requirements, emulator requirements, security requirements, network requirements

Practice Questions

1. What is Cloud computing?

   A. It is a new operational model and set of technologies for managing shared pools of computing resources

   B. It is the practice of using a network of remote servers hosted on the internet to store, manage and process data rather than using a local server or personal computer

   C. It is the on-demand delivery of computing resources through a cloud services platform with pay-as-you-go pricing

   D. All of the above

2. What is the advantage of Cloud computing?

   A. Increase speed and agility

   B. Go global in minutes

   C. Stop spending money on running and maintaining data centers

D. Benefit from massive economies of scale

E. All of the above

3. Which of the followings is a key cloud computing characteristic?

A. Broad network access

B. Multi-tenancy

C. On-demand self-service

D. None of the above

4. Which of the followings is a cloud service model?

A. SaaS

B. PaaS

C. IaaS

D. None of the above

5. Which of the following services provides the customers the ability to deploy onto the cloud infrastructure consumer-created or obtained applications created using programming languages and tools supported by the provider?

A. SaaS

B. PaaS

C. IaaS

D. NaaS

6. Which of the following is an example of Amazon EC2, Rackspace cloud servers?

A. IaaS

B. PaaS

C. SaaS

D. NaaS

7. What are the cloud deployment models?

A. Private Cloud

B. Public Cloud

C. Community Cloud

D. All of the above

8. Which of the following cloud services is more expensive but offers a higher level of privacy and security?

A. Private Cloud

B. Community Cloud

C. Public Cloud

D. Hybrid Cloud

9. What is a Private Cloud used for?

A. To offer an association that needs more control over data than using a third-party hosted service
B. To know which service provider makes resources, such as storage and application, possible to the overall public over the Internet or web applications/web services
C. It can be perceived where various associations have comparable necessities and very willing to share infrastructure in order to take in the advantages of cloud computing
D. None of the above

10. What are the advantages of cloud-based emails?

A. Server Space
B. Secure
C. Accessed Anywhere
D. Unlimited Backup
E. All of the above

11. What is cloud file storage?

A. It provides synchronized access for various users to a common set of file data in the cloud
B. The file system is a classified storage system that provides shared access to file data
C. It is used to store data in the cloud. It provides servers and applications access to data over shared file systems
D. None of the above

12. Which of the followings is a service of cloud file storage?

A. pCloud
B. IDrive
C. Google Drive
D. Mega
E. None of the above

13. What is IDrive?

A. It is the best cloud storage service for storing large media files
B. It is the best cloud storage service that mobile apps use to enable you to upload files or photos, and also sync clients with desktop machines
C. It provides continuous syncing of your files, even those on network drives; the web interface maintenances that share files by email, Facebook and Twitter.
D. All of the above

14. Which of the following is a smooth app and web interfaces that is companionable with Windows as well as MacOS and IOS devices and allots only 5GB storage for free?

    A. iCloud
    B. Google Drive
    C. pCloud
    D. Mega

15. What are the features of IDrive?

    A. Multiple Device Backup
    B. Online File Sync
    C. Disk Image Backup
    D. Continuous Data Protection
    E. All of the above

16. What are the benefits of application virtualization?

    A. Allows mismatched applications to run on a local machine simultaneously
    B. Lacks fewer resources compared to using a separate virtual machine
    C. Facilitates faster application deployment
    D. Maintains a standard, more active, and cost-effective OS configuration across multiple machines in a given association, independent of the applications being used
    E. All of the above

17. Which of the following features can be operated from the web browser and/or can be installed on desktops, smartphones?

    A. Cloud-Based Application
    B. Virtualization Application
    C. Virtual Desktop
    D. None of the above

18. What is a Virtual Desktop?

    A. A user's desktop environment (the icons, wallpaper, windows, folders, toolbars, widgets, etc.) that is stored remotely on a server, rather than on a local PC or other client computing device
    B. It is a desktop computer, which hosts a single guest virtual machine
    C. It is a data center technology, which supplies hosted desktop images to remote workers
    D. All of the above

Chapter 05: Hardware & Network Troubleshooting

Excellent troubleshooting skills are vital and are probably the most important for an IT technician to possess in any type of organization. To be able to troubleshoot an issue quickly and effectively, a technician needs to have detailed knowledge of the problem, the cause of the problem and the appropriate methodology for troubleshooting and fixing the problem. A troubleshooting methodology is a set of specific actions such as rebooting the computer or reinstalling a driver. It is a systematic process of identifying faults set out in an overall strategy.

In this chapter, we will discuss the methodology of troubleshooting and hardware and computer network problem resolution. We will look at the different phases of the troubleshooting lifecycle from finding the source an issue to finding resolutions. We will also learn about the troubleshooting procedure, practice isolating specific issues, look at the applicable troubleshooting tools, and develop proactivity using shared preventive maintenance procedures.

Best Practice Methodologies to Resolve Problems

A troubleshooting methodology is a systematic approach to dealing with any technical problems that may encounter during operation. The following section will discuss the theories and procedures of a methodical approach to troubleshooting, describing them in detail.

Always consider corporate policies, procedures, and impacts before implementing changes.

When encountering computer-related problems, consider the following:

1. Make sure to understand the corporate policies and procedures concerning computer usage, and consider the larger effect any changes might create in the wider computer system. For example, if a technician needs to take an important server offline for maintenance, they should consider the best time of day to do this and plan downtime when the server is least busy.

2. Before making any changes to a user's computer, check that users have made a backup of their data. If there is no backup, execute backups of data (at a minimum) and the whole system—provided the system is suitable for the task. If backups are not obtainable and there is no possibility of doing a backup, inform the customer that they may lose all their data— bad news is best served directly, but quietly.

3. Always have paper and pencil, tablet or smartphone, or some other means to record findings, actions, and outcomes. A digital camera or device with a camera is also handy for documenting the hardware before, after, and at various other stages of disassembly. Recording actions is a crucial aspect of the documentation that will be carried out at the end of the whole process.

4. Gather all the hardware and software troubleshooting tools. Several software troubleshooting tools are built into Windows. Also, check for hardware toolkits.

5. Now, apply the troubleshooting methodology.

Troubleshooting Methodology

CompTIA recommends a six-step troubleshooting methodology. Each step will be covered in detail in this section.

1. Identify the Problem

The first thing to be aware of when troubleshooting is that the symptoms are not the problem. When troubleshooting, it is critical to actually identify the basic problem—what is really causing the symptoms to manifest themselves. To do that, technicians must question the user. Ask detailed questions about when the symptoms occurred and why they may have occurred. It will be extremely useful if the user can re-create the problem. Define what, if anything, has changed that may have caused the problem. Importantly, before take any action, make a backup copy of the system so that you have a copy of everything as it currently is.

2. Establish a Theory of Probable Cause

When the problem that is causing the symptoms has been identified, the technician will establish a list of probable causes. When you have a full list of all probable causes, arrange it from the most likely to least likely. Incidentally, be sure to question the obvious. For example, if the symptom is a loss of power to the workstation, check that the power cord is plugged in and, if it is, check the outlet is actually receiving power. Assuming both are ok, it is now necessary move up the list to less probable causes.

3. Test the Theory to Determine the Cause

When you have established a theory of probable cause, take a moment to consider whether you can troubleshoot the issue on your own, or whether it needs escalating to a higher authority. If it falls within your capabilities, you should test your theory to determine whether it is indeed the actual cause. The best way to do this will depend on the cause. If your theory is confirmed, move on to the next step in the troubleshooting process. If the theory is disproved, you will need to go back to step two or step one, as needed, and work through the troubleshooting methodology again.

4. Establish a Plan of Action to Resolve the Problem and Implement the Solution

When you have determined and tested for the most likely probable cause, you will need to establish an action plan and then implement it. Simple problems require simple plans. However, a complex problem will require a written out plan to ensure it is implemented properly. This is another point at which you should consider whether it is necessary to escalate the problem to a more senior level.

5. Verify Full System Functionality

After executing the plan, you will need to verify whether the system is fully functional. If everything works—that's great. Based on the issue and your findings, may be able to implement preventative measures so that the problem does not occur again. If you have not achieved full system functionality, you will need to go back to step one and work through the troubleshooting methodology again.

6. Document Findings, Actions, and Outcomes

Once everything is fully functional, it is important to document the process. This is where you will document findings, actions, and outcomes. This is useful should the problem occur again, as you will have the information needed to walk someone through the troubleshooting and resolution.

This documentation also records a history of the equipment and the user so that you can identify any recurring issues. An important aspect of the documentation is to record both positive and negative outcomes. This can save time during future troubleshooting and prevent others from following any mistakes you may have made.

Mind Map of Troubleshooting Methodology

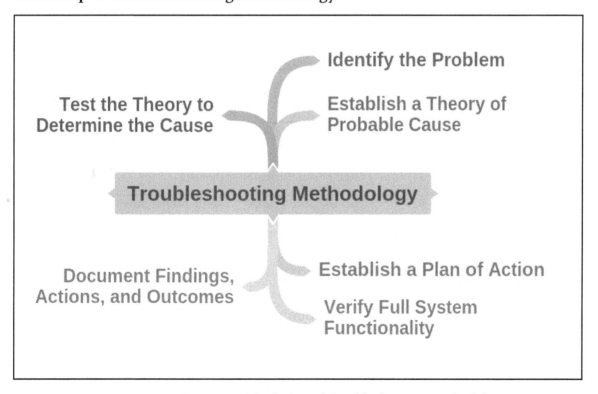

Figure 5-1: Mind Map of Troubleshooting Methodology

Troubleshoot Problems Related to Motherboards, RAM, CPUs, and Power

While problems can occur with an operating system with little or no physical warning, this is rarely the case when it comes to hardware problems. You will often be alerted of a problem by what you hear, smell, or see. This section discusses some of the common issues.

Common Symptoms

After troubleshooting for a while, technicians begin to notice patterns. With a few exceptions, in general the same problems occur over and over, usually after presenting the same warning signs. This section covers the common symptoms. Learning what these symptoms are trying to tell us will make your job easier.

Unexpected Shutdown

The table blow presents the general causes and prevention for unexpected shutdown:

Causes	Prevention
Dead short caused by loose screws, slot covers, or cards	Shut down the system and secure all metal components
CPU overheating	Check fan speed for CPU heat sink Clean fan if it is dirty Replace fan if it has failed or is turning too slowly Check power management settings and CPU drivers in the operating system to make sure that thermal throttling is functioning
Power supply overheating	Check the power supply fan and clean it if possible Replace the power supply with a higher wattage–rated unit if the problem persists
Power supply failure	Test the power supply to verify proper operation

Table 5-1: Causes and Prevention of Unexpected Shutdown

System Lockup

Here, the system just stops and does not react to any console information or mouse clicks. A system lockup differs from a blue screen, which comes with a dump message. With a normal lockup, things simply stop working. Like blue screens, lockups are less frequent than they used to be, particularly on more up to date Microsoft operating systems. One exception is with PCs that go into hibernate mode and cannot be coaxed out of it. If a lockup occurs, check the log files to see what is going on, for example, a driver may be loading, and find a way to correct it.

From a hardware perspective, freezes or lockups can be caused by memory problems, viruses or malware, and video drivers.

POST Code Beeps

On every device, during system boot-up, a Power-On Self-Test (POST) checks for functionality. If the system boots to the point where the video driver is stacked and the display is operational, any issues will be accounted for with a numeric error code.

If the system cannot boot to that point, issues will be accounted for with a beep code. Each manufacturer's arrangement of beep codes and their translation can be found in the documentation for the system or the website. Generally, one short beep dependably implies all is well. A few instances tested during this procedure incorporate the following as RAM, Video card, and Motherboard.

During startup, issues such as devices not loading, services not starting, etc., are written to the system log shown in Event Viewer. In the event that no POST error code prevents a successful boot, Event Viewer provides data about what is happening to the system and shows alerts, error messages, and records hence, aiding troubleshooting. Users can access Event Viewer through Computer Management or from the Administrative Tools in Control Panel.

Exam Note

The Power-On Self-Test (POST) will monitor the memory when the system boots. If you hear a beep that you do not recognize after installing RAM, double-check the installation.

Blank Screen on Boot-up

Sometimes after boot-up, the screen remains blank, although there are signs that the system has power and some functionality (maybe you can hear the fan or see lights on the system). The cause of this could lie in a few areas. Try these solutions:

- Ensure that the screen is on; it has its own power switch, so check it
- If the fan works but the system does not boot, it could be a problem with the power supply to the motherboard. Check and reset the motherboard's power connection
- Ensure that the link from the screen to the system is connects properly
- Replace the video card with one you know works to rule out a dud card
- Make sure that the brightness setting is set properly
- Where a PC is being used to direct output to a second display, ensure that the picture is being sent to the main display and not simply to the external monitor

BIOS Time and Setting Resets

Problems with BIOS time and settings resets are generally caused by problems with either the CMOS battery on the motherboard or the CMOS chip.

If date and time settings or other BIOS settings have reset to system defaults or show CMOS corrupted errors, replace the CMOS battery and reset the BIOS settings to the correct values. A CMOS battery, namely CR2032, should function properly for about three years before it needs to be replaced.

Attempts to Boot to Incorrect Device

The boot sequence listed in BIOS settings identifies which drives can be used to start the computer and in which order. If a non-bootable drive is in the boot sequence, the system will not start. For example, if a USB drive is listed first and a non-bootable USB drive is plugged in, the system will not start.

Change the boot order to list the location where the operating system is installed, such as the system hard drive, and restart the computer.

Continuous Reboot

Sometimes a continuous series of reboots is caused by a failed update or software corruption. More often, continuous reboot is caused by a failing motherboard component, RAM, the processor, or motherboard.

No Power

A situation of no power is easily diagnosable by the lack of noise from fan or drives and lights. Check whether all of your power sources, power strips, and wall outlets are good. Check the connections to the motherboard.

Overheating

This is a serious situation cause by potentially simple problems. The circuitry used in today's components can only cope with limited extremes of heat or cold. The biggest danger is heat. Usefully, sensors on the motherboard can detect temperature limits and either issue a warning or shut down the system. The causes of overheating include blocked airways impeding internal circulation, or excessive dust on air exchanging surfaces such as aluminum fins, fan/cooler or heat pipe assemblies. Unusual sounds inside the box could be from the heat sensor.

Loud Noises

Computers usually run quietly, so if you hear a loud noise coming from the power supply, it indicates a problem. A whirring, screeching, rattling, or thumping sound usually indicates a fan failure. If a fan built into a component such as a heat sink or power supply is failing, replace the component immediately.

Intermittent Device Failure

An intermittent failure can have a number of causes, from a failing processor, RAM, or motherboard to bad drivers. First, check the processor temperature then run RAM diagnostics. The following are the possibilities for intermittent device failure:

A bad motherboard can cause these types of problems once there are issues with its circuitry. Replace the motherboard or other failing component with a well-known motherboard or component.

Fans Spin, No Power to Other Devices

A fan is an important part of a processor and is used to maintain the temperature level of the processor. It is directly connected to the power supply and it starts working as the system turns on. If a fan spins but the computer shows no startup display, this could indicate a number of problems.

Check the following:

- Make sure the main ATX and 12V ATX or EPS power leads are securely connected to the appropriate sockets

- Make sure the CPU and memory modules are securely installed in the appropriate sockets

Indicator Lights

Most system components have a light indicating normal operation. Indicator lights are often found on the network interface card (NIC) as well as on the front of a desktop and in the display area of a laptop.

On an NIC, a light other than green can indicate more serious problems with the network. However, the absence of any light can indicate that the card itself has failed. CD-ROM, tape, hard drive, or DVD drive lights are on and blinking when the device is active. The power light must be a steady green.

Smoke

Anytime you smell or see smoke, shut the system down directly to prevent further damage. It usually indicates an overheating or burning component, commonly the CPU.

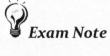

Exam Note

When power supplies fail, we can sometimes see smoke or smell burning components. New power supplies often release an odor for a short burn-in period, but they are not faulty. However, if you see smoke or sparks, remove the power supply immediately.

Burning Smells

A burning smell generally accompanies smoke but can also linger after the smoke has cleared due to a dead component that is burning. Try to identify the damaged component with a visual inspection; if that is not possible, replace one component at a time to determine which one is faulty.

Proprietary Crash Screens

Some operating systems have two proprietary methods of notifying the user that something bad may have just occurred. Two methods, BSOD (Blue Screen of Death) and Pinwheel, are defined below.

Blue Screen of Death (BSoD)

Blue Screen of Death (BSoD) is a Microsoft Windows operating system error screen that indicates system conflict and the potential for a crash. The term comes from the critical messages that are displayed on a blue screen.

BSoD errors relate to system temperature, hardware, resources, timing, or viruses. The error screen serves as an alert to prevent further computer and system damage. It is also known as stop error. BSoD error messages can help in troubleshooting the problem.

In the latest versions of Windows (Windows 7, 8, and 8.1), information from such crashes is written to XML files. When the system is established, a prompt generally appears asking for approval to send this information to Microsoft. Microsoft collects this data as a method of working with users to correct these issues.

BSOD error messages include the following:

- DIVIDE_BY_ZERO_ERROR: Occurs when an application tries to divide by zero

- IRQL_NOT_LESS_OR_EQUAL: Affected by a buggy device driver or actual hardware conflict

- KMODE_EXCEPTION_NOT_HANDLED: Affected by an incorrectly configured device driver

- REGISTRY_ERROR: System registry failure

- INACCESSIBLE_BOOT_DEVICE: Unable to read hard disk

- UNEXPECTED_KERNEL_MODE_TRAP: Check the Complementary Metal-Oxide Semiconductor (CMOS) for correct total of Random Access Memory (RAM) and Single Inline Memory Modules (SIMM) for speed and type

- BAD_POOL_HEADER: Latest changes introduced this error

- NTFS_FILE_SYSTEM: Specifies hard disk corruption

Pinwheel

In the Apple world, the pinwheel is similar to BSOD. It got its name from the pinwheel the cursor turns into, which stops you doing anything. The only solution is to force a shutdown and reboot.

Distended Capacitor

Many motherboards have distended capacitors that store electricity. They are short cylindrical tubes. A distended capacitor looks normal on the side, but the top of it will be a bit swollen and there may be brown residue coming out of the top of the capacitor. If a capacitor fails, the motherboard will not work.

Users have some options for fixing this:

- The first option is to replace the motherboard; whatever you do, do not touch the residue coming from a distended capacitor

- The second option is to drain the energy from the failed capacitor and replace it; only do this if you have specialized training on how to deal safely with capacitors because they can cause lethal shocks

Log Entries and Error Messages

Logs on a device are records kept to track the history of what has happened on the system. They record the tasks performed on the computer such as log in and out, opening an application, and so on.

Error messages indicate the something went wrong on the system, for example, a device failure or authentication rejection. These messages are helpful to IT professionals to solve the problem.

To access logs and error messages, go to "Control Panel" > "Administrative Tools" > "Event Viewer".

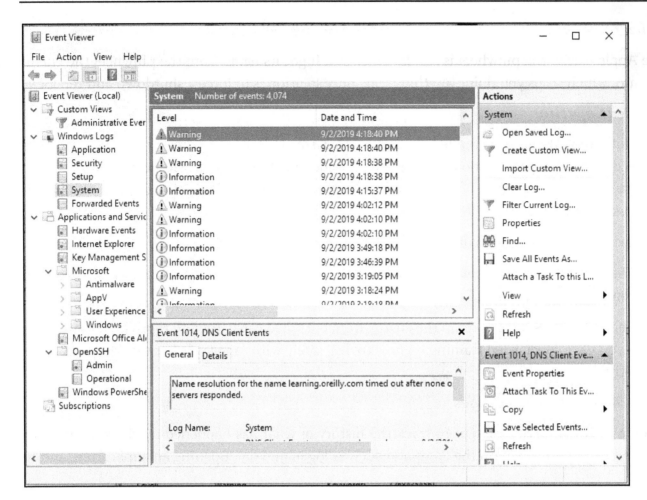

Figure 5- 2: Event Viewer

In Event Viewer, many types of logs are available in the different applications and system functions. In the system window tab, the "Warning" is highlighted with a yellow triangle indicating some failure and in this case; DNS requests.

Mind Map of Troubleshooting Problems for Motherboards, RAM, CPUs, and Power

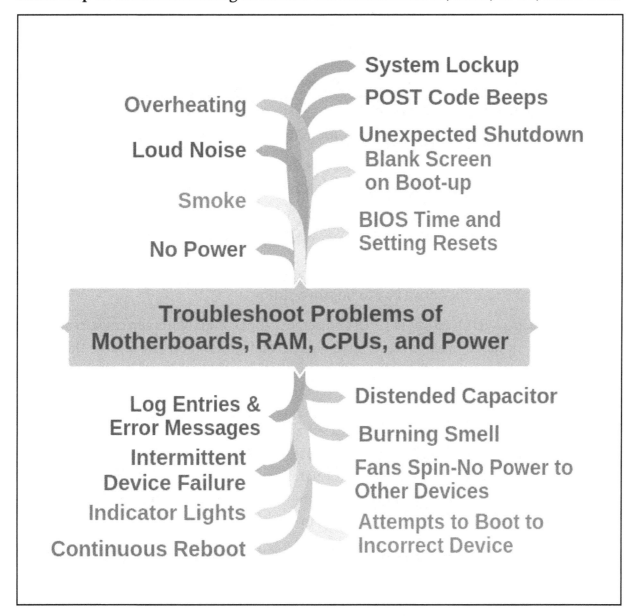

Figure 5-3: Mind Map of Troubleshooting Problems for Motherboards, RAM, CPUs, and Power

Troubleshoot Hard Drives and RAID Arrays

Hard drives contain useful and necessary data, so we tend to be highly reliant on our hard drives and RAID arrays working efficiently. For this reason, the drives need to be perfect. We can keep our drives healthy by adopting a variety of precautionary measures. Sometimes our system can be affected by unknown controls and system fails, so we need to troubleshoot the hard drives and RAID arrays.

Common Symptoms

The most common symptoms are discussed in this section.

Read/Write Failure

Read/write failures can take place for the following reasons:

Physical Damage to the Drive: Dropping any magnetic storage drive can cause damage to read/write heads and platters. The drive may stop spinning and start making a noise.

Damaged Cables: SATA cables are often integrated with new motherboards and are inexpensive to purchase. Replacing cables is an easy way to solve problems.

Damaged SATA Host Adapter on the Motherboard: Mostly motherboards have several SATA ports; use the original cable in different SATA ports on the motherboard.

Overheated Hard Disk: If you have two or more drives stacked on top of each other with limited airflow, move the drives to another drive bay to improve airflow.

Overheated CPU or Chipset: Overheated CPU, chipset, or other components can cause read/write failures. Remove loose or failed heat sinks, remove old thermal grease, and reassemble them with properly applied thermal grease.

Slow Performance

The applications running in a system affect the speed and performance of the system. The main cause of slow performance is applications that use most of the processing power, consuming too much of the system's resources and making the operating system and other apps wait for it. Performance slows when the hard disk is heavily fragmented because it then requires more time than usual to gather the files together and store them in memory.

In order to defragment the hard drive, use the built-in tool or a third-party application like Piriform Defraggler. Advanced Windows systems, such as Windows 10, automatically perform defragmentation and disk checks (in maintenance mode) on a regular basis, usually once a week. These settings can be changed through the Action Center according user requirements.

Loud Clicking Noise

Another symptom is a loud clicking noise from the hard drive. If users can isolate this noise to the drive and the drive is not working, it is probably physically damaged beyond repair. The smartest thing to do, if users cannot access any records on the drive, is to replace it and restore the data from the latest backup.

Failure to Boot

Quite often a computer will display a message saying there is a problem in booting. Now, this is a serious situation and can be checked at the BIOS settings of the computer. If these storage devices are mounted properly, then the problem is in the hard drive. It mostly makes data temporarily

inaccessible, meaning the hard disk cannot properly load data from the storage device. If the SATA or PATA are checked by reordering as primary and secondary memory and if the system does not respond properly, then either a mechanic or engineer needs to be called.

Drive Not Recognized

The computer system sometimes displays a message saying the drive is not found or recognized. The usually response is to check the disk and do basic defragmentation. But if the system continues to display the message, it suggests the drive needs to be replaced. This may be because the drive has lost contact with the hard disk. To do this, it is essential to back up all files as drive replacement will certainly result in a huge data loss.

OS Not Found

An Operating System (OS) not found error during boot can be caused by the following:

Non-bootable Disk in USB Drive: If a USB drive is listed before the hard disk in the boot sequence and it contains a non-bootable disk, the computer displays an error message saying it could not find the operating system. Remove the USB flash drive and restart.

Boot Sequence Does Not List Hard Disk: Restart the computer, start the BIOS setup procedure, and make sure the hard disk is listed as a bootable drive and is listed before options such as network boot.

Incorrect Installation of another Operating System: Windows automatically sets up its own boot manager for access to more than one Windows version if you install the older version of Windows first, followed by the later version. However, if you install a newer version first and install an older version later or install a non-Windows OS later, you cannot access the newer Windows version unless you install a custom boot manager.

RAID Not Found

A number of server devices today use redundant arrays or RAID arrays of independent disks. If you have issues with controller and then start up the computer, you might get a troubleshoot error command saying, "RAID not found". You can test the configuration of RAID on the computer and confirm whether the controller is working correctly. If it is faulty or something in it is missing, you may get a message at start up saying this controller is not yet configured. If so, it will not work correctly.

RAID Stops Working

If you view a message that describes an issue with the array, you can launch the RAID console to check the status of the drives. It differs for different RAID builders. Thus, you should check the documentation to see which process will work and compare the drives again with any physical drive inside the computer. Replace the wrong drive within the array.

Proprietary Crash Screens (BSOD/Pinwheel)

We discussed the Blue Screen of Death (BSOD) and Pinwheel in the previous section. Now let us look at the guidelines for these issues.

Sometimes, the system goes off after displaying a blue screen or a blue sign. This is a signal that the drives are not synchronizing with the hard disk, so the hard disk is not responding to the drive commands. The screen turning blue and automatically shutting down or restarting is known as BSOD. If this occurs once and does not happen again, then it is simply a hardware blockage. However, if the problem recurs many times or happens at every login, there may be a serious hard disk problem that needs technical support. However, before calling in support, you should make sure that all important data has been backed up.

S.M.A.R.T Errors

SMART stands for Self-Monitoring, Analysis, and Reporting Technology. It is a system incorporated into hard drives and solid-state drives that distinguishes and gives an account of drive dependability, in order to anticipate hardware failures. It requires software on the PC to read the data from the drives and plays out its analysis during startup.

Errors detailed by SMART should be taken as an indication that before long the drive will come up short, and users should back up all information at the earliest opportunity, even if the drive seems to be performing regularly and passes other disk checks. One error that users may be able to mitigate is overheating. If you are able to improve ventilation so that the error disappears, it is likely that you are safe to keep using the drive.

Mind Map of Troubleshooting Hard Drives and RAID Arrays

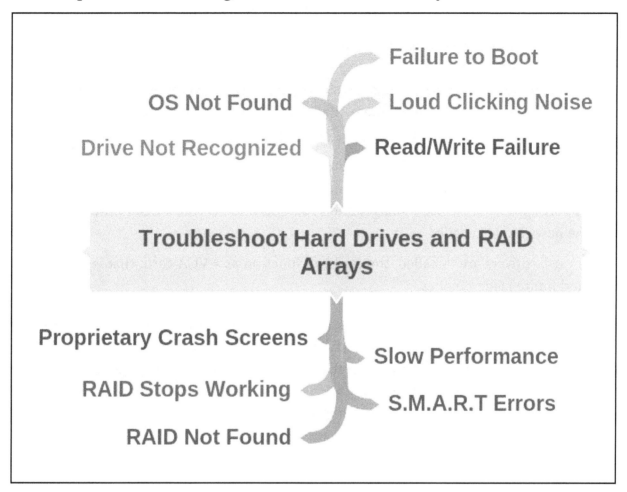

Figure 5-4: Mind Map of Troubleshooting Hard Drives and RAID Arrays

Troubleshoot Video, Projector, and Display Issues

Desktop, laptop, and mobile devices all have screens that can vary significantly. Use the following sections to learn how to diagnose and fix display-related problems with various display types.

Common Symptoms

In this section, we discuss the common symptoms and approaches to dealing with these problems.

VGA Mode

If Low-resolution mode or Safe mode has been selected at startup or if the correct drivers are not available, a Windows system starts in VGA mode.

Check the following:

- Many business desktops and most laptops use CPU-integrated graphics. Until chipset drivers are installed, these are used as ordinary VGA GPUs. Download the latest system or motherboard drivers from the vendor

- If the system is being upgraded from integrated graphics to a separate video card, be sure to install the new drivers after the card is installed. Download the latest graphics from the card vendor or GPU vendor: www.amd.com (Radeon, Fire GL) or www.nvidia.com (GeForce, Quadro)

- If the system is being upgraded by replacing an existing video card with a new video card with a different manufacturer's chipset, be sure to uninstall the current video card drivers and support apps from Device Manager and Programs and Features. Install the new drivers after the new card is installed

Until the new card's drivers are installed, the card will function as a VGA card, that is, with no 3D acceleration and limited video modes.

No Image Onscreen

When there is no image on the screen, the display is either dead or not receiving the signal from the computer. Check the cable from the back of the computer to the monitor, making sure that it is tightly screwed in place, and reset the cables if required. Also, make sure that the monitor is plugged into a functional power outlet and that the brightness settings are high enough. Finally, for a laptop, you should use the proper Fn key to guarantee that the signal is not being sent to an external monitor.

Overheat Shutdown

Video systems often shut down when they overheat.

To avoid overheating, check the following:

- Clean or replace filters when recommended; projectors with filters usually display a message onscreen when it is time to clean or replace the filter

- Make sure the projector has adequate ventilation

- Check air intake and exhaust ports for dust and dirt and clean as necessary

- Use lower brightness setting on projectors to reduce heat

- Be sure to allow the projector to cool down completely before removing it from power

- A video card (GPU) that overheats will usually display screen artifacts before shutting down

Dead Pixels

Pixels are small dots on screen that are the basic unit of programmable color on a computer image or computer display. The physical size of a pixel is based on how you set the resolution for the

display screen. Display screens have three transistors per pixel and one transistor each for green, red, and blue, called subpixels. Stuck pixels and dead pixels are two conditions that can occur.

A stuck pixel occurs when one or more subpixels remain activated when they are supposed to be off. A dead pixel occurs when an entire pixel or a group of subpixels remain dark when they are supposed to be on. Dead pixels (black pixels) typically result from manufacturing defects in an LCD screen. Check with the manufacturer of the panel or laptop to determine the number of dead pixels that are needed to qualify for screen replacement.

Artifacts

Artifacts are errors that occur during signal transmission or interpretation, commonly known as digital artifact. They can occur during transmission of a digital file or be created from the compression of a signal or data.

Artifacts can be created whenever hardware components such as the memory chip, processor, or cabling malfunction affect data corruption. They may be due to physical damage, but the first thing to check is whether the video card or graphic processor is overheating.

Incorrect Color Pattern

Sometimes, the image displayed uses incorrect color patterns or is garbled. The root of this problem depend on when the problem occurs. If the screen looks fine during POST but then goes bad when Windows starts to load, it is probably because of an incorrect video card setting. For example, the card may be set to do something it is incapable of doing. Restart in safe mode, which will make the system use the VGA driver and check all the card settings. You may also try updating the driver if a new one is accessible.

If this problem occurs from the moment you turn the system on, the problem is hardware, and you should check the card, monitor, and cable, replacing each with a component know to work until you isolate the failed component.

Dim Image

If the picture is fine but dim, firstly check the brightness setting, usually found at the front of the monitor. If it is a laptop, remember there are function keys that when hit inadvertently dim the screen.

If it is an LCD, the backlight may be going bad. We looked earlier at these pencil-sized lights behind the screen. They can be replaced in a laptop by following the procedure for opening the laptop lid (where the display resides) and replacing the backlight.

Flickering Image

When the picture is flickering, first of all, check whether the cables are seated properly. If that does not help, try different cables as the cable itself could be the problem. Another possible cause is a mismatch between the resolution settings and the refresh rate. If this is the problem, it will happen

only when using the higher resolutions. To solve it, increase the refresh rate to support the higher resolutions.

Distorted Images

Distorted images can be caused power problems. Try replacing the power cable, and if that does not help, try plugging the monitor into an altered wall outlet. Sometimes other devices on the same line (refrigerator, air conditioner, and so forth) can cause problems with the power supply to the monitor.

Distorted Geometry

Images on the monitor use a strict X-Y axis: X pixels high by Y pixels wide, with most monitors using 1024 by 768. In the clearest case, a perfect circle is input. Variations to either of the x or y values will result in an imperfect circle, possibly an egg shape.

A very obvious example of this is the short, fat, and stretched images of old television shows displaying on flat panel widescreen monitors. Distorted geometry is resolved by setting the monitor to a standard resolution.

Burn-in

Burn-in is a condition that affect CRT screens and still affects plasma and OLED displays. LCDs are not usually affected. The condition happens when pictures are left for extended periods of time on the screen. The early screen savers were intended to prevent this by showing a continually evolving picture.

Software and utilities can be used to cure burn-in. However, this will have little impact if the burn-in is serious. It is also important to realize that this solution will be least effective if it occurs on a new screen in its initial long periods of operation. DVDs can be obtained that will "break in" a screen, and at times, they can even wipe out existing burn-in if it is not extreme.

Oversized Images and Icons

Oversized images and icons in Windows can be caused by booting in Limited-resolution (VGA) mode. To fix the resolution problem, restart the system and select normal resolution from the Display properties sheet in the settings.

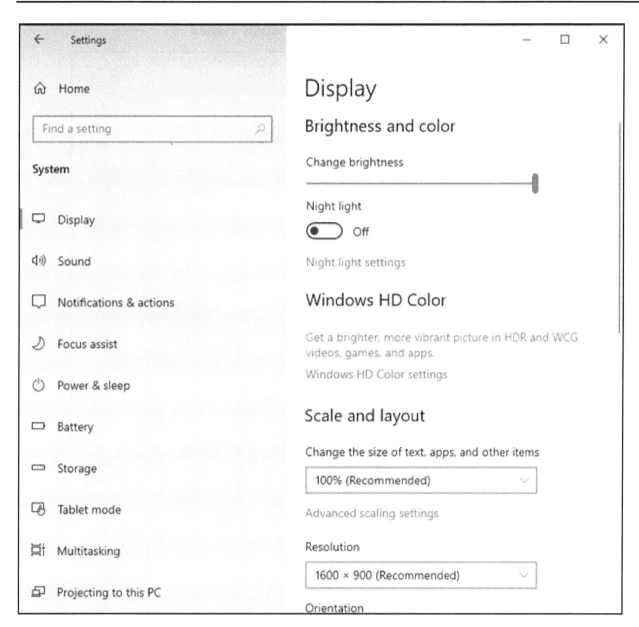

Figure 5-5: Display Settings Highlighted in Windows 10 Display Settings

Mind Map of Troubleshooting Video, Projector, and Display Issues

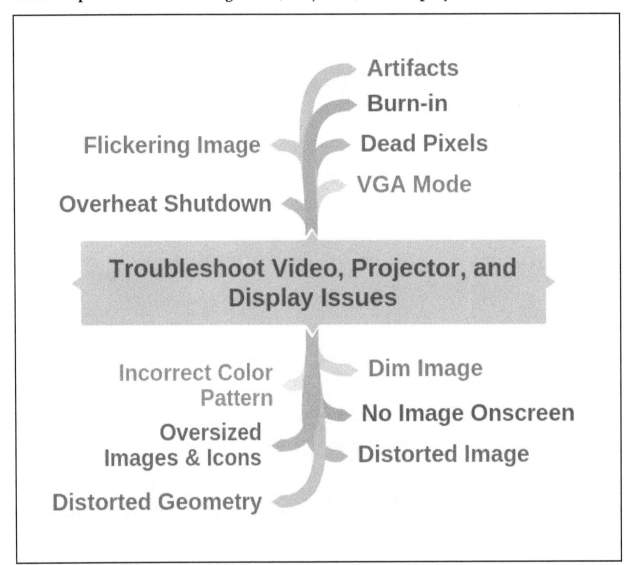

Figure 5-6: Mind Map of Troubleshooting Video, Projector, and Display Issues

Troubleshoot Common Mobile Device Issues While Adhering to Appropriate Procedures

With more organizations than ever before using laptops, tablets, and smartphones, it's important to know how to troubleshoot devices on the go. You need to understand the following concepts for the 220-1001 exam and to improve your technical skills.

Common Symptoms

Many mobile device problems have simple solutions that are really easy to identify and repair. It is often simple, as we will learn in this section.

No Display

When the device is powered on, a display will appear. If there is no display at all, first of all ensure that the smartphone is actually powered on. Failing this, replace the battery.

The display presents an EGA post screen or *Samsung* splash screen such as in the picture below:

Figure 5-7: Display of EGA Post Screen

In case of locked phones, the phone will have displayed an animation of the phone provider for example, O2.

If these kinds of displays occur, go to the display settings in the OS. Boot into the advanced startup menu by pressing the volume up (on most phones), select, and power keys at the same time while powering on the mobile device. Now choose the safe mode option where any misconfigured or changed display settings can be returned to normal.

In the case of a broken or cracked screen, the display will not necessarily stop functioning, although some parts of the display may not work. In this case, the entire screen needs to be replaced.

Dim Display

Sometimes, a phone will have a dim display, which can be varied by changing the brightness settings on the phone. These settings can be easily accessed by simply swiping down the settings menu. At the lower part of these settings, there is a brightness slider. It should be set to 50%, for regular use. If it is set to low setting, then the display may be unreadable.

Flickering Display

Flickering screens can be caused by video drivers, screen-fresh rates or loose connections. First, try to update the driver and make sure that the rate is set according to the documentation; remember as well that a cable connects the display to the motherboard. Another symptom that may appear is that more than one image is being displayed with the top image appearing to be transparent.

Sticking Keys

Sticking keys on a laptop or tablet usually indicate a problem with the keyboard. It is not always necessary to replace the entire keyboard. Several online vendors offer individual key replacements for laptops. If more than one or two keys are sticking, it may be most cost-effective to replace the entire keyboard.

If a tablet uses a removable keyboard, the keyboard can be replaced if keys are not available.

Intermittent Wireless

Here, mobile devices get intermittently disconnected from the wireless network while wired devices are still connected and work fine.

The following are possible causes:

- The distance of the device from the router; is it too far away to get a strong and stable signal?

- Is the router placed in a central location or is the router placed behind a large device such as a cupboard or refrigerator that may degrade or impede the signal's strength?

- Is there another device on the network sharing the same channel? What happens when other devices are disconnected?

- Is there a phone connection as well? Are all of the phone sockets in the building fitted with an ADSL micro-filter?

- Does a change in the wireless router channel make any difference?

No Power/Battery Not Charging

If a mobile device battery is not charging, then there is a simple test that can be carried out. First, check the green light on the AC adapter, and check that the battery is not overheated. Make sure the battery is not swollen. If the signs are good, let the battery charge for a normal period of time, then remove the AC adapter and attempt to power up the machine. If it works, everything is fine.

If it does not, remove all power from the machine and try using only the AC Adapter. If that works, the battery is dead and needs to be replaced.

No Wireless Connectivity

All mobiles have an Airplane mode option that when turned on, disables all radio communication from the device. Airplane mode was introduced to allow users to continue to use the mobile device while on an airplane, as any radio frequency communication may interfere or disturb the radio equipment used by the pilot.

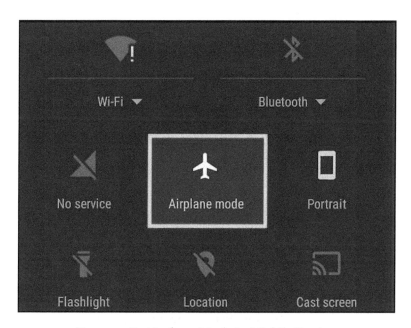

Figure 5-8: Airplane Mode in Mobile Devices

No Bluetooth Connectivity

Bluetooth consumes and drains power, so it is usually kept off in order to save battery life, and it needs to be turned on to make it functional. Further, users need to establish a Bluetooth connection between their device and the device they are connecting to using a four-digit pin code. Once the connection has been established, users are able to share data with that device.

Touchscreen is Non-Responsive

In some cases, the mobile device screen becomes unresponsive. If the device is kept inside a plastic protection case, its performance or touchscreen may be affected. To avoid this, wipe the screen with a lint-free cloth and make sure there is no dirt or oil. Parts with dirt or oil can become unresponsive. If the whole screen is not responding to touch, consider a restart.

> **Exam Note**
>
> If a user does not use the touchpad, it is best to disable it. This will prevent the user from accidentally causing the mouse pointer to jump around the screen.

Apps Not Loading

To solve the problem of an apps not loading, check the following:

- Check available storage space. If the system is almost out of space, apps cannot run. Uninstall apps that are never used

- If the device has adequate free storage space and still will not load an app, the device might not have enough free RAM. Close some apps

- For a web-enabled app, make sure the device has a good internet connection

Slow Performance

Mobile devices often suffer from slow performance. Here are some possible solutions; The first thing to look for is a virus attack. Also, check the space on the hard drive or memory. Defragment the hard drive and memory if necessary. Make sure the most recent updates are installed. Updates help to maintain the app and solve performance problems.

Extremely Short Battery Life

The early mobile device batteries had short lives and suffered from memory defects. Today, however, since the arrival of Li-ion batteries, this is rarely a problem.

Modern batteries charge well when they are properly charged using a fast charger, or giving regular top-ups. The battery is designed to be fully used and then fully charged.

Swollen Battery

Swollen battery occurs while the battery' cells are overcharged. Due to the lithium-ion, batteries react critically to overcharging. When you face a swollen battery, the only solution is to replace it.

Overheating

Overheating of a mobile device can be caused by the battery. If you find that is the source of the heat, replace the battery. Other than the battery, problems that contribute to overheating can be excessive browsing, excessive gaming, or using the device while charging.

Frozen System

When we talk about a "frozen" system, we are usually referring to a tablet or smartphone. A system lockup or freeze cannot be restored. The only way to do this is with a soft reboot. Each manufacturer has a different method for rebooting from a lockup.

No Sound from the Speakers

There are two main reasons for no sound emitting from the speakers. Smartphones and laptops have a mute button that will shut all sounds and this have been activated. The other reason is usually that the volume control has been set to 0% or a very low level.

There might be cases where the user gets sound from some applications but not from others. Often the problem here is that the sound on the site the user is using has been muted for example, YouTube videos. Remember that video websites have their own independent volume control and mute buttons.

GPS Not Functioning

If the GPS not functioning, Airplane mode may be turned on, which will shut down the GPS as well. Turn off Airplane mode and the GPS should come back on. If not, turn on the GPS in "Settings" > "Location" menu.

Disassembling Processes to ensure Proper Reassembly

Disassembling a laptop can be one of the biggest challenges and several simple steps should be followed. The following guidelines will ensure successful disassembly and reassembly when upgrading or servicing a laptop, convertible two-in-one, tablet, or smartphone.

Document and Label Cable and Screw Locations

A typical laptop may have 100 or more screws of varying sizes. A smartphone could have a dozen or more. Be sure to document and label cable and screw locations: As each screw is removed, note its location and size. A digital camera or smartphone camera is a useful tool, as you can use it to capture the device and the screws when they are removed.

Organize Parts

There are many ways to organize parts;

- Use a plastic divided-compartment lidded tray from a hardware store to keep screws and bolts organized. As you put each set of screws into a compartment, add a label to indicate which subassembly they go to

- Place static-sensitive materials (CPU, RAM, etc.) in antistatic bags

- Use antistatic bubble wrap for larger components, such as motherboards

- Use boxes to protect case and trim components

Refer to the Manufacturers' Resources

Prior to disassembling a device, make sure you have the information you need by referring to the manufacturer's resources:

- Get the manufacturer's service manual, if it is available

- To make your search easy, check the underside of a laptop or tablet to find the actual service number or catalog number – this is more useful than the marketing model number

Most manufacturers make this information readily available. Some third-party websites also provide service manuals, but do not use these resources unless you cannot download the service manual directly from the manufacturer's website.

Use Appropriate Hand Tools

Use the right tool for the job. Tools for working with mobile devices are smaller and have other differences from those needed for a desktop computer. For example, Apple now uses the five-point Pentalobe screw for external screws in its smartphones, although some models use the standard Phillips head for internal screws.

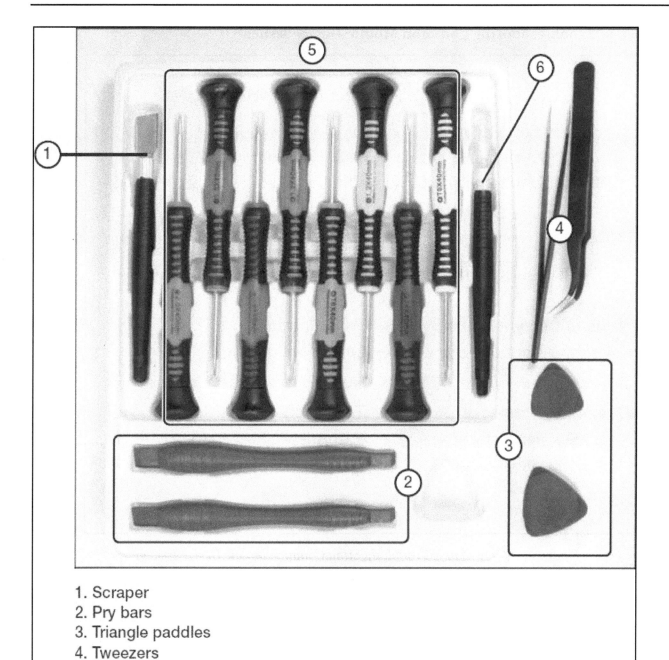

1. Scraper
2. Pry bars
3. Triangle paddles
4. Tweezers
5. Screwdrivers (Phillips, straight-blade, Torx, and 5-point/Pentalobe)
6. Precision cutting knife

Figure 5-9: A Typical Mobile Device Toolkit

Mind Map of Troubleshooting Common Mobile Device Issues

Figure 5-10: Mind Map of Troubleshooting Common Mobile Device Issues

Troubleshoot Printers

This section explores a variety of common printer issues. These issues can occur in both large organizations and small offices. A printer is a mechanical device. However, it is controlled by embedded firmware and by computers that manage it. In this section, we will discuss troubleshooting to solve common printing issues.

Common Symptoms

Depending on the environment, you may have to troubleshoot the following common symptoms on a daily basis.

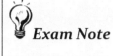

Exam Note

You will need to understand the basics of each of these printers. However, you will find that the CompTIA exams focus heavily on laser printers.

Streaks

Streaks are a vertical blank lines down the length of the page. On a laser printer, there are two reasons for this. One is that there is not enough toner in the cartridge. This can be temporarily fixed by removing the cartridge and shaking it to equally distribute the toner. However, the cartridge will soon need to be replaced.

With inkjet or dot-matrix printers, streaks can mean the print head needs cleaning. If cleaning does not help, try replacing the cartridge (inkjet) or the ribbon (dot matrix).

Faded Prints

Light or faded prints can be resolved by replacing the ink or toner and cleaning the ink cartridge head. Also, check the fuser and increase humidity if necessary.

Ghost Images

Prints with ghosted images can be resolved by replacing the cartridge. If this does not help, remember that the circumference of the image drum is considerably less that the length of the paper. An imaging drum will completely rotate close to 10 times to print a single page. This makes the cleaning procedure crucial. To determine the cause of the ghosting, measure the distance between the top of the page and the ghost image and consult the service manual for the printer. Clean or replace the defective component.

Toner Not Fused to the Paper

The fuser in a laser printer heats the paper to fuse the toner to the paper; fuser failure results in the toner not fusing to the paper. If the toner can be wiped or blown off the paper after the printout emerges from the laser printer, the fuser needs to be repaired or replaced.

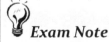

Exam Note

In some laser printers, the toner cartridge includes the imaging drum, the developer, and/or a cleaning blade used to clean off toner during the cleaning process. Therefore, when you replace the toner cartridge, you might also replace other components.

Creased Paper

Creased paper is usually caused by incorrect adjustment of the paper guides for feeding pages. If the paper guide is not set to the actual paper width, the paper might move horizontally during the feed process and become creased. Adjust the paper guides to the correct width for the paper or media in use.

Paper Not Feeding

If paper is not feeding into the printer, the pickup rollers may have solidified and lost their ability to grip the paper. Replacing these rollers most often fixes the issue.

Now and again, it is not the rollers but rather the paper-feed sensor. This tells the printer when it is out of paper. Always try cleaning the sensor first before replacing it. High humidity can likewise make the paper not feed appropriately.

Paper Jam

A paper jam can have a number of causes, depending on the printer type. Use the following options to solve paper jam issues:

1. Turn the printer on and off in the hope that the printer will clear the jam. This is known as power-cycling the printer. If that does not work, open the printer. Turn the printer off and unplug it before doing so.

2. Remove paper trays and inspect them for crumpled sheets that can be removed by grabbing both ends of the paper firmly and pulling or rotating the rollers to remove it. In general, clear the paper path.

3. Verify that the right paper type is being used. If the paper is too thin or thick, it might cause a paper jam. Also, check the paper has not been exposed to humidity.

4. Check for dirty or cracked rollers. A temporary fix for dirty rubber rollers is to clean them using isopropyl alcohol. A permanent fix is to replace the rollers.

5. Check whether the fusing assembly has overheated. Sometimes the printer just needs time to cool, or perhaps the printer is not in a well enough ventilated area. In rare cases, the fuser might have to be replaced. Be sure to unplug the printer and let the printer sit for an hour or so before doing so, due to the high temperatures of the fuser. The fusing assembly can usually be removed by removing a few screws.

6. Finally, check the entire paper path. Duplexing printers (ones that print on both sides of the paper) will have more complicated and longer paper paths, providing more chances for paper to get jammed.

No Connectivity

There are many software issues that can cause printer problems. Sometimes, it is difficult to tell exactly where the communication process between the PC and the printer is breaking down. It could be that users are not establishing a connection with the printer, or it could be that an incorrect setting or driver is preventing successful printing.

For a locally attached printer, make sure that the cable is properly attached. Try replacing the cable with a new one.

If this problem is with a network printer, ping the printer to see if it is available.

Garbled Characters on the Paper

This problem is usually caused by an incorrect printer driver. Install the most up-to-date version of the correct printer driver.

Vertical Lines on the Page

There are two types of vertical line:

- **Vertical black lines on the page**

Vertical black lines are caused by scratches on the drum or a dirty corona wire. If you suspect scratches on the drum, replace the toner cartridge. If you suspect the corona wire, try cleaning it first and if the problem persists, replace the toner cartridge.

For inkjet printers, try cleaning the print head or replacing the ink cartridge.

- **Vertical white lines on the page**

Vertical white lines are caused by foreign matter caught on the transfer corona wire. The solution is to clean the corona wires. Some printers come with a small corona-wire brush to help. To use it, remove the toner cartridge and run the brush in the charge corona groove on top of the toner cartridge.

For inkjet printers, first clean the print head then try replacing the cartridge.

Backed-Up Print Queue

In some cases, the printer will not print and all attempts to delete the print job or clear the print queue fail. It is as though the printer is simply frozen. When this occurs, it is best to restart the print spooler service on the PC that is running as the print server. Unfortunately, all clients will need to resend their print jobs. However, in most cases, the printer will be functional once more.

Low Memory Errors

Printer can have a few types of memory blunder. The most common is insufficient memory to print the page. Often this can be solved with the following:

- Turn off the printer to flush out its RAM, and then turn it back on: do this once more if necessary

- Print at a lower goal (alter this setting in the printer's properties in Windows)

- Change the page being printed so it is less complex

- Try using an alternative printer driver if your printer supports more than one PDL (For instance, try changing from PostScript to PCL, or vice versa)

- Update the memory, if the printer permits

Access Denied

If users get an Access Denied message when trying to print to a network printer, make sure their account has been granted access to the printer or to the computer hosting the networked printer.

Printer Will Not Print

It is unlikely that a print device will do nothing, so here the issue is with the printer object inside the OS. In the event that this has been set to disconnected mode, the printer will be at rest and not conveying to the printing device at that point.

Color Prints in Wrong Color

Inaccurate shades or shades that are faint or washed out are usually caused by a messy print head or that one of the colors is running out. Head cleaning is a critical part of maintenance that ought to be done once a month under ordinary usage. This is done in the printer properties (which vary by printer).

You should not perform this process if the ink cartridges are low as it requires ink to do it. Check that first, and if they are low, replace any cartridges before running the head-cleaning system.

Unable to Install Printer

By default, only domain administrators can install a printer, or AD member objects that have been given the right to install a printer. If a user is unable to install a printer, it is usually because they do not have sufficient privileges; you also need administrator access to uninstall a printer. If you are installing a printer in Windows, provide the administrator password when prompted by User Account Control.

Error Codes

Many laser printers contain LCDs for collaborating with the printer. When an error code appears, refer to the manufacturer's manual or website for information on how to interpret the code and resolve the issue.

Printing Blank Pages

If a printer is printing blank pages, try the following solutions:

1. The toner cartridge is empty or has failed. Install a new one. Toner cartridge failures could be associated with the developing and transferring stages of the laser printing process, with the developing stage being more common.

2. The toner cartridge was installed without the sealing tape removed.

3. The transfer corona wire has failed. If the transfer corona wire fails, there will be no positive (opposite) voltage to pull the toner to the paper. Replace the wire.

No Image on Printer Display

If there is no image on a printer display, check whether the printer is in sleep mode or off altogether. Printers cannot print RAW-format files but can print JPEG files. Verify that the printer is plugged in. In rare cases, the internal connector that powers the display might be loose.

Multiple Failed Jobs in Print Logs

To troubleshoot the print logs feature, reset the printer, analyze the controlling operating system or print server, clear the print queue, and reconfigure the spooler.

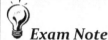

Exam Note

If print jobs back up in the queue, restart the spooler service. Each computer includes a printer spooler and a print queue so that it is possible for one user to print without any problems while the print queue on another computer is backed up.

Mind Map of Troubleshooting Printers

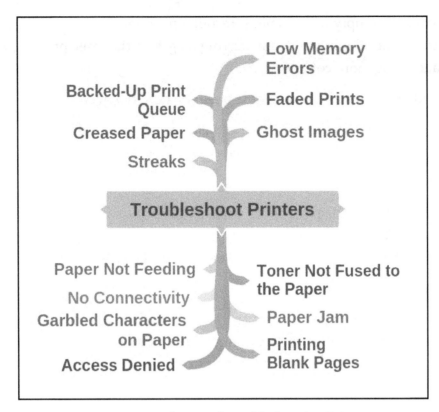

Figure 5-11: Mind Map of Troubleshooting Printers

Troubleshoot Common Wired and Wireless Network Problems

In this section, we will discuss troubleshooting network connectivity issues. Users will have to connect in a wired or wireless fashion and sometimes in both. Users have to be ready to support a variety of network connectivity issues. The goal of this section is to explain some basic troubleshooting techniques in a generic way, focusing on less complex procedures and the troubleshooting mindset that users should maintain. To perform their work, users need access to resources and network connectivity. So, a defective network connection means little to no available resources and, consequently, little to no work getting done. This should help to emphasize the importance of network connectivity.

Common Symptoms

Here, we concentrate on the common symptoms of networking issues.

Limited Connectivity

Limited connectivity happens when the user is restricted to send traffic just inside the subnet. In this situation, you should ping the router using its internal IP address first (the one on their subnet), and then an exterior IP address (for instance, one in the other subnet or the router services). If this second ping is successful, it demonstrates that the user's internal router is not the issue.

Next, try with the edge router; this is the gateway to the web and by pinging its open IP address, we are trying to get network.

Internet Service Providers rent public addresses temporarily and these can change regularly. Typically, this has no effect on the edge router and this router will follow and deal with the change of IP address.

In this way, connectivity is limited when the external network is not available.

Unavailable Resources

Network troubleshooting also involves access to resources. If any resources are unavailable, then users will not be able to get his or her work done, efficiency decreases, and the organization loses money. Resources can be broken down into two types: local resources—meaning ones on the LAN; and remote resources—ones that are beyond the LAN, possibly on the internet or another external network.

Internet-based Resources

If remote resources are not available to users, for example, websites, VPN connections, and streaming media services, then it could be that the IP configuration (especially the gateway and DNS settings) needs to be inspected and possibly reconfigured. If multiple users are having connectivity problems, then it could be the gateway itself or the DNS server that needs to be fixed (among other things). Escalate the problem if necessary.

Local Resources

You might find that users cannot browse the network or map network drives to network shares, or connect to network printers, or access an email server on the LAN. There are lots of examples, but the bottom line is this: if users cannot access local resources, then you need to troubleshoot the network connection. If multiple users cannot access resources, then it could be a more centralized problem. For example, a server is down; perhaps a DHCP server is not properly handing out IP addresses to clients, or a domain controller has failed and users cannot be authenticated to resources.

No Connectivity

When there is no connectivity with the network, troubleshooting should start at the physical layer and then proceed up the OSI model. As you decrease components at each layer considering them as the source of the problem, continue to the next higher layer. A simple yet effective set of steps are as follows:

- Check the network cable to confirm it is the correct cable type (crossover or straight through) and that it is functional. If in any doubt, try a different cable

- Confirm that the NIC is efficient and TCP/IP is installed and functional by pinging the loopback address 127.0.0.1. If required, install or reinstall TCP/IP and/or replace or repair the NIC

- Check the local IP configuration and confirm that the IP address, gateway, and subnet mask are correct. If the default gateway can be pinged, the PC is configured properly for its local network and the problem lies outside the router or with the destination device. If pings to the gateway are unsuccessful, confirm that the IP configurations of the router interface and the computer are compatible and in the same subnet

When allocating with a wireless network, make sure that the wireless card is functional. The wireless card is simply disabled with a keystroke on a PC and should be the first thing to check. If the network uses a concealed SSID, confirm that the station in question is configured with the right SSID.

Exam Note

When troubleshooting connectivity issues, ping and ipconfig are two of the most commonly used tools. Other commands are effective, but you can often identify a problem by first checking the IP configuration with ipconfig and then checking connectivity with ping.

APIPA/Link Local Address

APIPA/Link Local Addressing is used to assign an IP address to a user. The Windows nodes on a network will self-assign non-routable addresses to themselves until the server is able to run an address.

Intermittent Connectivity

Local connectivity and intermittent connectivity are all addressed with the same basic troubleshooting methods. Begin by trying to access a well-known IP address on a local network. This will help to determine whether the problem is with the physical network or the programs and protocols being used.

- First, check the lights on the NIC and devices

- Test out the cable

- Check switches and indicator lights on wireless connections

- Also on wireless connections, be aware of radio power and frequency issues, including line of sight

- Start the next phase by deciding if you want to do the command line interfaces first or the programs. If it is the command line, open a command prompt by clicking the icon or typing **cmd** in the search window

- You can use a few commands and varieties to diagnose the NIC and establish its relative location. First, check that the NIC, its drivers, and the protocol stack are functioning properly. Ping the local host name (ping local host) and number (ping 127.0.0.1), then a common internet address; most DNS servers will in all probability have looked up google recently. Its IP address is simple, 8.8.8.8. Ping that to validate connectivity

IP Conflict

An IP Conflict occurs while two IP-based machines use the same address. Duplicate addresses are not allowed by the TCP/IP addressing scheme.

One interesting approach to give connection a little poke is to use stock functions like variations on the ipconfig utility. Users can check the settings on a new DHCP server by using it to generate Renew and Refresh IPv4 and IPv6 addresses. Using this process, the addressing can be systematically modified whenever required.

Real World Scenario

Background

An IP conflict arises when two or more than two hosts in the same subnet are configured with the same IP address. When this happens, communications with the two conflicting hosts are scrambled. One host may receive packets that belong to the other one, and vice versa.

Challenges

How to detect an IP conflict?

Both Windows and Mac operating systems notify the user via pop-up notification when an IP conflict is detected with another computer.

Detecting an IP conflict is still more difficult if it is affecting remote network devices that are not end-user workstations. It is more difficult because you do not have local access to the host and you are not able to have a consistent remote session.

In this scenario, one way to detect an IP conflict is to first ping the remote IP address. If the ping test results high packet loss, then it is worth continued troubleshooting.

To troubleshoot this problem, you should:

1) Get access to the router that works as the default gateway of the subnet where the conflict is occurring.

2) Examine the router's ARP cache and check whether the MAC address related to the conflicting IP changes constantly. To verify this, you have to execute every two or three seconds the command that returns the ARP cache.

Solution

If you have identified an IP conflict in your network, you will need to correct the IP settings of the device that is "squatting". Preferably, you or someone else on your team has access to the device, to ensure that the correct IP settings can be set. If there is no way for you to locally access the affected host, then you have few options.

One option is to remove the host from the network by shutting down the switch port that it is connected to. Make sure that you do this during off hours when there are no users on the network. Also, make sure that your changes will not cause any further damage to applications or network services.

Conclusion

IP conflicts have very impulsive effects on the affected hosts. Hosts may experience uninterrupted connections and disconnections. This is something that should be addressed as soon as the problem arises.

Slow Transfer Speed

In a situations where resources are influenced by the number of users on a segment or link, the advertised connection speed is measured when no other devices are competing for the resources. As the number of users increases, the comparative speed of the connection decreases. You should be aware of the number and type of connections in use by your device at any given time. Monitor and end any app that is using resources and is not proving to be a useful service.

Low RF Signal

The quality of the wireless signal is indicated by a progression of five bars, or as a rate. If the signal quality is more than three bars (55% or higher), the signal is said to be satisfactory and the session can proceed. The shortcoming of the signal means that it is more diligently to hear and that the signal will be inclined to interference, or crosstalk, implying that the measure of error packets will increase.

This will back off transmission as packets should be disliked. At the point when the signal drops under resistance (distinctive on each device but as a rule around 50%), the session may break and network will drop.

SSID Not Found

Service Set Identifier (SSID) is used as both a network name and in some cases the magic word that allows access to the network in 802.11 WLAN. First approach to increasing the security of a WLAN (not sufficient in and of itself but a good addition to layered method to WLAN security) is to "hide" the SSID: this is referred to as disabling SSID broadcast. This is completed by setting the AP to not list the SSID in the reference frames. These frames contain the data that is utilized to populate the rundown of available wireless networks when "checking" for a wireless network on a wireless device.

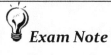

Exam Note

The best way to protect a wireless network is to use a strong security protocol such as WPA2 and a strong passphrase that cannot be easily guessed. You can hide a wireless network from some wireless devices by disabling the SSID, but this does not provide any security.

At the point when the SSID is concealed, the main way a device can interface with the WLAN is to be configured with a profile that incorporates the SSID of the WLAN. While each operating system is slightly different, to do this in Windows 10, follow these steps:

1. Open "Control Panel" and select "Network and Internet" > "Network" and "Sharing Center".

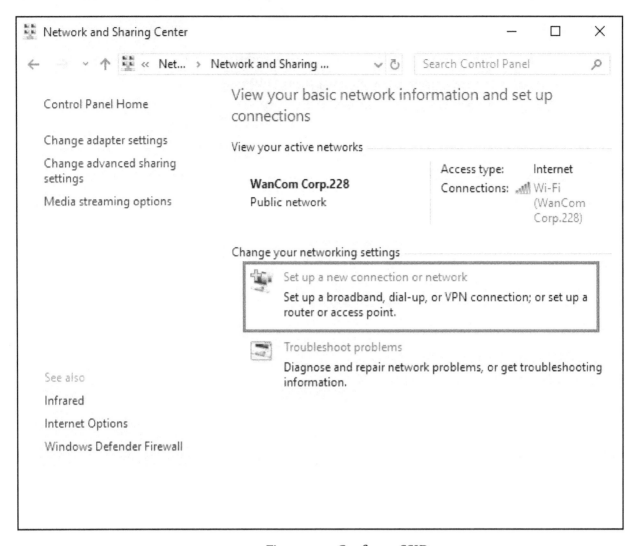

Figure 5-12: Configure SSID

2. Click "Set Up a Connection or Network".

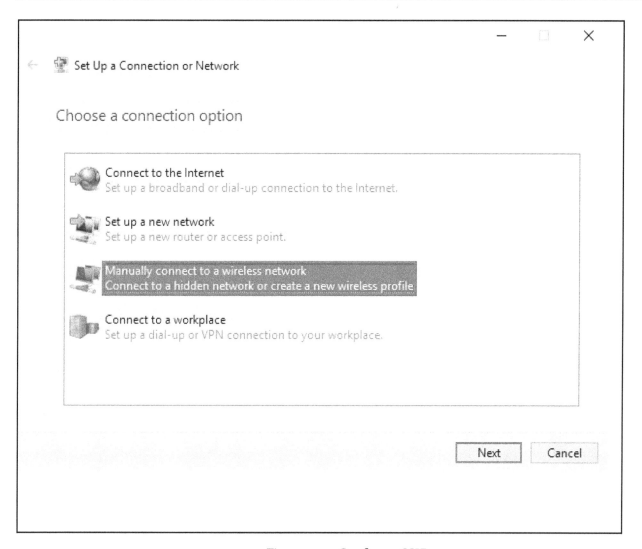

Figure 5-13: Configure SSID

3. Click on "Manually connect to a wireless" network and select "Next", opening the dialog box.

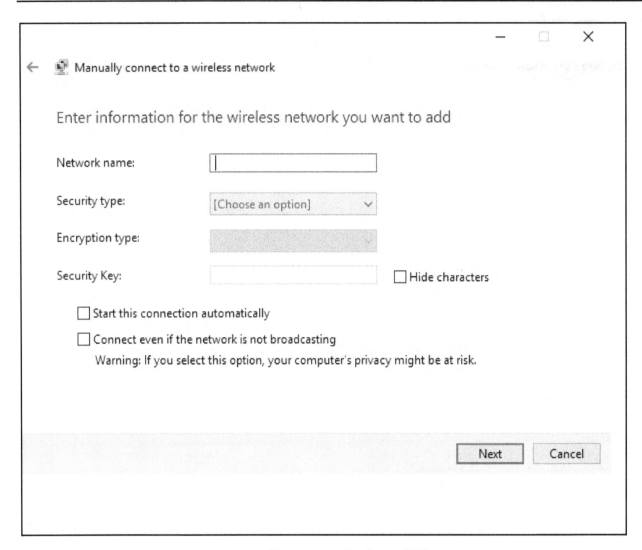

Figure 5-14: Configure SSID

4. Fill the "Network name", "Encryption type", "Security type", and "Security key" and click on box connect even if the network is not broadcasting and select "Next".

When the profile is complete, you should be able to connect to the "hidden" network. To make it easier for users, you may also need to check the box to start this connection automatically.

Mind Map of Troubleshooting Common Wired and Wireless Network Problems

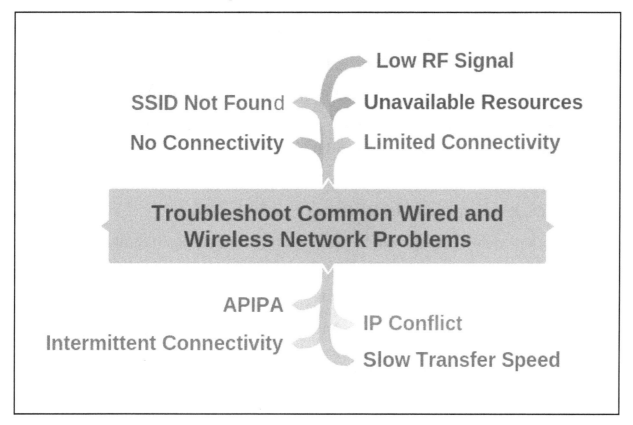

Figure 5-16: Mind Map of Troubleshooting Common Wired and Wireless Network Problems

Summary

Use the Best Practice Methodology to Resolve Problems

- Understand troubleshooting theory, procedure, and methods in detail and take a methodical approach to troubleshooting theories and procedures

- Always consider corporate policies, procedures, and impacts before implementing changes

- Follow the CompTIA six-step troubleshooting methodology: Identify the problem, establish a theory of probable cause, test the theory to determine the cause, establish a plan of action to resolve the problem and implement the solution, verify full system functionality, document findings, actions, and outcomes

Troubleshoot Problems Related to Motherboards, RAM, CPUs, and Power

- Motherboards contain jumpers for different purposes, and almost all motherboards contain jumpers that are used to clear the BIOS password and all BIOS settings

- Motherboards include connectors used to run wires to the front panel of a computer. These are used for LED indicators, a power button, audio, and USB connections

- Common BIOS configuration settings that users can manipulate are the boot sequence, enabling and disabling devices, and the date and time. If the BIOS loses time, if time needs to be reset frequently, or if the system generates CMOS errors, replace the battery

Troubleshoot Hard Drives and RAID Arrays

- Hardware RAID is more efficient than software RAID. Ensure that you have the correct drivers for a hardware RAID enclosure

- Clicking noises from a hard drive indicate a hard drive crash. Back up data as soon as possible

- Use tools such as chkdsk, Check Disk, defrag, and Disk Defragmenter to maintain drives

Troubleshoot Video, Projector, and Display Issues

- Desktop, laptop, and mobile devices each have screens that can vary significantly

- A Windows system starts in VGA mode if Low-resolution mode or Safe mode has been selected at startup or if the correct drivers are not available

- Burn-in is a condition that affects CRT screens and still affects plasma and OLED displays. LCDs are commonly not affected

Troubleshoot Common Mobile Device Issues While Adhering to the Appropriate Procedures

- With more organizations than ever before using laptops, tablets, and smartphones, it's important to know how to troubleshoot devices on the go

- Many mobile device problems have simple solutions that are really easy to identify and repair

- Disassembling a laptop can be one of the biggest challenges unless several simple steps are followed

Troubleshoot Printers

- A printer is a mechanical device; however, it is controlled by embedded firmware and by computers that manage it

- The print spooler service coordinates sending print jobs to a printer. If the print queue backs up, restart it

- Many printer problems have clear symptoms, causes, and solutions. You will often find that taking steps to clean a printer resolves many problems. Additionally, replacing a toner cartridge on a laser printer resolves many problems

Troubleshoot Common Wired and Wireless Network Problems

- Users have to connect in a wired or wireless fashion and sometimes in both. Users have to be ready to support a variety of network connectivity issue

- The goal of this section is to explain some basic troubleshooting techniques in a more generic sense–meaning, less complex procedures and more of the troubleshooting mindset that users should maintain

- To perform their work, users need access to resources and have network connectivity. A defective network connection means little to no available resources and, consequently, little to no work getting done

Practice Questions

1. How many steps of troubleshooting methodology are there?
   A. Four
   B. Five
   C. Six
   D. Seven

2. According to troubleshooting theory, what should you do immediately after establishing a theory of probable cause?
   A. Identify the problem
   B. Test the theory to determine the cause
   C. Document findings, actions, and outcomes
   D. Establish a plan of action to resolve the problem

3. What is the most common reason for an unexpected reboot?
   A. Overheating
   B. ESD Damage
   C. RFI
   D. Memory Leak

4. Which of the following is typically not a cause of system lockups?
   A. Memory Issues
   B. Virus
   C. Video Driver
   D. Bad NIC Driver

5. What is the proprietary screen crashes called in Windows?
   A. Pinwheel
   B. BSOD
   C. Bomb Screen
   D. PSOID

6. Which operating system uses the pinwheel of death as a proprietary screen crash?
   A. Apple
   B. LINUX
   C. Windows
   D. UNIX

7. What process may generate beep cores during reboot?
   A. SMART
   B. POST
   C. DCDIAG
   D. BIOS

8. Which of the followings is a BSOD error message?
   A. REGISTRY_ERROR
   B. DIVIDE_BY_ZERO_ERROR
   C. INACCESSIBLE_BOOT_DEVICE
   D. All of the above

9. What is the full form of RAID?
   A. Relative Array of Independent Disk
   B. Redundant Array of Independent Disk
   C. Redundant Array of Independent Device
   D. None of the above

10. Which of the following statements occurs when one or two subpixels remain activated even when they are supposed to be off?
    A. Dead Pixel
    B. Stuck Pixel
    C. Both of them

D. None of the above

11. What are the small dots on the screen that are filled with color called?
   A. Cells
   B. Capacitors
   C. Hypervisor
   D. Pixels

12. What are visual anomalies that appear on the screen called?
   A. Cells
   B. Pixels
   C. Artifacts
   D. Dead Spots

13. What is the light in the device that powers the LCD screen called?
   A. Backlight
   B. Inverter
   C. Reflector
   D. Charger

14. Which of the following is a user interface feature designed by HTC?
   A. Type I
   B. Type II
   C. Container-based
   D. TouchFLo

15. Which of the following indicates that the fuser is not fusing the toner properly on the paper?
   A. Streaks
   B. Black Spots
   C. Blank Spots
   D. Garbled Output

16. Which of the following indicates that the toner cartridge is just about empty?
   A. Streaks
   B. Faded Prints

C. Garbled Output

D. Black Spots

17. If you can ping resources by IP address but not by name, _____ is not functional.

A. HTTPS

B. DNS

C. ARP

D. DHCP

18. Which of the following should be set to the IP address of the router interface connecting to the local network?

A. IP Address

B. Subnet Mask

C. Default Gateway

D. DHCP Server

19. What is the reason for having blank pages come out of a laser printer?

A. Damaged Roller

B. Failed Transfer Corona Wire

C. Failed Primary Corona Wire

D. Failed Fusing Assembly

20. What is the reason for having black lines on printouts?

A. Damaged Roller

B. Scratch on the laser printer drum

C. Damaged transfer corona wire

D. Scratch on the fusing assembly

21. What to do first when removing a paper jam?

A. Turn off the printer

B. Take the printer offline

C. Clear the print queue

D. Open all the doors of the printer

22. What is a possible sign of a failing CPU?
    A. CPU is beyond the recommended voltage range
    B. PC will not boot
    C. BIOS reports low temperatures within the case
    D. Spyware is installed into the browser

23. Which of the following are possible signs of hard drive failure? (Select two)
    A. System Lockup
    B. Antivirus Alerts
    C. Network Drive Errors
    D. Failing Bootup Files
    E. BIOS does not recognize the drive

24. Which of the following tool should be used to fix the problem if one computer loses connectivity and all connectors and settings appear to be correct?
    A. PSU Tester
    B. Loopback Plug
    C. Cable Tester
    D. Multimeter

25. Which of the following could be the problem if mobile device of a user is overheating? (Select two)
    A. Excessive gaming
    B. A damaged battery
    C. The brightness setting is too low
    D. The device is not in a case
    E. The charging cable is defective

Answers

Chapter 01: Mobile Devices

1. B

Explanation: Hard-disk drives consist of rotating magnetic platters paired with read/write heads that moves over the platters' surfaces to record or retrieve data. As the speed of platter rotation increases, the faster the hard drive performs.

2. A

Explanation: Hybrid Disk Drive or Solid State Hybrid Drive is a blend of Hard Disk Drive (HDD) and Solid State Drive (SDD). This ultimate solution provides you with improved storage performance and greater capacity at a low cost.

3. C

Explanation: Random Access Memory is volatile so the data in RAM will be retained here as long as the computer is on, but it will be lost once the computer is turned off. The OS and other files are reloaded into RAM again from other storage devices like HDD or SSD, when the computing device will be rebooted.

4. D

Explanation: Accelerated Graphics Port (AGP) slots are specially designed to be a direct connection between the PC's memory and the video circuitry.

5. D

Explanation: The display or monitor of a laptop is an integrated component, just as the keyboard. It can have LCD, LED or OLED.

6. A

Explanation: Function keys are a set of programmable keys that are horizontally present on the top of the keyboard. They perform their special tasks assigned by the current application program as well other than their regular function.

7. C

Explanation: To gain access of the special functions of the function keys, press a function key "Fn" (generally, located at the lower left corner of your laptop) along with some other key to allow alternate functions. Alternate functions are usually written in different color, smaller, light type, or, written or drawn on the edge of the key.

Special functions include changing the display's brightness, adjusting the volume, using Num Lock, and switching between the built-in monitor and an external monitor.

8. C

Explanation: A port replicator is a device to be attached to a laptop or notebook computer. The port replicator contains all of the laptop's ports, including serial and parallel ports. In addition, it also contains ports for devices like musical instrument digital interface (MIDI) and joystick.

Docking station is a more advanced version of port replicator, that provides all the ports that a port replicator does. Additionally, it provides slots for PCI cards and also floppy drives, CD drives and additional media/accessory bays.

9. A

Explanation: E-readers or E-book readers are mainly designed for reading E-books and magazines that are in digital and downloadable form. E-readers have either an LCD or E-ink display.

10. A

Explanation: Universal Serial Bus (USB) is one of the most common port you can see in all mobile or computing devices. USB ports are used to transfer data between your mobile device and other devices like laptops, storage disks, smartphones etc.

11. C

Explanation: In Client-Based Email, you need an application or program on your device, which needs to be configured properly in order to enable email transactions

in your device. Examples of client-based emails are Microsoft Outlook, Outlook Express, Pegasus Mail, etc.

12. **D**

Explanation: Web-Based Email accounts, like Outlook.com, Gmail, iCloud, or Yahoo mail, do not require specification of a sending and a receiving server. You just need to enter the correct credentials to gain the access of your emails.

13. **D**

Explanation: **Username** – Your name will become the first part of your email address, but not always. First part of your email may differ if it is already occupied by some other email user.

Password - Your password is used to access approval or to prove your identity to get access to a resource.

SMTP Server Address - To begin your email transaction, you need the address of your Simple Mail Transfer Protocol (SMTP) server that receives your outgoing emails and forwards it to an email server.

IMAP or POP server address - To enable your account to receive mails, there are two servers; Internet Message Access Protocol (IMAP) and Post Office Protocol 3 (POP3) server.

14. **C**

Explanation: Ports must be defined for the incoming and outing email servers along with the security settings. By default, port 25 is used for outgoing email, but you can vary ports setting according to the requirements.

15. **B**

Explanation: Multi-Purpose Internet Mail Extensions (MIME) is an extension of the email protocol. This protocol allows people to exchange different kinds of data files on the Internet other than email message text such as images, audio, video, application programs, ASCII text and other kinds of data. This protocol allows new file types to be added to "mail" as a supported Internet Protocol file type.

16. B

Explanation: The Preferred Roaming List (PRL) is a type of database that is stored in your mobile device. It allows the device to be able to roam or get service from outside of your cellular network. It contains all necessary information used for connecting mobile devices to the cellular service towers.

17. D

Explanation: Dropbox is one of the most popular example of cloud storage services. All kind of data that you place into your Dropbox folder gets backed up online and can be downloaded at any other device that is logged in to the Dropbox by using the same account. Similarly, there are synchronization apps for Android and IOS such as OneDrive and iCloud.

18. E

Explanation: You can synchronize data such as Contacts, Applications, Email, Pictures, Music, Videos, Calendar, Bookmarks, Documents, Location data, Social Media data, E-books, and Passwords between two devices.

19. D

Explanation: Single Sign-On (SSO) is a technique in which a user needs only one set of credentials to gain access of multiple resources.

SSO issues a security token (credentials, usually username and password) for the first time you log in and then you can log in into multiple applications by using the same set of credentials or security token.

20. A

Explanation: Inside your mobile devices or smartphones are some specific identification numbers, which differentiates your cell phone from the others. International Mobile Equipment Identification (IMEI) is the standard used to identify a physical phone device. This code serves as a tracking number for the device.

Chapter 02: Networking

1. **A**

Explanation: There are two types of Internet Protocol (IP):

Transmission Control Protocol (TCP) and User Datagram Protocol (UDP)

2. **A**

Explanation: TCP is connection-oriented, which ensures end-to-end reliable packet delivery with efficient flow control, full-duplex operation, multiplexing, and data streaming service.

3. **B**

Explanation: The usage of UDP is suitable for applications that require fast, efficient transmission, such as games. UDP's stateless nature is also useful for servers that answer small queries from huge numbers of clients.

4. **A**

Explanation: The full form of FTP is File Transfer Protocol.

5. **A & B**

Explanation: Secure Shell (SSH) opens a secured network channel that promotes confidentiality and integrity for network services over an unsecured network using public key cryptography, this makes it a cryptographic network protocol. It is used to secure remote network logins and other confidential data.

6. **C**

Explanation: Telnet is a remote access protocol for creating a connection with a remote machine over TCP/IP network.

7. **C**

Explanation: SMTP is an internet standard protocol that allows the transmission and delivery of email over the Internet. SMTP uses TCP port 25 for internet mail transmission.

8. **B**

Explanation: The Domain Name System (DNS) is the way that Internet domain names are located and translated into internet protocol (IP) addresses.

9. **B**

Explanation: Remote Desktop Protocol (RDP) is a secured network communications protocol designed for remote management, as well as for remote access to virtual desktops, applications, and RDP terminal server.

10. **A**

Explanation: The full form of SMB is Service Message Block.

11. **C**

Explanation:

The Service Location Protocol (SLP) is a protocol or method of arranging and locating the resources (such as printers, databases, schedulers, disk drives) in a network.

12. **A**

Explanation: Dynamic Host Configuration Protocol (DHCP) is a network management protocol used to dynamically assign an Internet Protocol (IP) address to any device, or node, on a network so that they can communicate using IP.

13. **B**

Explanation: Router is a network device that forwards data packets from one network to another.

14. **A**

Explanation: There are two types of switches:

- Managed Switch

- Unmanaged Switch

15. C

Explanation: A firewall is a network security device that monitors incoming and outgoing network traffic and decides whether to allow or block specific traffic based on a defined set of security rules.

16. A

Explanation: The full form of NIC is Network Interface Card.

17. C

Explanation: The NIC contains the electronic circuitry required to communicate using a wired connection (such as Ethernet) or a wireless connection (such as Wi-Fi). A network interface card is also called network interface controller, Local Area Network (LAN), or network adapter.

18. A

Explanation: Static IP address are the types of IP addresses, which once assigned to a device on a network, they never change. They provide a simple and reliable way for the communication and serve as a permanent internet address.

19. D

Explanation: Some advantages of Dynamic IP address are:

- It does not cost you anything extra

- It is automatic, carefree and reliable with very little work on your end

- It is the most effective use of IP addresses, for your ISP

20. C

Explanation: Some advantages of subnetting are:

- Subnetting breaks large network in smaller networks and smaller networks are easier to manage

- Subnetting reduces network traffic by removing collision and broadcast traffic, that overall improves performance

- Subnetting allows you to apply network security polices at the interconnection between subnets

- Subnetting allows you to save money by reducing requirement for IP range

21. **B & C**

Explanation: Gateway is a network device that establishes a connection between the local network and external network with different structure; it connects two dissimilar networks. In simple words, it is a node on a network that serves as an entrance to another network and it expands the functionality of the router by performing data translation and protocol conversion.

22. **C**

Explanation: Virtual Private Network (VPN) is an encrypted communication channel or tunnel between two remote sites over the internet. VPN is a logical network that allows connectivity between two devices.

23. **A**

Explanation: There are two types of VPN:

- Remote access VPN

- Site-to-site VPN

24. **B**

Explanation: The remote access VPN feature allows an endpoint to connect to the secure LAN network of an organization. These endpoint devices include smartphones, tablets, laptops etc.

25. **B**

Explanation: Near-Field Communication (NFC) allows data to be exchanged between devices through short-range, high-frequency wireless communication technology by combining the interface of a smartcard and reader into a single device.

26. A

Explanation: Radio-frequency identification is the information exchanged between tags and readers that is rapid, automatic and does not require direct contact or line of sight. RFID readers may be handheld units or fixed units connected to a remote computer system.

27. B

Explanation: Digital Subscriber Line (DSL) is an internet connection. This uses existing 2-wire copper telephone line, which is connected to one's home service. It is delivered at the same time as landline telephone service.

28. D

Explanation: Some advantages of ISDN are:

- ISDN is used to facilitate the user with multiple digital channels. These channels can work simultaneously through the same one copper wire pair

- The digital signals broadcast across the telephone lines

- ISDN delivers high data rate as of digital scheme, which is 56kbps

- ISDN network lines are able to switch multiple devices on the single line such as computers, cash registers credit cards readers, faxes, and many other devices. All these devices can work in an organized manner and can directly be associated with a single line

- ISDN takes only 2 seconds to launch a connection while other modems take 30 to 60 seconds for creation

29. B

Explanation: Tethering is a way to provide internet access that allows you to connect your cell phone to a laptop or desktop computer through USB or Bluetooth. It allows

devices using the phone's cellular connection to provide mobile connectivity to another device. This connection is a one-to-one connection share.

30. **C**

Explanation: Wireless Mesh Network is the concept of mesh networking that can be applied to both wireless networking and physical.

Chapter 03: Hardware

1. **E**

Explanation: Cable Internet connections use RG-6 coaxial cable (generally) with an F-connector at the end. DE-9 (or DB-9) is a serial connector used with RS-232 connections. RJ-45 is the connector used on twisted-pair patch cables. BNC is an older form of connector used by coaxial networks. LC is sort of a fiber optic connector.

2. **C**

Explanation: A crossover cable is used to connect similar devices: PC to PC or switch to switch. Straight-through cables do not connect similar devices. T568B is the typical wiring standard in twisted-pair cables; T568A is the less common standard. SATA is used to connect hard drives internally to a laptop or desktop computer.

3. **C & D**

Explanation: Category 5e and Category 6 are used for 1000-Mbps networks. Category 3 is used for 10-Mbps networks only. Category 5 is used for 100-Mbps networks.

4. **D**

Explanation: The RS-232 standard had been commonly used in computer serial ports. A serial cable uses only one wire to carry information in every direction; all the rest are wires for signaling and traffic control. An RJ-11 is a standard connector for a telephone line and is used to link a PC modem to a phone line. It is similar to RJ-45 but is noticeably smaller.

5. **C**

Explanation: DDR4 SDRAM is an abbreviation for double data rate fourth-generation synchronous dynamic random-access memory. DDR4 is not compatible with any earlier sort of random-access memory (RAM).

6. **C**

Explanation: DDR3 is a 240-pin architecture. 184-pin is the DDR first version (DDR1). DDR4 is a 288-pin architecture.

7. **A**

Explanation: SATA Revision 3.0 drives can transfer 6 Gb/s, which after encoding amounts to 600 MB/s. SATA Revision 3.2 is 16 Gb/s (1969 MB/s) but needs SATA Express or M.2. 50 MB/s is a typical write speed for Blu-ray discs and some flash media. 90 MB/s is a typical write speed for an SD card.

8. **C**

Explanation: RAID 5 stripes information parity across three or more disks. RAID 0 does not stripe parity; it stripes data only and can use two disks or more. RAID 1 uses two disks only. RAID 10 has two sets of mirrored disks that are then striped.

9. **A**

Explanation: Blu-ray has the largest storage capacity, at a typical maximum of 50 GB. CDs top out just under 1 GB. DVDs have a maximum of 17 GB.

10. **A**

Explanation: The lithium battery (or CMOS battery) provides power to the CMOS when the computer is turned off. The reason is that the CMOS is volatile and would otherwise lose the stored settings when the PC is turned off.

11. **B**

Explanation: 6-pin or 8-pin PCIe connector normally powers a video card. The 24-pin power connector is the primary connector that leads from the power supply to the motherboard. Molex is used for fans, older IDE drives. 3.5-mm TRS is an audio connection.

12. **C**

Explanation: To perform hard drive encryption, some motherboards come with a Trusted Platform Module (TPM), a chip that stores encryption keys that can be enabled in the BIOS.

13. **C**

Explanation: Hyperthreading enables an operating system to send two simultaneous threads to be processed by a single CPU core. The OS views the computer core as two virtual processors.

14. **B**

Explanation: Brightness is a description of light output, which is measured in lumens (not watts).

15. **D**

Explanation: Smart TVs, touchscreens, KVMs, and headsets are considered both input and output devices.

16. **C**

Explanation: The SATA power connector consists of 15 pins, with 3 pins designated for 3.3V, 5V, and 12V and with each pin carrying 1.5 amps.

17. **A**

Explanation: A thick client is a desktop computer system. It has the applications installed locally and will need to have sufficient resources to support the applications.

18. **C**

Explanation: Molex connectors provide 12 volts and 5 volts.

19. **C**

   Explanation: A NAS (Network Attached Storage) device enables users to access files and stream media; it normally has a gigabit NIC and a RAID array.

20. **D**

   Explanation: The fusing step uses heat (up to 400 degrees Fahrenheit/200 degrees Celsius) and pressure to fuse the toner permanently to the paper.

---

21. **A**

    Explanation: The laser printer is the most-often-used shared network printer in businesses.

22. **D**

    Explanation: Inkjet is the type of printer that applies wet ink to paper.

Chapter 04: Virtualization & Cloud Computing

1. **D**

   Explanation: Cloud computing is a new operational model and set of technologies for managing shared pools of computing resources. Cloud computing is the practice of using a network of remote servers hosted on the internet to store, manage and process data rather than using a local server or own computer. It is the on-demand delivery of computing resources through a cloud service platform with pay-as-you-go pricing.

2. **E**

   Explanation: There are many advantage of cloud computing such as go global in minutes, increased speed and agility, stop spending money on running and maintaining data centers, benefits from massive economies of scale.

3. **A, B, & C**

   Explanation: Key cloud computing characteristics are on-demand self-service, broad network access, rapid elasticity and scalability, multi-tenancy, resource pooling, and measured service.

4. **A, B, & C**

   Explanation: SaaS, PaaS, NaaS, IaaS are the cloud service models.

5. **B**

   Explanation: PaaS (Platform as a Service) provides customers the ability to deploy onto the cloud infrastructure consumer-created or obtained applications created using programming languages and tools supported by the provider.

6. A

Explanation: Amazon EC2, Rackspace Cloud Servers are the example of IaaS (Infrastructure as a Service).

7. D

Explanation: Cloud deployment models are Private Cloud, Public Cloud, Hybrid Cloud, and Community Cloud.

8. B

Explanation: A Community Cloud is more expensive but offers a higher level of privacy and security.

9. A

Explanation: Private Cloud offers association that needs more control over their data than using a third-party hosted service.

10. E

Explanation: Server space, accessible anywhere, secure, unlimited backup, iron-clad security, and collaboration are the advantages of Cloud-Based Email.

11. C

Explanation: It is used to store data in the cloud that provides servers and applications access to data over shared file systems.

12. A, B, C, & D

Explanation: There are many Cloud files storage services such as IDrive, pCloud, Mega, OneDrive, iCloud, Google Drive, Box, Next Cloud, and Spider Oak.

13. C

Explanation: IDrive provides continuous syncing of your files, even those on network drives. The web interface maintenances share files by email, Facebook and Twitter. It is easy to use, fast, and with no two-factor authentication.

14. A

Explanation: iCloud is a smooth app and web interface, which is companionable with Windows as well as MacOS and IOS devices. 5GB storage is given for free.

15. E

Explanation: Multiple devices backup, online file sync, disk image backup, continuous data protection, manage computers, security, and privacy, and go mobile are the features of IDrive.

16. E

Explanation: There are some benefits of application virtualization, which are:

- Allows mismatched applications to run on a local machine simultaneously
- Lacks fewer resources as compared to using a separate virtual machine
- Facilitates faster application deployment
- Maintains a standard, more active, and cost-effective OS configuration across multiple machines in a given association, independent of the applications being used
- Facilitates security by separating applications from the local OS
- Allows applications to be copied to convenient media and used by other user computers, with no necessity for local installation
- Easier tracing of license usage, which may save on license costs
- Increases the capability to handle high and diverse/variable work volume

17. A

Explanation: The Cloud-based application can be operated from the web browser and/or can be installed on desktops, smartphones, etc.

18. A

Explanation: A user's desktop environment (the wallpaper, icons, folders, windows, widgets, toolbars, etc.) that is stored remotely on a server, relatively than on a local PC or another user computing device is called a Virtual Desktop.

Chapter 05: Hardware and Network Troubleshooting

1. **C**

Explanation: There are six steps of troubleshooting methodology:

1. Identify the problem
2. Establish a theory
3. Test the theory
4. Establish a plan
5. Verify full systems
6. Document findings, actions, and outcome

2. **B**

Explanation: After establishing a theory of probable cause, test the theory to determine the cause.

3. **A**

Explanation: One basic reason behind shutdowns is overheating. Often when that is the situation, however, the system reboots instead of simply shutting down.

4. **D**

Explanation: A bad NIC driver would cause the NIC to not work but would not cause a system lockup.

5. **B**

Explanation: Once a regular occurrence when working with Windows, blue screens (also known as the Blue Screen of Death) have become much less frequent.

6. **A**

Explanation: In the Apple world, the pinwheel is similar to BSOD. It is named due to the cursor that turns into a pinwheel and does not let you do anything else. The only solution is to force a shutdown and reboot.

7. **B**

Explanation: During the boot-up of the system, a Power-on Self-Test (POST) occurs and each device is checked for functionality.

8. **D**

Explanation: BSOD error messages are as followings:

- REGISTRY_ERROR
- DIVIDE_BY_ZERO_ERROR
- INACCESSIBLE_BOOT_DEVICE
- IRQL_NOT_LESS_OR_EQUAL
- UNEXPECTED_KERNEL_MODE_TRAP
- BAD_POOL_HEADER
- NTFS_FILE_SYSTEM

9. **B**

Explanation: The full form of RAID is Redundant Array of Independent Disk.

10. **B**

Explanation: A stuck pixel occurs when one or more than one subpixels remain activated even when they are supposed to be off and a dead pixel occurs when an entire pixel or a group of subpixels remain dark even when they are supposed to be on.

11. **D**

Explanation: Pixels are the small dots on the screen that are filled with color.

12. **C**

Explanation: Artifacts are visual anomalies that appear on the screen. They might be pieces of images left over from a previous image or a "tear in the image".

13. A

Explanation: The backlight is the light in the device that powers the LCD screen. LCDs can become dimmer over time and need to be replaced, and it can also be held captive by the inverter.

14. D

Explanation: Touch flow, or TouchFLO, is a user interface feature designed by HTC. It is used by dragging the finger up and down or left and right to access common tasks on the screen.

15. A

Explanation: With laser printers, streaks usually indicate that the fuser is not fusing the toner properly on the paper. It could also be that the incorrect paper is being used.

16. B

Explanation: In laser printers, faded print usually indicates that the toner cartridge is just about empty. Users can usually remove it, shake it, and replace it and then get a bit more life out of it before it is fully empty.

17. B

Explanation: It is possible to ping the entire network using IP addresses, but most access is done by name, not IP address. If it is not possible to ping resources by name, DNS is not functional, meaning either the DNS server is down or the local machine is not configured with the correct IP address of the DNS server.

18. C

Explanation: If the PC cannot connect to the default gateway, it will be confined to communicating with devices on the local network. This IP address should be that of the router interface connecting to the local network.

19. B

Explanation: There is no way for the toner to be "attached" to the paper. If the transfer corona wire has failed, it will result in blank sheets coming out of the printer.

20. B

Explanation: A scratch on the laser printer drum can be the cause for black lines showing up on printouts.

21. A

Explanation: Turn off the printer before working inside of the printer. Make sure it is turned off (and unplugged) before putting hands inside of printer. Turning it offline is not enough in this case.

22. A

Explanation: If the CPU is operating beyond the recommended voltage range for extended periods of time, it can be a sign of a failing CPU.

23. A & D

Explanation: System lockups and failing bootup files or other failing file operations are possible signs of hard drive failure.

24. C

Explanation: Use a patch cable tester to check the patch cable and possibly use a continuity tester to test longer network cable.

25. A & B

Explanation: Damaged battery and excessive gaming are the possible reasons that cause the mobile device of a user to overheat.

Acronyms:

ADC	Analog-to-Digital Converter
ADSL	Asymmetrical Digital Subscriber Line
AFP	Apple File Protocol
APIPA	Automatic Private IP Addressing
ATX	Advanced Technology eXtended
BD	Blu-ray Disk
BNC	British Naval Connector
CAD	Computer-Aided Design
CAM	Computer-Aided Manufacturing
CAN	Cash Area Network
CD	Compact Disk
CMOS	Complementary Metal-Oxide Semiconductor
CRT	Cathode Ray Tube
DAC	Digital-to-Analog Converter
DCE	Data Communications Equipment
DDR	Double Data Rate
DHCP	Dynamic Host Configuration Protocol
DLP	Data Loss Prevention
DPCP	DisplayPort Content Protection
DRM	Digital Rights Management
DSL	Digital Subscriber Line
DTE	Data Terminal Equipment
DTV	Digital Television
DVD	Digital Versatile Disk
DVI	Digital Visual Interface

EAP	Extensible Authentication Protocol
EMI	Electromagnetic Interference
GPU	Graphical Processing Unit
HDCP	High-Bandwidth Digital Content Protection
HDD	Hard-Disk Drive (HDD)
HDD	Hard-Disk Drives
HDMI	High Definition Multimedia Interface
IaaS	Infrastructure as a Service
IBSS	Independent Basic Service Set
IDE	Integrated Developed Environment
IDS	Intrusion Detection System
IGP	Integrated Graphics Processor
IPS	Intrusion Prevention System
ISDN	Integrated Service Digital Network
ISP	Internet Service Provider
KVM	Keyboard, Video and Mouse
LAN	Local Area Network
LC	Lucent Connector
LCD	Liquid Crystal Display
LCD	Liquid Crystal Display (LCD)
LDAP	Lightweight Directory Access Protocol
LED	Light-Emitting Diode
LED	Light Emitting Diode (LED)
LGA	Land Grid Array
MAN	Metropolitan Area Network
MIMO	Multiple-Input Multiple Output
MMF	Multimode Fiber
MT-RJ	Mechanical Transfer Registered Jack

NAT	Network Address Translation
NetBIOS	Network Basic Input/Output System
NFC	Near Field Communication
NFC	Near Field Communication
NFC	Near Field Communication
NGFF	Next-Generation Form Factor
NIC	Network Interface Card
NIC	Network Interface Card
NIC	Network Interface Card
NIC	Network Interface Controller
NLX	New Low-Profile
NVME	Nonvolatile Memory Express
OLED	Organic Light-emitting Diode (OLED)
PaaS	Platform as a Service
PAN	Personal Area Network
PATA	Parallel Advanced Technology Advancement
PCB	Printed Circuit Board
PCI	Peripheral Component Interconnect
PCI	Peripheral Component Interconnect
PCIe	Peripheral Component Interconnect Express
PCIe	Peripheral Component Interconnect Express
PCMCIA	Personal Computer Memory Card International Association
PGA	Pin Grid Array
PoE	Power over Ethernet
POST	Performs the Power-On Self-Test
PVC	Polyvinyl Chloride
QR	Quick Response
RAID	Redundant Array of Independent/Inexpensive Disk

RDP	Remote Desktop Protocol (RDP)
RFID	Radio-Frequency Identification
RG	Radio Guide
RJ	Registered Jack
RS	Recommended Standard
SaaS	Software as a Service
SATA	Serial Advanced Technology Advancement
SC	Subscriber Connector
SCSI	Small Computer Small Interface
SD	Secure Digital
SDSL	Symmetric Digital Subscriber Line
SLP	Service Location Protocol
SMB	Service Message Block
SMF	Single-Mode Fiber
SMT	Simultaneous Multithreading
SNMP	Simple Network Management Protocol
SODIMM	Small Outline Dual In-line Memory Module(s)
SSD	Solid-State Drive (SSD)
SSHD	Hybrid Disk Drive/Solid State Hybrid Drive (SSHD)
SSL	Secure Sockets Layer
ST	Straight-Tip
STP	Shielded Twisted Pair
TCP	Transmission Control Protocol
TPM	Trusted Platform Module
USB	Universal Serial Bus
UTM	Unified Threat Management
UTP	Unshielded Twisted Pair
VGA	Video Graphics Array

VLAN	Virtual Local Area Network
VM	Virtual Machine
VMM	Virtual Machine Monitors
VPN	Virtual Private Network
WAN	Wide Area Network
WMN	Wireless Mesh Network
WPANs	Wireless Personal Area Network
xD	eXtreme Digital
ZIF	Zero Insertion Force

References:

http://www.mdmsecured.com/Mobile-Document-Sync.asp

https://learning.oreilly.com/library/view/comptia-a-core/9780135301265/ch01.xhtml

https://learning.oreilly.com/library/view/Complete+A++Guide+to+IT+Hardware+and+Software:+A+CompTIA+A++220-1001+_+220-1002+Textbook,+First+Edition/9780135291542/ch10.html#ch10

https://learning.oreilly.com/library/view/CompTIA+A++Cert+Guide+Core+1+(220-1001)+and+Core+2+(220-1002),+5th+Edition/9780135300053/ch01.html#obj1_7

https://www.outlook-apps.com/outlook-com-pop-settings/

https://www.nytimes.com/2016/12/14/technology/yahoo-hack.html

https://www.theguardian.com/technology/2016/dec/14/yahoo-hack-security-of-one-billion-accounts-breachedhttps://en.wikipedia.org/wiki/Yahoo!_data_breaches#cite_note-wash1-5

https://www.lunawebs.com/blog/2012/07/27/why-duplicate-emails-happen-with-pop3/

https://www.google.com/amp/s/whatis.techtarget.com/definition/POP3-Post-Office-Protocol-3%3famppo

https://redmondmag.com/articles/2016/02/29/outlook-2016-pop3-problems.aspx?m=1

https://itstillworks.com/stop-microsoft-outlook-receiving-duplicate-emails-8507.html

https://www.lifewire.com/smart-locks-4159894

https://www.lifewire.com/smart-speaker-4145037

https://www.swann.com/blog/types-of-security-cameras/

https://www.lifewire.com/introduction-to-internet-controlled-thermostats-817748

https://learning.oreilly.com/library/view/comptia-a-cert/9780135300053/ch02.html#ch02

https://learning.oreilly.com/library/view/complete-a-guide/9780135291542/ch13.html

https://www.internetsociety.org/resources/2018/state-of-ipv6-deployment-2018/

https://www.spamhaus.org/news/article/719/a-survival-guide-for-the-small-mail-server

https://learning.oreilly.com/library/view/comptia-a-certification/9781259859397/ch21.html

https://learning.oreilly.com/library/view/comptia-a-certification/9781787127302/1a757a10-424c-4903-bea9-8673ae941a19.xhtml

http://193.140.54.45/donanim/ComptiaA_Certification.pdf

http://willypritts.tripod.com/OLD%20FILES/itstudy/SybexACertificationStudyGuide.pdf

https://www.elprocus.com/types-power-supplies/

https://www.online-tech-tips.com/computer-tips/blu-ray-disc-formats-ultra-hd/

https://fcit.usf.edu/network/chap4/chap4.htm

https://www.computerhope.com/jargon/r/risecard.htm

https://searchstorage.techtarget.com/definition/IDE

https://learning.oreilly.com/library/view/CompTIA+A++Core+1+(220-1001)+and+Core+2+(220-1002)+Exam+Cram/9780135301265/ch09.xhtml#ch09

https://learning.oreilly.com/library/view/CompTIA+A++Cert+Guide+Core+1+(220-1001)+and+Core+2+(220-1002),+5th+Edition/9780135300053/ch03.html#obj3_1

https://learning.oreilly.com/library/view/comptia-a-cert/9780135300053/ch03.html

https://learning.oreilly.com/library/view/complete-a-guide/9780135291542/toc.xhtml#toc

https://learning.oreilly.com/library/view/complete-a-guide/9780135291542/ch01.xhtml#ch01

https://arstechnica.com/information-technology/2018/11/intel-cpus-fall-to-new-hyperthreading-exploit-that-pilfers-crypto-keys/

https://thehackernews.com/2018/11/portsmash-intel-vulnerability.html

https://www.theregister.co.uk/2019/05/14/intel_hyper_threading_mitigations/

https://www.tomshardware.com/news/infineon-tpm-insecure-rsa-keys,35668.html

https://learning.oreilly.com/library/view/CompTIA+A++Core+1+(220-1001)+and+Core+2+(220-1002)+Exam+Cram/9780135301265/ch16.xhtml#ch16

https://learning.oreilly.com/library/view/comptia-a-cert/9780135300053/ch04.html#ch04

https://learning.oreilly.com/library/view/architecting-the-cloud/9781118826461/

About Our Products

Other Network & Security related products from IPSpecialist LTD are:

- CCNA Routing & Switching Technology Workbook
- CCNA Security v2 Technology Workbook
- CCNA Service Provider Technology Workbook
- CCDA Technology Workbook
- CCDP Technology Workbook
- CCNP Route Technology Workbook
- CCNP Switch Technology Workbook
- CCNP Troubleshoot Technology Workbook
- CCNP Security SENSS Technology Workbook
- CCNP Security SIMOS Technology Workbook
- CCNP Security SITCS Technology Workbook
- CCNP Security SISAS Technology Workbook
- CompTIA Network+ Technology Workbook
- CompTIA Security+ v2 Technology Workbook
- Certified Information System Security Professional (CISSP) Technology Workbook
- CCNA CyberOps SECFND Technology Workbook
- Certified Block Chain Expert Technology Workbook
- Certified Cloud Security Professional (CCSP) Technology Workbook
- CompTIA Pentest Technology Workbook
- CompTIA A+ Core II (220-1002) Technology Workbook

Upcoming products are:

- CCNA 200-301 Technology Workbook
- CCNP Enterprise (ENCOR) Technology Workbook

Note from the Author:

> Reviews are gold to authors! If you have enjoyed this book and it has helped you along certification, would you consider rating and reviewing it?

Link to Product Page: